THE SENATOR AND THE SOCIALITE

Also by Lawrence Otis Graham

Our Kind of People
Member of the Club
Proversity: Getting Past Face Value
The Best Companies for Minorities

THE
SENATOR
AND THE
SOCIALITE

*The True Story of America's
First Black Dynasty*

Lawrence Otis Graham

HarperCollins*Publishers*

HarperCollins books may be purchased for educational, business, or sales promotional use. For information, please write: Special Markets Department, HarperCollins Publishers, 10 East 53rd Street, New York, NY 10022.

FIRST EDITION

Designed by C. Linda Dingler

Printed on acid-free paper

Library of Congress Cataloging-in-Publication Data.

Graham, Lawrence.
   The senator and the socialite : the true story of America's first Black dynasty / Lawrence Otis Graham.—1st ed.
      p. cm.
   Includes bibliographical references and index.
ISBN-10: 0-06-018412-4
ISBN-13: 978-0-06-018412-4
   1. Bruce, Blanche Kelso, 1841–1898. 2. Bruce, Josephine. 3. Legislators—United States—Biography. 4. African American legislators—Biography. 5. Legislator's spouses—United States—Biography. 6. United States. Congress. Senate—Biography. 7. Bruce, Roscoe Conkling, 1879–1950. 8. Bruce, Blanche Kelso, 1841–1898—Family. 9. Bruce family, I. Title.
E664.B865G73 2006
929'.208996073—dc 22

2005055146

06 07 08 09 10 NMSG/RRD 10 9 8 7 6 5 4 3 2 1

To my mother,
Betty Johnyce Walker Graham,
for challenging bias
with courage and grace.

To my father,
Richard Charles Graham,
for remembering our
people's history.

To my wife,
Pamela Thomas-Graham,
for everything else.

Contents

Preface and
Acknowledgments

⤳⧢⧢⤳

HE WAS A FORMER SLAVE WHO LIVED IN MISSISSIPPI AND UNDERSTOOD
how to exploit the harsh rules that governed black-white relations during the post–Civil War period. She was the daughter of a wealthy black
doctor whose family socialized with and drew on their black Northern
society connections in Philadelphia, Cleveland, and Washington. He
was a shrewd political operative who learned how to forge ties between
newly freed blacks and white Republicans while also building a real
estate portfolio that would fund his political career. She was the sophisticated educator who could bring polish, style, and an understanding of
black and white society to the union. Together, they straddled the black
and white upper-class worlds with a calculated finesse that made their
work seem almost effortless.

The family forged between Senator Blanche Kelso Bruce and his
wife, Josephine Willson Bruce, was an extraordinary one, which came
to represent wealth, position, academic accomplishment, notoriety, and
power in both black and white circles. It was a family that united two
very different people from two very different circles.

I wrote this book in order to tell the story of how a slave born in
1841 rose from being a minor landowner in Mississippi to becoming the
first African-American to serve a full term as a United States senator.
Through his friendships with President Ulysses S. Grant, Frederick
Douglass, Booker T. Washington, and many white Republicans and

Democrats, Bruce gained appointments under four presidents and was twice named to a Treasury post that placed his name on U.S. currency.

In researching the lives of Senator Bruce and his wife, Josephine, I found something more than the accomplishments of two individuals who thrived in spite of the racial discrimination that surrounded them. By following three fascinating generations of this upper-class family from 1841 to 1967, I discovered America's first true black dynasty.

While the family moves from Virginia to Mississippi to Washington, DC, to Tuskegee to Boston and, finally, in the late 1920s, to New York, the important events in our nation's history unfold with dramatic consequences. Along with this political history comes a social history that describes the rise and fall of America's first black upper-class family.

This is a family that produced successive generations of Ivy League graduates: a son who graduated from a prestigious East Coast WASP establishment school, Phillips Exeter Academy, and went on to become a Phi Beta Kappa graduate of Harvard University; a daughter-in-law who entered Radcliffe College in 1901 and who, while at Boston University Law School, became the first woman of any color to serve as president of a law review. Their grandchildren were similarly educated at Exeter, Harvard, Radcliffe, and Harvard Law School—all at a time when members of the black upper class lived awkwardly and quietly between a black America that didn't understand them and a white America that feared or despised them. It was a family that at one time owned an 1,100-acre plantation, summer homes, residences in three states, and town houses in Washington where they entertained the most powerful black and white political figures of the nineteenth century.

The family story of Blanche and Josephine Bruce shows how a black U.S. senator and his black socialite wife became a lightning rod for politics, social discourse, and racial intrigue that mystified most whites and angered many blacks. It is a story that bridges the Civil War, Reconstruction, "Southern Redemption," northern migration, the 1929 economic depression, and the modern civil rights period.

In their later generations, the Bruce family enhanced their status by forging a ten-year relationship with multimillionaire philanthropist John D. Rockefeller Jr.; by producing a superintendent of the Washington, DC, segregated school district; and by marrying into families that brought them additional contacts. When the senator's granddaughter eloped with the light-skinned son of an elite black Washington family, her father attempted to annul the marriage out of fear that it would jeopardize her admission to Radcliffe. Years later, the marriage would become even more complicated, when the husband passed for white in order to succeed as an actor in Hollywood and on the New York stage. This decision required the senator's granddaughter to "divorce" her family and relinquish her black identity.

But the Bruce family also made enemies by taking on public battles with many people, such as nineteenth-century conservatives in the Senate; the twentieth-century black newspaper publisher who chased them out of Washington because he felt the Bruces acted "too white"; the president of Harvard who, in 1923, refused to allow one of the Bruce children to move into an all-white dormitory; and powerful Harlem residents who felt the Bruce family looked down on those around them. Because their loyalties to the black working classes were questioned in Washington and again in Harlem, they had an awkward relationship with many blacks in America. But they similarly offended whites, because they demanded respect for their own race and position.

Finally, they faced economic losses and public humiliation when the senator's grandson, also an Exeter and Harvard alumnus, was sent to prison in 1937 for a crime that dominated national headlines. After decades of ostentatious wealth, it was a loss that, in the end, put the family on the rolls of New York City's welfare department.

I first became intrigued by the Bruce family during a presentation to an audience of Harvard students several years after I had graduated. I was there to speak about my book *Our Kind of People*, a social history of America's black upper class. The audience, which consisted of college students and several adults from the community, had just finished asking me questions about my research, when one student approached me after the discussion. Holding a copy of the book, he pointed to a 1969 photo that showed Edward Brooke, the black senator from Massachusetts, standing next to a black Detroit debutante. After reading the picture's caption, this student, an eighteen-year-old freshman, was incredulous and announced, "I thought Carol Moseley-Braun was the first black senator!"

To my surprise, no one in the group offered a correction. I perused the audience, stunned to discover that the collective memory—or understanding of our black history—was this shallow. "No," I answered. "Ed

Brooke was elected to the U.S. Senate in 1966. And about a hundred years before that," I added, to drive my point home, "there were two black senators—Hiram Revels, who was elected to a partial term; and Blanche Bruce, who was the first black elected to a full six-year term. In fact, Bruce's son went to college here."

I walked away from the conversation, disturbed that a college student could be so unaware of a basic historical fact, but also very embarrassed that I, myself, didn't have much more knowledge of the circumstances that made it possible for a black man to be elected to the U.S. Senate *and* to send his son to Harvard in the 1890s. So, this book started as a project to educate myself, as well as to record the story of a fascinating American family.

My research was aided by several institutions and many more individuals. They are: Howard University and its Moorland-Spingarn Research Center, which shared the many private letters written by Senator Bruce, Josephine Bruce, Clara Bruce, Roscoe Bruce Sr. and Jr.; the reference staff of Harvard University Archives in Nathan Pusey Library, which shared the school records, personal letters, and other data related to Roscoe Bruce Sr. and Jr.; Jane Knowles, archivist at Radcliffe College, who provided letters, school records, and other data on Clara Washington Burrill Bruce and Clara Washington Bruce; Fern Coleman of the Office of the Registrar of Harvard Law School, who provided school records on Burrill Bruce; the Schomburg Library; the New York Public Library; the Library of Congress; Boston University Law School archives, which supplied student information on Clara Burrill Bruce; Peter Knapp, archivist at Trinity College who provided information on Bruce family friend T. John Syphax, later known as T. John McKee; Leigh Bonney, a good friend who opened the doors of Phillips Exeter Academy for me; Ed Desrochers, archivist at Phillips Exeter, who provided records on Roscoe Bruce Sr. and Roscoe Bruce Jr. during their years at the school; Tuskegee University, which shared its records during the time that Roscoe Bruce worked for Booker T. Washington; Columbia University's Keith Walton, Susan Hamson, and Jocelyn Wilk; Betty Koed, assistant curator in the U.S. Senate Historical Office, who opened many files on Senator Bruce, Senator Revels, and others who served in the U.S. Senate during the 1870s and 1880s; Melinda Smith of the U.S. Senate Curator's Office, who provided information on the senator's term as well as on the creation of the senator's official portrait and its unveiling.

Special gratitude is owed to two institutions that three generations of the Bruce family held dear: Harvard University and Howard University. I am especially grateful to the following people at Harvard who made my four years of research at the school possible. They are President Lawrence Summers, Barbara Graham, Robert Cashion, and Barbara Meloni. At Howard University and its Moorland-Spingarn Research Center, I am gratful to Thomas Battle, Donna Wells, Clifford Muse, Jean Currie Church, and Joellen El Bashir.

I also thank Sandra Miranda and her staff at the White Plains Public Library; Mount Vernon Public Library; Mark Hasskarl and his staff at the Chappaqua Public Library; Scarsdale Public Library; Mississippi Department of Archives and History in Jackson, Mississippi; the staff of the Library of Congress, which shared files of clippings, personal letters, and notes written by Senator Bruce; Historical Society of Washington, DC; the staff of the Charles Sumner Museum of the Board of Education of Washington, DC, for their records on Roscoe Bruce when he served as superintendent of the Colored Schools; Mary Edwards of the Curator's Office at the Department of the U.S. Treasury, who gave me facts concerning Senator Bruce's time spent as register of the U.S. Treasury; Nan Card, curator at the Hayes Library and Rutherford B. Hayes Presidential Center; William Pickens; the Association of the Bar of the City of New York; and Sigma Pi Phi's Khephra Burns and Peyton Williams.

I learned details about a whole new generation of Bruce family members from the following people, and I thank them: Marnie Pillsbury in David Rockefeller's Office at the Rockefeller Family Office in Manhattan, who allowed me to collect data on the ten-year period when Roscoe and Clara Bruce worked for John D. Rockefeller Jr. in the 1920s and 1930s; Kenneth Rose, Michele Hiltzik, and the research staff at the Rockefeller Family Archive Center at Pocantico Hills, who shared dozens of letters written to Roscoe Bruce, bank documents and articles and photos that chronicled the years when the Bruce family was employed by the Rockefellers at the Dunbar Apartments and Dunbar National Bank. I thank Andrew Tisch and Mary Schmidt Campbell, dean of New York University's Tisch School of Arts, for giving me access to historical information on the Bruce family in New York and elsewhere. I am grateful to Bruce family descendant Dr. Norma Rozelle, who was kind enough to give me two very long interviews as she shared details from her family's personal records. I also thank friends who assisted me in my research—Gregory Schwarz and Jamil French—who helped in between college, law school, and their new careers. I thank Stephen Gura, Jeannie Goldie, New York *Amsterdam News* archives, Keith Walton and Aubria Corbitt, Cathy Hemming, Susan Weinberg, and Jane Friedman at HarperCollins for believing in me.

There were many friends and colleagues who assisted me in ways that went beyond my library and archival research. Within that group, I must include Rev. James Forbes of Riverside Church, Tina Brown and Harold Evans, Vernon Jordan, Ann and Andrew Tisch, Bill Lewis, Jackie Leo, Brian Duffy, Pamela and Leonard Yablon, Lisa Linden, Judy Marcus, Lawrence and Teresa Hamdan, Jay Ward, Debbie Perry, Marcella Maxwell, Earl Graves, Hazel Dukes, Percy Sutton, Roscoe Brown, Paul and Ammie Williams, Helen and Milton Williams, Judith Riggs, Dorothy and Vicki Holloway, Janet Wells, Anita Jackson, Lynne Perry-Bottinger, Dauna Williams, Jordan Horvath, Larry and Laura Gordon, Charles Ogletree, and Derrick Bell.

I am honored to have an editor like Marjorie Braman, because she demanded the best from me—and gave the best of herself—over an extended period that included the deaths of both of my parents and other losses. This history is more complete because of her, and she helped turn that period of researching and writing into one of triumph. I thank my literary agent, Esther Newberg, for taking me through this process all these years. And I thank Tammy Richards, Kathy Schneider, and especially Peggy Hageman for keeping the papers flowing in the right direction. On my own home turf in New York and Chappaqua, I thank the people that make my life run smoothly. They are Carmen Villar, Laurie Lotz, and Carol Rodriguez, because they organize and inspire every day. And there is my family—Searcy O. Graham, Richard E. Graham, Delores Harris, Claudia Foston, Jean Walker, Mirian Calhoun Hinds, Sandy Eulinberg Fletcher, Magnolia Williams, and dear Margaret Morton and Barry Cozier—who have given me a lifetime of reasons for getting our people's history right.

When this project began, my parents, Betty and Richard Graham, were a continual resource for me as they opened their personal address books and called their contacts in Harlem, Memphis, Tuskegee, and Washington, and connected me with people who gave me information on the Bruce family and the institutions the family was associated with during its three generations. I am grateful to them and all our friends in Jack & Jill, Horace Mann School, the Links, and Sigma Pi Phi Boulé for their networks that helped me.

I thank my children, Gordon, Harrison, and Lindsey, for giving me their patience and enthusiasm. And finally, I express my greatest gratitude to my brilliant wife, Pamela Thomas-Graham, whom I continue to admire as she balances her own corporate career and writing career while also giving me advice and inspiration. I thank her for giving me support every step of the way.

LAWRENCE OTIS GRAHAM

Chappaqua, New York

Cast of Characters

BLANCHE KELSO BRUCE—Born a slave in 1841 in Prince Edward County, Virginia, he later moved to Mississippi and became a Republican politician. Married Josephine Beal Willson in Cleveland, Ohio. Father of Roscoe Conkling Bruce Sr. Elected to the U.S. Senate from Mississippi in 1874, later served as register of the U.S. Treasury under Presidents James Garfield, Chester A. Arthur, and William McKinley. Served as recorder of deeds for Washington, DC, under President Benjamin Harrison.

JOSEPHINE BEAL WILLSON BRUCE—The wife of Senator Blanche K. Bruce and mother of Roscoe Conkling Bruce Sr. Born in Philadelphia in 1853 to Dr. Joseph Willson and Elizabeth Harnett Willson. Married Blanche Bruce in 1878 in Cleveland, Ohio, and became a respected socialite hostess among Washington's white liberals and the black elite. Originally an elementary school teacher, she was hired in 1899 by Booker T. Washington as lady principal (dean of women) at Tuskegee Institute, and in 1901 ran unsuccessfully for the national presidency of the National Association of Colored Women.

ROSCOE CONKLING BRUCE SR.—The only child of Blanche and Josephine Bruce. Born in Washington in 1879, he graduated from Phillips Exeter Academy and Harvard University. Served as head of Education Department at Tuskegee Institute, then as superintendent of Washington, DC, Colored School System, then as manager of John D. Rockefeller's Dunbar Apartments in New York City. Married childhood friend Clara Burrill.

CLARA WASHINGTON BURRILL BRUCE—The childhood friend and later wife of Roscoe Bruce Sr. Mother of Clara Jr., Roscoe Jr., and Burrill Bruce. Born in 1880, she attended Radcliffe College and Boston University Law School, where she became president of the law review, and the first black woman to pass the Massachusetts bar. Published essays and poetry in several publications, including the *Saturday Evening Post*. Served as assistant manager of Rockefeller's Dunbar Apartments.

CLARA BRUCE JR.—Oldest child and only daughter of Roscoe Bruce Sr. and Clara Bruce Sr. Born in 1904, attended Washington, DC, Dunbar High School and Howard University, and Radcliffe College in Massachusetts. Against parents' wishes, married Washington friend Barrington Guy. After having two sons, Clara and Barrington began passing as Indian and white in the 1940s.

ROSCOE CONKLING BRUCE JR.—Oldest son of Roscoe Conkling Bruce Sr. and Clara Washington Burrill Bruce. Born in 1906, attended Phillips Exeter Academy and Harvard University. The subject in 1923 of a nationwide public battle, in which he was initially denied a room in white freshman dorms at Harvard. Hired by Prudential Insurance to manage Richard B. Harrison Apartments in New Jersey and was sent to state prison in 1937, after staging a false robbery to conceal his mismanagement of rent monies.

BURRILL K. BRUCE—Youngest son of Roscoe Conkling Bruce Sr. and Clara Washington Burrill Bruce. Born in 1909, attended Cambridge Latin School, New York University, and Harvard Law School. Practiced law in New York City.

BARRINGTON GUY JR. (LATER KNOWN AS BARRINGTON SHARMA)—Washington, DC, childhood friend of Clara Bruce Jr. Eloped with Clara when she was entering Radcliffe and refused parents' wishes to annul the marriage. During the 1920s and 1930s, he performed as a black actor and singer in New York plays and nightclubs, and in movies. In 1940, changed last name to "Sharma" in order to pass for white or Indian, and performed in nonblack clubs and venues.

POLLY BRUCE—Mother of Blanche Bruce. Worked as a house slave for white owner, Lemuel Bruce. She was later owned by Lemuel Bruce's daughter Rebecca Bruce Perkinson and Rebecca's husband, Pettis Perkinson. Died in Leavenworth, Kansas, in the 1880s.

HENRY CLAY BRUCE—One of Blanche K. Bruce's older brothers. Became active in the Kansas State Republican Party, served as doorkeeper of the State Senate, and ran unsuccessfully for Kansas State Legislature in 1880. Later worked in Washington, DC, for U.S. Pension Department. Published his autobiography, *The New Man: Twenty-nine Years a Slave, Twenty-nine Years a Free Man*, in 1895.

JOSEPH WILLSON—The father of Josephine Willson and father-in-law of Blanche Bruce. Born in 1817, he was one of the few black dentists in Philadelphia during the mid-1800s. He was born in Georgia, raised in Philadelphia, and educated in Quaker schools. He authored a book on the black elite in 1841, *Sketches of the Higher Classes Among the Colored Society in Philadelphia*. According to the Richmond County, Georgia, archives, his father, John, was a founding director, in 1810, of the Bank of Augusta.

ELIZABETH HARNETT WILLSON—The mother of Josephine Willson and mother-in-law of Blanche Bruce. Like her husband, Joseph, she was born a free black person in Georgia.

LEONIDAS WILLSON—Brother to Josephine Willson and brother-in-law to Blanche Bruce. Born in Philadelphia in 1846, he was one of the most successful black attorneys in the city and later in Cleveland. After his first marriage, he ended his ties to the black community and with his black family during the late 1890s.

EMILY WILLSON HARANG—Oldest sister to Josephine Willson. Her husband became the manager of Josephine and Blanche Bruce's Mississippi plantation after the senator's death in 1898.

MARY WILLSON—The first of Josephine Willson's two unmarried younger sisters who taught grammar school in Indianapolis.

VICTORIA WILLSON—The second of Josephine Willson's two unmarried younger sisters who taught grammar school in Indianapolis.

LEMUEL BRUCE—Original white slave owner of Blanche Bruce's mother, Polly. Father of Rebecca Bruce Perkinson.

REBECCA BRUCE PERKINSON—Daughter of Lemuel Bruce. Married to Pettis Perkinson and owner of Blanche Bruce.

WILLIE PERKINSON—White son of Blanche Bruce's slave owners, Pettis Perkinson and Rebecca Bruce Perkinson, in Virginia. Childhood playmate of Blanche; later joined the Confederate Army.

GEORGE CORNELIUS SMITH—Close black friend and confidant to

Blanche Bruce in Ohio, Mississippi, and Washington. Often served as personal secretary and adviser on Senator Bruce's correspondence and speeches. Wrote articles about Blanche.

ADELBERT AMES—Liberal white Republican supporter of Blanche Bruce, who served as provisional governor of Mississippi in 1868–1870, then was U.S. senator representing Mississippi in 1870–1874, and later served as governor of Mississippi in 1874–1876. Born in Maine, he was a graduate of West Point and served as a corporal and brigadier general for the Union Army.

JAMES ALCORN—White Republican supporter of Blanche Bruce up until the time Bruce was elected to the Senate. Alcorn wavered between moderate and liberal positions, and served as governor of Mississippi in 1870–1871, then as U.S. senator representing Mississippi in 1871–1877. Refused to "present" Bruce to the Senate body on the day of Bruce's swearing in at the Capitol.

ROSCOE CONKLING—Liberal white Republican U.S. senator representing New York (1867–1881), and mentor of Blanche Bruce when the latter joined the Senate. Was the namesake for Blanche's only child, Roscoe Conkling Bruce. A powerful political boss, Conkling got Bruce named to various Senate committees. He later fell out of favor with President James Garfield.

JOHN ROY LYNCH—Black friend and political adviser to Blanche Bruce. Served as speaker of the House in Mississippi legislature. Elected to U.S. House of Representatives in 1872, and then again in 1882. By the 1890s, became one of the wealthiest blacks in Washington. Worked with James Hill to maintain control over Mississippi Republican Party.

JAMES HILL—Black friend and Mississippi political adviser to Blanche and John Roy Lynch. Served as Mississippi secretary of state and worked with John Roy Lynch and Blanche Bruce to maintain control over Mississippi Republican Party during 1870s and 1880s. Later resented Bruce's national success and felt unappreciated after keeping Bruce's power base in place.

PINCKNEY BENTON STEWART (P. B. S.) PINCHBACK—Wealthy black Republican Louisiana politician and friend of Blanche Bruce. In 1868, elected to the State Senate, then served as lieutenant governor and governor of Louisiana, and published the black weekly newspaper,

The New Orleans Louisianian. Was elected to the U.S. Senate, but was never allowed to be seated. Later moved to Washington, DC.

GEORGE HOAR—White liberal Republican friend and Senate colleague to Blanche Bruce. Powerful U.S. senator from Massachusetts—serving 1877–1904—who hailed from aristocratic New England family of politicians. Descendant of Harvard president Leonard Hoar and brother of U.S. Attorney General Ebenezer Hoar. Graduated from Harvard and sat on the school's board of overseers. Helped Blanche Bruce's son gain entrance to Phillips Exeter and Harvard.

FREDERICK DOUGLASS—Born a slave in 1817 in Maryland, he became one of the most prominent abolitionists in the nation. Supporter, adviser, and friend to Blanche and Josephine Bruce. Served as minister to Haiti, recorder of deeds, and president of Freedman's Savings and Trust Co. Asked Blanche and Josephine Bruce to serve as his witnesses at his controversial second marriage—to Helen Pitts, a white feminist newspaper editor and teacher—in 1884.

ARCHIBALD HENRY GRIMKÉ—Black friend of Blanche and Josephine Bruce. An 1874 Harvard Law School graduate, Grimké was appointed by Bruce to represent Massachusetts in the Colored Exhibits at the World's Industrial and Cotton Centennial Exposition in New Orleans in 1885, but Grimké later publicly denounced the worldwide gathering because its exhibits were racially segregated. Grimké's brother, Francis, was the prominent Washington minister at Fifteenth Street Presbyterian Church.

T. JOHN MINTON SYPHAX (LATER KNOWN AS T. JOHN MCKEE)—Black childhood friend of Roscoe Sr. Attended Phillips Exeter with Roscoe, then Trinity College and Columbia University School of Law, where he changed his name and began passing as white. Became Wall Street lawyer and married a white woman in New York City. Later, in the 1940s, publicly acknowledged his true black identity in order to claim the remainder of his black grandfather's two-million dollar estate. Descendant of black elite Syphax family who donated their land to enlarge Arlington National Cemetery.

LUCIUS Q. C. LAMAR—White Democratic Mississippi politician who served as leading spokesman against Reconstruction and against black equality. Served in U.S. House of Representatives before and after Civil War, and as U.S. senator in 1877–1885. As junior senator from Mississippi, had cordial relations with senior senator Blanche Bruce. Although a segregationist, he reportedly recommended Bruce for cabinet post and later served on the Supreme Court.

BOOKER T. WASHINGTON—Founder of Tuskegee Institute and influential educator who advised blacks to embrace trade schools and industrial labor rather than liberal arts colleges and professional careers. With the political and economic support of white industrialists, such as Andrew Carnegie and J. Pierpoint Morgan, became the most powerful black man in America. Hired Josephine Bruce as lady principal in 1899; paid Roscoe Jr. to "spy" on Booker's opponents in Boston while Roscoe was a Harvard student. Later hired Roscoe to head Tuskegee Institute's Education Department in 1903. Disliked by many among the black elite.

ROBERT TERRELL—Black Washington lawyer and friend to Blanche and Josephine Bruce. Class of 1884 graduate of Harvard College, lawyer and municipal judge in Washington. Married to Mary Church of Memphis, daughter of Robert Church, the wealthiest black man in the American South. With his politically active wife, Mary—who later sat on the Washington, DC, Board of Education—he served as mentor to Roscoe C. Bruce Sr.

ULYSSES S. GRANT—Eighteenth president of the United States. Served in 1869–1877. Liberal Republican who supported Reconstruction policies and befriended Blanche Bruce. Hosted Senator and Mrs. Bruce in Europe during their 1878 honeymoon.

RUTHERFORD B. HAYES—Nineteenth president of the United States. Served in 1877–1881. Although he served as a Republican, his election was a key element of the Compromise of 1877, which led to the end of Reconstruction and advanced the racial goals of white Democrats and Southerners.

JAMES GARFIELD—Twentieth president of the United States. Served in 1881. Ohio Republican who appointed Blanche K. Bruce as register of the U.S. Treasury. Became a foe of Bruce mentor Roscoe Conkling.

CHESTER A. ARTHUR—Twenty-first president of the United States. Served in 1881–1885, after Garfield's assassination. Kept Bruce as register of the U.S. Treasury.

BENJAMIN HARRISON—Twenty-third president of the United States. Served in 1889–1893. Indiana Republican who opposed putting blacks in important government roles, but was pressured into appointing Blanche Bruce recorder of deeds for Washington, DC.

WILLIAM MCKINLEY—Twenty-fifth president of the United States. Served in 1897–1901. Ohio Republican who appointed Blanche K. Bruce as register of the U.S. Treasury.

WILLIAM WINDOM—Republican politician from Minnesota. Served as U.S. senator during Bruce's time in the Senate. Appointed secretary of the Treasury by President Garfield; Bruce's boss when the latter became register of the Treasury in 1881.

CALVIN CHASE—Attorney and publisher of the black Washington newspaper *The Washington Bee*, which he ran from 1882 to 1921. Was a friend to Blanche Bruce, serving as a pallbearer at the senator's funeral. Was a major critic of Roscoe C. Bruce Sr., and led an aggressive and successful campaign to have Roscoe fired as superintendent of the city's Colored Schools. Was critical of elite blacks who made compromises with whites.

A. LAWRENCE LOWELL—President of Harvard University from 1909 until 1933. Born into a prominent New England family, he graduated from Harvard College and Harvard Law School, and established the school's "house system." Created discriminatory housing policy that barred blacks from the freshman dormitories in Harvard Yard. Lost a public fight to keep Roscoe Bruce Jr. out of the all-white dormitories.

JOHN D. ROCKEFELLER JR.—Philanthropist, powerful New York businessman, and investor in real estate. Son of Standard Oil founder John D. Rockefeller. Built the Dunbar Apartments complex in Harlem in 1926, which was the first housing development for the black middle class in New York City. Hired Roscoe C. Bruce and Clara B. Bruce to manage the Dunbar from 1927 to 1936.

CHARLES O. HEYDT—Chief real estate adviser to John D. Rockefeller Jr. and senior executive at Rockefeller's office, which ran the Dunbar Apartments in Harlem. Beginning in 1927, served as liaison between John D. Rockefeller Jr. and Roscoe C. Bruce Sr.

HARRIET SHADD BUTCHER—Washington family friend of Roscoe and Clara Bruce's, who moved to New York City in 1920s. Served as a teacher in Washington's Colored Schools, then later became superintendent at Russell Sage Foundation in New York City. Helped Roscoe get a job at Rockefeller-owned Dunbar Apartments. Had many New York City "dates" (possibly an affair) with Roscoe while his wife, Clara, was living in Cambridge and attending law school. Won a public 1929 lawsuit, humiliating Roscoe, after accusing him of not repaying her several thousand dollars.

❦

CHAPTER ONE

1875

A Senator Is Sworn In and a Dynasty Begins

ON THE FRIDAY MORNING OF MARCH 5, 1875, THE FIRST BLACK MAN elected to a full term as senator of the United States, Blanche Kelso Bruce of Mississippi, sat in seat number two of the Senate Chamber, awaiting his swearing in. Behind him, in the mammoth room, stretched the crescent-shaped arrangement of wide wooden seats. There were three rows of chairs with a desk for every seat—seventy-four in all— one for each of the two senators from the thirty-seven states that, in 1875, made up the Union. Tall Corinthian pilasters framed the room.

Thanks to windows high above in the thirty-five-foot iron-and-glass ceiling, the otherwise windowless room was not as dim as the new senator from Mississippi might have expected. As Bruce sat there on his first day, dressed in a black waistcoat, bow tie, and a stiff cotton shirt, with his handlebar mustache and a fourteen-karat gold pocket watch, he might have convinced himself that he was the very picture of a Reconstruction survivor who had succeeded and who proved that leaders could be elected and accepted, regardless of their color. He might have convinced himself that he was living proof that race and class no longer mattered in the United States, that it was possible for a black former slave from Virginia to overcome poverty, bigotry, and political differences in order to enjoy the same success that white men of achievement were enjoying. But it would have been almost impossible to really believe those things.

By the time Blanche Bruce arrived in Washington, DC, for his swearing-in ceremony, Reconstruction policies had been in place for nearly ten years, making it possible for blacks in Southern states not only to vote but also to run for office and receive municipal, state, and federal appointments.

But now that Bruce finally had been elected, the tide was already starting to turn against blacks—particularly in his home state of Mississippi. Although the Northern states were in step with the liberal Republicans who controlled Congress, Mississippi residents were unwilling to allow this national liberal mood to continue sweeping through their state, even if it meant they had to rely on coercion and illegal activity. There, the white Democrats and hate groups such as the Ku Klux Klan were inciting racial violence and organizing aggressive ballot-stuffing in order to discourage black citizens and black candidates from voting or running for office. At the very moment Bruce sat in the Senate, his white constituents back home were contemplating methods for driving black legislators out of office, and his primary mentor, Governor Adelbert Ames, was losing control of Mississippi to renegade groups. Even the newspapers in his home state were supporting the suppression of black freedmen as a means to stomp out Reconstruction and return to the old order.

It was clear to Bruce and many other black political figures that Reconstruction's underpinnings were never fully accepted by white Southerners. It had been undermined at each step since it was first introduced by President Lincoln in 1865. When the liberal Republican anti-slavery president was shot just five days after the Confederate Army surrendered to General Ulysses S. Grant, black Americans inherited a new pro-slavery president. Besides being a virulent racist and former Tennessee Democrat, Andrew Johnson did not believe in black equality and sought to veto all congressional acts that attempted to give the recently freed blacks an education, job training, or even citizenship. He also opposed any military protection for blacks against violence from newly established hate groups such as the Klan. As a native Southerner himself, Johnson was so sympathetic to the vanquished Confederate states he permitted them to establish discriminatory Black Codes that severely limited the movement, activities, and rights of recently freed blacks. Bruce's home state of Mississippi had been the first to create these codes. It was not until the Reconstruction Acts of 1867, which provided for military rule in Southern states, that black citizens finally benefited from the new legal rights and opportunities that were promised to them at the end of the Civil War. It was then that blacks could finally play a role in drafting new state constitutions and run for positions in political party conventions. Almost immediately, in 1868, the first black was elected to the House of Representatives.[1]

By 1875, many of the Democratic newspapers in Mississippi and other parts of the South argued that white citizens should begin voting along "color lines" and using "the aggressive instincts of the white people" to defeat the blacks and the Republicans.[2] During the same month that Bruce was sworn in to the U.S. Senate, one of his own state's newspapers, *The Hinds County Gazette*, would run a pro-Democrat editorial that said, "[Governor] Ames and his negroes [have] swept away every vestige of republican government in Mississippi" and that the people "have been robbed of their birthright."[3] This message of racial hatred was beginning to turn the tide against the freed blacks, even as Blanche Bruce won the right to represent his state in the Senate.

Bruce must have been nervous as he looked around the poorly ventilated Senate chamber, waiting to be sworn in. Staring down at him was the broad second-floor gallery that wrapped around all four sides of the chamber. Only a few rays of light broke through the twenty-one glass ceiling panels. Crowded toward the front, the seventy-four desks and their occupants all faced the lectern and the vice president's desk, where Bruce and twenty-two other men would be sworn in that day.

At noon, Vice President Henry Wilson called the room to order. "O Thou Almighty and everlasting God, the maker of heaven and earth," began Reverend Byron Sunderland, the Senate chaplain, as he offered the opening prayer. "Give them to see eye to eye, in all the grave matters of this nation committed to their charge, and in all their labors and responsibilities may they lean upon Thy arm for support. Through Jesus Christ. Amen."[4]

Next, the chief clerk read a proclamation from President Ulysses S. Grant declaring that the special session of the Senate was permitted to convene that day. Surrounding the senators' seats were 1,700 yards of floral-patterned purple carpeting and ornate walls with heavy plaster crown molding. Wilson, himself a former senator from Massachusetts, had already asked more than a dozen newly elected senators to proceed to the front of the grand room, each escorted by the senior senator from the same state. For this group of senators-elect, the tradition of using escorts was, indeed, necessary, since nineteen of the twenty-three senators to be sworn in that day were completely new to the governmental body.

Then it was Bruce's turn.

"Senator-elect Blanche Kelso Bruce of Mississippi," called Vice President Wilson's voice into the large ornate chamber.

Bruce unclasped his hands and stood slowly as he looked at the men around him.

"Senator-elect Blanche Kelso Bruce," the loud voice at the front repeated. "Of Mississippi!"

Three long rows of men, many of them white-haired, turned to Bruce and waited with curious expressions. They watched and waited for Bruce's escort to come to the black man's side.

But no escort came. The senior senator from Mississippi, James Lusk Alcorn, did not move. He remained in seat number fourteen, his face hidden behind a newspaper.

The lone black man in the room, Bruce finally moved to the end of his row and then glanced back at Alcorn, who remained in his seat. Seeing that Alcorn was not going to follow proper protocol and lead the senator-elect to the front, Bruce looked to the front, adjusted his coat, and strolled slowly down the purple carpeted aisle by himself.

As Bruce advanced a few steps, he was suddenly joined by a thin, full-bearded man with a receding hairline.

"If I may, Mr. Bruce," the courtly white gentleman said with a slight nod as he took Bruce's arm. "Permit me. I am the senator from New York, Roscoe Conkling."

The room of white men watched in stunned silence as the two reached the front. Bruce would later share his experience with the *National Republican*:

> When I came up to the Senate, I knew no one except Senator Alcorn, who was my colleague. When the names of the new Senators were called out for them to go up and take the oath, all the others except myself were escorted by their colleagues. Mr. Alcorn made no motion to escort me, but was buried behind a newspaper, and I concluded I would go it alone . . . [Conkling] linked his arm in mine and we marched up to the desk

together. I took the oath and then he escorted me back to my seat. Later in the day when they were fixing up the committees, Conkling asked me if any one was looking out after my interests, and upon my informing him that there was not and that I was myself more ignorant of my rights in the matter, he volunteered to attend to it, and as a result, I was placed on some very good committees.[5]

He and Conkling would eventually enjoy a long friendship in the Senate (Bruce would ultimately name his own son after the white Republican senator from New York), and Bruce would never again feel so vulnerable in the Senate Chamber as he felt that day.

For even though he was reaching the greatest heights of power and dignity possible for a black man in America, he simultaneously could see how easily all of it could be taken away—both in that chamber and back home in Mississippi.

At that moment, Bruce was certain that he had reached the pinnacle of his career. He was a thirty-four-year-old black man who had begun life as a fatherless Virginia slave and risen to become a powerful U.S. senator. Between the time he had escaped bondage in 1863 and now—just twelve years—he had left his siblings and mother in Missouri, studied at Oberlin College in Ohio, taught school in Kansas, and taken up residence in Mississippi, where Reconstruction policies made it possible for him to join and quickly rise through the ranks of the Republican Party. By cultivating the right white mentors, like Mississippi governor Adelbert Ames, and the powerful white scalawags, like Senator James Alcorn, he got himself appointed or elected to such positions as county sheriff, tax collector, school superintendent, and county commissioner in northwestern Mississippi's Bolivar County. None of his white benefactors, including Alcorn, had expected him to move beyond the status of local government official. And it was because people always underestimated Bruce's ambition and his talents that his white colleagues never felt threatened by his accomplishments.

Always clever and forever expressing gratitude to those who had helped him in the past, he learned how to perform favors for those who could help him in the future. He also learned how to both buy and foreclose on properties for which he had been assigned to collect overdue taxes. By doing so, Bruce managed to amass enough rental property in his own Mississippi town to supplement the salaries from his overlapping municipal jobs. With these earnings, he was eventually able to purchase an eight-hundred-acre plantation that produced enough cotton, corn, and livestock to finance his political and social ambitions.

Throughout this time, he identified other bright and ambitious black men who expressed an interest in politics and business. Together with them, he assembled a black political machine that reached out to the large number of black freedmen who were eager to exercise the voting rights that they had been denied as slaves. Soon, Bruce and his black political colleagues were noticed by white Republican carpetbaggers and scalawags who saw how the Republican Party could benefit from an association with Bruce and the black voters who believed in him. These were the same whites who recognized how the nation's 450,000 black Republican votes made it possible for President Grant to defeat his Democratic opponent by 300,000 votes.

It would not be long before the white Mississippi Republicans saw that they could exert true dominance over the Southern Democrats once they embraced the blacks and made them a part of their Republican Party structure. And this consolidation of forces—one white and one black—was the factor that precipitated Blanche Kelso Bruce's rise to power and ultimately got him elected to the U.S. Senate in 1874 and brought him to the Senate chamber on this day in March of 1875.

At that moment, Bruce probably felt he had done all that a black man could possibly dream of. Only four days earlier, Congress had passed a Civil Rights Act that ended discrimination in all public accommodations. He had become a national figure at an important time in America's history. His very presence there allowed him to occupy a page in the history books. But there would be many more goals for this man to reach, and many barriers for him to break as he advanced in the world of politics and business.

Here was a man who would not only be the first black to serve a full term in the U.S. Senate but also serve as a power broker among white and black political figures in both parties for the next twenty years. Even as Reconstruction was to be unraveled on a national level, and segregation began to undermine the gains that blacks had gotten in government and elsewhere in society during this period, Bruce would be nominated for vice president, gain the friendship of President Grant, serve as head of the Mississippi State Republicans, and ultimately receive top appointments in the Treasury Department and elsewhere from Presidents Garfield, Arthur, Harrison, and McKinley. And, surprising to even him, two of these presidents would make it possible for him to be the first black man to have his signature printed on U.S. currency.

Perhaps even more interesting, Bruce would establish the first black American dynasty—one that mirrored the white dynasties formed by his contemporaries, such as the Hoars of Massachusetts, the Roosevelts of New York, the Frelinghuysens of New Jersey, and the Harrisons of Ohio. He ruled over a black Washington society that included such friends as abolitionist Frederick Douglass, hotel owner James Wormley, attorney and minister to Haiti John Mercer Langston, educator Booker T. Washington, and Memphis-born millionairess Mary Church Terrell and her Harvard-educated husband, Judge Robert Terrell, who would later help Bruce's son gain admission to Harvard College. Two years into his six-year Senate term, Bruce would solidify his position by marrying into an upper-class black family that brought him prestige and access to a larger freeborn black elite community that had previously been closed to him as a former slave. At the time, his net worth was estimated at just over $150,000—more than $2.5 million in today's dollars—an astounding sum at the time, for a black or a white.

Marrying the educated and light-complexioned Philadelphia-born Josephine Willson enabled Bruce to parlay his money, his vast real estate holdings, and his career credentials into a package that made him attractive to the liberal white Washington community as well. Josephine was sufficiently elegant and respected that their 1878 wedding became the first black nuptials to be reported in the society columns of the *New York Times* and the *Washington Post*.[6] As the daughter of a freeborn black dentist and the granddaughter of the founder of the Bank of Augusta, Josephine had all the credentials and exposure to prepare her for the life of Washington's first black socialite and hostess to the world's black elite. Many of the nation's newspapers wrote stories about her afternoon teas, and made predictions about which Senate wives and Supreme Court wives would be willing to cross the "color line" and return the black hostess's invitations. The expensive wedding clothes purchased at New York and Washington department stores by the bride and groom, as well as their subsequent honeymoon to Europe, where they toured London and Paris and visited with former president Grant, all became a part of the background for Bruce's historic ascent.

With the subsequent birth and naming of his son in 1879 after his white Senate mentor, Roscoe Conkling, Senator Bruce launched the second generation of the Bruce dynasty. Following the example of his New Orleans friend Pinckney B. S. Pinchback—Louisiana's first black governor and lieutenant governor—Bruce and his wife moved into a palatial red-brick Washington town house at 909 M Street NW and hosted numerous high-profile social events. Wanting his son to enjoy the same opportunities as the children of other prominent political figures, he relied on the advice of his white political friends and, in 1896, took his fifteen-year-old boy out of Washington's all-black M Street High School. He sent him to boarding school in New Hampshire, at Phillips Exeter Academy, where young Roscoe was one of six black students. Roscoe would eventually enter Harvard University in 1898—just months after Blanche was named register of the U.S. Treasury by President McKinley—and then ultimately graduate Phi Beta Kappa. Like his father, Roscoe would be paired with a daughter of the black elite— this time, a woman who had gone to both Radcliffe and Boston University Law School. Later, through the family's ties to such power brokers as Booker T. Washington and John D. Rockefeller Jr., Roscoe's children would be the second generation of Bruces to attend Exeter and Harvard, and they would also go on to make history in such places as Boston, Washington, and New York City.

As the senator stood there with his hand on the vice president's Bible that Friday afternoon of March 5, 1875, in the United States Senate Chamber, he had no idea how wide-ranging his legacy would be for a whole race of people. He had no idea how many complicated twists and turns his life was still to take in the coming years, and how those experiences would impact the fortunes and misfortunes of the future generations of his own—and America's first—black dynasty.

CHAPTER TWO

⋧⊙⊚⊙⋬

1841–1861
Blanche Bruce's Slave Family
in Virginia and Missouri

THE STORY OF BLANCHE KELSO BRUCE BEGINS IN VIRGINIA, ON A RUS-
tic Prince Edward County plantation where he was born into slavery
on March 1, 1841.[1] Sixty miles west of Richmond and just east of the
Blue Ridge mountain range, this rural Virginia setting served as a mid-
point for horse-drawn coaches brimming with the corn, wheat, and
tobacco that had been harvested by slaves and sent east to city merchants in Richmond by country farmers. This bucolic area would gain
a nineteenth-century prominence for being just a few miles from Confederate General Robert E. Lee's surrender at Appomattox, and a
twentieth-century footnote for being the infamous county that fought
school desegregation so hard that its schools became one of the five
defendant school districts represented by the landmark 1954 *Brown v.
Board of Education* Supreme Court case.[2]

But in the early 1840s, just ninety years after its founding in 1754,
Prince Edward County had little political or economic influence on the
rest of Virginia. It was fertile farmland to be worked, and it was a
sixty-square-mile area to be passed through on the way to larger metropolitan areas in the east, such as Richmond, Norfolk, and Chesapeake.

The county, with its sleepy towns of Worsham and Farmville, was
composed of simple farming communities populated with large plantations owned not by the sophisticated white gentry—"the planters"—

found closer to larger cities along the Mississippi or Atlantic coast but by slave masters who supplemented their incomes by hiring out their slaves to work on the plantations or farms owned by others. This was the case for Blanche Bruce's family, who spent the 1830s and early 1840s as slaves on various lands that sat along the road leading east to Richmond.[3] That well-worn dirt road brought commerce back and forth between the eastern and western halves of the state.

Each day, from morning until late afternoon, the most trusted black slaves were charged with manning coaches with the highly valued harvests of their owners and bringing profits back from the city dealers who conducted business with them. Each day, the coaches would pass along the road that cut through and in front of the Lemuel Bruce plantation, where Blanche's slave family worked.

The son of wealthy planters from Scotland, Lemuel Bruce owned the tobacco plantation with his wife and lived there with his slaves and his two children—a son, William, and a daughter, Rebecca. Among these slaves were Blanche's mother, Polly, who was born in Virginia in 1800. Raised to be a house slave, Polly was responsible for inside labor: cooking, cleaning, and taking care of her owner's wife and two children. Born to an African slave woman who had been raped by a slave trader, Polly lived in a slave cabin on Lemuel's property but worked exclusively in the master's main house.[4]

Polly's work as a house slave—or "house nigger," as she was called—was considered to be less punishing than the grueling outdoor labor of picking tobacco or cotton. In this role of "maid and mammy" to Master Lemuel Bruce's family, she was in an environment where she could learn to read and write and observe the lifestyle of her owner's family. But, along with this access to the owner came a hardship that she had to endure for more than twenty years: like many female house slaves, she was forced into sexual relations with her owner.

Lemuel Bruce and his wife had two white children, William and Rebecca, but he also fathered Polly's first five children, including her oldest son, Sandy, born in 1823, as well as Calvin, James, and Henry. The fifth child was a daughter, whose name is unclear.

The net result was that the Bruce's had a line of white family members and a line of black family members. Lemuel kept a family Bible in which he wrote his name at the top center of a page. Below it, he drew a vertical line down the center of the page. On the left side of the page, he wrote the names of his white wife and their two white children. On the right side of the page, he wrote a much longer list. There he put Polly's name and the names of his black children. This Bible was used as a record for him when he later decided to leave money and property to certain family members.

Among the Bruce plantation slaves, Polly was considered to receive the best treatment, but it was because of her relationship with Lemuel Bruce that she and her children were not treated as harshly as the other blacks on the plantation. When Lemuel died in 1836, Polly and her oldest sons by Lemuel were each left between $125 and $300. Although it was disturbing to Lemuel's white children, this custom was not unusual.

At Lemuel's death—five years before Blanche's birth—he left all his slaves to his two white children, Rebecca and William B. Bruce. Polly and her children became the property of Rebecca, while William became the owner of several other slaves.

Although they were owners of this slave family, Rebecca and William were under twenty-one and lived with their aunt, Prudence Perkinson. Soon thereafter, Rebecca Bruce married a distant cousin, Pettis Perkinson; and Polly continued as the house slave for Master Perkinson, Rebecca Bruce Perkinson, and their new family. It was believed by many family members both on the white Bruce family line and the black Bruce family line that at that time Polly's new master, Pettis Perkinson, forced her into a sexual relationship similar to the one she had with her prior master, Rebecca's father, Lemuel Bruce.[5]

Shortly after Pettis fathered a white son, William E. Bruce, with his wife, Rebecca, he fathered a slave son with his house slave, Polly. That slave son was Blanche Bruce, who was born March 1, 1841.

Delivered without any medical complications in a small wooden cabin on a farm plantation known as Linwood, Blanche was actually originally given the first name "Branch," which he would later change to "Blanche" when he was in his late teens.[6] In addition to the siblings that had already been born to his mother with Lemuel Bruce, Blanche was to have at least five other siblings that were born to his mother with Pettis Perkinson. Among this younger group of siblings, there were brothers named Howard, Edward, and Robert, and sisters named Eliza and Mary. All of them were assigned slave status.

What was remarkable about Polly's life as a slave mother was that unlike most other slave parents, she never had a master sell her children away from her. They were often hired out to different farms on a temporary basis, but the family was never broken up or sold away to other owners or traders. While both Lemuel Bruce and Pettis Perkinson broke up other slave families on their plantation, Polly's offspring were accorded special treatment.

Despite this forced sexual relationship, Polly's long and relatively healthy life bears out the fact that she was given certain advantages not available to most slave mothers. Up until her emancipation during the Civil War, she never worked in the fields. After the war, she lived in Leavenworth, Kansas, until her death at age eighty-nine in 1889.[7]

In 1841, the year of Blanche's birth, the United States was reaping great benefits from developments in transportation through the building of turnpike roads and railroads. The South was still primarily an agrarian economy, but improved transportation made it easier for Southern plantation owners to sell their goods well beyond their boundaries. Rural communities, like the tiny towns in Prince Edward County, Virginia, were certainly not as populated or as sophisticated as the larger Southern cities of Richmond, Charleston, Atlanta, or Memphis, but they had gained access to the goods bought and sold in these communities through railroad lines and the traveling salesmen who transported their goods across south-central Virginia.

The country had recently added Arkansas and Michigan as states, and was pushing for greater western expansion after seeing Texas gain its independence from Mexico. President John Tyler was in the White House following William Henry Harrison's sudden death after one month in office, and the Northern cities of New York, Boston, and Philadelphia were the cultural, industrial, and intellectual centers of the nation.

The country, which then consisted of twenty-six states—thirteen of them slave states and another thirteen of them free states—had a population of 17 million. Roughly 2,874,000—16.8 percent of the population—were black. Because of the heavy demand for slaves, blacks already outnumbered whites in Mississippi and South Carolina.

In 1841, the United States had little involvement with international affairs, except for dealings and negotiations with nations that held title to North American territories that the United States coveted. Its two-party system of Whigs and Democrats had been strengthened a decade earlier, and now seemed to be focused on the one major issue that separated the two: the issue of slavery, and how the nation's expansion would impact this American enterprise.

Since 1836, when the Republic of Texas had first declared its independence from Mexico, there were ongoing disputes between Northern states, which opposed annexing new territories if they were to be slave states, and Southern states, which opposed annexation of land if they were to be free states.

Much of the disagreements among congressional leaders fell along these lines, and despite the fact that other countries, such as Denmark and France, were headed toward abolishing slavery during the 1840s, the American South's focus on increasing production of cotton, sugar, and tobacco made it seem as if the institution was going to remain a permanent part of the economic and social fabric in that region of the United States.

Typically, Whig party members—like most Northerners—cared more about industrialization, public education, and equal rights for blacks, while Democratic Party members cared more about maintaining states' rights and specific territorial expansion that would preserve slavery. Hence, the battle lines between the two parties in the 1840s remained rather consistently centered on slavery and its place in American society. The Southerners feared that additional free states would upset the balance of power in the Senate, and Northerners, who already controlled the House, were afraid that new slave states would dilute the power they were already wielding in Congress.

Although brought to the presidency by the Whigs, being a slave owner himself, President Tyler more often sided with Southern Democrats, who argued that any new territories should be annexed as slave states, not as free ones. Tyler would later work closely with the Democrates and encourage Southern secession during the 1860's.

With a cabinet of advisers who were equally pro-slavery, he often turned to his secretary of state, John C. Calhoun, to advance the issue. A South Carolina native, Calhoun had been one of the most aggressive and most articulate pro-slavery advocates in the South. Having earlier served as vice president under both John Quincy Adams and Andrew Jackson, he eventually used his position as senator to pass pro-slavery resolutions in Congress in 1838, which supported states' rights in maintaining slavery without any interference from abolitionists or the federal government.

Northern anti-slavery advocates were represented by such outspoken white New Englanders as William Lloyd Garrison, publisher of the *Liberator*; Wendell Phillips, a Harvard Law School graduate who served as president of the American Anti-Slavery Society; and two brothers, Lewis and Arthur Tappan, wealthy businessmen who helped fund the Underground Railroad. Since the early 1830s, they had been using the American Anti-Slavery Society to sponsor lectures and distribute articles that argued that this "peculiar institution" was a sin against man as well as a sin against God.

More than three decades earlier, in 1808, both England and the United States had made it illegal for their citizens to participate in the *international* importing of slaves, and by 1833, England had ended slavery altogether in its colonies in the West Indies. The Northern segments of the United States had similarly abolished slavery in all of their states by 1820, with the State of Maine also giving black men the right to vote beginning in that year. But the American South, seeing great profit in slave labor and recognizing that their agrarian economy was intensely dependent upon slavery, continued not only the legalized domestic purchase, sale, and "breeding" of black slaves, but also the illegal international trading, by employing renegade slavers who kidnapped slaves from Africa as late as the start of the Civil War.

In 1841, when Blanche was born, slavery was facing some major challenges—challenges that didn't end the institution but had an impact on future black generations. It was the year that Frederick Douglass, the country's most outspoken black civil rights leader, launched his career as an abolitionist. Born a slave twenty-four years earlier in Maryland, Douglass had escaped to freedom in Massachusetts as a sixteen-year-old. It was in 1841, on the Massachusetts island of Nantucket, that he gave the first of hundreds of anti-slavery speeches. Three decades later, Douglass would form an alliance with Blanche Bruce as they both worked to provide opportunities to freedmen who sought to live with dignity in a short-lived Reconstruction atmosphere throughout the South. Douglass would also ask Bruce and Bruce's wife to serve as witnesses at his controversial 1884 marriage to a white woman in Washington.[8] These two couples would alternately share the enmity of black Washingtonians who would eventually accuse them of preferring to live among whites rather than with the blacks who first supported them.

During the same week of Blanche Bruce's birth, the United States Supreme Court issued one of its strongest opinions on slavery when Justice Joseph Story wrote the majority opinion on how to deal with the fifty-three African slaves who staged the most famous slave mutiny in the nation's history. Two years earlier, after being kidnapped from their native Africa, Joseph Cinque and fifty-two other slaves took over the *Amistad* slave ship, killed their Spanish captors, and sailed to Long Island, New York, where they were ultimately arrested.

In a dramatic opinion written by Justice Story, it was decided that the fifty-three slaves should be set free, because, as the court explained, they had been "kidnapped free men from Africa and were illegally detained and restrained on board the *Amistad*."[9]

Although these were favorable moves on behalf of the anti-slavery movement, the American South that Blanche Bruce was born into remained an aggressively racist and slave-centered environment. The nation showed incredible divisions. The South, too, was divided— between coarse country farmers in Kentucky or Tennessee and planters in the more gentrified Southern states like Virginia who, while unwilling to surrender the institution that made them rich, were at least willing to offer their slaves modest privileges and less physical abuse. Young Blanche, his mother, and his older siblings belonged to a family that fell into the second group.

Before he died, Lemuel Bruce was considered a decent master in that he permitted his slaves to be well fed and clothed and to receive some minor on-site schooling. This attitude continued to the next generation; Rebecca Bruce Perkinson and her new husband, Pettis Perkinson, were slave owners who, if it could be said, treated their slaves as property to be protected rather than abused.

Blanche's older brother Henry Clay Bruce recalled the manner in which he and his family were treated during the 1840s and 1850s by the Bruce-Perkinson family when he and Blanche were still children. In his 1895 autobiography, *The New Man: Twenty-nine Years a Slave and Twenty-nine Years a Free Man*, he wrote of his owner, "It is but simple justice to Mr. Perkinson to say, that though [related to] a family known in that part of the country as hard task-masters, he was himself a kind and considerate man . . . We were tenderly treated."

Henry, who later became a Kansas politician and government worker in Washington, qualifies that statement very clearly by pointing out that this "tender" treatment was relative to how other masters treated their slaves and by also noting the young age of himself— eight—and his brother Blanche, still only three years old. According to Henry Bruce's autobiography, slaves were distinguished among white slave owners based on the social standing and class of the slave-owning family. The wealthier, better educated families—the planters—usually treated their slaves with greater care, and the poorer white slave owners or slave drivers abused their slaves mercilessly. He explains,

> During the slave days, these poor whites seemed to live for no higher purpose than to spy on the slaves . . . Their ambitions were gratified if they could be overseers or slave drivers . . . This class was conceived and born of a poor blood, whose inferiority linked its members for all time to things mean and low. They were the natural enemies of the slaves, and to this day they have sought to belittle and humiliate the ambitious [black] freeman, by the long catalogue of [Jim Crow] laws framed with the avowed intention of robbing him of his manhood rights . . . the high-toned Negro would not associate with him if he could.[10]

Henry and other members of the Bruce slave family knew that, as slaves, they were relatively well off working for the Bruce-Perkinson family. Their living quarters consisted of shabby, unheated cabins, their food made up mostly of leftover pork parts or animals they hunted themselves, and they were not permitted to travel, own property, or attend church, but their fellow slaves on neighboring farms fared far worse in terms of physical brutality. Even though the Bruce-Perkinson slaves were often hired out to other families or plantations for short periods, physical beatings and family-member separations would still, for the most part, be controlled by a relatively sympathetic Pettis Perkinson. Henry knew that the treatment received at the hands of less advantaged white masters would have been far less humane.

As was the case with many slave children who had been fathered by their white masters, Blanche and his siblings were favored over the plantation slaves who had no blood relation to the white Bruce and Perkinson families.

When Rebecca Perkinson died in 1844, Blanche's mother, Polly, became responsible not only for her own children but also for helping to care for her master's white son, young William E. Perkinson. Because of their close age and the Perkinsons' belief in having one or two minimally educated slaves, Blanche and Henry were occasionally tutored alongside young William over the next few years. Pettis permitted an informal friendship to develop between William and the two slave boys, because Henry could teach him athletic activities and Blanche's intellectual curiosity reinforced William's interest in school. By the time he was six, Blanche would already be able to recite the alphabet and read numbers and dates—an unusual skill for a slave child, given that it was then illegal to teach slaves anything beyond the most rudimentary skills.

In April of 1844, just after Blanche's third birthday, Pettis Perkinson and his deceased wife's brother, William B. Bruce, decided to move Blanche and his mother and siblings—along with their other slaves—from Virginia to Missouri, where Pettis's brother, Jack, lived in Chariton County.

Chariton County was a rural area located near the Chariton and Missouri Rivers in north-central Missouri, about two hundred miles west of Kansas City. It was becoming known as fertile territory for flourishing tobacco plantations. Recently settled and distinctly Midwestern, its small communities of Brunswick, Chariton, and Keytesville were a world away from the Bruce-Perkinson Southern plantation home that Blanche and his family had known for the past several years. Many years later, these Missouri communities would become the established home for his mother and most of his siblings.

One of the motives behind Perkinson's decision to leave Virginia was an economic one. The agrarian way of life for midsized Virginia planters in the late 1830s and early 1840s was not a wildly successful one. Perhaps because of its reliance on slaves as the primary "engine" behind the farming industry, very few technological improvements had been developed to revolutionize the profession. Compounding this lack of progress was the fact that both the population and the development of Virginia's urban centers were losing ground to the better-financed urban centers in the North.

Not only was Virginia's major city, Richmond, dropping in rank compared to American cities in the North, but the state as a whole had seen its population increase only by a minuscule 3 percent during the prior ten years. In fact, the old adage "cotton is king" surely had far greater relevance to the Deep South than to border states like Maryland or Virginia by then.

As the years proceeded, the center of the cotton industry began moving to states farther west, like Mississippi, because it was discovered that unlike sugarcane, hemp, or tobacco—all farm products that required special soil, cultivation, or equipment—cotton could grow in even poor soil and required only the simplest of farm equipment, making it an accessible business for the newest and smallest of farmers throughout the South.

Virginia and its plantations were losing ground to other cotton-producing states for two reasons. First, there was increased competition from planters who were operating in the Deep South, in states like Georgia and South Carolina, and now there were new farmers moving into former Indian territories west of the Mississippi. As this land, much of it in Tennessee and Kentucky, was taken from the Indians, it was quickly cultivated for cotton, further flooding the export market. So, not only did states like Tennessee and Kentucky become more populated, their political leaders—many of them cotton growers—became wealthier and more influential in national government because of their own farms and because of the growing number of successful citizens they represented.

The second setback for Virginia was a problem that was not unique to the Commonwealth, but which was becoming a disappointing pattern for most of the Southeast: outside of farming, there was little industry or employment. In fact, since the 1820s, more than 80 percent of Southerners made their living through work connected to farming, and with no growth in other industries, there was little to attract new immigrants or others who were looking to settle in a new home. These people were, instead, attracted to the North or the Midwest, where opportunities seemed almost infinite.

As Midwestern cities such as St. Louis, Kansas City, and Louisville grew, they and their respective outlying rural areas were suddenly attractive destinations for such Southern slave owners as Pettis Perkinson.

The journey to Chariton County would take two months and was conducted using three covered wagons, two carrying the slaves and the third carrying the owners' family members. It was the first time that Blanche and most of his siblings had ventured outside of the South.[11]

It was already early summer when they arrived in Missouri. They unloaded the three wagons at the border of a community called Keytesville, a town which had been named for a local businessman and Methodist preacher, James Keytes, who had donated the town's land several years earlier, in 1833.

Since tobacco production was a major business in Chariton County, Blanche's family members were immediately hired out to work in local tobacco factories. As he and his eight-year-old brother, Henry, were too young to work in the factories—slave children were generally put to work at age ten—they had local chores to supplement their hours that were also spent fishing, hunting, and planting the small plot of vegetables that the slave family was allowed to grow for its own consumption.

According to Blanche's brother Henry, in January of 1845, Pettis hired the family out to work for James Means, a brickmaker, whose business was several miles south, in Randolph County. "Mr. Means also owned a girl about fourteen years old called Cat," recalled Henry Bruce, "and as soon as spring came, he commenced work on the brick yard with Cat and me as offbearers. This, being my first real work, was fun for a while, but soon became very hard and I got whipped nearly every day, not because I did not work, but because I could not stand it. Having to carry a double mold [of bricks] all day long in the hot sun, I broke down."[12]

In early 1846, Blanche's family was thrown into a much more vulnerable working and living situation when Pettis decided to leave his slaves with his brother-in-law, William, and return to Virginia. Over the next year, Blanche, his mother, and his siblings would all be hired out to work for tobacco factories, ironworkers, and middle-class families who owned small farms in the Chariton County area of Missouri. "I was then about ten years old," explains Henry as he recalls that year when his younger brother and siblings were hired out to a Judge Applegate, who ran a tobacco factory in Keytesville, "and although I had worked at Mr. Means' place . . . at Judge Applegate's I was kept busy every minute from sunrise to sunset, without being allowed to speak a word to anyone." The Bruce children were often whipped during the months they worked for Applegate, because of their inability to work hour after hour without breaks. Henry described that year's work as both grueling and monotonous:

> It was so prison-like to be compelled to sit during the entire year under a large bench or table with tobacco, and tie lugs all day long except during the thirty minutes allowed for break-fast and the same time allowed for dinner. I often fell asleep. I could not keep awake even by putting tobacco into my eyes. I was punished by the overseer, a Mr. Blankenship . . . But I soon became used to that kind of work and got along very well the balance of that year.[13]

During this time, the nation was expanding rapidly and aggressively. In 1845, Texas and Florida had both become states. And in 1846, Iowa became a state, and the nation declared war on Mexico as a means of expanding the southern boundary of Texas to the Rio Grande River as well as of expanding slavery and American annexation farther west across the continent. What was argued by President Polk as a way of defending the United States because "Mexico has invaded our territory and shed American blood upon American soil" was really American Southerners and Westerners pushing U.S. imperialism for mostly economic reasons. Within two years, as a result of the Mexican War, Mexicans would be driven out of the California territory.

Only one year later, in 1847, the indecisive Pettis Perkinson decided that he did not want to return to Missouri, where his slaves were working. He wanted to remain in Virginia, and asked William Bruce, his brother-in-law, to bring his slaves back to him. In April 1847, William escorted the slaves out of Brunswick by steamboat to St. Louis.

Prior to the time of Blanche's family's departure, there was an increasingly active group of abolitionists working in Ohio and other Midwestern states. That was the year Frederick Douglass was elected president of the New England Anti-Slavery Society, a leading abolitionist group that sponsored speeches and demonstrations to denounce slavery. Along with outspoken abolitionists like William Lloyd Garrison, publisher of the *Liberator*, and Theodore Weld, author of the 1839 book *Slavery as It Is*, Douglass gained the sympathy of religious leaders and other liberals in the North and Midwest.

But despite all that the white and black abolitionists were doing to combat slavery throughout the South, the large, uneducated slave population was unaware of the abolitionists and their success in bringing blacks to freedom through the Underground Railroad and other paths North. Blanche's family was similarly oblivious of the work of the abolitionists, and suffered for it when they lost a valuable chance to reach freedom during their 1847 trip from Brunswick, Missouri, back to Virginia.

As Henry Bruce explained in his autobiography, he, Blanche, their owner, and their siblings were being transported on the steamboat southeast to St. Louis, heading for Cincinnati in spring of 1847, when some whites on the boat secretly informed the slaves that when the boat arrived in Ohio, there would be abolitionists coming on board to take them from their owners. Although the slaves probably knew that Ohio was free soil, they had never heard of an "abolitionist" and suspected that they were some sinister group—possibly taking them to an even worse fate. Henry Bruce explains,

> I must tell a little incident that happened, which explains why we were not landed at Cincinnati, but taken to the Kentucky side of the River where we remained until the steamboat finished her business there and crossed over and took us on board again ... Just before reaching Cincinnati, Ohio, some of these white [deck passengers] told my mother [and our other women] that when the boat landed at Cincinnati the abolitionists would come aboard and even against their will take them away. Of course our people did not know what the word abolitionist meant; they evidently thought it meant Negro-trader and they were frightened ... so they went to W. B. Bruce and informed them what they had been told. He was greatly excited and went to the captain of the boat ... My mother says he paid the captain a sum of money to have us landed on the Kentucky side of the River. [We] remained there until the steamer transacted its business at Cincinnati and then crossed over and picked us up ... The ignorance of [our slave] women caused me to work as a slave for seventeen years afterward.[14]

Upon his return to Virginia, six-year-old Blanche was reunited with his white master's son, Willie Perkinson. Now living together again, Blanche and Henry were permitted to practice their reading with young Willie.

Henry recalled, "Willie took great pride in teaching me his lessons of each day from his books." The two slave boys secretly practiced their reading until a year later, when Willie's aunt objected to it. "She insisted that it was a crime to teach a Negro to read, and that it would spoil him, but our owner seemed not to care anything about it. I learned that he was glad that his Negroes could read, but he was opposed to their being taught writing."[15]

By 1848, when Blanche was seven, it was evident that he was a bright child. "My younger brother, B.K. Bruce (now an Ex-Senator) had succeeded me as playmate and guardian of Willie, and being also anxious to learn, soon caught up with me, and by Willie's aid went ahead of me and has held his place during all the years since."[16]

In the fall of 1849, Pettis Perkinson sold his Virginia farm and moved his family and slaves farther south to Mississippi, where his sister Susan Perkinson Greene and her husband, Thomas Greene, lived just outside Holly Springs. Although his mother and siblings all remained together for the trip, Blanche saw other relatives separated and sold to other slave buyers on their route farther south. "While en route to Mississippi," Blanche's brother recalled, "Uncle Walt was taken sick and had to be left near the line of Virginia and Tennessee. His wife, Aunt Martha, did not want to be separated . . . they were sold to the man with whom they were left."[17]

Upon the slave family's arrival in Mississippi in December, the children were sent directly to the cotton fields to pick with the adults. At eight years old, it was Blanche's first introduction to relentless daily labor. His brother Henry recorded the experience:

> We were in the field by daylight, sometimes, before it was light enough to see the cotton balls, and kept steadily at work till noon, when dinner was brought to us . . . as soon as the last mouthful was swallowed, the order was given to go back to work. From noon until dark we were driven by the overseer who carried a long whip called a blacksnake. At dark, the females were allowed to go to their quarters, but the men and boys were divided into squads of five; each had a bale of cotton to turn out. Gins run by mules had been going all day, making

lint cotton which had to be put in bales, and each bale had to stand under the press about twenty minutes, so that the last squad seldom got through earlier than nine o'clock; and this went on each day except Sunday.[18]

Such was Blanche's childhood for the next year in Mississippi, as Perkinson kept them working on the plantation of his sister and brother-in-law. After that year, the itinerant owner once again decided to move his slaves back to Brunswick, Missouri.

Blanche's brother expressed the family's frustration at being moved from state to state with such frequency, but there was little they could do to influence the indecisive Pettis Perkinson, who appeared not to know whether he wanted to farm tobacco or cotton, or whether he wanted to raise hogs or horses.

Despite the constant movement, Blanche surely must have been grateful that his fate and that of his immediate family was relatively stable, and that they didn't get sold like his uncle Walt and aunt Martha, or separated and sold to different families.

It is not clear whether Blanche knew, at this age, the true identity of his father, and to what extent he would have understood why Perkinson was willing to sell some of Blanche's relatives, but never to separate Polly's children from her or from each other. While it is clear he knew he was the mulatto child of a white man, it is not clear whether his mother shared the details with him.

Blanche's family were to remain as slaves in the Midwestern community of Brunswick, from 1850 to 1862, while farming tobacco, splitting rails on uncultivated land, and being hired out to various farms. It was an extremely difficult and intellectually barren existence.

Although he was hardly ever to refer to events that led to his emancipation, Blanche's departure from the slave state of Missouri took place in 1862, around the same time as twenty-one-year-old Master Willie left home to join the Confederate Army.[19]

Angry and disappointed that Willie was not supporting the battle for emancipation in the way that he had always discussed with Blanche, the young slave told his brothers and siblings that he was also going to be leaving. At the time, his eventual goal was to travel to Ohio. He had told his brother Henry that he might first try to earn money in Kansas before traveling north.

There isn't much known about the specific events on the day of Blanche's departure, but it is acknowledged in the family history that he did not have to sneak off in the dead of night or in the manner in which Henry escaped a year later with a slave girl whom he later married. It is believed that Blanche was manumitted by his owner, Pettis Perkinson, but that he still had to be cautious in his movements as he left Missouri, out of fear of being captured and then illegally sold back into slavery. This is why it was important for him to travel to Ohio, a state where he could live under the protection of a large abolitionist community.

To Blanche, Ohio held promise. Even parts of Kansas held more promise than life in Missouri—a state that still didn't believe in freedom. He needed to be in a place that believed in something better for his kind. Some place that offered more than just farms and unheated dirt-floor cabins.

Blanche thought the possibilities were limitless if he could just stay out of Missouri. Maybe he would work at one of those Northern newspapers. Maybe he would take school courses. Maybe he would do things that he and Master Willie had read about all those years before. He didn't know what it would be, but this future senator knew that his future wasn't going to be found on a plantation in Missouri.

As Blanche ventured deeper into Kansas, not knowing if he'd reach Ohio or simply settle in this new, more racially liberal state, he knew he was moving physically, intellectually, and emotionally away from his family. At that time and during the few years that followed, many of his family members would remain with the familiar. After the war, as freed slaves, they all came back to work on farmland, sometimes living in the kinds of quarters they had known before. As depressing as the picture appeared to an outsider, their past migratory life as slaves had been sufficiently harsh for them to alter their expectations and find satisfaction in simply being together and calling the plantation town of Brunswick home.

CHAPTER THREE

᪥

1841–1860

The Free Aristocratic Family of Josephine Willson

AT THE SAME TIME THAT BLANCHE BRUCE WAS BEING TRANSPORTED as a slave from Prince Edward County, Virginia, to Brunswick, Missouri, with his white master by covered wagon, the family of Josephine Willson, Blanche's future wife, was making news in a different part of the country with the publication of *Sketches of the Higher Classes Among the Colored Society in Philadelphia*, her father's controversial new book about the black upper class of Philadelphia.[1] Coming at a time when most American blacks were still enslaved, the book gave a close analysis of the lifestyle of well-educated, well-to-do American blacks. Each of the six chapters shared specific advice on how an upper-class black person accomplishes everything, from decorating a home to entertaining guests and conducting himself in the company of wealthy guests or coworkers.

While the Bruce family had been slaves in the South and Midwest, most of Josephine's family had been free blacks in the Northeast. Her father, Joseph, had a particularly interesting family background, which he was able to trace back to the late 1700s in Georgia and South Carolina.

In 1841, the same year as Blanche's birth, Josephine's father, a Philadelphia dentist, published the book that both intrigued and outraged blacks throughout the Northeast. Although it was originally published anonymously and aimed at educated whites, upper-class blacks in Philadelphia immediately recognized its author, and both he and the book became the subject of parlor gossip for several years. The residents of the Spring Garden neighborhood, in particular, were engaged in discussions as they contemplated if their neighbor had intended to mock them or flatter them with his book on proper manners. The fact that Willson's friends and in-laws included some of the wealthiest blacks in the city and the country created further intrigue for people who bought the book.

Joseph Willson had been born February 22, 1817, in Augusta, Georgia, to Elizabeth Willson, a free black woman from South Carolina. Although Elizabeth took the surname of Joseph's father, John Willson Jr., a wealthy white man of Scots-Irish background who had been one of the founders of the Bank of Augusta, she had actually never married him.[2]

Elizabeth had given birth to four children by the time John decided he could no longer maintain a clandestine relationship with a black woman. He gave Elizabeth two hundred shares in his bank and enough money to buy a three-story home in Philadelphia, where she moved in 1833 with sixteen-year-old Joseph and her three daughters, Caroline, Emily, and Elizabeth. Joseph was enrolled in the exclusive Pennsylvania Abolition Society's Clarkson School, a Philadelphia school started by Quakers to educate black middle-class children.

The family joined an Episcopal church that served many of the city's prominent black residents. Among their fellow black churchgoers was James Forten, the wealthy sailmaker who had outfitted hundreds of ships in the Northeast through his sail-manufacturing business that employed more than forty black and white workers.[3]

Other influential residents who socialized with the Willsons were the Cassey, Prosser, Dorsey, McKee, and Minton families. During the ensuing years, many of these families would develop additional social, business, and family ties with one another. They were all joined by the family of yet another black real estate speculator, Robert Purvis, after he was left a $120,000 inheritance in 1826.[4]

With their rather comfortable lifestyle, the Willsons socialized with educated black and white neighbors and befriended Frederick Augustus Hinton, a wealthy black businessman who owned the exclusive Gentleman's Dressing Room, a men's barbershop and perfume shop that served wealthy white Philadelphians. In 1837, four years after the Willson family arrived in Philadelphia, Hinton married one of Joseph's sisters, Emily.

Joseph soon became a protégé of the successful businessman and his new brother-in-law. Upon Joseph's mother's suggestion, Hinton contacted his close friend in Boston, William Lloyd Garrison, to ask if he would give Joseph his first job. Garrison, already known as the liberal white publisher of the *Liberator*, was an outspoken abolitionist, having established the New England Anti-Slavery Society in 1832. Garrison immediately hired Willson to work for the newspaper in Boston, and took him under his tutelage. Willson would remain there for two years, and assist Garrison on articles as well as lectures.

In the early 1840s, the country was focused on the annexation of Texas and a general embrace of manifest destiny as Americans pushed toward settling all lands until they reached the Pacific Ocean. White Southerners were focused on expanding slavery farther west, and white Northerners were passing legislation that limited the civil rights and civil liberties of free Northern blacks. Black abolitionists like Sojourner Truth were traveling around the Midwest and Northeast to galvanize support in their fight against the expansion of slavery. In a way, Willson's book about the black upper class, while well written and documented, seemed anachronistic. With most of black and white America focused on the enslavement—and brutal treatment of—blacks, it seemed beside the point to be writing about ways in which educated upper-class blacks differentiated themselves from poor or middle-class blacks. But the book was heralded by many as being courageous and fiercely honest in its account of the class divisions among blacks in the nineteenth century.

Cities in both the North and South took notice of Willson's new book. At the time, he was just getting to know his future wife, Elizabeth Harnett, and discovering that they had a lot in common. Her mother had been a free woman of color from Georgia and her father had been an immigrant from Scotland. Like his own, Elizabeth's family wealth defied the stereotype that there was only one class of black people in America. In fact, the upper-class and middle-class black population consisted of free born blacks who had been educated at schools like Oberlin, or at Quaker-sponsored schools in the Northeast. Also among those classes were black slaves who had been manumitted by their masters and sometimes given inheritances with which they started small businesses or purchased land.

The other black social classes included those who worked as slaves but were allowed education and taught skills so that they could work inside plantation homes as butlers or upstairs servants rather than in the fields with the most deprived slaves. The class lines drawn both on and off the plantation highlighted the complexity of the black social structure.

Elizabeth had been intrigued by Joseph's new book. They both felt it was important for whites, and other blacks as well, to understand the range of black experiences in the United States. At the time, in June 1841, the New York paper *The Colored American* reviewed the book and said, "This work is on a delicate subject, and we should think it required more than an ordinary share of moral courage, even in an anonymous author, to handle it."[5]

What made Joseph's book so extraordinary was how narrowly he defined the black elite. For him, the group members were more than well educated and refined. They were also necessarily economically advantaged. As he explained in the book, the higher-class Philadelphia blacks whom he was addressing were "that portion of colored society whose income, from their pursuits or otherwise, enables them to maintain the position of house-holders, and their families in comparative ease and comfort." At the time of the book's publication, Philadelphia probably had a larger black professional community than any other American city. Notwithstanding these facts, the very discussion of this subject created a great deal of discomfort for blacks both inside and outside Philadelphia.

Three years later, while the controversy over the book continued, Joseph Willson and Elizabeth Harnett married. With his newspaper-office training from Boston and his experience as a published author, the entrepreneurial Willson opened a printing business. In 1846, Elizabeth gave birth to a boy they named Leonidas. According to an 1847 census, which listed families by name and which was conducted by the Society of Friends in Philadelphia, Joseph was now worth about $25,000. The report indicated that he was living with his wife and baby son at their Morgan Street home, and that also living there were his mother and brother, John. Later that year, his mother died. Following his mother's prior wishes, he began to pursue dentistry—a profession that was to elevate many blacks into the upper classes. With the financial assistance of his wealthy brother-in-law

Frederick Hinton, Joseph became a popular dentist among the black community in Philadelphia.

In 1852, Joseph and Elizabeth had a daughter they named Emily, and in 1853, baby Josephine was born. His first daughter was named after his closest sister, and he named his second daughter after himself. By the time Josephine was born, the Willsons had amassed a considerable amount of money. With family investments in Georgia, added to moneys left to his sister and him by his brother-in-law Frederick Hinton, who died in 1849, and earnings from his printing and dental business, the family was able to move to a larger home on Shippen Street in Philadelphia. Only a few months later, they moved to Cleveland, Ohio, where Joseph felt that abolitionism and greater numbers of liberal whites would further enhance the economic and educational opportunities for upwardly mobile blacks.

While blacks in Philadelphia were not targeted with the same bad treatment that slaves and freeborn blacks received in the South, Joseph believed that Philadelphia whites had no political interest in what happened to the blacks outside their city. With Ohio's history of abolitionism, the people there were more politically involved in trying to bring about an end to slavery.

Although Elizabeth wanted to remain optimistic for their three children, she still wasn't so sure about Cleveland yet. She may have wondered if they cared about the future of colored people here only because there were so few of them in Cleveland. According to the 1850 census, the city only had 224 black residents.

Cleveland was, however, known for its upper-class black population, and its black community benefited from integrated schools, which invested more in black children. Also, many of its liberal white residents had come out of abolitionist centers, like nearby Oberlin. Because of the greater liberal beliefs of its residents, white as well as black patients supported Willson's dental practice, thus making it even more successful than the one he had established in Philadelphia.

Although the family remained close to their Philadelphia friends, they also eventually socialized with the families of other well-to-do blacks in Cleveland, like John P. Green, an attorney who later served in the Ohio state legislature, and local political leaders John Malvin and George Vosburgh. In fact, Vosburgh's oldest daughter would later become engaged to Senator Bruce in 1876, and then die before a marriage date was set. Despite their social interactions with others in the city, much of the Willsons' time was spent on building Joseph's practice and on raising their growing family. In 1854, Elizabeth gave birth to a third daughter, Mary, and two years later, in 1856, to a fourth daughter, named Victoria.

One day, after his last patient left his office, Joseph asked his wife if, perhaps, they were attending the wrong church. They had joined Saint Paul's Episcopal when they had arrived in town four years earlier, but now he was considering resigning. He wondered if it was wise for them to remain in a virtually all-white congregation.

Elizabeth was detecting a concern and fear in her husband that she hadn't seen since the days following the publication of his book in Philadelphia. She understood he might be concerned that certain less wealthy blacks in Cleveland might not want to patronize his dental office if they felt the Willsons didn't care for most blacks, but the fact was that she and her husband *didn't* care for most blacks in that city. They did not socialize with people who had less money than they did, or who were much darker than they were.

Perhaps Elizabeth believed that she should not lower her social standards simply because the socioeconomic background of black people in this town was not the same as the larger group of black Philadelphians. It was her husband, Joseph—not she—who felt the strongest ties to black people. And it was he who feared telling his black patients that he attended a white church.

Elizabeth and Joseph had come to Ohio in search of friendlier white people. Having been the state with the most Underground Railroad stops, the greatest number of anti-slavery societies, and the first to establish a college for blacks—Wilberforce College, in 1856—Ohio had been regarded as more hospitable to blacks than any other. But with this move, the Willsons lost the large number of the kind of blacks they liked to associate with: light-complexioned, well bred, well educated, and well-to-do.

Elizabeth was determined to make the best of their situation. She honestly believed that Saint Paul's introduced her husband to whites who became his patients, and that there were not enough middle-class blacks in the city to support his practice, no matter what church they attended. She also believed that since their children could attend the best white schools, they would get a fine education. And after they played second fiddle for so long to black Philadelphia families like the Prossers and the McKees, it probably felt good to finally be at the top of the black social strata.[6]

Even though he would always miss the large upper-class black community in Philadelphia, Joseph was also surprised by how satisfied they'd become in this city by the lake, a city that felt like a small Midwestern town, in contrast with the big-city atmosphere of Philadelphia. Things were, indeed, going well for them and their children.

It would be several years before the Willsons would join the Social Circle, an exclusive, by-invitation-only black Cleveland social club founded in 1869. For now, they had to be satisfied with the notion that one day they might again be able to enjoy the company of a larger black upper-class community. Joseph agreed with his wife that their life was destined to be an uncommon one, and that they might as well remain in a whiter, upper-class environment like Saint Paul's Episcopal Church rather than seek out the friendship of blacks who were not their kind of people.

CHAPTER FOUR

⤸⤸⤸

1862–1870

Bruce Finds Kansas Freedom, Ohio Education, and Mississippi Reconstruction

I was in Lawrence, Kansas, when Quantrill sacked the town and
butchered so many people. My life was saved by a miracle.
Quantrill's band certainly would not have spared a colored
man . . . The night before the Quantrill raid I had been watching
and nursing a sick friend, and when the day broke, I heard firing.
Looking out of the window I saw armed men riding by firing pistols,
and immediately realized that the enemy was upon us. To remain
with my sick friend would have been to invite certain death, so I
bade him adieu, . . . got out of the house and hid in the bushes.[1]

AFTER LEAVING HIS FAMILY IN MISSOURI ONLY A FEW MONTHS EAR-
lier and enjoying his freedom in the thriving, liberal, abolitionist town
of Lawrence, Kansas, Blanche was awakened one morning by what
became known as a historic attack that proved how vulnerable life
remained for emancipated blacks living in what was considered free,
"friendly" territory.

Although he hated to recall that early morning of August 21, 1863,
whenever Blanche explained his eventual albeit temporary move from
Kansas back into Missouri, it centered around the famously bloody

attack that Colonel William Quantrill and several dozen Confederate white supremacists made on the blacks who lived alongside Blanche in Lawrence. The early morning riders burned, shot and hung over 150 defenseless people, as well as every black military man who was stationed in the town.

Attacks like this were only the latest example of deep racial problems for the nation. Blanche thought he'd be leaving all that behind when he'd left home the previous year. He had held hopes of getting to Ohio or a similar place that was far removed from the threat of racial attacks, but he hadn't found the money to get him farther than Lawrence, a town that held the promise of racial open-mindedness and opportunity.

A year earlier, in the summer of 1862, as Congress and the president debated over two "confiscation acts" and an Emancipation Proclamation that would free certain slaves while leaving others in bondage, the United States had become an embarrassing anomaly as political leaders representing the North and South continued to argue over slavery, states' rights, western territories, and the unequal economic developments that were galvanizing the North and further weakening the South. These debates not only eroded the liberal edges of communities, but they invited into bordering areas angry white supremacists, who were determined to spread their own pro-slavery ideology into neutral or even anti-slavery communities.

While slavery and its expansion beyond the original Southern states were at the heart of the North-South dispute, there were also some important cultural issues driving the two regions apart. The Southern Democrats, who, in the past, had not focused on industrial development or public education, were now seeing how much farther ahead the Northern cities were progressing in both the economic and the intellectual arenas. Republicans in the North had been advocating for their corporate and industrial constituents while also supporting an expansion of public schools, thus improving the education and employment opportunities for citizens of all socioeconomic groups. Not surprisingly, this created great envy among residents of the South.

To compound the friction already at work, the North was bent on pushing its abolitionist views on the South. While some Northerners— particularly Quakers—were deeply offended on a religious level by the South's practice of buying and selling black people, many more of them opposed it simply because their less-agrarian economy and lifestyle saw no benefit to the outdated institution of slavery. Southerners resented the fact that Northerners were imposing their own views on the South.

Two years earlier, Blanche and his slave family in Missouri had some sense of what was going on politically in the South and the North, because young Willie Perkinson, his father, Pettis, and his uncle, William Bruce, often talked about party issues and political disputes. What Blanche and his brother Henry had also come to learn, as slaves who could read and interpret the world around them, was that there were two important skills that could help them in life: first, the ability to know which white people to trust; second, the ability to educate themselves.

Blanche and Henry also understood class lines, and that, in turn, helped them decide which whites to align themselves with. While the white race would consistently belittle and look down on blacks, these two young men understood how the class differences among whites could determine their own fate. Years later, in 1895, Henry pointed out that he and his family discovered very early that the greatest enemy to the black race were uneducated, less affluent whites. In speaking about the working-class white man in the South, Henry wrote, "He is not far enough up the scale to see the advantage of education, and will not send his children to school, nor allow the Colored child to go, if it is in his power to prevent it. The [white] aristocracy and the Colored people of the South would get along splendidly, were it not for these poor whites."[2]

The other important life skill shared by the ambitious Bruce brothers was their interest in education, an interest that Blanche was to develop even before his older brother. Years later, Blanche would attend Oberlin College, and then, later still, insist that his son go to Phillips Exeter and Harvard, institutions that only wealthy whites attended. Not surprisingly, this interest in education began early, while Blanche was still a slave. As Henry explained years later,

> There was a trait of character running through my mother's family, a desire to learn, and every member could read very well when the war broke out, and some could write. The older ones would teach the younger, and while mother had no education at all, she used to make the younger study the lessons

given by the older sister or brother, and in that way they all
learned to read. . . . Slavery in some portions of Missouri was
not what it was in Virginia, or in the extreme South, because
we could buy any book we wanted if we had the money to pay
for it.[3]

While rare to find in a slave family in the rural South or even the
Midwest, this understanding of both class differences and the value of
education was of great advantage to Blanche Bruce as he planned his
rise through Mississippi politics—a white arena that would demand all
his skills as an orator, businessman, and strategist.

In early 1862, while Blanche was still working as a Bruce-
Perkinson family slave, Master Willie was talking fervently about his
interest in supporting the Union side of the national conflict, in order
to keep the slave states and the free states together in one union. He
told Blanche that he did not care that his own father and uncle supported the Confederate side, because he was set on standing in support
of the Union.

Only a few months later, Master Willie went back on his word; he
enrolled in the Democratic Party and joined the Confederate Army, as
his father and uncle had wished. It was not up for debate: if the family
wanted to keep their slaves, they would have to fight with the side that
supported slavery. It was a pattern that Blanche would see in the
future, among other whites who professed to be liberal civil-rights pro-
ponents.

This had been a turning point for Blanche. His disillusionment with
his childhood companion and the realization that he could be stuck on a
plantation forever was what motivated him to leave Missouri.

Following the passage of the Fugitive Slave Act in 1850, Northerners were incensed that Southern slave owners could reach into Northern states and either reclaim runaway slaves living in free states or—in
many cases—simply kidnap free blacks and sell them into slavery with
the help of federal commissioners. Northern liberals saw this as an
infringement on personal liberty and on their own laws opposing slavery. At the same time, the outspoken abolitionist Horace Greeley, who
published the *New York Tribune*, worked hard to show his influential
readers how wrong slavery was for the nation. Although his concerns
would become more far-flung in 1872, when he was nominated for

president, in the 1850s and 1860s Horace Greeley focused primarily on ending slavery and getting the North and South to see eye to eye on the issue. Perhaps the final straw that caused abolitionist political leaders to decide that the Democratic and Whig Parties were no longer representing their interest was the passing in 1854 of the Kansas-Nebraska Act, which created Kansas and Nebraska and allowed the citizens of both territories to decide whether they were to be free or slave states. The fury that resulted from this among Northern politicians is what gave birth to the Republican Party. Although the party would not successfully elect its first president until the 1860 victory of Abraham Lincoln, the Republicans were galvanized by the Dred Scott Supreme Court decision, which permitted a slave to be brought into the free territory of Minnesota and remain a slave when his master wished to bring him back again to the slave state of Missouri. Northern Republicans argued, unsuccessfully, that residence in a free state gave Scott the status of a free man. With such deep divisions along political and geographic lines, it was no surprise when, in 1860, South Carolina became the first of seven southern states to secede from the Union.

In later years, Blanche was deliberately vague in recounting the way in which he escaped from Missouri slavery into Kansas freedom. Perhaps it was because he didn't want it to appear as if he had abandoned his slave family, or because he thought it was an unappealing story for a U.S. senator to relive in a public forum.

Another theory was that because Bruce was the mulatto offspring of his white slave master, Pettis Perkinson, he would have to openly acknowledge a fact that he would have found embarrassing or difficult to embrace. Although it was well known that many black slave women had been raped and forced into ongoing sexual relations by their white owners, Blanche would have known it was not a scenario that white constituents wanted to be reminded about.

For whatever reason, Blanche rarely discussed the early moves back and forth between Kansas and Missouri, though it is clear that he left the slave state of Missouri while many of his family members remained enslaved there.[4]

The first time that Bruce ever publicly described his 1862 escape from slavery was in 1886, when he wrote a short piece for the *Kansas City Times*. In the article, he wrote: "[A]fter the firing on Fort Sumter and the opening of the rebellion [I] concluded I would emancipate myself. So I worked my way to Kansas, and became a free man before the emancipation proclamation was issued by President Lincoln."[5]

Although the act of "departing" slavery surely had to have been a crucial event in Bruce's life, he waited twenty-six years to share it with the public. Interestingly, he revealed it with the greatest subtlety, while weaving it into an almost romantic story that spoke more of other events. It is also interesting that Bruce shared this story only after it would have almost no impact on his future success; by the time he wrote about it in 1886, he had already served in the Senate and completed his first appointment as register of the U.S. Treasury.

It is true that a small number of slaves escaped to freedom in late August 1861, when Union Army General John Fremont issued a proclamation emancipating Missouri slaves who were owned by Confederate sympathizers. Although President Lincoln rescinded the unapproved emancipation only days later, there were a few blacks who left during that time, but there is no evidence that Blanche or his family members were able to take advantage of that small window of opportunity for freedom.

Whatever reason Bruce had for remaining reticent about his departure from Missouri, it is clear that he left many family members behind. In fact, neither he nor his brother Henry, who was rather specific in his recounting of the family history up to 1895, ever explains how or why Blanche was suddenly alone in Lawrence, Kansas, in 1863 when, up to that time, the Bruce family had remained together—whether they were in Prince Edward County, Virginia; Chariton County, Missouri; or Holly Springs, Mississippi.

It is possible that Blanche realized there was no favorable way to recount his activities in 1862 in detail without alienating black freedmen who would think he had deserted his family, or without antagonizing white Southerners who would learn he had "abandoned" his owner when Willie Perkinson departed to serve in the Confederate Army. It was a calculated decision for him to almost erase that story from his biography and then just pick up again in 1863, after his emancipation.

Blanche resumed his autobiography in detail in August of 1863, in Lawrence. It had been his intention to try to get to a Northern place like Ohio, but Kansas was closer and easier—particularly given his lack of funds. He chose Lawrence because it had a large community of residents that opposed slavery, encouraged the education of blacks, and practiced other abolitionist teachings. With the help of the members of a local Congregational church, he was further educated and was able to establish the area's first school for black children. As Confederate sympathizers learned about the liberal activities in Lawrence, it drew the ire of whites who resented the possibility of black upward mobility. There was further white resentment aimed at Lawrence because two squads of black federal troops were stationed in the town.

By the time Blanche found himself caught in Lawrence during William Quantrill's 1863 killing spree, he realized life was dangerous even in free territory. It was to force him back to Missouri.

> I saw the fighting going on, and the guerrillas rode by without discovering me, although they pursued every man in sight. At last I had a clear field, ran down to the Kaw River as fast as I could and jumped in. My flight was observed, and several armed men rode furiously toward me. Fortunately, keeping my head under water, I managed to hide ... The troopers rode in the river, searched everywhere without discovering my retreat, although they came within a few feet of me ... I remained concealed in the river all day ... until after night fall, when the town had been sacked and burned.[6]

The incident made frightened and destitute Blanche realize that he had to return to Missouri, a place that felt less foreign and terrifying. As the Civil War advanced, he remained in the state, creating in early 1864 a school in Hannibal, which had the distinction of being Missouri's first school for blacks.

The racial and political landscape surrounding Blanche in 1864 was an intimidating one in both the South and the North. One of the few bright spots was the reelection of President Lincoln. While on June 28, 1864, Congress passed laws that repealed the Fugitive Slave Act, and while the Union Army was scoring well in their efforts against the South by winning major battles in Atlanta and Richmond, there was increased rioting against blacks in the North among poor white Irishmen. The whites resented being drafted for a war they believed was being fought on behalf of blacks, a war they couldn't afford to buy their way out of, as their affluent WASP counterparts could.

This anti-black sentiment was becoming more and more popular in the North, where poor whites argued that if they joined the war effort, blacks might come to their cities and take their jobs while they were away. Many of these whites ignored the fact that blacks were fighting, too, with more than 386,000 blacks enlisted in the Union Army and Navy. In fact, blacks made up 10 percent of the Union's troops even though blacks made up only 1 percent of the North's population. The black troops were, for obvious reasons, anxious to join the fight. Twenty-four black enlistees received the Congressional Medal of Honor for their combat service.

On April 9, 1865, the nation's attention was turned toward Virginia, when Confederate General Robert E. Lee and Union General Ulysses S. Grant met at Virginia's Appomattox Courthouse, where Lee offered an unconditional surrender, thus ending the four-year war. Just five days later, President Lincoln was assassinated by Confederate sympathizer John Wilkes Booth.

By early 1865, Blanche had gotten a job working on a Missouri newspaper's printing press. It allowed him to further educate himself, to hone both his reading and writing skills. Also from this position, he could view how the nation responded to the emancipation of blacks and the establishment of their rights. It was his former home state, Mississippi, that more than any other state in the Union or former Confederacy resisted congressional edicts supporting blacks. For example, on November 24, less than a month before Congress passed the Thirteenth Amendment, making slavery illegal, the State of Mississippi passed Black Codes, to penalize and limit the activities of blacks. These Black Codes made it illegal for blacks in Mississippi to be educated in the same schools as whites, to serve on a jury, to carry a gun, to hold meetings, to testify against a white person, or to be outdoors beyond a special "black curfew time." These new Mississippi laws even stated that any black adult male who did not have a job could be legally arrested and hired out to a white employer against his will.

Only a week before the Senate created the Committee on Reconstruction, the official act that began what would be the twelve-year Reconstruction Era, Congress convened on December 4, 1865, in

Washington. Once again, Blanche's former home state of Mississippi held the dubious distinction of being the only state that was not in step with the rest of the South. The Mississippi legislature was the only governing body that refused President Andrew Johnson's conditions for being readmitted to the Union.

Blanche returned to Missouri in early 1866, after the war was over, and again saw his family working a tobacco plantation in Chariton County. It seemed as though the war had changed nothing.

Blanche would never be satisfied working in Missouri and watching his family continue to toil in the same work they had suffered through during slavery. In the summer of 1866, he joined his friend George Cornelius Smith on the route east, headed for Oberlin, Ohio. There was a college Smith had heard about, where blacks could obtain a good education. On their trip of several weeks, George told Blanche more about Oberlin College, the rural Ohio school that was relatively well known for its abolitionist background and progressive attitudes on educating blacks since its founding in 1833.

In a June 27, 1891, article that Smith later wrote for the *Freeman*, he discussed his first year of schooling with Bruce. He says of Bruce,

> He at once joined the class and from the start, was its recognized leader; especially was this true in mathematics, in a class, too, where there were many freshmen who were making up these studies. After remaining there some time, his funds gave out and he was upon the eve of leaving to earn more and return—for he, at that time, intended completing a full course and fit himself for the Congregational ministry—when I begged him to remain and seek a loan from a source from which I had reason to believe he might succeed.[7]

As Smith explains, Blanche applied for a loan, but once it was denied, he realized that he had to leave Oberlin. Smith recalled the day that Blanche found out he would not be receiving money to help pay for the tuition: "I can never forget his utterances and the look of determination written in every muscle of his face when the letter finally came, declining to grant the accommodation. He said to me: 'I am truly glad that the money did not come. I shall leave for St. Louis tomorrow.

I can and will win my way without it; there is a place for me and money, too. Both shall be mine.' "[8]

Blanche kept in touch with Smith even after leaving for St. Louis and getting a job as a steamship porter. During that time, Reconstruction was opening up opportunities for blacks in the South, and Smith encouraged him to consider relocating back there to take advantage of the new possibilities. It was his friend's comment about Reconstruction opportunities in the South that first caused Blanche to begin reading Republican newspaper accounts of what was happening in Washington and the South.

The liberal Republicans and President Andrew Johnson were in heated conflict throughout 1867 over various Reconstruction issues, with Congress passing the First Reconstruction Act over the president's veto. This news was encouraging to Blanche as he realized that Congress, at least, was serious about improving the opportunities for blacks in the South.

Ulysses S. Grant, riding his wave of post–Civil War popularity and taking advantage of support from black voters, was able to win the presidency in 1868. Knowing Grant's strong ties to the black cause, Blanche was convinced that the Southern black could probably benefit from Grant's presidency. He decided he should return to those Southern roots and reap some of the opportunities that Grant and other Republicans were promising.

Bruce arrived back in Mississippi in February 1869. The Republican newspapers were reporting that blacks were now being elevated to government positions for the first time in the South—with Jackson, Mississippi, holding a political convention that included seventeen black delegates. Blanche hoped that this state, which was not yet readmitted to the Union despite its majority black population, would offer him the opportunities that Reconstruction in Louisiana had offered to such blacks as P. B. S. Pinchback and Oscar J. Dunn, two men who had served as lieutenant governor in the state. In Louisiana, where there were far more educated blacks than in Mississippi, the Republican Party had begun to allow black freedmen as well as freeborn blacks to participate more fully in their political activities.

Pinckney Benton Stewart Pinchback (or P. B. S. Pinchback, as he was known) and Oscar Dunn were both black former captains in the Union Army who rose quickly in New Orleans politics.

Pinchback, the founder and publisher of the *New Orleans Louisian-ian*, had been educated in Cincinnati before working as a boat steward and then joining the Union Army. In 1868, he had been elected to the Louisiana State Senate, where he was an outspoken critic of the state's public accommodation laws that discriminated against blacks. As an astute black political leader who also understood the power of the press, he would later become a close friend and adviser to Blanche once the latter entered the Senate. During Pinchback's eventual term as lieu-tenant governor, he would be elevated to the governorship for a brief time in late 1872 and early 1873.

Dunn, a Louisiana native, began politics as a member of the New Orleans City Council and in April 1868 was elected Louisiana's lieu-tenant governor, serving with the white governor Henry Warmouth. Dunn would face strong opposition but still win the chairmanship of the 1870 Republican State Convention.

By the time Bruce reached Mississippi in early 1869, he had already spent a few months in Little Rock, Arkansas, and Memphis, Tennessee. What caused him to keep traveling south toward Mississippi was the determination to find a city or county where it was clear that ambitious black men would be accepted for meaningful positions in work and soci-ety. Instinctively, he knew that this would occur only where blacks made up a substantial percentage of the population. Mississippi was one of those states where blacks outnumbered whites in many of its counties. In Mississippi, with its large black population, black Republicans were likely to be offered employment or entry-level government positions.

In fact, Blanche had read that a Mississippi black man, Isaiah Montgomery, who had been a former slave of Confederate President Jefferson Davis, was appointed to public office as justice of the peace in 1867, in a town called Davis Bend. This could only have happened in a state where blacks held a large segment of the population, and where Republicans saw potentially strong support for their party. In 1868, Mississippi held the "Black and Tan Convention," which took place in Jackson and included black Republican delegates. It was a pivotal event, because it was the first time that the state had ever held a con-vention that included nonwhite representatives. Of the one hundred delegates participating in the convention, seventeen were black. The remaining eighty-three consisted of white Democrats, white Republi-cans from the North, and white Republicans from Mississippi.

But the event that had the greatest impact on Blanche's decision to choose Mississippi as his home, and on his interest in holding political office, was his attendance at an 1869 speech given by James Lusk Alcorn, the Republican candidate for governor of the state. By then, the federal government's Reconstruction programs in the South were well under way. A provisional Mississippi governor named Adelbert Ames had already been appointed in 1868 by the president. Federal troops were in place to protect black freedmen. Southern scalawags like James Alcorn—a wealthy Delta planter who had earlier supported the Whig Party—had fallen into line and realized that if they wanted to keep their land, their wealth, and political positions, they'd have to adopt the more liberal attitudes that the Republicans in power were espousing. They knew that if they wanted to win political office, they would have to offer the blacks something.

In his speech, Alcorn announced that black men should and *would* be given positions in his administration if he was elected. He also declared that the country was changing—and that the black man must have a role in it.

Within days after hearing Alcorn's speech, Blanche began attending more Republican meetings in the northwestern part of the state. By the spring, Blanche caught the attention of several advisers of then-governor Ames, who agreed to name the new Mississippian to the position of conductor of elections for Mississippi's Tallahatchie County. This role, while not very prestigious or challenging, gave him an immediate introduction to the political process and to the various players in the state Republican Party.

Several weeks later, in November 1869, the forceful and charismatic Alcorn was elected as the new provisional governor of Mississippi. Alcorn continued to aggressively advance the argument that whites had better start accepting the fact that Negroes now had rights that could not and should not be threatened. He also criticized those who had supported Mississippi's secession from the Union.[9]

Blanche continued to catch the eye of the state Republican Party leaders. On January 13, 1870, he was nominated for the positions of postmaster and official doorkeeper for the Mississippi House of Representatives. Although he lost the elections to these posts, Mississippi State Senator Henry Paine nominated him again, and he was eventually victorious in his election to sergeant-at-arms for the Mississippi State Senate.[10]

Blanche's first full year in Mississippi offered a great deal of hope—much more than he could have contemplated when he had lived there as a slave in the 1840s and 1850s. Whites and blacks that lived in the Reconstruction South were seeing dramatic changes. Not only did the Fifteenth Amendment give black men the right to vote, but Mississippi, Virginia, and Texas were readmitted to the Union. Given the fact that Mississippi had one of the largest black populations of any state, it was no surprise that its state legislature was suddenly one-fourth black.

Further north, in South Carolina, changes were also being made. Joseph Rainey became the first black congressman to be both elected to and seated in the U.S. House of Representatives. That same year, Richard T. Greener, a man who would later play a controversial role in Bruce's and other high-profile blacks' lives, would become the first black college graduate from Harvard University. 1870 was a year that made Blanche feel justifiably optimistic.

He knew that his ambitions to find professional success and wealth—even as a recently arrived black man in Mississippi—were achievable. He was twenty-nine years old, and for the first time in his life, he felt a boundless optimism toward his future.

CHAPTER FIVE

⤥⟋⟍⤦

1870–1874

*Bruce Builds a Base of Power in Mississippi
and Is Elected to the U.S. Senate*

BY 1871, THERE WERE ONLY A SMALL HANDFUL OF BLACKS IN THE
North and the Middle Atlantic who had established themselves as successful businessmen. They included such people as John McKee and
Henry Minton, two wealthy Philadelphia caterers; James Wormley, a
real estate and hotel entrepreneur in Washington; and Isaac Myers, a
founder of the Chesapeake Marine Railway & Dry Dock Company,
a black-owned Baltimore shipyard. Black entrepreneurism was not as
widespread in the Southern states.

While not having the same type of economic opportunities as their
Northern brethren, blacks in the South, with the help of Reconstruction, were finding greater success in the political arena. With the support of white Republicans in the North, black carpetbaggers and their
white counterparts saw a chance to fill the political void left once the
South had lost the Civil War. Blanche was benefiting in the South
through these same opportunities.

In 1871, there were more than 4.8 million blacks in the United
States, almost 13 percent of the entire population.[1] Although some
blacks had begun to leave the Southern plantation and farm areas in
search of better living and working conditions in the cities, most blacks
remained rooted in their rural communities.

By this time, Reconstruction and its various programs such as the Freedmen's Bureau and the Freedman's Bank had brought improved opportunities for blacks in the South. It was during this period that some of the well-known black colleges were being established and expanded in the South. Since the Civil War, schools like Howard University, Morehouse College, Atlanta University, and Fisk University had positioned themselves as important destinations for upwardly mobile black students.

The Freedman's Savings and Trust Company, a bank that was created in 1865 and run by the Freedmen's Bureau for the purpose of doing business with blacks, had more than thirty different branches in the South. Recently freed blacks now were learning how to save and invest their small earnings with the government-run bank. This Reconstruction program was the best source of the optimism that was felt by many Southern blacks.

Although he was well on his way to advancing in county and local government, it is interesting that Bruce's political career had started a year earlier in *state* government. He had come to the attention of white Republican Party leaders while attending local party meetings in 1869. They had been looking to identify and elevate some competent black ingenues in this heavily black-populated county and suggested Bruce for a job in the statehouse.

It was on January 17, 1870, that the Mississippi State Senate elected Bruce to the position of sergeant-at-arms after he had been nominated by Republican state senator Henry Paine.[2] Earlier that month, the Mississippi legislature's 140 members had convened in the city of Jackson, with the plan to fulfill the requirements that had been outlined by President Grant for those Confederate states still awaiting readmission to the Union. With Republicans making up more than three-fourths of the legislature, it was no surprise when the majority agreed to ratify the U.S. Constitution's Fourteenth and Fifteenth Amendments, which, respectively, gave blacks citizenship and the right to vote.[3]

During that same month, in preparation for readmission to the Union, the Mississippi legislature also had to elect new men to represent it in the U.S. Senate. While members of the House of Representatives were elected by the general population, in 1870, U.S. senators were still being elected by members of the various state legislatures.[4] In January 1870 the legislature had to fill three seats—two unexpired terms that would be seated immediately, and one full six-year term that would be seated in 1871.

The legislature easily voted Alcorn in for the full Senate term that was to begin in 1871. (From March 4, 1871, until December 4 of that year, he simultaneously served as both U.S. senator and Mississippi governor.) Next, after some debate, provisional military governor Adelbert Ames was picked for the longest unexpired term.

At this point, the black legislators were furious. As the Republicans had full control during the Mississippi legislature's debates, black leaders had demanded that at least one of the three seats should be given to a black Republican, emphasizing the loyalty and dedication of black voters to the Republican Party. Now they insisted that their colleagues consider a black man for the last Senate seat, a short unexpired term that had originally been held by Mississippi native Jefferson Davis, who had become infamous as president of the Confederacy. Following long discussions of possible white candidates, the legislative body finally acquiesced to pressure from the more liberal legislators and considered a black politician named Hiram R. Revels, who had already served as an alderman in Natchez and as a Mississippi state senator.

Born free in Fayetteville County, North Carolina, Revels had been a pastor in Illinois, Indiana, and Missouri before moving to Mississippi. Like Blanche Bruce, he also had a background in education. In 1863, he had opened a school for black children in St. Louis. Although whites were angered by the idea of elevating a black to the Senate, Revels's calm demeanor and respectable background in the church and government softened their resistance. They finally voted eighty-five to fifteen to admit Revels to the third Senate seat. Southern whites were assuaged by the fact that his term would only last one year.

Within weeks, on February 23, President Grant signed the bill readmitting Mississippi to the Union. Two days later, Hiram Revels was seated in the U.S. Senate. Although Revels was the last of the three Senate candidates to be voted in, he was actually seated first, prior to Ames.

On March 10, 1870, James Lusk Alcorn, who had already proven to be a major supporter of Bruce's, was sworn in as governor of the state. Alcorn's Senate term would not begin until 1871. In Alcorn, the Republicans saw that they had a Mississippian who spoke more aggressively than virtually any other white Southerner about the importance of welcoming blacks into the political arena. Cynical and calculating, Alcorn recognized that the tide had turned, leaving Southern whites with no alternative if they wanted to maintain any political influence. They would have to acknowledge that the Northern Republicans were controlling the federal government and, hence, controlling the newly readmitted states. Embracing political expediency better than most white Southerners, Alcorn saw the large numbers of newly enfranchised black Republicans, and he knew he'd better be on their side while also anointing a handful of "black lieutenants" who would aid his advancement. Bruce would be among that chosen group.

Later that month, on March 24, after considerable debate, the state legislature finally seated General Adelbert Ames for the second Senate seat. A man with markedly less political savvy than Alcorn, Ames had been named provisional governor in 1868, while the state was still under military rule. Having been a military commander who arrived as a carpetbagger from New England, he knew very little about the Mississippi natives, and therefore had no compunction about overlooking local whites and appointing black freedmen to minor local offices. This practice made him popular among blacks and radical Republicans. His most significant order on behalf of the freedmen had come in 1869, when he ordered that blacks should be allowed to serve as jurors.

After being acknowledged by a state Republican newspaper as "one of the most promising young men in the State," in his role of recruiting blacks to register with the Republican Party, Bruce again caught the attention of Alcorn, who was now exerting his power as governor. Later in 1870, Governor Alcorn responded to Bruce's rising popularity among blacks and among white Republicans by appointing him to the position of tax assessor of Bolivar County, a position that allowed Bruce to earn a 7 percent commission on major properties that were now being assessed for the first time. Bolivar County, which was located in the northwestern quadrant of the state, hugged the Mississippi River and sat just across the Arkansas border. The county, while not densely populated, had many plantations and farms that could be newly assessed and added to the tax rolls. More important for Bruce, more than three-quarters of Bolivar's voting population consisted of black freedmen—making it easy for a black man to win any county-wide election. At that time, the thirty-four-year-old county consisted of 2,084 black voters and only 590 white voters.

It was the spring of 1871. Bruce had just been sworn in as Bolivar County tax assessor. He shook the hands of the men who had attended the ceremony. He gazed into the warm afternoon sunlight, looking for no one in particular. The group of forty or fifty people was mostly white, with maybe six or seven black men standing on the fringes of the enthusiastic crowd.

As he watched his audience once again break into applause on the steps of the tiny courthouse, Bruce knew that he had more than satisfied the men who stood before him. But despite all the kind words and praise that he heaped on the audience, he knew that he had gotten this appointment because Mississippi Governor James Alcorn, the white Southern scalawag, had forced it through.

Just a year earlier, in 1870, Blanche had gotten the position of sergeant-at-arms in the Mississippi Senate by befriending the white carpetbagger Adelbert Ames, who had been the military governor before being seated in the U.S. Senate on March 24, 1870. Now, he had moved on and was benefiting from his relationship with the newest most powerful man in the state, James Alcorn, who was out to build a power base among blacks throughout the state. In many ways, Alcorn was a rival of Ames's for the various spoils that were available to white Republicans who were positioned to exploit Mississippi's Reconstruction policies. Alcorn had been inaugurated as Mississippi governor only a year earlier, on March 10, 1870, but he was determined to maintain a foothold in every section of the state—particularly where Republican majorities were in existence.[5]

By the fall of 1871, Bruce was emboldened by his growing popularity among black and white Republicans. Although there was a white Democrat opposing him, he decided to run for the job of sheriff and tax collector of Bolivar County. He later described the experience in a *Kansas City Times* newspaper article:

At my first canvass for sheriff, my democratic opponent . . . challenged me to meet him in debate. I was reluctant to do so . . . But being pressed to accept the offer, we agreed to divide time at a meeting held in a precinct where the democrats were largely in the majority. My competitor said . . . that I had been a slave and therefore was unfit to fill the high office of sheriff. I hardly knew how to meet this logic [except to] turn the laugh on my adversary . . . I frankly admitted that I had been a slave . . . but I had outgrown the degradation. [I said] had he been a slave . . . he never would have risen superior to his original condition, and would be performing menial offices even now. This was so well received by my opponents, my competitor never invited me thereafter to debate.[6]

During the next several days, Bruce continued to campaign throughout the county and easily won the election on November 7, 1871. In his role as county sheriff, a position that only twelve blacks held during the Reconstruction period throughout the state of Mississippi, Bruce wielded great economic and political influence. He not only collected county and state taxes but also directed the selection of men who would serve on trial juries and chose the election registrars. Bruce's early wealth, no doubt, was tied to the fees and commissions that he was able to earn in his role as sheriff and tax collector. In a county of Bolivar's wealth, it is estimated that Bruce would have earned fees as high as fifteen or twenty thousand dollars in his first year as sheriff and tax collector.[7]

Shortly after he had been elected to those two offices, the Mississippi state board of education appointed him to the position of county superintendent of education. His friendship with Governor Alcorn aided him in getting the position. With Republicans exerting control in the reorganization of the state's affairs, Bruce was able to become a new and powerful force in the county—holding three positions simultaneously and exerting control in every aspect of its citizens' lives.

It was true that the Republicans were aggressively appointing and recruiting their own in order to ensure that the Democrats were kept out of all powerful positions, and thus often unqualified—but available—Republican cronies received appointments for which they were ill suited. Bruce, on the other hand, found himself well prepared for the position of superintendent of education, since he had previously founded schools in both Kansas and Missouri. In fact, the two years he held the position, Bruce established seven new schools in the county, bringing the total to twenty-one schools, which educated more than one thousand children.

By 1871, Blanche Bruce was finding that Bolivar County and other areas in northwestern Mississippi had become fertile ground for his ambition, but the state still lagged behind other states, such as South

Carolina and Louisiana, in terms of providing political opportunities for blacks. In fact, South Carolina had already placed blacks at the highest levels of government. There, residents had elected a black, Jonathan Jasper Wright, to its Supreme Court; a black secretary of state, Francis L. Cardozo; and a black lieutenant governor, Alonzo J. Ransier.[8] Furthermore, blacks had made up the majority of the South Carolina state legislature since 1868.

What was encouraging to Bruce's political career ambitions in Mississippi was not only the seating of Hiram R. Revels in February of the prior year, but also the ongoing status and power wielded by Governor Alcorn. With Alcorn on Bruce's side, the young black leader was able to appear even more influential to onlookers. Having such a powerful mentor proved invaluable to Bruce when the latter faced his November 7 election day for the office of county sheriff and tax collector. Who could defeat a candidate backed by a senator and governor—especially when that candidate's party was now running the state and the nation?

Perhaps a statewide position was the next goal. He just had to determine how to make himself even more useful to the state leadership, so that they saw he could do more than just help them locally. Bruce was already strategizing for the long term.

In 1872, Bruce was able to broaden his power so it reached beyond the borders of Bolivar County and into more of the Delta region, when he was named to the Board of Levee Commissioners for a district that included three counties along the Mississippi and Arkansas Rivers. That region was well populated with farmers and residents who needed help with the frequent flooding that resulted from the overflow of the two rivers. Articulate and charismatic, Bruce quickly used his position on the board to acquaint himself with prominent people in the other two counties. His stature in the party grew quickly, as was evidenced when the state Republican party chose him as the delegation's secretary for the 1872 national convention where President Grant was nominated for a second term.

Another black who was gaining favor among Mississippi Republicans at the time was John Roy Lynch. Like Bruce, Lynch had also been born a slave. Living in the more populated and cosmopolitan city of Natchez, Lynch had greater ties to the top party leaders than Bruce had at the time. In 1869, Mississippi's provisional governor Adelbert Ames had named the twenty-one-year-old Lynch justice of the peace in

Natchez. The following year, he was elected to the Mississippi state legislature. Lynch would, more so than Bruce, maintain close ties to the state of Mississippi after his service in the nation's capital. In fact, Lynch remained the head of the Mississippi Republican executive committee until 1892.

Following a political trajectory that was even faster than Bruce's, Lynch was popular as a state legislator. With the urging of James Alcorn, the State House of Representatives chose Lynch as their speaker.[9] With this new position, Lynch became a powerful legislator, and by the time he and Bruce worked together in the Mississippi delegation to the 1872 Republican National Convention, Lynch was talked about as a contender for a U.S. House of Representatives seat.

Although Lynch's successful 1872 congressional campaign would help him reach the national stage two years before Bruce, and keep him there for multiple terms, Bruce would find significant economic wealth before any other black leader in the state, including Lynch. In 1872, Bruce helped found the town of Floreyville, which became the Bolivar county seat, a move that allowed him to turn his political and civic connections into financial opportunities for himself. Not only was he able to buy land in sections of the town that would prove advantageous, but he was able to profit from the large fees that he earned while collecting taxes. With $500, he purchased nine pieces of property in Floreyville, using one of them to erect his home, the first house to be built in the new county seat.[10] By April 1873, he was not only a significant landowner in the town but also had been elected to the town's Board of Aldermen. As recorded by the *Annual Report of the Auditor of Public Accounts of Mississippi* that year, as sheriff and tax collector, Bruce collected state taxes of $28,804.15.

Given the powerful positions that he held in the county, it is also possible that wealthy landowners and others who wanted to curry favor with the Republican Party could have offered Bruce money or goods as payment for his assistance. This was a practice that became commonplace in Mississippi and other states where disenfranchised white Democrats still owned land but needed to remain on good terms with the local Republican officials. In fact, an 1872 congressional subcommittee investigation revealed that many county government officials contributed to the financial corruption that took place in the first two years of Mississippi's readmission to the Union. While he was never personally accused of such corruption, it is likely that Bruce's fast-emerging wealth at this time can be traced to the large fees that he was paid by wealthy landowners. Always cautious and diligent in his record-keeping and service to residents, Bruce maintained the respect of constituents in Bolivar as well as the surrounding counties.

But it still remains a question why whites would have allowed Bruce to gain so many positions and so much power. When most whites at the time had so little regard for blacks, why would they have given so much authority to Bruce? The answer is not so complex when one looks at the needs of the various white citizens of Mississippi. First, there were the white Republicans who were most concerned about maintaining political power over the county and the surrounding region. They realized that close to 75 percent of the residents of the county were black freedmen, and the Republicans wanted to be sure that these freedmen remained loyal to the Republican Party now and in the future. To gain the trust of the blacks, the Republicans knew they could not place only white men in leadership roles, as it would have offended the blacks and made them suspicious of the white-dominated party. The Republicans knew that Bruce would articulate their party platform, and remain loyal to them, and all the while keep the blacks within the party tent.

The white Democrats' motivation for accepting Bruce as a rising figure in their county was slightly different. They knew that the Republicans outnumbered them and could continue to outmaneuver them so long as the state Democrats and the nation's Democratic Party were voted out of power. So, if not one of their own, their second choice would be a figure who would serve their economic interest in keeping their plantations and businesses thriving. And since their primary labor source was black freedmen, these white landowners lived in constant fear of an unstable black labor force. They needed a local leader who would keep the blacks satisfied, and keep them working. Bruce could accomplish that because he was a moderate, because he was a black man with business acumen, and also because he was a man who owned land and understood the need to maintain a stable labor force in an agricultural economy. Despite his different race and political party, the white Democrats saw that he and they at least had the same economic interests.

Recognizing the political and racial dynamics that put him in power, Bruce was determined to act quickly and use his power and money wisely. He was enough of a realist to know that these advantages would not last long.

On March 28, 1874, he took out a loan from the Marine Bank of Georgia in order to purchase an eight-hundred-acre plantation that had belonged to William Stark, a wealthy Mississippi Delta landowner. It would become the home of the Bruce plantation that would remain in his family for several decades. He would increase the plantation's size significantly by purchasing additional parcels during the next decade.

Owning his own plantation put Bruce in the position of being compared to the successful white political leaders that he knew in the Republican Party. But despite the gains that Bruce was making in the state, similar political successes were not enjoyed by many other aspiring black politicians living there. Unlike South Carolina, North Carolina, and Louisiana, where black populations were high and were able to elect multiple blacks to high levels of government, Mississippi remained a state where a large black population was able to elevate only a few blacks to important elected positions.

With blacks finally making some advances in Mississippi, hate groups such as the Ku Klux Klan were increasing their reign of terror throughout the state. By burning property, threatening and killing blacks, the Klan was quickly gaining power and influence in white Democratic areas where resentment against Republicans and blacks was high.

As Bruce made his plans and became a serious contender for a statewide position, it became more and more evident that Mississippi was seeing the emergence of a generation of smart black power brokers. There were inevitable comparisons to be made between Blanche Bruce and John Roy Lynch, who started their political careers in 1869 and later found themselves in Washington in the mid-1870s. What would also prove similar about the two men was their success in real estate. Although he would never be as wealthy as Bruce, Lynch would own a considerable amount of land and four plantations by the time he retired from Congress. Some believed that Lynch and Bruce were driven to compete with each other. It was said that because Lynch had entered politics earlier and had deeper state party roots than Bruce, it had been the latter's goal to match or outperform Lynch. When Lynch was elected to Congress first, in 1872, in the House of Representatives,

Bruce was determined to outshine Lynch by aiming for the U.S. Senate. This is possibly why Bruce had turned down offers, in 1873, to run for governor on a ticket with Senator Alcorn or to run for lieutenant governor on a ticket with Senator Adelbert Ames.

Extremely competitive, Lynch was determined not to be outdone in years of service—even if already outdone in rank. Even after losing his House seat in 1876, he ran again and regained his seat in 1882, until finally losing it to Henry Van Eaton, a white Democrat who had fought for the Confederate Army. Lynch therefore served in Congress three years beyond Bruce's last year in office. He also competed with Bruce in terms of land ownership—ultimately surpassing the senator in the number of acquired parcels. By 1891, he owned four plantations in Mississippi—most of them in or around Natchez. One of them, known as Grove Plantation, consisted of more than 1,500 acres. By 1898, John Roy Lynch was worth more than $90,000—which would translate into approximately $1.7 million in today's dollars.

But despite their competitive natures, the coalition that Bruce and Lynch put together to advance themselves, other black leaders, and the rights of black people, far outweighed any jealousies that they might have felt. In fact, most would have argued that they were extremely close friends, advisers, and confidants to each other.

A lot of what Lynch was able to do in the Mississippi legislature contributed to the success that Bruce would have both in the state and on a national level. To begin with, in 1873 Lynch took advantage of the large number of blacks and Republicans in the state legislature by pushing through a civil rights bill that made it illegal to discriminate against blacks in public accommodations like hotels, restaurants, and train seating. Although the bill would be ignored by many, and eventually undermined when public restaurants and hotels started to declare themselves private clubs who could "host" their "invited" patrons, the bill's initial passing demonstrated the power that blacks, and Lynch in particular, now exerted in Mississippi politics.

Another Lynch—no relation to John Roy Lynch—was James Lynch, the first black in Mississippi to hold a state office. When James Lynch died in 1872, the race to become the most prominent black leader was on. Bruce and his young contemporaries fashioned themselves after the popular leader and courted his prior supporters.

A post–Civil War transplant, James Lynch had first arrived in Mississippi in 1867 from the North, after being sent there to act as a bishop for the Methodist Church. Embracing Republican politics as firmly as his religious beliefs, the eloquent and bright Lynch was soon speaking on behalf of the Republican Party and organizing freedmen in Jackson and elsewhere to spread the word about the party and its potential role in helping blacks throughout the state.

It wasn't long before Lynch became publisher of his own weekly newspaper, the *Jackson Colored Citizen*, which he founded in 1868 in order to further popularize Republican politics among blacks in the state. From then until he died in 1872, he was perceived as the preeminent black political leader among Mississippi Republicans.

Although there were other rising black political stars, such as James Hill, Ham Carter, and John Roy Lynch, vying for the role, Bruce felt he was the natural heir, and that the death of James Lynch offered him an opportunity to step into the position as the state's leading black politician. Since Bruce was the only one in the group who was liked by both the moderate Republicans and the radical Republicans, his chances of succeeding were good. It had been proven in the presidential election of 1872 that there were many divisions in the party, and that such divisions could be exploited if there was no single candidate to represent each group's interests. In fact, when the liberal Republicans had put forth the former abolitionist and newspaper publisher Horace Greeley as their candidate to run against mainstream Republican Ulysses S. Grant, the conservative Southern Democrats got behind Greeley simply because they wanted to punish Grant for having empowered blacks and forced Reconstruction policies onto their region. Although Greeley lost the election, his strong showing revealed how effective the anti-Republican forces were as they chipped away at the mainstream Republican power base.

Hence, it was necessary for the Republicans to identify the one individual who attracted the widest range of registered Republicans— black, white, moderate, liberal, and radical—in order to prevent outsiders from entering the fray and further dividing the party. Bruce was the person who fit that profile best.

Moreover, Bruce had received a wealth of political experience during his four years of living in Mississippi. Since his arrival there, he had held the positions of sergeant-at-arms for the State Senate, as well as sheriff, tax assessor, tax collector, superintendent of the county schools,

Floreyville town board member, and a member of the Second District Levee Board. While he held each position only a short period, these jobs gave Bruce the confidence that he needed in order to pursue a position beyond the local and county level.

It was the 1873 Mississippi gubernatorial campaign that set the stage for Bruce's rise to the Senate. In that year, both of Mississippi's U.S. senators, Adelbert Ames and James Alcorn, were seeking the Republican nomination for governor. Ames had held his Senate seat since 1870, and Alcorn had taken his in 1871. The current governor, Ridgely Powers (who had been lieutenant governor when Alcorn was governor two years earlier), was a moderate. Early on, he had disappointed many black leaders when they realized he had close ties to white conservatives who had advanced the many Mississippi laws passed to discriminate against black freedmen in 1865. For many of the black leaders who wanted to see aggressive moves toward racial equality, a slow-moving white moderate Republican was viewed as not being much better than a white conservative Democrat. Powers had appointed too many conservatives in important positions to ever win back the black vote. In fact, the only well-known blacks who supported Powers were Hiram Revels, who had long before lost black support with his moderate stands—and James Lynch, who had recently died.

In addition to losing black support, another early threat to Powers's reelection was the candidacy of radical white Republican activist Robert Flournoy, who, although he had owned slaves in Mississippi, was now urging the integration of public schools and equal rights for blacks in all areas of life.[11] Although Flournoy was never able to establish himself as a serious candidate, his radical views made Powers's past seem all the more conservative and threatening to the black voters. And Powers began making such major mistakes in office—like asking for the military to return to Mississippi—that his party forced him to withdraw his candidacy.

Now the only two Republican candidates for governor were Alcorn and Ames. Alcorn had held the job two years earlier, and was eager to return despite the fact that he was still in the early part of his Senate term. At the time, Senator Ames was closely affiliated with the radical wing of the Republican Party, while Senator Alcorn was associated with the moderate wing—a group that had done very little to aid blacks—despite his prior promises to the freedmen. Since Ames had the support of President Grant as well as of the majority of the black population, Alcorn was anxious to secure any foothold he could find in the black community. He thought that he could accomplish that by getting the popular Bruce to run on the same ticket. Often willing to promise blacks more than he would actually deliver, Alcorn assumed he could win the support of Bruce and blacks by merely publicly *promising* to give Bruce a good position after the election. The offer was made in late August, while all of them were in Jackson for the Republican state convention. Bruce was immediately suspicious, because he had already watched Alcorn's past moderate rhetoric slowly transform itself into conservative policy and programs that were consistently disrespectful to the black community.

The liberal Ames was more aggressive in his wooing of Bruce to his gubernatorial campaign. He directly offered Bruce a position on his campaign ticket—as his running mate and lieutenant governor. As many, including Bruce, knew, the offer to run as Ames's lieutenant governor was better than it sounded, for it was a known fact that it was Ames's goal to win the governorship, hold it for several months, and then run for the Senate again. Such a plan would automatically make Ames's lieutenant governor—Blanche Bruce, in this case—the new governor of Mississippi.

Black and white Republican leaders assumed that Bruce would jump at the chance to align himself with one of the two gubernatorial candidates. They all assumed that Ames's offer would be the most attractive to Bruce. If Ames won, this would be Bruce's opportunity to rise from Bolivar County sheriff to lieutenant governor—and then, in a year or so, to governor.

But he turned it down.

Bruce was willing to give political support to Ames, but he didn't want to be on a gubernatorial ticket with him or anyone else. He had another plan in mind. He knew that if Ames won, within five months, the Mississippi legislature would have to select a new senator to replace him. Bruce wanted to be available for the job. Knowing that he had to keep both the liberal white Republicans and the black Republican contingent energized, Ames next turned to an undistinguished black political activist, Alexander K. Davis, and selected him as his running mate for lieutenant governor. He also included another black man on his ticket, James Hill, as his candidate for Mississippi secretary of state.

To combat Ames's appeal to the black voters, Alcorn rounded out his mostly white moderate ticket by adding two black candidates. And to hedge his bets, just in case the black voters failed to support him in large enough numbers, he and his team also started making overtures to white Democrats in order to undermine the Ames ticket. He figured that the Democratic vote could easily offset any advantage that the black voters would give to Ames. This was all Republicans and blacks needed to hear in order to decide who should receive their vote. Three months later, Ames and his running mate, Alexander Davis, won the election, with 69,870 votes for Ames and 50,090 for Alcorn.[12]

Also important about this November 1873 election was its impact on the racial and political party makeup of the Mississippi state legislature. After the election, there were nine blacks out of a total of thirty-five in the Republican-dominated state Senate, and the House now consisted of seventy-six Republicans and only forty Democrats. Fifty-six of the seventy-six Republicans were black, which meant that not only did the Republicans control the House but the black House members actually controlled the Republican vote in the House. Since white Republican legislators were still divided by their radical and moderate factions, the only cohesive group among both the House Republicans and the Senate Republicans were the black legislators. So, for now, this generally meant that so long as the white Republicans did not vote along with the white Democrats—and they never did, during this period—the black legislators were able to dominate both the Republican caucus and the overall legislature vote. Since the selection of U.S. senators was the province of the state legislature, this unique pro-black, pro-Republican environment was one that could only enhance Bruce's likelihood for being nominated to the U.S. Senate.

The makeup of Governor Ames's new administration was an additional factor in Bruce's eventual rise to the Senate. Because the black Alexander Davis was an unpopular choice for lieutenant governor among even the most liberal Republicans, the party leaders told Ames that they would not support him in executing his original plan to hold the governor position for a short time and then depart in order to again run for the Senate, leaving Davis to be governor. Although he would have to stay in his new position, Ames was still grateful to Bruce for not helping Alcorn's candidacy. As repayment, he agreed to assist Bruce in his quest to be nominated to the Senate in January 1874. In the mean-

time, Bruce was back home, campaigning for a second term as tax collector and sheriff of Bolivar County. In November 1873, he easily won
reelection to his county jobs and was sworn in two months later.

In January 1874, the newest debate in the Mississippi legislature
focused on the vacant Senate seat that had to be filled now that Ames
had been elected governor. At this time, James Alcorn still held the
other Senate seat from Mississippi. Since blacks made up a large percentage of the state legislature, and since black support was the primary
reason that Ames had won his election in the first place, the black legislators had the clout to demand that their pro-Ames Republican colleagues support Bruce in his candidacy for a full six-year Senate term
rather than for the short term left open by Governor Ames's resignation from the Senate.

The Mississippi legislature was now faced with the task of filling
two Senate terms. They had to consider candidates who would vie for
completing Ames's term, which, by then, had a little more than a year
remaining. They would simultaneously hold an election for a full six-
year term that would begin immediately after the short term ended.
For the short term, the leading candidate quickly became Henry
Roberts Pease, who had served as a captain in the Union Army and
who had distinguished himself as superintendent of education for black
freedmen in Mississippi in 1867 and then later as state superintendent
of education, beginning in 1869. An architect of Mississippi's public
school system, Pease was a moderate Republican who had been born in
Litchfield County, Connecticut, and had worked as a teacher and
lawyer in Washington before the Civil War.[13]

Bruce was very concerned about how he would convince the white
legislators that he should be the candidate to fill the longer, six-year
term. This would essentially make him the successor to Senator Ames,
since the short-term post would be but a footnote in history. Since
Bruce assumed that there would be a number of men jockeying for the
nomination to the longer term, he knew that the best person to argue
on his behalf was Ames himself. So, Bruce was extremely grateful
when Ames agreed to support him over two white politicians who
challenged him for the nomination. His opponents were G. Wiley
Wells, a U.S. district attorney who had become popular among blacks
because of his aggressive enforcement of the Ku Klux Klan Act during

the prior three years, and Congressman George McKee, an Illinois native who had been a brigadier general in the Union Army before settling in Vicksburg. Both had the antipathy of Governor Ames. In the past, Wells had done little or nothing to assist Ames's career ambitions, and McKee had earlier accused Ames of being a carpetbagger who didn't identify with the Southern people.

In the end, the Republican caucus nominated Bruce with a vote of fifty-two to thirty-six, and the following month, on February 3, 1874, at the age of thirty-two, Bruce was elected to the Senate by the legislature. Out of thirty-four senators, twenty-five voted for him, and of the one hundred twelve House members, he received the support of seventy-four.[14] With similar ease, thirty-eight-year-old Henry Pease was elected to the short term. Pease would begin his term immediately.

Despite the fact that Bruce was suddenly the first black to be elected to a full term in the U.S. Senate, his election was not met by a firestorm of publicity. Republican newspapers generally agreed that his election was the natural outcome of the rise to power of the moderate Republicans in the state. Political leaders also said that his election was the result of the unity displayed by black officials within the Republican Party. Still attempting to undermine his successful rise to power and legal election to the Senate, newspapers influenced by conservatives, Southern "Redeemers," and others tried to advance ludicrous and nefarious explanations for his success. One such paper waited two years before it suggested that Bruce had bribed thirty Mississippi House members and three Mississippi Senate members in order to earn their votes in the U.S. Senate election.[15] Given the fact that blacks controlled the House and would all have been unified behind Bruce, this theory was ludicrous on its face. Furthermore, since the three state senators that this paper suggested Bruce had bribed also happened to be three black senators who were all, once again, likely to be backing Bruce anyway, the "bribery theory" failed to gain credibility or support beyond one or two out-of-state newspapers.

Overall, it was an anticlimactic election for Bruce, the public, and the press, because it would be more than a year before he would even move to Washington to begin his term. In Mississippi, Henry Pease became the immediate focus of the public's attention. And with a new governor in position and a new senator in Washington, political leaders were focused more on how Ames would run the state and how Pease would work with Alcorn in representing Mississippi's interests in a Washington that was becoming increasingly uninterested in pulling the South out of its racial, political, and economic quagmires.

On March 5, 1875, thirteen months after the election, Blanche Bruce was sworn into his new position as U.S. senator, a job where he would earn the annual salary of $5,000. In the meantime, he quietly returned to his local political positions and activities in Mississippi. He spent his time managing his rental properties and running his eight-hundred-acre plantation in Bolivar County. For these months, he could act as a true gentleman planter with no financial or career concerns to trouble him. Although he did not know it at the time, despite his incredible financial and political success in the state, these would be his last calm days in the South, for the racial unrest that was to follow soon would make it impossible for this black Mississippi leader to remain physically rooted in the place he now called home.[16]

CHAPTER SIX

⁓◎◎◎⁓

1875–1877
The Start of a Senate Career

ALTHOUGH THE 1874 ELECTION WAS A TRIUMPH FOR BRUCE AND those black Americans who found pride in seeing the first black man elected to a full term in the U.S. Senate, the outcome could not have been more different for most of the other Republicans who were running for seats in the House and the Senate during that year. In fact, Bruce's victory was so much of an aberration for the party in the congressional elections that the story surrounding it was rather short-lived and nearly buried by news articles that reported on the bigger share of congressional elections, which spelled out an overwhelming loss for the Republican Party.

By the time all the elections for the Forty-fourth Congress (the Congress for which Bruce was elected) would be complete, it would be obvious that the Republicans were no longer the force they had been at the close of the Civil War. Of the twenty-three Senate seats that were up for election, fourteen were won by Democrats. And even more devastating were the results in the House races. Before the election, the House was controlled by the Republicans, with a two-thirds Republican membership. But after the election, the Democrats controlled the House with a three-fifths Democratic membership.

Nevertheless, Bruce had a lot to celebrate in February of 1874. Both the Republican papers and the Democratic papers applauded his victory, with surprisingly little space devoted to his racial background. A Vicksburg newspaper, the *Times*, was more typical of the Republican press's response: it referred to him as a leader who was "winning and retaining the respect of his associates."[1] Two days after his election, one conservative Mississippi paper, the *Jackson Weekly Clarion*, referred to Bruce as "well thought of by his political opponents, as a man of moderation and integrity."[2] Coming from a newspaper that typically displayed open derision toward blacks and Republicans, the *Clarion*'s words sounded like a ringing endorsement.

For the most part, the press resisted the temptation to question whether a black man was fit to represent an entire state, or whether he was capable of addressing issues that went beyond the black community. And neither Republican nor Democrat editors mentioned the possibility that his election would exacerbate the problems between black freedmen and white conservatives who opposed Reconstruction policies. Since widespread, regularly published black-owned newspapers did not come of age until the late 1870s and early 1880s, there was little reported black public comment on the election.[3] Even the *New York Times*, which occasionally reported on blacks in the South and Midwest, as well as the increasing number of black lynchings at the time, was silent on both the election and seating of Bruce in 1874 and 1875.[4] It was not until June 1878 that the paper actually reported on Bruce, and when it did, it was to report on his wedding and then later on his trip to Europe with Josephine, and the couple's plans to visit with President Ulysses S. Grant.[5]

There are perhaps two reasons why there were not more articles written about Bruce at the time of his election. For one, Hiram Revels's election in 1870 removed the novelty of a black man being elected to the Senate. Although Revels served for only one year and Bruce had actually earned a full six-year term, the shock value of elevating a black man to such a position had passed through the white Mississippi community's psyche long before Bruce's election in 1874. Another reason why Bruce's election did not elicit great emotion from the press was because the editors probably knew that although Revels was permitted to be seated in 1870, there was a strong possibility that Bruce might never be allowed to assume his position in the Senate. Many black politicians of the period, such as John W. Menard of Louisiana, Josiah T. Walls of Florida, and P. B. S. Pinchback of Louisiana, had experienced the humiliation of winning their hotly contested congressional elections and then being denied their seats when they arrived in Washington.[6] This had also happened in state legislatures in several Southern states by this time.[7]

The Democrats were probably intensely aware of the constitutional challenges that they could raise when it came time to seat Bruce. They knew that Bruce was a former slave and, therefore, could not have fulfilled the constitutional citizenship period requirement, which stated that a senator must have reached "the age of thirty years, and been nine years a citizen of the United States."[8]

Bruce's detractors could easily interpret his citizenship as having been awarded at the time of the Fourteenth Amendment's ratification on July 23, 1868, when it was stated: "All persons born or naturalized in the United States, and subject to the jurisdiction thereof, are citizens of the United States and of the State wherein they reside."[9] If it was true that he did not gain his citizenship until 1868, then he would not be constitutionally qualified for the Senate until nine years later, in 1877. If the public interpreted his citizenship as having been awarded in 1865, when he was freed by his owner, Pettis Perkinson, then he had fulfilled the citizenship requirements of the Constitution by the time of his 1874 election. Although never used on the floor of Congress, these were all arguments that Democrats considered using if it was determined that Bruce's seating should be denied.

Knowing that such challenges could be raised by his opposition right up until the time he was to be seated in early 1875, many members of the press were not necessarily certain that Bruce would ever get to serve in the Senate, so they failed to write much about him, and, hence, the public response to his election was limited.

As Bruce awaited his time to move to Washington, he remained focused on his business activities and his work as the Bolivar County tax collector. For the most part, as he waited in Mississippi, he withdrew from the national scene and statewide political activity.

Thoughtful and deliberate, Bruce used this time at home to assess what type of political leader he intended to become. He looked toward Grant and other powerful Republicans and watched as the press began to accuse the president and his colleagues of rumored corruption. As Bruce also considered the recent political events of the last two years, he understood that Reconstruction, and the opportunities it presented, were not going to last forever. He was proud to acknowledge that one of the era's policies, the establishment of free public schools, had taken hold in most of the Southern states. But he knew that many of the other advances made by the radical Republicans would be short-lived. First of all, the economics of the South and of the nation could not support ongoing spending for improvements in the South. Second of all, white citizens would eventually object with legal measures or violence if they felt that blacks were gaining too much too fast.

Going back more than a year earlier, when President Grant began his second term in 1873, many blacks believed that the Republican White House could keep Reconstruction policies in place. After all, blacks had made tremendous strides that year in Mississippi and throughout the South. Black Mississippi speaker of the house, John Roy Lynch, took his seat in the U.S. House of Representatives, bringing the total number of blacks in Congress to seven. With black U.S. congressmen representing districts in Mississippi, South Carolina, Alabama, and Florida, Reconstruction seemed unstoppable. In Little Rock, Arkansas, a black Oberlin College graduate, Mifflin W. Gibbs, became the nation's first black city judge, and in several Mississippi cities, such as Natchez, there were black sheriffs, county treasurers, and magistrates, which demonstrated that white residents were sharing power.

By 1874, some of these positive signs for blacks were continuing as I. D. Shadd followed John Lynch to become the second black speaker of the house in the Mississippi legislature; as Georgetown University in Washington named a black priest, Patrick Healy, as its president; and as black abolitionist Frederick Douglass was named president of the Freedman's Savings and Trust, a bank with forty branches and deposits of over $3 million.

But all of this confidence in the future of Reconstruction and black advancement was quickly eroded as a cloud began to form over the national and state Republican Party. It started when it became evident that many of Grant's appointees were stealing, embezzling, and using other measures to violate the public trust. Several members of Grant's administration were involved in a scandal wherein they received illegal payments from executives of the Union Pacific Railroad and a related construction company called Credit Mobilier. Republican members of Congress had also advanced legislation that gave Congress an incredible 50 percent salary increase, which was also retroactive to cover the preceding two-year period. Along with scandals involving Grant's U.S. minister to England, U.S. minister to Brazil, Treasury Department, and Interior Department—where land speculators were taking serious advantage—these incidents put the Grant administration and the Republicans in a negative light.

And all this corruption in Washington was made worse by a tremendous financial collapse that had begun back in September 1873 and worsened over the following months. Many argued the collapse had been brought on by the surplus farm crops that went unsold as the supply coming from the ever-expanding agrarian economy of the South and West outstripped foreign and domestic demand. In addition, American banks had overextended themselves when granting loans to unworthy ventures and businesses. By the fall of 1873, several major businesses and railroad companies collapsed, with even the New York Stock Exchange shutting down for a week. The disastrous economic condition got worse in 1874.

Even as Senator Bruce was being elected to the Senate, the South had been feeling an awful financial pinch that it blamed on what the Southerners now believed was a corrupt Republican presidential administration. And now, as economic conditions made whites suffer in both the North and the South, these citizens started to point to Reconstruction policies and black freedmen as the cause of their problems and the drain on the nation's pocketbook. Democratic Mississippi congressman Lucius Q. C. Lamar would advance this notion and win credibility for it during his famous eulogy in Congress following the death of Massachusetts senator Charles Sumner. Lamar, who had become a leading spokesman against Reconstruction, used this congressional eulogy to both praise the Northern senator and attack the Reconstruction policies that the popular Massachusetts leader had embraced. This April 27, 1874, speech, laced with conservative propaganda, was heavily responsible for convincing many citizens in the North that Reconstruction had been a corrupt and immoral influence on the South.[10]

It was not long before these theories gave credence and encouragement to the messages of white hate groups and white Democrats who were now bent on "redeeming" the South and taking back their government from Republicans and the handful of elected blacks who had seen moderate success during the prior half dozen years. The White League, a violent paramilitary white supremacist group that had been founded in Opelousas, Louisiana, on April 27, 1874, had been growing in strength. The White League and the Ku Klux Klan began working in tandem with Democrats to force blacks in many counties in Mississippi and other Southern states to resign their positions or face death.

In late August of 1874, black and Republican elected officials in Louisiana were beginning to fear that white Democrats might not wait for the next election in order to take back their political offices for the white Democratic community. They had been hearing threats that the whites might simply band together and kill any official who was black or Republican. On August 30, this was exactly what happened to sixty Republicans—some black and some white—in Coushatta, Louisiana. Only days later, Louisiana blacks called on President Grant with a petition signed by one thousand black citizens, asking that they be protected by federal troops or removed to Liberia, or any place in the United States where the white Democrats would not be able to harm them.

Grant's military did not move fast enough because, on September 14, the Louisiana State House was taken over by armed white Democrats who murdered two dozen blacks and white Republicans in order to discourage further support of the Republican Party.[11]

While white Democrats led the massacre of innocent blacks in Louisiana in both August and September, it was not until December 7 that a concerted effort to kill blacks in Mississippi took place. Working with the Ku Klux Klan, white Democrats killed as many as seventy-five black residents of Warren County when the county's black sheriff Peter Crosby had a disagreement with whites in the community.

In the fall of 1874, Sheriff Crosby had been the target of more than five hundred angry whites who lived within his Warren County jurisdiction. Sheriff Crosby, who also served as tax collector for the Vicksburg–Warren County area, drew the ire of white residents when he refused to resign after being accused of financial mismanagement in the county. Many of the white citizens had also alleged that he showed favoritism toward three black local officials who recently had been charged with fraud.

Despite the angry whites' threats, Mississippi governor Adelbert Ames supported Crosby and told the sheriff that he should return to Vicksburg and build his own militia from local blacks if it appeared that the whites would use physical force to remove him. Sheriff Crosby followed the advice of Ames and traveled the county, imploring local blacks to join his posse in order to maintain peace. In the end, the rioting whites who assembled throughout the county not only outnumbered the blacks helping Crosby but were better armed with rifles, pistols, and other weapons. The angry whites spread out aggressively and launched a killing spree throughout the county, leaving more than six dozen black citizens dead.

The fact that only two whites died in the conflict only underscored how little the governor had helped the black sheriff who had been ordered back to Vicksburg. After the slaughter had already taken place, Governor Ames approached President Grant and convinced him that federal troops were necessary in order to prevent any ongoing racial conflict in the Vicksburg area.

This Vicksburg conflict ended up becoming a model for how white conservatives in Mississippi would later violently take back their cities and political positions from the Republicans and blacks who were gaining ground. This violent "Mississippi plan" would eventually be adopted by other Southern states that admired the speed with which Mississippi Democrats would claim "Redemption" for whites who would no longer tolerate blacks with equal rights in their state.

Similar attacks were made on blacks in Clinton, Meridian, and other Mississippi towns where whites felt they could send a message to black voters and political leaders that they would be killed if they continued to vote or run for office.

Not surprisingly, Republicans and black citizens continued to ask the president to send federal troops to protect the blacks and turn away the white hate groups. As a result, Grant sent the Seventh Cavalry to Louisiana, and he also concluded that the military needed to monitor and assist in the protection of blacks in Arkansas and Mississippi.

But even as the black residents in Mississippi and elsewhere appealed to Grant and other Northern officials, Bruce was strangely silent. Even when the president sent federal troops to Vicksburg on January 5, 1875, Bruce played no public role in the act. While Bruce was not to be sworn in as senator until March of that year, one would have expected him to make some public statements or actions on behalf of his future constituents. His silence makes him seem oddly detached, at best, and extremely calculating or opportunistic, at worst.

It is possible that Bruce had two strong reasons for not taking a more public stand on the issue of white-on-black violence in his state. For one, Bruce knew that he was already a controversial choice for the Senate, and since he had not yet been seated, it was very possible that

Democrats and even some white Republicans might become threatened by an outspoken black leader and decide to raise challenges to his seating in the Senate. Bruce would not have to have been unreasonably cynical or paranoid to believe this, since he had already seen this happen to several black leaders in Washington. Only two weeks earlier, on December 23, 1874, Senator Henry Pease had presented Bruce's credentials as the senator-elect to Congress.[12]

The other possible reason Bruce did not get involved in calling on President Grant was out of respect for his former mentor Adelbert Ames, who was serving as governor. Since Ames had been responsible for endorsing Bruce's candidacy early enough to discourage other challengers, Bruce refrained from joining those individuals who argued that Ames was losing control of the state and needed federal assistance. He knew that it would be disrespectful and alienating for him to join that chorus. He could not risk losing Ames as a supporter even before he arrived in Washington.

It must have been obvious to Bruce, as it was to many others, that Ames was not managing the legislature or the problems of the citizens very well. In addition to racial conflicts, tensions were also boiling over because of the rising taxes that threatened to bankrupt farmers and other Mississippi citizens. As a wealthy planter who owned several hundred acres of plantation land that raised cotton and other farm products, Bruce would have had intimate knowledge of the tax burdens on Mississippi landowners.

When Governor Ames had been inaugurated, he had promised to address the issue of tax reform, particularly since the financial collapse of 1873 had created ongoing effects that made people even more desperate by the end of 1874. But Ames seemed unable to motivate the Republican-controlled legislature in the area of reducing taxes. Whether it was because the legislators lacked the economic skills to determine how to reduce taxes in the face of a national and local economic recession or because of the legislators' arrogant belief that they did not *have* to respond to constituent demands so long as they were certain of ongoing Republican control, it is clear that the Republican legislators waited too long to respond.

In the end, the Democrats took advantage of racial divisions and the burdensome taxes on plantations and other property by publicly linking the two. They argued that black legislators were to blame for the government's irresponsibility, and the Republicans were to blame for elevating the black legislators. They established taxpayers' leagues, local organizations of citizens who were asked to put pressure on their legislators. According to the *Natchez Democrat*, the purpose of the leagues was to address the fact that "the state and county tax to which Mississippi people have been and are now subjected is enormously excessive, unequal, unjust, oppressive, and incompatible with good government."[13]

In the beginning, the groups seemed completely legitimate. They focused only on getting the government to create tax relief legislation. At the end of 1874, the *New York Times* reported that black property owners in Mississippi were also joining a few of the leagues.[14] But it wasn't long before several of the leagues around the state transformed themselves into distinctly white Democratic groups focused on getting blacks out of office and on keeping black freedmen from voting.

Governor Ames encouraged Republicans to support the tax relief ideas, but the radical Republicans refused. They perceived the leagues as nothing more than thinly disguised racist groups that were bent on advancing white rule.

In early 1875, the state legislature adjourned and the Democrats and many other whites were furious that the tax issue had not been resolved. The Democrats took advantage of white citizens' economic hardship by directing their anger at black legislators and suggesting that they use the upcoming March elections to seek revenge. Their goal was to get all the Republicans out of office, but their method was to focus white citizens' ire on black legislators in particular. They determined that although blacks did not make up the majority of the Republican legislators, they were a significant enough and visible enough group for their purposes. Making use of the inherent racial antipathy that Southern whites felt toward blacks, the Democrats knew the blacks would be easy scapegoats, and could also be scared away from the polls and from campaigns with physical threats or outright violence. Since Mississippi had decided not to hold its 1874 congressional elections until 1875, when it would hold its state and local elections, the Democrats had plenty of time to organize their anti-black and anti-Republican "Redemption" movement.[15]

Adding further fuel to the fire was the fact that other states in the South, by early 1875, had already reclaimed their governments by chasing out most black officials and many of the Republican leaders. This gave encouragement to the Mississippi Democrats.

During this time, there also seemed to be a strong public relations effort that was being launched to forever characterize Reconstruction as a horrid period of Negro rule—replete with corruption, disorganization, and immoral behavior. Democrats, white Southerners, and white Northerners who had no personal familiarity with blacks in the South, jumped on a bandwagon together to make black freedmen the scapegoats for everything that had gone wrong in the South since secession: blacks were the cause of the Civil War, blacks were the cause of costly Reconstruction programs, blacks were the cause of burdensome taxes, black legislators were the cause of ineffective state governments and of ineffective federal government.

This simplistic message worked well at the time and was embraced by white journalists and alleged scholars from both the North and South who attempted to describe the Reconstruction period without discarding their racial biases and without attempting to discover facts and experiences that went beyond resentful Democrats and other "Redeemers." Few of these journalists or "scholars" ever attempted to interview black leaders or other blacks who could at least assist the writers in assembling a balanced account of the Reconstruction years. What is noteworthy is that these same journalists overlooked the fact that the corruption and waste that were taking place in New York under Boss Tweed and his Tammany Hall were far more extensive and far more costly to the public. But because its participants were white politicians rather than black freedmen, some of these biased journalists preferred to make an example of the blacks.

It worked well for the white Southern racist agenda for its journalists to create a propaganda that would stick forever—a kind of standard "rap" on Reconstruction, which stated that it was a corrupt period when illiterate blacks and crooked liberals ran the country into the ground. One of these pieces of propaganda, masquerading as research, was a book that had a great impact in the mid-1870s, titled *The Prostrate State*.[16] The author, James Pike, was a former ambassador to the Netherlands who had long expressed anti-black opinions in his writing. Amazingly, he wrote a book about South Carolina's Reconstruction but failed to interview any blacks who lived or worked there. Taking his cues from the white Democrats who informed him with their own agenda, he was among the first to popularize the characterization of the Reconstructed South as being a region run by black barbarism.

Other writers jumped on this anti-black bandwagon, urging their book editors, magazine publishers, and newspaper publishers to one-up each other with tales of how ignorant blacks had taken over. Even thoughtful magazines like *The Nation* occasionally joined in the fray without conducting legitimate research or interviews beyond the white Democrats or sympathetic white Republicans who pointed their fingers at the convenient scapegoats: black freedmen. In April 1874, *The Nation* ran an article that stated that black elected officials in South Carolina had an intelligence that was just "slightly above the level of animals."[17] Of course this was written by the same author—E. L. Godkin—who three years earlier had written in *The Nation* that the people of the Dominican Republic should not be given U.S. citizenship because they were "ignorant Catholic spanish negroes."

Racist books and articles like these were encouraged by white Southerners, and were being read by Northern whites who had a general curiosity about their Southern brethren. They were getting a one-sided picture from these articles and books on the real cause of the South's problems: black people. Although liberal journalist Horace Greeley had used his *New York Tribune* to advance sympathetic views about blacks throughout the 1860's and early 1870's until his death in 1872, the more popular message was one that white bigots and disingenuous journalists advanced as they pretended to define and explain the South's situation throughout the mid 1870s and for many years to come.

When 1875 arrived, Bruce was feeling confident that he would soon be sworn in as the junior senator from Mississippi. His credentials had been presented to the Senate body just before Christmas, and the discourse both inside and outside the Capitol had been without controversy. Looking back on the heated debate that had occurred when the credentials for Hiram Revels were presented to the Senate, Bruce recalled a dialogue that showed how opposed many of the white senators were regarding the admission of a black man to their chambers. Senator Garrett Davis from Kentucky had said, "This is certainly a morbid state of affairs. Never before in the history of this government has a colored man been elected to the Senate of the United States . . . The black race—I do not know why the law of the universe permitted that race to be brought here . . . unless it was to cause and create another devil for the white man."[18]

Although Bruce was to be the first black elected to a full Senate term,

Revels had borne the brunt of being the first black in the Senate—even though it was just for a one-year period. The vitriol that had been expressed over Revels was not so apparent when Bruce's credentials were discussed, or when his March 1875 swearing-in date approached.

Bruce arrived at the Capitol on the morning of March 5, 1875, for his swearing-in ceremony. It was the first day of a special session of the Forty-fourth Congress. The session would only last three weeks, and then Congress would be on break for several months until December, when the first regular session of the Forty-fourth Congress would begin.[19] President Grant was serving his seventh year as president, and Bruce felt triumphant as he joined his Republican colleagues and walked through the long hallways paved with handsome Minton tiles. The brightly colored floors led the way to the Senate chamber, and Bruce walked inside and past the wooden desks that weaved across the room.

As Bruce sat in his front-row desk, at seat number two, he over-heard several of the senators remarking that the day's session would probably not even last an hour. In the end, Bruce's first day in the Sen-ate would only last twenty-three minutes, because there would be a recess, and then an adjournment until Monday, March 8. But before those first twenty-three minutes elapsed, Bruce would hear his first two Senate resolutions that day. And, ironically, they both related to his friend P. B. S. Pinchback, the black political leader in New Orleans who had previously served as Louisiana lieutenant governor and gover-nor and was subsequently elected (but not seated) to the U.S. Senate.

The resolutions put before Bruce and his colleagues that afternoon by Indiana Senator Oliver P. Morton were to ask that the U.S. Senate acknowledge the William Pitt Kellogg government of Louisiana as the legitimate and legally elected governing body in that state, and to admit Pinchback as the duly elected U.S. senator from Louisiana with a six-year term to have begun March 4, 1873. The two resolutions were tabled until the next meeting of the Senate, which was to be the follow-ing Monday, March 8. Since Bruce knew that this special session of the Senate was to last only twenty days, until March 24, he hoped Pinch-back's situation would be resolved quickly.

On Bruce's second day in the Senate, the body returned to a lengthy discussion of Pinchback and the political disputes that had been carried on in Louisiana since 1873. As Bruce and his colleagues listened, Senator Morton of Indiana proceeded to tell the genesis of Pinchback's rise to power in the state, and why he should be admitted to the Senate seat for which the Louisiana legislature elected him. He said,

> In 1871, Lieutenant Governor Dunn of Louisiana died. At the next session of the legislature, Pinchback, a member of that body, was elected president of the senate. By operation of law, this election of Pinchback as president of the senate made him the lieutenant governor of the state. In the month of December 1872, after the election of that year, Governor Warmouth convened the new legislature . . . What that legislature convened, the House of Representatives proffered articles of impeachment against Governor Warmouth . . . [which] had the effect to suspend the governor, and Pinchback became the acting governor of Louisiana.
>
> Afterward, on the first Monday of January 1873, [William Pitt] Kellogg, who had been declared elected . . . was declared to be the governor of the state and was inaugurated. Afterward, on the second Tuesday after the convening of the [Louisiana] legislature, Pinchback was elected a member of the Senate of the United States for the term commencing the 4th of March, 1873.[20]

Although the debate over Pinchback would continue for several more days, driven mostly by the racial bigotry and party allegiance of the senators—most of whom did not want another black senator and many of whom did not want another Republican—there was a break in the discussion on March 9, to assign committees.

Bruce had remained silent for these first days as he watched the other senators, many of whom had already served in the House of Representatives or in their respective state legislatures, and kept close watch on his new friend Senator Roscoe Conkling of Utica, New York, who sat in seat thirty-two, halfway across the semicircle. With the help of Conkling, he found himself appointed to three Senate committees that excited him. The first of the appointments was due to, and would make use of, his background as a teacher: the Committee on Education and Labor. The other two were the Committee on Manufactures and the Committee on Pensions.

What seems remarkable is that Bruce did not make a single comment on the seating of Pinchback during this special session. Even

though he was intimately aware of the details of the Louisiana governmental activities, he yielded to others. (For the next five years, this
would generally be Bruce's method of operation. He avoided issues that
would cause too great a conflict, and he commented on those that were
the least controversial.) When the special session finally adjourned at
five o'clock in the afternoon on Wednesday, March 24, Bruce left a Senate floor that would not be as welcoming for Republicans for many
years to come.

During the remaining months of 1875, Bruce's—and the Mississippi Republicans'—fortunes changed. In the spring, summer, and
early fall of 1875, before the Forty-fourth Congress was to open its first
session in December, the Democrats worked aggressively with white
league groups and the Ku Klux Klan to develop a strategy that would
sweep out blacks and Republicans in the upcoming fall elections in the
state. They determined that violence, threats of violence, and ballot
stuffing would have to be used in order to ensure victory for the state
legislature races as well as for the U.S. House seats. It was obvious to
Bruce and other Republicans that their own party under Governor
Ames had been so split between moderate and radical Republicans that
they were ripe for the attack.

It is unclear where Senator Bruce spent most of his time during the
eight months of recess before Congress was to resume in December
1875. Since his constituents would have expected to communicate with
him in Mississippi, and since he had vast landholdings in the state, it is
likely that he spent a great deal of time there. But because of the widespread attacks by whites on black people and black-owned property, as
well as because of threats made against both black and white Republican activists and officials, it is probable that Bruce did not venture into
many of the Mississippi counties where Democrats were building resistance, because his life would have been in danger.

The white supremacy groups and the Democrats had focused their
rioting, beatings, and lynchings in twenty-two Mississippi counties—
none of which included Bruce's home county of Bolivar. Although the
targeted counties seemed to be spread throughout the state, from north
to south and from east to west, many of them lined the Mississippi
River. From De Soto County in the north to Washington County just
south of Bolivar, down to Warren and Claiborne Counties, the hate
groups and Democrats worked to intimidate blacks from voting and to

keep white and black Republicans from running for office. In the center of the state, they terrorized blacks and Republicans in Hinds County, where the city of Jackson is located; Yazoo County; and Lowndes County, where the city of Columbus is situated.[21]

During the widespread violence throughout the state, the senator was written to frequently by constituents—most of them Republican—who sought relief from the violence and corruption that the Democrats and white hate groups were spreading. He was also called on by Republican Party leaders around the state, asking his help in bolstering the counties where the Republicans needed to shore up their support. On April 10, 1875, he received a letter from a Republican constituent complaining of a postmaster in Leflore County, an area situated to the east of Bolivar. In the letter, M. W. Randolph wrote,

> I will . . . tell you what we want done in Leflore. In the first place, we want a change made in our post office at Greenwood . . . Likely you know who the postmaster is . . . he has been an obstacle and as the election approaches, he seems odious and cumbersome to the party. . . . get rid of him . . . I hope you will spare no time in doing what you can for us. . . . you will have contributed to the good of our party.[22]

A few weeks later, on May 7, Bruce wrote to Randolph, promising to remove the postmaster as requested. Such token gestures to fend off the Democrats and bolster the Mississippi Republicans were as much as Bruce seemed to be willing to do at the time. And this is probably the case either because he was genuinely frightened about antagonizing white Democrats in neighboring counties out of fear for his life, or because he honestly did not believe that the Democrats would be successful in their murderous campaign to take back the government. Given that Bruce had his ear to the ground through party operatives, and given that he surely read news reports of Mississippi activities in every corner of the state, it is unlikely that he thought the Democrats were not a threat. The more likely reason for his inaction was fear of retribution.

By the fall of 1875, the Mississippi Democrats had sufficiently terrorized the blacks and Republicans that they had no problem winning Democratic victories in areas that were overwhelmingly Republican.

It was not until March 31, 1876, that the Senate finally responded in a meaningful way to the violence that had taken place in Mississippi during the summer and fall of 1875. Indiana Senator Oliver P. Morton had submitted a resolution on December 15, 1875, acknowledging the violence and fraudulent election activity that had been aimed at blacks in the state and at those who had protected them.

The issue of the Mississippi violence was then postponed until after the winter, until Morton's resolution was taken up again in mid-December. The resolution read, in part,

> Whereas it is alleged that the late election in Mississippi was characterized by frauds committed upon and violence exercised toward the colored citizens of that State and the white citizens disposed to support their rights at the election, and especially the colored voters, on account of their color, were by intimidation and force, deterred from voting . . . and that such intimidation has been continued for the purpose of affecting future elections . . .
>
> Resolved, that a committee of five Senators be appointed to investigate the truth of those allegations, and to inquire how far these Constitutional rights have been violated and to report to the Senate what further legislation is necessary to secure to said colored citizens the enjoyment of their constitutional rights; and that said committee be empowered to visit said State, to send for persons and papers, to take testimony.[23]

Bruce was the first to speak. With a stack of papers in front of him and a pen in his hand, he began to address his colleagues and the Senate president. Many of the Democrats in the room wore nonchalant expressions. Many of them had seen him working during the last few days, at his desk before the session opened as well as during lunch recess, in preparation for his presentation. Like many of the senators, Bruce worked in open view of his colleagues. At the time, the Senate did not provide office space for its members, so the politicians either conducted their work at home or at their desks during breaks. Only the wealthiest official could afford to rent his own office space in a nearby building.

As was typical for Bruce's speeches, he opened by begging the indulgence of his audience. He first apologized for speaking so forcefully when he was still but a new addition to the Senate body. He said, "I had hoped that no occasion would arise to make it necessary for me to claim the attention of the Senate until at least I had acquired a larger acquaintance with its methods of business . . . but silence at this time would be infidelity to my senatorial trust and unjust to both the people and the State."[24]

While Bruce often dealt with powerful whites with a tone and style that was so deferential that it almost seemed obsequious, there was no question that this quality would be beneficial at this time. He knew that the Democratic senators, as well as many of the Republican senators, held sufficiently negative ideas about black people that they were ready to dismiss anything he said regarding his own people. But with measures of modesty and outrage, he was able to gain their attention. He began by backing up his points with statistical evidence regarding the 1873 elections, when the Republicans carried the state by a twenty thousand majority, and then pointed out that in the 1875 elections, the Democrats carried the state by a thirty thousand majority. He pointed out that simple, uneducated people in rural states like Mississippi do not so quickly and so decidedly change their party support as would be suggested in the election returns. He compared it with New York State, "where free speech and free press operate upon intelligent masses—a state full of railroads, telegraphs, and newspapers—on the occasion of a great national [election]" might cause such a change in political views of the people. But he said such things did not happen to people in a mostly rural state, where they were not kept as informed on the changing political activities and issues.

Bruce then pointed to a specific county, Yazoo, to further demonstrate that there was obvious pressure from Democrats. "This county gave in 1873," he began, "a Republican majority of nearly two thousand. It was cursed with riot and bloodshed prior to the [1875] election and gave but seven votes for the Republican ticket." And to show how the Democratic Mississippi newspapers encouraged the violence, he quoted from an October 1875 issue of the *Yazoo Democrat*, " 'Let unanimity of sentiment pervade the minds of men. Send forth the soul-stirring announcement that Mississippians shall rule Mississippi though the heavens fall. Hit them hip and thigh, everywhere and at all times. Carry the election peaceably if we can, forcibly if we must . . . Try the rope on such characters. It acts finely on such characters here.' "[25]

Bruce continued his speech, making cogent points and supporting them with documented facts and numbers. In a calculated effort to get his fellow senators to take seriously the lives of black people, he went on to point out how much black freedmen in Mississippi had accomplished since their emancipation. He gave the statistics of the increased number of black property owners, the increase in marriages, the steady growth of black preachers and churches, as well as the annual increase in black shoemakers, black farmers, et cetera. By noting these numbers, he hoped to demonstrate that black Mississippi citizens were productive people who deserved the right to vote and the right to be protected from menacing night riders and others bent on abusing them.

Toward the end of his speech, he added:

> The vicious and exceptional political action by the White League in Mississippi has been repeated in other contests, and the colored voters have been subjected therein to outrages upon their rights . . . I have felt, as the only representative of my race in the Senate, that I was placed upon the defensive, and I have consequently endeavored to show how aggravated and inexcusable were the wrongs worked upon us . . . there are some considerations that justify frankness, and even boldness of speech.
>
> I represent the interest of nearly a million of voters, constituting a new, hopeful, permanent, and influential political element . . . They number more than a million producers, who, since their emancipation, [have made] their contributions to the production of sugar, rice, tobacco, cereals, and have furnished nearly forty million bales of cotton [worth] $2,000,000,000, a sum nearly equal to the national debt.

In his closing and his final underscoring of the need for a committee to report on the abuses in Mississippi, he made what sounded like a simple request. He said, "we ask such action as will not only protect us in the enjoyment of our constitutional rights, but will preserve the integrity of our republican institutions."

As articulate and as thoughtful as Bruce's speech was, it was immediately clear that the Democrats in the Senate simply didn't care about the facts that he presented. Given that they embraced the notion that blacks were vastly inferior to whites and had to be kept in that position, there was absolutely nothing that was going to make them feel sympathy for the abused blacks. Liberal and moderate Republicans would certainly have been moved by the statistics that reported on the increased productivity and responsible nature of blacks who were now running businesses, building homes, and marrying, but these facts simply enraged Southern whites and Democrats who hated to see these "inferior beings" making any progress at all. Rather than engendering respect, it created jealousy.

As soon as Bruce sat down, the Democratic Tennessee Senator David Key stood and boldly ignored all that Bruce had just said. Instead, he talked about the need for Northerners to be more patient with the Southerners as the latter group slowly learned to accept the changes that the Civil War and the end of slavery had brought to Southern life. With dishonesty equal to that of the Mississippi Democrats, Key said that Southerners "have no disposition to deprive the colored people of any of their rights of citizenship or of their free exercise."[26] He said that it was simply a slow process to get white Southerners to adjust to the new, post-slavery way of life. He also noted that these white Southerners were not to be blamed, because they had not started slavery, they had inherited it from a prior generation.

As the debate continued over the creation of a Senate committee, others weighed in on the wisdom, and even the constitutionality, of appointing such a committee. By the time the senators were asked to vote on the resolution, Bruce was exhausted. But the fight had been worth it, because although twenty-five senators were absent and nineteen voted against the resolution, there were twenty-nine senators who voted in favor of establishing a committee to visit and report on the Mississippi elections of 1875. Selected to chair the committee was Republican Senator George S. Boutwell from Massachusetts. Bruce was encouraged by Boutwell's position in the committee, as were other Republican colleagues. A former governor of Massachusetts, secretary of the Treasury, commissioner of Internal Revenue, and member of the Board of Overseers of Harvard, Boutwell was held in high esteem. Working with him on the committee were Delaware's Thomas Bayard, Wisconsin's Angus Cameron, Indiana's Joseph McDonald, and Minnesota's Samuel McMillan.

During the spring and summer of 1876, the committee traveled to

Mississippi, where they stayed for six weeks. They interviewed more than 150 witnesses and collected evidence to help them decide if whites and Democrats had won the election through violence and corruption. They spoke to local Republican officials who were forced to leave town rather than see their homes burned down. They were told of armed men who stood at the polling places to make sure that only Democrats could vote. They heard wives testify about their husbands being taken out of their homes and shot on Christmas Day. In some of the cases, in order to humiliate the families of the dead blacks and Republicans, the Democrats prevented anyone from selling caskets to them. So horrid were the atrocities that even the chairman of the Mississippi Republican Committee, General Warner, was afraid that he would be killed. As the report stated, "Warner owed the preservation of his life on the day of the election to the intervention of General J. Z. George, chairman of the Democratic State Committee." George had sent a letter to two Democrats in Canton, Mississippi, which read, "If Warner goes to Madison, see by all means that he is not hurt. We are nearly through now, and are sure to win. Don't let us have any trouble of that sort on our hands..." The Mississippi Democrats returned a telegram to the Democratic state chair that read, "To General George: Your telegram of last night saved A. Warner at Calhoun.—Gart. A. Johnson."[27]

As the committee continued to collect its data, Bruce was selected as a delegate to the Republican National Convention to take place in Ohio during the middle of June. The Democratic Convention took place in St. Louis shortly after, and it was there that the Democrats would choose New York governor Samuel Tilden as their presidential candidate. During Bruce's trip to Ohio for the Republican Convention in Cincinnati, he met a large Ohio contingent of hosts who invited him to Cleveland. It is not specifically known who made the initial introductions, but he was introduced to the small circle of black elite Cleveland families at this time. Among the group that he met was the family of Josephine Willson, his future wife. It was shortly after that summer time visit that Blanche began corresponding with Josephine on a frequent basis. Josephine, who was a young Cleveland schoolteacher at the time, had known that the Senator had already been engaged during late 1875, to a young woman in Cleveland. The woman had died suddenly from a short illness. Six months later, he met Josephine.

In August, after resuming their session in Congress, the committee looking into Mississippi violence finally reported the findings Bruce had expected. Recognizing that there had been widespread violence aimed against blacks, against whites who sought to protect them, and against Republicans of both races, the committee assembled a report in excess of 1,800 pages. In the report, they stated,

> The committee finds that outrages of the nature set forth in this report were perpetrated in the counties of Alcorn, Amite, Chickasaw, Claiborne, [list of eighteen more counties], and that the Democratic victory in the state was due to the outrages so perpetrated. The committee finds that if in the counties named there had been a free election, Republican candidates would have been chosen, and the character of the Legislature so changed that there would have been [a majority of Republicans rather than a majority of Democrats] . . . and that consequently the present Legislature of Mississippi is not a legal body.[28]

Despite the overwhelming evidence, the Democrats still denied that anything out of the ordinary happened to the black people of the state. Nevertheless, there was hope among the Republicans that when Congress reconvened in December and early 1877, the Democrats would be made to pay for their corrupt and violent practices.

During the fall of 1876, Bruce returned to Mississippi to manage his property and to assist the national party to the extent that he could in a state that was now controlled by Democrats. He traveled where he believed it was safe, and gave speeches in support of Rutherford B. Hayes, the Republican candidate for president. The election left Tilden the victor, in terms of the popular vote. He had at least 250,000 more votes than Hayes, but there were still electoral votes from four states that had to be settled. After Congress set up an Electoral Commission that was staffed completely along political lines, a deal was made to hand Hayes the presidency with an electoral vote of 185 to Tilden's 184. As a part of this famous compromise, which ultimately took place in March 1877, when Hayes was sworn in, he had to agree to end Reconstruction in the South and call off all federal protection of blacks who lived there.

On March 6, 1877, the very day after Hayes was sworn in as president, the Democrats were emboldened. They knew their reward was "Redemption"—a chance to take back the South. One of the first orders of business was to get one of their friends and leaders seated. They called for the seating of Mississippi Senator-elect Lucius Q. C. Lamar, who was clearly the beneficiary of the state violence against Republicans and blacks during the 1875 election. Having been a leader at the 1875 Mississippi Democratic Convention, and one of the key negotiators of Hayes's final compromise, he was immediately powerful and threatening to the liberal Republicans.

Senator Oliver P. Morton, Republican of Indiana, argued that Lamar should not be seated, because the Mississippi government was illegally elected and the situation in Mississippi was no different than it was when the Senate had earlier decided that the Louisiana government was illegally elected. He said that it was unfair to rule that Pinchback was illegally elected in Louisiana and yet declare that Lamar was legally elected in Mississippi. New Hampshire Senator Bainbridge Wadleigh agreed with him. This brought back an important issue that Bruce and others had long been waiting to see resolved. They wanted closure on the committee's report, which clearly stated that violence against blacks allowed the Democrats to win state legislature and House elections in 1875. If it was ever to be taken seriously, its application was to be considered while they decided on the seating of Lamar.

So, again in March of 1877, the Senate listened to the committee's report on the violence that took place prior to and during the 1875 Mississippi elections. As Bruce sat in the front row of the Senate chamber, he observed that a great portion of his colleagues were ignoring the report as it was retold by Senator Morton. Morton restated the gruesome discoveries by the committees, which included beatings, nighttime raids on black and Republican families, lynchings, and threats of violence in order to keep the blacks from voting and to put Democrats into office.

Finally, in the middle of the report, Democratic Georgia Senator John Gordon stood up and asked that the remainder of the report not be read to the Senate. When Alabama Senator George Spencer responded, saying, "That report is not very long, and I am very anxious that the Senate shall hear it," Gordon looked around at his fidgeting colleagues and added, "It must be very apparent to the senator that nobody is listening to it."[29] And like Bruce, the other Republicans were appalled by the way the Democrats were boldly talking through, and ignoring, the reading of the Senate report.

Nevertheless, Senator Morton finally said to his colleagues, "If it is right to seat Mr. Lamar, it was a great wrong *not* to seat Mr. Pinchback. The Democratic Party of this Senate were unanimous in refusing to seat Mr. Pinchback, and I presume will be unanimous in favor of seating Mr. Lamar. My purpose was to call attention to this extraordinary change of position."[30]

In a shocking vote, which showed almost complete unanimity among Democrats and Republicans—except for Republican New Hampshire Senator Bainbridge Wadleigh—the Senate voted to seat Lamar. This vote served as a repudiation of everything that the Mississippi committee had found. That the Senate body could completely turn its back on all the report's evidence demonstrated the new power of the Democrats to resume control over the South and the lack of concern that Republicans had over the ongoing abuse of blacks in the country.

But despite all of this, the most troubling aspect of the long debate was that Senator Blanche Bruce had surrendered and voted in support of Lamar with no comment or criticism of the man who had not only incited much of the racial conflict and engineered the folding of Reconstruction policies, but also had served as the defense attorney for Mississippi Klansmen who had murdered blacks and Republicans in their home state. Bruce had raised important points and made a powerful argument the prior year when speaking about the atrocities in his state and pleading for a committee to report on the 1875 election. Now, for some reason, he remained silent.

Bruce recognized the handwriting on the envelope as soon as he walked into his office. It had a Natchez return address on it. He had spent the entire morning in the Senate chamber, listening to a debate that the Republicans were sure to lose once a vote was called. He now had two hours for his lunch—time enough to relax and read through his personal mail. It was a welcome respite from the daily beatings that he and his Republican colleagues were receiving from the Democrats. A letter from his pal and adviser John Roy Lynch was a welcome one.

"Dear Friend," the letter began warmly. It was penned in a broad script, written with the same fine ink pen that Lynch used for most of his letters. Bruce had counted on the advice and encouragement that Lynch offered in his letters from Mississippi each week. As the best-connected black politician in the Mississippi Republican Party, Lynch always had his ear to the ground and could keep Bruce posted on the news back home. The letters were often peppered with witty and upbeat messages. This one, however, quickly took a turn for the worse. "Politically speaking," Lynch wrote, "everything is going one way. I don't believe there is a county in the State [of Mississippi] where the Republicans will make straight out nominations. I see the *Tribune* says that a U.S. Senator from Mississippi is actually afraid to come home. Have you seen that article? What will your Bolivar County Democratic Friends think of that?"[31]

Bruce had to stop reading. He knew that Lynch's analysis was a clear one. Like Bruce, Lynch had been born a slave and later rose through the state party machine. Capturing plum positions before Bruce had, Lynch had served as speaker of the Mississippi State House, then was elected to the U.S. House of Representatives in 1872 and then again in 1874. He was an expert at reading the political "tea leaves," and always offered a realistic analysis of public attitudes about himself as well as about Bruce. And now that Lynch was out of Congress, and living home in Mississippi, he was even more in touch with the conventional wisdom being shared by his Southern neighbors.

Bruce knew that Lynch always offered important advice, but it was more than he could take right now. Yes, he had seen the article Lynch was describing, and yes, it was obvious that he was the senator to which it referred. But what was he to do now that the White League groups, the Ku Klux Klan, and the Democrats had taken over the state? Even though he was a U.S. senator from Mississippi, he was a *black* U.S. senator from Mississippi, and he knew he could get himself killed if he started campaigning for the Republicans in any county that was much beyond his own. It was 1877, and although a Republican was in the White House, a new regime was controlling the South and pulling the strings in Washington. It would be another two years before Bruce would find the confidence to fight for legislation and issues that would assist and advance blacks and other disadvantaged Americans. In 1877, he was clearly intimidated and overwhelmed by the hostile mood of many of his colleagues.

Things had changed radically since Blanche Bruce had been elected on February 3, 1874.

CHAPTER SEVEN

1877–1878

A Senator and a Socialite Marry Despite
Family and Class Conflicts

AS FREEBORN BLACKS WHO HAD LONG BEEN AT THE CENTER OF BLACK
elite society in Philadelphia and Cleveland, Dr. Joseph and Elizabeth
Willson had strong opinions about people outside their social class.
Since the Senator had first met the Willsons and their daughter,
Josephine, during his June 1876 visit to the Republican Convention in
Ohio, he corresponded regularly with the 22-year-old Cleveland school
teacher. On more than one occasion, Bruce visited Cleveland and dined
with Josephine and her family. As one of the more prominent black
families in the city, the Willsons were surely flattered by the fact that
they were hosting such a prominent man. But as the relationship
between Bruce and Josephine advanced, it is likely that their own concerns about class and skin color caused them to worry about the Senator's slave background. One can imagine how they responded when
their daughter Josephine made it clear to them that she intended to
marry a former slave, after all the money they had expended on their
son and three daughters since uprooting them from their comfortable
position among Philadelphia's black elite and then reestablishing themselves as leaders among colored society in Cleveland.

Their daughter's choice represented much of what their class of black
people was trying to leave behind. Not only were his complexion and features considered too Negroid for the light-complexioned, straight-haired

blacks that formed their social circle, but Blanche Bruce had been a slave from Mississippi. He claimed not to know the identity of his father, and his illiterate mother had given birth to children by at least two white men. The Willsons' world, while mostly black, was a world of educated Northeasterners and Midwesterners who felt far removed from slavery and the Deep South. They were a group that looked down on blacks from that region, because these uneducated people reminded them of their own less-advantaged ancestors. Their children were well schooled, sophisticated, and could almost pass for white, because of their coloring, while two of their four daughters were Negro in appearance (their only son eventually did pass), and their Northern accents as well as the comfort with which they moved among the liberal whites in Philadelphia and Cleveland. They had little in common with former slaves from southern regions beyond Washington or Baltimore. Their closest black friends in Cleveland—the John Malvins—were as insular and affluent as the John McKee and Cyrus Bustill families that they had befriended during their years in Philadelphia.

The Willsons' large, comfortable home at 228 Perry Street was outfitted with oil paintings, plaster molding, marble fireplaces, heavy mahogany furniture, and gleaming oak floors, much like the houses of their white professional neighbors. While not rich, the Willsons had long lived a comfortable life, with fine possessions adorning their home.[1]

Joseph Willson's father had been one of the founders of the Bank of Augusta in Georgia. His Negro mother, Betsy, had directed the slaves who worked in her own Georgia home and kitchen. His sister had married the wealthy black Philadelphia entrepreneur Frederick Hinton, a friend and colleague of liberal editor William Lloyd Garrison. Elizabeth's mother had been a free woman of color from Georgia. In his *Sketches of the Higher Classes of Colored Society in Philadelphia*, published in 1841, Joseph Willson had revealed his own elitism and strong belief in class divisions when it came to friendship and marriage. He wrote, "It is not my desire to be understood as an advocate of universal social union. Far from it. Such a union would not only be impractical, but even could it take place, would, to say the least, be highly injudicious and prejudicial. If the virtuous and exemplary members of society should not keep aloof from the worthless, they would furnish no example to the latter to strive to make themselves reputable . . . By associating with such persons we not only thereby give countenance to their doings, but we degrade ourselves to their level. Hence, distinctions and divisions on this ground, are in every respect commendable, proper and just."[2,3]

With friends in the elite black communities of Philadelphia, Cleveland, and Washington, the Willsons were probably aware of the conversation that was surrounding their daughter's name as she prepared to marry Bruce and move to Washington, a city that was more segregated and race-conscious than any place she had ever lived. Still living in their Cleveland home, Josephine received almost weekly letters from Blanche, letting her know that both black and white Washingtonians were speculating about which white hostesses in the capital would welcome her in their homes. Bruce attempted to joke about it, but the subject was raised frequently in his letters to her. In a December 5, 1877, letter to Josephine, he writes,

> *My Dear Miss Josie,*
> *. . . A great deal of curiosity is manifested here, for what reason I know not, to know where you will stop . . . It is very amusing. Washington is all ablaze to see you . . . I will meet you at the depot.*
> *Will our babies come home during the holidays?[4] I doubt if they can remain away from Ma and enjoy their turkey. How are they getting on with their school, do they like it better than when they first went to Indianapolis . . .*[5]

If Josephine's parents were privy to these letters arriving at their home, they might have wondered if Bruce was using their daughter's family credentials as a means to aid his own popularity among white and black elite Washingtonians who might be more inclined to accept the modest-backgrounded, dark-complexioned senator once he was paired with an educated, light-complexioned wife. [Although the only surviving photograph of Bruce suggests that he was a light- or medium-complexioned black man with somewhat Negroid features, news accounts written by blacks and whites during his life always referred to his skin color as being brown, and his features as being definitively Negroid. Among the Willsons' social circles and others among the black elite families, even a café au lait-complexioned black with curly hair and Negroid nose would have been described as "dark."] At the very least, Doctor and Mrs. Willson

would have been concerned that their daughter might face a hostile reception from bigoted Southern whites—a group she had never before
encountered. They had always lived in cities where wealthy blacks and
whites mixed. Their other two daughters, Mary and Victoria, were teaching in a white grammar school in Indianapolis. The racial attitudes of
Washington citizens, and the treatment accorded by white congressmen
and their wives, would take considerable adjustment for Josephine. One
issue that Josephine would have to adjust to was the ongoing discussion of
her skin complexion. Although she was considerably fair, her racial ancestry shows that she was the child of a Negro mother and a half-Negro
father—thus making the newspapers' labeling of her as an "octoroon"—
one-eighth black—inaccurate. She was, in fact, three-fourths black.

Josephine's parents knew of Bruce's ambition and his meteoric rise
in Mississippi, a state where he had resided only a few short years. They
had first heard of him two years earlier, when he became engaged to the
daughter of one of their black Cleveland friends. Only a few months
after the engagement was announced, his young fiancée died suddenly.
Less than a year later, Bruce began calling on Josephine Willson.
Many in Cleveland must have thought it odd that a Mississippi-based
senator who lived in Washington would be courting women in Ohio—
particularly when he had no friends or family there. But there must
have been many questions that the Willsons had for their daughter—
many of which may never have been answered: Who were his parents?
Is "Bruce" a slave name or a new name? Would the newspapers and the
public make the mistake of assuming that Josephine or her parents had
been slaves? Would Senator Bruce's former owner attempt to attend the
wedding?

Back in Washington, much had changed since Senator Bruce had
arrived in the fall of 1874. While there were nine blacks in Congress
when he joined, there were now only three: Bruce, and the South Carolina representatives Robert Smalls and Richard Cain. Even though
Frederick Douglass had just become the first black to be appointed to a
major position as U.S. marshal for Washington, the setbacks for blacks
were coming swiftly and surely. Senator Bruce now had to work alongside racist Southern Democrats, who were quickly being brought back
into power, including South Carolina general Matthew Butler. Butler
had become famous for attacking the largely black town of Hamburg,

South Carolina, two years earlier and leading the killing of black residents and the ransacking and burning of their homes and businesses because white area residents resented the black people's power and number in the town. Almost as a reward for his anti-black defiance in the middle of Reconstruction, the state elected him to the U.S. Senate in 1876. It was just one more indignity for Blanche to suffer, as he wrote to Josephine:

> *I have just been honored with an invitation and hope to be able to attend, but on account of the equality of parties in the Senate, I fear I shall not be able to get away. You know we have just passed through a fiery ordeal which ended with the admission of Hamburg Butler. We do not know at what moment the Democrats will spring some unseen trap on us, and taking us unawares, defeat us.*[6]

Bruce felt powerless after being handed defeats like this. These losses, no doubt, shook his confidence and made him even more cautious in his work. His reticence disturbed his friend John Roy Lynch, who had stood up to greater white opposition when he helped shepherd through the Civil Rights Act of 1875. Lynch, who was first elected to the House of Representatives in 1872, was unapologetic in his support for his fellow blacks in Mississippi and elsewhere. He had hoped that Bruce would be the same. Lynch expressed that concern in a letter he wrote to Bruce in the fall of 1877: "You are very particular and guarded in what you [say], thus demonstrating the fact that you possess a good deal of Senatorial diplomacy."[7]

Lynch was not far off the mark in his analysis of Bruce. In fact, there were many situations where Bruce pulled his punches with people who had openly disrespected him. For example, Bruce found amusement in telling the story of how he had been insulted by a white Democrat's racist remark years earlier, before both of them were elected to the Senate. In the 1850s, when Bruce was a young teenager in St. Louis, he was approached by a white man, Lewis Bogy, who offered Bruce a quarter if he would carry his suitcase to a waiting steamboat. After the young Bruce carried the luggage, Bogy refused to pay the money. When Bruce countered that he would turn over the bag only in exchange for the promised quarter, Bogy snatched the bag, called Bruce a "black rascal," and shook his fist at the insulted teenager. More than twenty years later, in 1877, when Lewis Bogy was a Democratic U.S. senator from Missouri, he approached Bruce and asked the black Republican senator to support him on a bill. Upon realizing that Bogy did not recognize him, Bruce reminded him of the incident that took place between them in St. Louis two decades earlier, and added, "You were the gentleman and I was the colored boy." In recalling the experience to the *Washington Post*, Bruce added, "Senator Bogy laughed heartily at the reminiscence, and we shook hands. I helped him pass his bill, just to demonstrate that strange things frequently happen in this world and I bore him no malice."[8]

There were many blacks who, like John Roy Lynch, felt that Bruce was too passive, or downright submissive, when dealing with bigoted whites. But Bruce had been feeling particularly uncertain of his position since President Rutherford Hayes had been sworn into office. Since that time, blacks in the South were becoming more frightened, as federal troops, who had been there to protect them against white hate groups, started withdrawing. By April, the troops had already been removed from South Carolina and Louisiana. As Bruce attempted to explain to his black Mississippi constituents, the fact that the new president was a Republican was irrelevant; Hayes was not on the side of Southern freedmen. In fact, in numerous letters between Bruce and Lynch, it becomes clear that Bruce felt somewhat overwhelmed by the cynicism that he has seen in his own party, particularly since the February meeting where Rutherford Hayes's Ohio representatives cut their infamous deal with the Democrats. Although Lynch was emboldened to speak more forcefully because of the deal, he, too, acknowledged the cynicism of his party. He wrote, "Politically speaking, I look upon the result in Ohio as a condemnation of the Southern Policy."[9]

The infamous deal that disturbed Bruce and Lynch was a February 26 meeting between four Southern Democrats and five Ohio Republicans who represented Rutherford Hayes. Interestingly, the meeting took place at the Wormley, a downtown Washington hotel owned by one of Bruce's black friends, James Wormley.[10] Since the presidential election of 1876 was still being contested in Congress because Democratic candidate Samuel J. Tilden was disputing the electoral college results for Hayes well into the new year of 1877, Democrats had approached Hayes and his representatives with a compromise.

This compromise, which came to be known as the Compromise of 1877, was an opportunity for the Southern Democrats to demand an end to Reconstruction, a removal of federal troops from the South, and a return of unfettered power to the white Democrats in the South, and a chance to remove blacks from public office as well as to reenact laws that limited the activities, rights, and mobility of blacks. What the four Southern Democrats offered to Hayes's five representatives was a compromise that basically stated that the Democratic Party would relinquish its support for Tilden's candidacy and offer it to Hayes if Hayes agreed to give the white Democrats the control they wanted over the South and over the black freedmen who lived there. Hayes and his representatives agreed, which gave him the presidency and brought an immediate downfall to the rights and safety of blacks who had been living under the protection of federal troops and nondiscriminatory laws. With this deal, Reconstruction was officially over.

What made the Compromise of 1877 so unsettling to the characteristically savvy Bruce was that he did not see it coming—not even after Tilden began complaining about the electoral vote issue. Senator Bruce and his brother Henry had earlier commented on the danger of Tilden's candidacy and the degree of protection that they and other blacks would receive from the Ohio-bred Hayes. Months earlier, Henry had agreed with his brother in a letter saying they had to do everything necessary to prevent the Democrat Tilden from coming to power, because he would try "to be President by fraud and intimidation."[11] He and Henry naturally believed that if they could keep the conservative Tilden out of the White House, their black brethren in the South would be secure. They quickly discovered their miscalculation.

Bruce found a welcome relief from his Senate duties as his wedding day approached. He wrote out a three-hundred-dollar check to Saks and Company in his First Washington Bank checkbook and sent it to Josephine.[12] He wanted to be sure that when he and Josephine left their nuptials and arrived at the Hoffman House Hotel in New York City, they were dressed in the best manner possible. Their new wardrobe would be used during their four-month honeymoon in Europe. Even before the articles were published, he knew that blacks and whites in DC, Mississippi, and Ohio would be following the details of this wedding.

During the last few months of their engagement, Josephine's parents had become more civil to him, but whenever he visited Cleveland to call on her, he never stayed in their four-bedroom home. He stayed at Forest City House, one of the city's top hotels. When he visited the Willsons' home, Josephine and her mother would tell him about the plans they had made. The house would be completely repainted. The ceremony would take place in the parlor, which opened up to a library on one end and a large foyer on the other end. The hors d'oeuvres and food would be provided by Henry Weisgerber, a popular Cleveland caterer. Calla lilies would be arranged throughout all of the first-floor rooms.

They would also show him the gifts that had already begun to arrive: four crystal vases from the Herkomers, a silver berry dish from the Huntingtons, a silver butter dish from the Boyds, silver and crystal from the Vosburghs, silver vases from the Morgans, and so forth.[13]

Finally, the wedding day arrived. At seven-thirty p.m. on June 24, 1878, the Willson family hosted the wedding of their daughter to the most prominent black man in America.

By the next afternoon, newspapers around the country—in New York, Baltimore, Atlanta, Vicksburg, New Orleans, Indianapolis, and Chicago—were publishing the details surrounding the nuptials of the black senator and his new wife. Since no black member of Congress had been as wealthy or as well connected to both the black and the white political establishment as Bruce, there had never been much interest in the families of previous black congressmen. The *Cleveland Gazette* reported on June 26, two days after the event:

THE MARRIAGE OF SENATOR BRUCE
TO MISS JOSEPHINE WILLSON

The marriage of Senator Blanche K. Bruce, the only colored member of The United States Senate, and the second colored man who has ever held a seat in that body, and Miss Josephine Willson, took place at the Residence of Dr. Willson at 7:30 o'clock Monday evening.

Dr. Willson lives at No. 228 Perry Street, a few doors from Prospect Street, in a neat two-story frame house standing a few feet back from the street. The interior of the house, as well as its exterior surroundings, give evidence of the good taste and enlightened ideas of the occupants. The parlors are carpeted with soft, light-colored Brussels of a pretty pattern, and the walls are tastefully hung with paintings and engravings, many of them from the hands of well-known artists . . . The front windows were heavily curtained to keep out the gaze of the inquisitive crowd, who hung about the fence and lined the sidewalk in front of the building.

The guests, who numbered some sixty in all, were met at the door by an usher and shown to the cloak room upstairs. The gentlemen were nearly all in full dress, black broadcloth and white kid gloves, and the toilettes of the ladies were becomingly elaborate and brilliant. Promptly at the appointed hour, the bridal party entered the rear parlor . . . The bride and groom took their places under an arch near one end of the room, which was prettily trimmed with smilax, and calla lilies hanging over the bride's head. The bride was attired in a beautiful white silk cut in the princess style and trimmed in white satin. The dress was covered with satin orange blossoms, and the veil worn over the head reaching to the floor like a cloud. The bridesmaids were attired in white muslin.

After the impressive ceremony of the Episcopal Church was performed and the benediction pronounced, Dr. Rulison introduced to the assembly "the Senator and Mrs. Bruce," . . . and many repaired to the front parlor where the presents were displayed . . .[14]

By the time Blanche married Josephine Willson, he had well established himself in the press and in the minds of white colleagues he sought to impress as a wealthy and well-spoken man. He never spoke of his experiences as a slave in Virginia and Missouri, presumably because those details would underscore that the Mississippi senator was not, in fact, from Mississippi and was no different from the other Republican carpetbaggers. And while other blacks in Congress had often made reference to their families' slave experiences as a means of showing deference to white colleagues or demonstrating their empathy for their less-advantaged constituents, Blanche made no such attempts. He avoided making any public speeches or published writings that referred to his life prior to his 1869 arrival in Mississippi. As far as he and his public were concerned, Blanche Bruce's biography began in 1871 when he became tax assessor of Bolivar County.

The senator likewise chose to assume a low profile in the wedding preparations. In a move uncharacteristic for any political leader celebrating a happy event, the senator avoided the media. He gave no interviews, extended no high-profile invitations, and even consented only to a very private wedding, outside Washington, inside a private home, with few observers. One might presume that he was protecting himself and his future wife against the stories of his slave past rearing their ugly heads in the press.

The wedding at 228 Perry Street, the Cleveland home of Dr. and Mrs. Joseph Willson, was an elegant albeit small one—particularly for the wealth and stature of the two people being married. It included roughly sixty people, no other elected officials among them. And no member of the senator's family was present for the wedding.

The wedding was almost a metaphor for what the senator's experiences were going to be for the rest of his life: publicly glamorous and triumphant, but privately reticent and guarded. Why would a U.S. senator with great personal wealth fail to have any fellow political leaders—black or white—at his wedding? And more important, why would he fail to have any of his own family members present? Several of his siblings, including his brother Henry, the Missouri politician and writer, were living less than two hundred miles from where the wedding took place.

As Senator Bruce and his wife, Josephine Beal Willson Bruce, left the next week for an extravagant four-month European honeymoon cruise, which would include a Paris visit with ex-president Grant, they sailed closer toward a life that Blanche had been contemplating for the last several years. It was a life that would exclude any family members who lacked their social status. They would display grace and sophistication as they accumulated greater wealth, power, and prestige, but they were going to do it by themselves.

❧⦿⦿❧

CHAPTER EIGHT

1878

A Black Dynasty Begins

BY LATE JUNE 1878, AFTER HIS WEDDING TOOK PLACE, WASHINGTON was still abuzz with conversation about the senator's new bride. There were dozens of articles in both black and white newspapers still specu-lating about the bride's social and ethnic background. One paper spoke of her resembling "a beautiful Spanish lady [with] no one cognizant of her African blood," while the senator's physical appearance was described derisively as "of the color designated in the south as 'nigger-colored,' and a 250-pounder."[1] Such remarks were not limited just to the Democratic newspapers that had an additional motive for insulting the Republican senator. The various Washington political observers continued guessing how the capital's white political wives and hostesses would deal with the new Mrs. Bruce. People were wondering if this black woman, who could easily pass for white, would be invited to the social teas and lunches where other Senate wives were entertained. Southern journalists asked if this high-toned, well-bred Northern woman would identify with her husband's Southern constituents, who were not so educated and worldly. Northern Republicans were hoping that a black wife with her credentials would further humiliate the racist Democrats in the South. Blacks in the North and the South were still asking if the light-complexioned woman was, indeed, black. Only a few newspapers acknowledged that her mother was a "full Negro" and her father was half Negro.

"Josephine fever" was finding its way into the newspapers that chronicled the activities of Washington's elected officials. For the next few months, each paper tried to develop a new weekly angle on the story, using it to comment on the state of race relations, the implications of Reconstruction, or the ongoing divisions between North and South or between Republicans and Democrats. As the months advanced, black readers, in particular, relished learning new facts about this new power couple. The Bruces' relatives, friends, trips, and clothes were all grist for the mill—beginning as early as the date of their four-month honeymoon, which was chronicled in many papers during the summer and fall of 1878. One New York paper said the following:

THE EXODUS TO EUROPE
Departure of Senator Bruce and His Bride

B.K. Bruce, the colored United States Senator from Mississippi, and his bride, were the social lions among the throng of passengers who sailed on the *Algeria*, of the Cunard Line for Europe, this afternoon. The happy pair reached the steamer in a Hoffman House coach an hour prior to moving out into the stream, and during the interval were the center of a group of friends of both races, and the object of interest for scores who stood at a distance inspecting and commenting upon their appearance.

The Senator is a splendid specimen of his race, standing nearly six feet in his stockings with a finely formed head and pleasing countenance . . . He was dressed in a black suit with a broad-brimmed black felt hat. His bride was elegantly attired in a plum colored silk dress elaborately trimmed with velvet of the same color, a jaunty chip hat, with a waving feather of a grayish tint, setting off to advantage her very handsome features.

The contrast between them as regards color was very marked, she being a pale brunette with light colored hair and would readily be taken for a white woman.

It was [the senator's] intention to . . . proceed directly to London, where he would remain for a fortnight . . . Italy would be his objective point, and . . . he would go to Berlin and Vienna, reaching the French capital during the latter part of August.[2]

Prior to the Bruces, no white newspaper had included black politicians in its society columns. Even if the rare black politician had been present at an important social event, his presence or role had never been as closely observed as that of Josephine and Blanche. Many articles were brutally honest in revealing their reporters' nineteenth-century racist views regarding the color line, and they oftentimes portrayed the senator and his wife as some new species—too dark to be white yet too well-bred to be authentically black. They were a conundrum that was used to entertain readers. But even when the journalistic envelope was pushed, however inexplicable this couple might appear to white readers, Josephine was still usually portrayed favorably, even if, at the same time, her positive attributes served to highlight negative qualities that whites might unfairly observe in the senator.

At times, Bruce would complain to his friends John Roy Lynch or James Hill that the articles might be causing too much controversy, but they usually argued that the stories raised his profile and placed him in the mainstream by reminding the public of his wife's credentials. On November 20, 1878, yet another article questioned whether whites would welcome Josephine Bruce, even despite her upper-class background and beauty.

OUGHT WE TO VISIT HER

Senator Bruce, who has been travelling in Europe with his bride since his marriage in June, is expected to arrive soon, and has engaged a handsome residence on Capitol Hill for the remainder of his senatorial term. There is some social agitation here with regard to the manner in which Mrs. Bruce will be received by the "swells" of Washington.

She is a lady of fine personal appearance, an octoroon, and is, perhaps, better educated than most of the women who intend to snub her if she presumes to enter society . . . her husband has sufficient wealth to gratify any taste she may have in the way of personal adornment or equipage. It is whispered that a wardrobe purchased by her in Europe would be prized by any of our belles. It is a requirement of official etiquette here that all the Cabinet ladies and the wives of Congressmen shall make the first call upon a Senator's wife.[3]

Articles like this found a sympathetic audience in the Northeast, but the controversy surrounding the treatment of Josephine was so titillating, its coverage reached beyond the East Coast, landing in papers in the Midwest as well. It gave Republicans in the North and Midwest the chance to wag their tongues at the Southerners who shunned the black couple. Of course, this was both self-serving and disingenuous in that these Northerners and Midwesterners themselves had virtually no social interaction with blacks. It was just that, to these non-Southerners, the senator and his wife seemed like the kind of blacks (i.e., rich, intelligent, famous, light complexioned, and well respected) that any white person should be willing to welcome—if they really had to. Blanche took the attention as a mixed blessing. The threat of being ignored was an insult to him, but the fact that the newspapers continued to write stories about it served as vindication for his outrage.

Using the simple headline "Snobbery," a Wisconsin weekly paper with Republican leanings carried an 1879 editorial about the treatment accorded Josephine in Washington.

SNOBBERY

It was a reasonable expectation, that when emancipation became a practical reality, and the new relations became properly adjusted, the old slaveholding aristocracy would ignore their prejudices of caste, and would accept the new order of things . . .

But that the reverse of this is true, is amply illustrated by the treatment which the wife of a United States Senator has lately received at the National Capitol . . . His wife is an educated, refined and highly accomplished lady . . . but at least one eighth of her blood is transmitted from the same lately oppressed and enslaved race. This made no difference to Republicans. The wife of the President

(Hayes), and the wives of the Cabinet officers and Republican Senators paid their respects to Mrs. Senator Bruce . . .

Not so the southern Democrats. They have studiously ignored her existence. They have allowed themselves to be controlled by the old race prejudice . . . Worst of all, their shameful example has been followed by Northern Democrats. It having been reported that the wife of Senator Thurman had called on Mrs. Bruce, that high toned gentleman and Presidential aspirant hastened to make an earnest denial, and thus set himself right with his Southern masters.

No more humiliating exhibition was ever made in Republican America . . .[4]

Stories like this continued to give smug Republicans in the North a great deal of satisfaction, because such newspaper accounts characterized Southerners, who prided themselves on decorum, as uncouth bigots.

When the new couple returned to Washington from Europe, they had looked forward to settling into a five-year-old four-story brick town house that Blanche had found at 909 M Street NW. Built in 1873, it was an imposing ten-room house with an ornate mansard roof. The Second Empire–style architecture matched that of other town houses on the block. Because of extensive renovations that Bruce was having done on the town house, he had decided to live elsewhere until it was complete. He decided that he and Josephine would temporarily live in a house a few blocks away. It was called Hillside Cottage.

Most blacks who lived in Washington or were familiar with the city at the time understood the significance and suitability of Hillside Cottage, a freestanding fourteen-room home that had once been the mansion inhabited by John Mercer Langston. Most members of Washington's black and white elite knew the Langston family's ties to the city's black upper-class community. Born in 1829, Langston had earned a master's degree from Oberlin College and had been admitted to the Ohio bar in 1854. Langston was married to another black Oberlin graduate, Caroline Wall, who was from a wealthy North Carolina family. Not only had Langston been the first black elected to any public office in the country when he was elected town clerk in his Ohio town, but he had also been inspector general of the Freedmen's Bureau, as well as Howard University's law dean and the school's acting president before he was appointed minister to Haiti in 1877 by President Rutherford B. Hayes. He and Caroline had made their home, Hillside Cottage, an important destination on the Washington social entertaining circuit.[5] The reason Hillside was available to the Bruces was that John Langston was currently living abroad, serving in his minister to Haiti position for another two years.

In such a home, Blanche and Josephine's busy social schedule could continue. And it did. In fact, because the senator had made their honeymoon such a priority in those first months of marriage, staying in Europe for so long, visiting with European dignitaries and Americans abroad, such as former president Ulysses S. Grant, he and his wife were eager to start entertaining locally. And the publicity that had continued during their European trip had prepared the Washington locals for their fall arrival.

In Washington, Josephine and Blanche entertained many of the white Republican political leaders and a large upper-middle-class group of whites who, while unaccustomed to socializing with blacks, felt honored to be in the company of a high-profile senator and his socialite wife. During those first months at Hillside Cottage, their social schedule was dizzying.

In fact, the only people who seem *not* to have been included in their activities and communications were the middle-class black community and the senator's family members. While it soon became apparent to some of the local black journalists that the Bruces were not going out of their way to find black friends beyond the small and well-insulated light-complexioned black elite community in the city, it was not so obvious that the senator's family members were also being left out. Blanche had never made many efforts to include his Missouri family in Washington affairs or even to make reference to them in the many articles that profiled him and chronicled his rise to power. Now that he was married to Josephine and had tied himself to an honest-to-goodness upper-class black family, he demonstrated even less interest in mentioning his own family. There were never remarks about his parents, his deceased or surviving siblings—or even recollections about his childhood in Virginia, Missouri, or Mississippi.

What is so shocking about Blanche's treatment of his family during this period is not just that he failed to mention them in public settings or in personal correspondence with his wife and her family members, but that he did not seem even to keep them abreast of the most basic events in his life. He appeared to be trying to keep them out of his life altogether.

For example, as late as December 16, 1878, practically six months after his marriage to Josephine, two of his brothers, Calvin and James, each wrote separate letters to Blanche, to ask if it was true that Blanche had gotten married. Not only did Blanche fail to invite his family members to his wedding, he did not even inform them that he was marrying.

James, who at that time was serving in the prestigious role as treasurer for the Masonic lodges based in five states—Minnesota, Iowa, Colorado, Nebraska, and Missouri—wrote to Blanche on official treasurer's stationery from Brunswick, Missouri:

> Dear Brother, I write to say we are all well. I see in quite a
> number of newspapers that you have just married—is it
> so or not? If so, my wife says you must send her your wife's
> photograph . . . I want you to do all you can for W.V. Hall as
> he put all confidence in you. Please let me hear from you
> soon . . . My wife sends her best regards to you and your new
> family if you have one. My son is at the Lincoln Institute
> [University] attending school . . .[6]

That same week, Blanche's brother Calvin wrote a three-page letter inquiring about the stories he had heard regarding his brother's marriage. Calvin, who was far less educated and in far worse health than his brother, seemed to also make a plea to Blanche for closer contact:

> Dear Brother, I take the pleasure to ask you for a Christmas gift
> for I have not seen you for so long . . . Well, I am glad to hear that
> you are married . . . My sight is getting very bad and I can't hardly
> see to write a note . . . I sent you my photograph, please let me
> know whether you got it. All of the people here speak well of you,
> white and colored, every day . . .

*I wish that you would write to me anyhow and just let me
know how you are getting along as you are living a new life. All
of the family is well and hearty at this present time. We have the
largest snow here now that we ever had in Brunswick. It was three
feet deep.*
          Yours truly, Calvin Bruce[7]

*P.S. You must excues [sic] my pencil writing to you. My hand
is so nerffes [sic] that I can not write with a pen and ink.*

While there is evidence that Blanche was indeed in communication
with his brother Henry, who was a successful produce dealer in Atchison,
Kansas, and with two other brothers who were tobacco farmers in
Meridian, Mississippi, he did not inform them of his marriage, either. If
Blanche distanced himself from his family members because he believed
that they would reflect negatively on him, it is clear that he made no distinctions between those who were educated and those who were not.

In spite of his own personal dilemmas involving his siblings and
the new home for his wife, there were many more burning issues facing the senator once he returned to Washington from his honeymoon
in the fall of 1878. For one, his state had been devastated by a severe
yellow-fever epidemic earlier that year, which killed thousands of people and caused great disruption in civic and social affairs, since whole
communities in Mississippi and other Southern states along the great
river had to be secured and quarantined for several months.

Bruce also returned to the United States in time to see the continued unraveling of black voting rights throughout the South, as well as
the weakening of the Republican Party in Mississippi and other Southern states. President Hayes's Compromise of 1877 had gutted the
Republican Party, and with its removal of troops to protect black voters
in the South, had handed everything to the Democrats, who were seeking "Redemption" after the fall of Reconstruction.

By late 1878, the Redeemers in Mississippi had so effectively gone
about the state terrorizing blacks with Black Codes, house burnings,
and lynchings, Blanche had to severely limit his travels to the state he
represented. Many of the Mississippi newspapers were Democratic, and
they helped to spread untrue stories about Reconstruction and mythic

tales of dishonest, lecherous, and greedy black elected officials who purportedly had been corrupting and cheating the state of money and integrity.

Through the use of well-placed propaganda and their own crooked judges and press, the Redeemer Democrats were effective in convincing white Mississippians that the blacks and the Republicans were bad for the state. These lies fanned the anger of white mobs and white Democrats, who saw further reason for stuffing ballot boxes.

In fact, the Southern voting corruption was so bad in the 1878 congressional election that although blacks had customarily voted Republican, many black counties in Mississippi, Louisiana, and South Carolina did not record a single Republican vote. Among the 294 counties that had black majorities, according to the recorded ballots, only one-fifth supported Republicans—when just two years earlier, the black majorities had swung their support to the Republicans by twice as much. What the white Southern Democrats were unable to accomplish by threats against blacks they simply achieved by tossing out Republican ballots and replacing them with illegally stuffed Democratic ballots. On the rare occasion when white Southern Democratic election workers were arrested for voter intimidation or fraud, there was no jury who would be willing to convict them.

In late 1878, when the third session of the Forty-fifth Congress convened, Blanche and his colleagues were focused on voting law violations in the South and Chinese immigration in the West.[8]

By the end of 1878, it was clear that the Democrats, from a political standpoint, had taken advantage of what President Hayes had given them, and had more than made up for what they felt they had lost during Reconstruction. Democrats now controlled both houses in Congress, and there was nothing that Hayes or Republicans could get through without their approval. And to add insult to injury, eighteen of these recently elected Democratic congressmen were former Confederate generals.

Like other Southern leaders, upon his return Senator Bruce faced the ongoing economic depression that had begun in 1873 and was still a problem in 1878. And the economy of the state had not gotten any better once the white Democratic Redeemer leaders took over, so the Southern farmers still faced severe problems.[9] The hostility that Mississippi whites had felt toward the Republicans and black citizens during Reconstruction was exacerbated now that even the Redeemers hadn't turned their economic fortunes around. Blanche knew that this was no place for him to be campaigning; he maintained his property holdings there but focused his energies on his work in the Senate and in the Washington social scene.

Throughout all of this dissension in the South and in the divided Congress, Blanche was still focused on further establishing his family's name and presence in the company of prominent white Republicans in Washington. Already in his late 30s it was essential to him that he and his wife quickly present themselves as an all-American family. By the fall of 1878, he felt he was well on his way to accomplishing that when Josephine learned that she was expecting a child. This news was not something that would slow the couple down. In fact, as 1879 began, Blanche and Josephine entertained aggressively. One Boston paper took note of the New Year's Day gatherings that the Bruces hosted at the fourteen-room home they were renting while waiting for the renovation of their M Street town house:

MRS. SENATOR BRUCE'S NEW YEAR'S

Many called upon Mrs. Senator Bruce, the colored bride of the colored Senator from Mississippi. She made her debut into Washington society on this occasion, and nowhere were callers more gracefully welcomed or more hospitably entertained. Mrs. Bruce is a lady of great personal beauty, of the Andalusian Type, and wore a magnificent black velvet dress made for her by Worth during her recent visit to Paris, and handsome diamonds.

She was assisted in entertaining by her sisters, the Misses Willson, of Cleveland, both of them handsome and accomplished ladies. Senator Bruce is living temporarily at the house of John Langston, Minister to Haiti, near Howard University, but he is fitting up a house, into which he will soon move. The house is on M Street, formerly occupied by Secretary Delano. He will have as his neighbors Representative Blair, of New Hampshire, and District Attorney Wells.[10]

Although there was not much press available to him in his home state—generally the most likely place for a senator to be able to flaunt his popularity and power—Blanche was adept at keeping his name in papers farther north. He understood that the more connections he could draw to the upper-class Washington establishment, the more fascinated the news editors would be in writing about him and his wife. The fact that Josephine wore diamonds and velvet at her own dinners and teas offered yet another dimension to the "status-boosting"—yet factual—stories that their current home had been owned by the minister to Haiti and their future home was previously owned by a cabinet member and was now adjacent to a prominent congressman and the district attorney. The implication of these stories was important to Blanche, because they further substantiated the fact that the Bruces were as prosperous and as important as the very wealthy and powerful white people who lived around them.

During this time, Senator Bruce was beginning to rely heavily on the advice of his New Orleans friend P. B. S. ("Pinckney") Pinchback. Bruce had great respect for Pinchback, for he had demonstrated an indomitable spirit throughout his own political career. The black politician had been elected to the Louisiana State Senate in 1868, and then also served as lieutenant governor of Louisiana. He eventually served as governor in December 1872 and January 1873, when Governor Henry Clay Warmouth was impeached in 1872 for "high crimes and misdemeanors." Pinchback was elected to the House of Representatives in 1872 and then to the U.S. Senate in 1873, but miraculously, the Democrats refused to seat him in both cases. Hence, Pinchback had the kind of experience and political savvy that made him a reliable adviser as Bruce found himself facing controversial issues.

One issue that Bruce asked Pinchback about was the Liberian emigration movement. As a Southern senator, Bruce found himself close to the center of a controversy regarding black Southerners who were considering emigration to the African republic of Liberia as a means of escaping bigotry in the Deep South. Publicly, Bruce was uneasy speaking about it. He was, indeed, opposed to this movement, which had begun in 1877 and continued into 1878, and had discussed it in letters to Pinchback, who was now editor of the New Orleans weekly *The*

Louisianian. He finally expressed his public opinion in the pages of the Ohio newspaper *Cincinnati Commercial.* Bruce wrote:

> The Negro of America is not African, but American—in his mental development and biases, in his religious beliefs and hopes, and in his political conception . . . He is not a parasite, but a branch, drawing its life from the great American vine . . . as readily and unreservedly as his Caucasian brother. None of the conditions exist in Liberia as to make a general exodus of the Negroes of the South either desirable or practicable.[11]

While these provocative words appeared in print for thousands to read, Blanche was not willing to say such things on the floor of the Senate. He understood the concept of floating trial balloons before they became a part of the *Congressional Record.* Before approaching other newspaper editors with his remarks, he would often "test" them with Pinchback's editorial sensibilities. Once his opinions were screened and approved by Pinchback and then by another party—in some cases, other black newspapers—Blanche was willing to expose himself to the permanence of placing his opinions in the Senate records.

Throughout the year and well into 1879, Bruce and Pinchback exchanged correspondence, discussing the 1880 presidential elections, in particular. In many of these letters, Pinchback asked Blanche for help in obtaining a government appointment. It was time for Blanche to return the favors that Pinchback had bestowed on him in the past. What Pinchback recognized in Blanche was the influence that the senator had with President Hayes, a rare power for any black to have exerted with an American president. But the reason why Blanche was able to exert any influence on the president was because of the impression that the senator gave, of still controlling the political activities of his home state. Once Mississippi senior senator James Alcorn stepped down in 1877, Blanche was the senior senator and the sole Republican senator from the state.

He further solidified his position of authority over the state Republicans back home by continuing to build an alliance with black Mississippi politicians, including James Hill, a former secretary of state, and his friend John R. Lynch, a former congressman. Together, the three of them controlled the Republican Party in Mississippi, thus making it possible for Blanche to insist that the Hayes administration consult them on patronage positions and other Mississippi-related interests. This was an arrangement that would work for several more years—even while white Republicans in the South were becoming less and less powerful. This was the kind of black alliance that would help Blanche maintain his power even after leaving his position as senator.

CHAPTER NINE

 споĝ

1879–1880
A New Child and a New Redemption Congress

WHEN THE FORTY-SIXTH CONGRESS CONVENED IN MARCH OF 1879, Blanche was the only black to be found in either house. Since 1869, there had always been at least two blacks in the House of Representatives, and as recently as 1876, there had been as many as eight blacks in Congress. But Southern Democrats' scare tactics and violence toward black voters had been successful.

He remembered that first day of the Forty-sixth Congress very well. He remembered it because he noticed that he was no longer assigned to a seat next to George Hoar of Massachusetts, a Republican colleague with whom he had begun a great friendship. The scion of a New England dynasty that espoused liberal Yankee ideals, Hoar and his family members had all attended Harvard, and they were outspoken on the issue of racial equality.

After sitting in the same seat since 1875, he had now been assigned to seat number one, which placed him at the very end of his row.[1] Of course, in the Senate Chamber senators were commonly permitted to move their desks where they wanted—sometimes exchanging places with others, and most often trying to sit together as a party—but the *official* seating chart now showed Blanche with only one person next to him: Orville H. Platt, the new Republican senator from Connecticut. At each new Congress, the secretary of the senate would offer the more senior senators a chance to select the better seats in the chamber.

It was twelve o'clock on Tuesday, March 18, when the session was called to order and Senate chaplain Reverend Byron Sunderland offered the prayer. Then it was time to swear in the new senators. As the new senators were sworn in, there weren't many whispered remarks until a few people quietly noted that the senator-elect from Louisiana, Benjamin F. Jonas, was Jewish—only the second practicing Jew to ever join the Senate.

It was earlier in 1879—during the third session of the Forty-fifth Congress—that serious issues had arisen. Bruce had long been thought of as reticent and willing to confirm only the Republican platform that was espoused by his party's leaders. In January and February of 1879, Blanche confirmed for others that he was willing to speak about race issues going beyond the treatment of black freedmen in the South.

In February of that year, the Senate and the House were still debating how to deal with the continued immigration of Chinese people into California. It was an issue that had been raised in 1878. West Coast political leaders were arguing that this influx of immigrants was taking jobs away from white residents and placing a heavy burden on their communities.

Although hundreds of thousands of immigrants had been entering the U.S. from Germany, Ireland, Austria, Italy, Russia, and Scandinavia, Congress did not consider federal regulations to limit immigration until it came to addressing immigrants from China in 1879. Prior to that time, the states were allowed to regulate immigration for themselves. Although the Chinese were far outnumbered by both the Germans and the Irish, white Californians had begun making demands on Congress to stop the flow of Chinese people moving to their state. Bigoted attitudes toward the race, religion, and customs of the Chinese was, no doubt, a major factor. Ironically, it had been the white Californians who had encouraged the Chinese to settle there in the first place in 1849, when gold was first being mined in the state. Viewed as inexpensive labor, the Chinese workers were utilized for mining as well as for the work on the Central Pacific Railroad. But by 1879, many white residents and Irish workers were becoming resentful of this new immigrant group's presence and its collective willingness to work for less pay than the white workers.

In making his argument to the Senate on behalf of his white constituents back home, California's Republican senator Aaron Sargent

said, "Chinese immigration presents in California a present evil as great
as any ever ascribed to slavery in the Southern states."[2]

While the idea of allowing other immigrants to enter the United
States but stopping the Chinese seemed patently racist and un-
American to the liberal Republicans, the Democrats and many moder-
ate Republicans indicated that they would support a bill limiting
Chinese movement into the country. Finally, on February 14, 1879,
Blanche spoke out against the bill. In his characteristically noncon-
frontational style, he said:

> I desire to submit a single remark. Representing as I do a peo-
> ple who but a few years ago were considered essentially dis-
> qualified from enjoying the privileges and immunities of
> American citizenship, and who have since been so successfully
> introduced into the body politic, and having large confidence
> in the strength and the assimilative power of our institutions, I
> shall vote against the pending bill.[3]

Bruce's friend George Hoar, Republican senator from Massachusetts,
was on the same side of the issue. A longtime champion of equal rights,
Hoar easily and forcefully opposed the bill limiting Chinese immigration.
Never afraid to openly confront his white colleagues, Hoar recalled in his
1903 autobiography how he had asked his Jewish Senate colleague,
Louisiana's Benjamin Jonas, why he did not demonstrate empathy for
another mistreated race of people. Hoar said to Senator Jonas, "Why will
you not remember the terrible history of the men of your race and blood,
and help me resist a like savage treatment of another race?"[4]

According to Hoar, Jonas replied, "Mr. Hoar, the Jews are a superior race. They are not to be classed with the Chinese."

Two days after Bruce's comments on the bill, several newspapers,
including the Detroit *Plaindealer*, remarked on the irony of a black man
having the opportunity to vote on the treatment of another racial group.
The paper wrote, "All eyes were seemingly turned to the Senator from
Mississippi, who would meet with some embarrassment on that question
by having to play the difficult role of American and Negro."[5] Despite
Bruce's and Hoar's opposition to the bill, they failed to persuade their colleagues. The Senate quickly passed the bill, and it was not until it reached
the desk of President Hayes that the discriminatory legislation was vetoed.

Right on the heels of the Chinese immigration debate, another major race issue arose in the nation: a black exodus from the Deep South to the Midwest. With scores of black freedmen feeling cheated by the corrupt sharecropping system of farming and feeling defeated by the violence and indignities aimed at them throughout the South by hate groups such as the Ku Klux Klan, there began a ground swell of support for an exodus out of the South to safer territory where whites could not control them economically or harass them and their families.

This issue not only had an impact on white-owned plantations, it affected Blanche and Josephine's plantation in Bolivar County. If the black farmworkers left the South, they'd be leaving their plantation as well. These black Southerners—a great portion of them from Mississippi, Arkansas, and Louisiana—had decided that they would rather face an uncertain future in a Midwestern state, like Kansas, than continue being abused by Southern Democrats who resented the blacks for their recently acquired freedom and right to vote. The white Southern farmowners continued to work the blacks for long hours and then sometimes claimed not to have enough money to pay them. Since there were no other employment opportunities for these black farmworkers, they were forced to accept the abuse.

Despite his own self-interest as a plantation owner, Blanche understood how his colored brethren felt on the issue, because a decade and a half earlier, he himself had left home and all that was familiar to him, in order to escape the indignities and cruelties of slavery. Even though his current life as a wealthy politician was so completely in contrast to theirs, there were still aspects of the black experience that were not so foreign to him.

But given his situation, Blanche did not find it politically expedient to comment on the floor of the Senate on this crucial issue of a Kansas exodus. He unashamedly avoided entering the discussion.

Many found it shocking that the country's only black U.S. senator remained silent on the issue of the exodus, particularly since he had been publicly opposed to the planned black emigration to Liberia two years before, in 1877 and 1878. He was so willing to oppose that back-to-Africa movement, some observed, why was he silent on this movement? Had more people known of his vast land interests in Mississippi, they might not have wondered about his reticence.

Although he knew that his sharecroppers did not suffer the other abuses that were practiced on neighboring white-owned farmland, Bruce's plantation in Bolivar County employed poorly compensated black sharecroppers who lived in flimsy wooden shacks. Like those of his fellow plantation owners, his interests as a landowner were better served by keeping the blacks in their jobs as sharecroppers. Who else would work the land? Bruce certainly didn't want to see his own workers leave and move to Kansas. It would be a detriment to his own income and to the income of his white constituents. But at the same time, he knew how unpopular he would become among black citizens if he openly opposed the exodus—thereby forcing his "own" people to stay and accept the abuse.

Bruce's friend Frederick Douglass, who was then U.S. marshal for the District of Columbia, was willing to speak publicly against the exodus in September 1879. Other blacks, like former congressman John Lynch, U.S. Minister to Haiti John M. Langston, and Howard Law School dean Richard T. Greener, publicly supported the fifty thousand blacks who sought a more racially hospitable environment in Kansas for their families. Greener, an 1870 graduate of Harvard, debated Frederick Douglass on the issue and insisted that the exodus was a viable alternative to living amid corruption and racial abuses in the South.

Bruce was so cautious with the subject that he avoided attending a June 1879 Senate vote on a resolution to establish a committee to investigate the causes of the emigration out of the South. This was a political hot potato that he didn't want to touch on the floor of the Senate. It was also an issue that his wife, Josephine, had mixed feelings about, because while she often lent her name to charitable causes that aided disadvantaged blacks—as she did as a board member of the National Association for Relief of Colored Women and Children—she usually supported only those causes that were embraced by wealthy white liberals.

Even though Bruce managed to remain silent on the emigration debate, his words found their way to the Senate lectern when it was revealed that on April 18, 1879, Bruce had written a letter to a Mississippi resident who had invited him to attend a convention and discuss the exodus. Not realizing that the constituent letter would be saved and then later read into the *Congressional Record*, Bruce candidly wrote about the exodus. While it was written in the same guarded style that he used in his public discourse, the letter reveals more than he was willing to share with his colleagues in Congress:

From the best information that I can obtain, the exodus of the colored people from the South is referable mainly to two considerations: first, the feeling of insecurity and uneasiness ... springing from the unfortunate race collisions and violence that have sometimes existed in certain southern localities; and, second, from the fact that the colored laborers have not in many instances received satisfactory returns from the products of their labors.[6]

Unwilling to acknowledge openly that he could see how black Southerners were afraid of being further terrorized by white Democrats or cheated by their sharecropper bosses, Bruce avoided placing blame through his deft use of qualifiers and understatement. The black senator was well skilled at avoiding unpopular issues. And he made use of this talent for at least a year while the Kansas exodus became more and more controversial.

It was not until February 1880, when thousands of black "exodusters" had begun dying in Kansas from starvation, their farms having failed, that the senator spoke out on the matter. It was a late Friday afternoon, on February 20, after a long week in the chambers. Vermont senator Justin Morrill had just read a House bill that provided for food and clothing to be made available to the dying blacks in Kansas. The provisions had actually been sent to the United States from England and only needed congressional approval in order to be distributed by the government. The House had already passed the bill authorizing distribution of the British donations, and Bruce was astounded that his Senate colleagues found it so difficult to approve such a simple measure. It revealed how deeply they held their bigotry and resentment toward blacks. After his friend Roscoe Conkling argued in favor of the bill, pointing out that it would not cost the U.S. government anything, Bruce stood up.

He turned to his Senate colleagues and demanded that no matter how they felt about the original purpose of the exodus, they at least must have felt enough compassion to offer this free emergency aid to the dying blacks. He said,

I have studiously avoided giving expression to my views on this floor, touching the movement of colored people from the

South, and I have hoped no occasion would arise for me to engage in that discussion. I shall not do so now . . . It is not now a question of how they came there or why they went there; it is not a question of whether they ought to have gone there or not; but that they are there and they are in distress . . . It seems to me that the only question involved now is whether or not we will relieve suffering humanity . . . in Kansas . . . [and] permit a charity which the English people have sent here to pass through the custom house free of duty. . . . In the name of the hundreds of colored people now starving in Kansas, I appeal to the Senate to pass the pending measure . . .[7]

While his colleagues refused to earmark any U.S. government funds for the starving families, Blanche was at least able to get the Senate to approve the release of England's duty-free aid to the blacks in Kansas. Despite his embarrassingly late comments on the issue, he managed to bring some benefits to the needy Kansas transplants.

There would be other legislative issues for Blanche to face in the Senate with regard to race relations in the 1879–1880 period. One involved West Point and the ongoing mistreatment at the school of black cadets (e.g., James Smith, Henry Flipper, John Alexander), who had been racially harassed, ostracized, and encouraged to drop out by white students and staff who still opposed the integration of the prestigious military academy. The most recent instance was mentioned on April 9, 1880, when Illinois senator John Logan introduced a resolution regarding "the recent mutilation of one of the cadets at West Point."[8] This referred to a young black cadet named Whittaker, who'd had his ears cut off by his fellow West Pointers. Bruce and his friend Senator Hoar were horrified. The preposterous defense that West Point administrators were advancing was that racial hostility and harassment did not exist at the school, and that what had actually happened was that the black student cut off his own ears. Although it would be hard to believe that anyone would do such a thing to himself, only Bruce and Hoar raised the obvious points. Like others, they knew that the academy had preferred to remain all white, and that the cadets resented the one or two black students who had been admitted during the past several years.

It was the liberal senator George Hoar who made the point that the cadet was black and was, no doubt, mutilated by the whites who had been harassing him in order to get him to leave. After Hoar and Bruce had become exasperated with the senators' feigned confusion over what might have happened, Hoar said, "The treatment of the colored pupils at West Point stands by itself alone. The colored boys who have entered West Point have been subjected to a course of treatment there, which, if it cannot be put a stop to, will result in the abolition of the institution itself."[9]

Also disturbed that his colleagues were even considering the outlandish "self-mutilation theory," Bruce added, "It is asking entirely too much of me when I am called upon to believe that young Whittaker . . . would thus mutilate himself." And in pointing out that West Point hazing was vastly different from the hazing at other colleges and institutions, he cautiously added,

> I once said to a young colored man who asked me for my influence to secure him an appointment at this institution, that if he were my enemy, and I desired to inflict a severe punishment upon him, I would send him to West Point. But in cases of this sort it makes no difference whether the cadet is white or colored, and I have not for a moment stopped to consider that phase of the question . . . The Senate ought to know all the facts in [this] case, and the guilty parties should be promptly and adequately punished.[10]

Although Bruce qualified his remarks with words that suggested a "racial color blindness" on his part—a frequent and almost exasperating habit that he practiced in order to gain the support of white colleagues—he allowed his voice to be used in the case of a black man whom few others had intended to assist. He had clearly come to terms with how he was going to offer support to his own race while offending the fewest moderate white political leaders. By this time, his last year in the Senate, he was finally at ease about pursuing issues of particular interest to the larger black community.

On the morning of May 22, 1879, barely a month after giving birth to her baby boy, Josephine Bruce saw her name in the *Washington Post* society column. The *Post*'s headline read simply "Roscoe Conkling Bruce." It was the first time she had ever seen her son's name in print. The story followed underneath:

There was a small gathering of friends at the house of
Senator Bruce last evening to celebrate the first month of
the existence of his infant son and to select a name for him.
With great unanimity "Roscoe Conkling" was selected.
The christening will be celebrated on the occasion of the
visit of Senator and Mrs. Bruce to Cleveland, it being
deferred to that time in order that the ceremony may be
performed by the former pastor of the lady.[11]

On the very same day, an article about the naming of their child
also ran in the *Washington Republican*.[12] While nearly as ambitious as
her husband, Josephine was always fairly reticent about her private life.
In fact, having grown up in an upper-class black family where children
were appropriately named after deceased or living relations who were
dearly beloved (she was named after her father; her sister Emily was
named after her aunt; her aunt Elizabeth was named after her grandmother), she still thought it peculiar that they should be taking a family
name that bore no ties—except the professional ties of her husband—to
her family's blood or history. She braced herself for the often-told story
of how Senator Roscoe Conkling was the kind New York senator who
had escorted her husband to the front of the Senate Chamber on the
day Blanche was first welcomed to Congress.

But these were the public compromises that Josephine had to
accept as she and her husband maneuvered through the white Washington society that lay before them. Only days later, when Blanche presented her with an engraved set of silver from Senator Conkling, it
must have become clear to her why Blanche believed that these compromises paid off. The inscription on the silver cup read "To Roscoe
Conkling Bruce from his friend, Roscoe Conkling, 1879."

Blanche also attached an article from a Boston newspaper, that
demonstrated how his own compromises had very quickly become
hers. It read:

There was an interesting social event at the residence of
Senator Bruce this evening. A number of friends were
invited to take part in selecting a name for his babe—a
boy. It was finally agreed that the election should be left

with Mrs. Bruce, and she knowing the cordial relations of
her husband and the Senior Senator from New York,
decreed that the son's name should be Roscoe Conkling
Bruce.[13]

With that, Josephine knew that she could no longer say that it was
only her husband who had agreed to render their private lives public.
With the assistance of a cook, a personal maid, and a nanny for their
only child, Josephine continued to serve as a busy hostess at their four-
story town house on M Street. Interestingly, although both he and his
wife had grownup with several siblings, neither one of them showed an
interest in having a large family. Since there was no shortage of money
and no indication that she had any medical complications during the
childbearing years, it is likely that Blanche's career ambitions and his
related professional and social demands on Josephine were likely reasons for their decision to only have one child.

The strategizing that went into making decisions about the Bruces'
personal lives was no less rigorous than that which was used to decide
the senator's stand on political issues. As much as he cared about helping blacks and representing the black experience, Bruce walked the
fine line between the two races in an effort to remain in power and not
offend either group. It was an approach that was quietly antagonizing
the black press and other black observers whom he had not fully
befriended. And it was further evidence for people who had watched
the senator oppose the back-to-Africa movement in 1877, and who had
watched him remain deafeningly silent on the 1879 Kansas-exodus
movement.

The fact that Blanche had spoken out strongly on behalf of Chinese
immigrants might have endeared him to white liberals who thought
this was evidence of his fearlessness on race issues, but it did little to
help him in the eyes of blacks. They were left even more certain that
Blanche acted on behalf of blacks when he needed their support, and
acted *against* them when it would help create a politically expedient distance from them. They perceived him as wanting to be seen as black
but not "too black."

For those black constituents who knew the details surrounding his
private life, Blanche's behavior was even more troubling. Many members in the black community were honored that one of their own repre-

sented the race so eloquently and with such dignity that racial stereo-
types about black people were laid bare. Nevertheless, some blacks were
becoming weary of seeing what they perceived as an upper-class black
family avoiding contact with the black masses. These black constituents
and otherwise proud onlookers started to conclude that the Bruces
wanted little to do with ordinary blacks. Their wealth, their mostly
white social network, their membership in the white First
Congregational Church of Washington, as well as their insistence on
championing issues that had multiracial support rather than those
that had only black support, served to distance the Bruces from the
working-class blacks in Washington and the blacks back home in
Mississippi.

It was an issue that would continue to worry the senator, for
although he wanted to preserve his political viability, his frequently
stated goal was to improve the lives of black people who no longer had
black leaders in Congress. The problem for him was that he justifiably
worried that the white power structure would take away his power if
he was perceived to favor his own people above whites.

One way in which he demonstrated this passion for creating a
black legacy was the effort as well as the personal and political capital
he used in order to investigate and salvage the financial losses suffered
by more than seventy thousand black families when the Freedman's
Savings and Trust Company failed and lost $57 million in black-owned
funds and real estate. The bank had originally been established at the
end of the Civil War, and had been created as a place to accept money
deposited by blacks, as well as to make small loans to black freedmen
who wanted to buy land or build homes. During its final months, after
years of mismanagement, Congress had asked Frederick Douglass to
head the bank. A short time after that, the bank was closed by the federal government. Although Douglass was not given the position until
after the bank had already begun its spiral toward insolvency, many
Republicans feared that the Democrats would ignore the nine years of
mismanagement that preceded Douglass and try to pin the bank's failure on the black politician's four-month tenure, as a way to embarrass
him, blacks, and the Republican Party.

In April 1879, the Senate appointed Bruce to head a committee to
investigate the collapse of the bank, which had operated more than
thirty branches located throughout the South. Angus Cameron, Repub-

lican from Wisconsin; Augustus Garland, Democrat from Arkansas; John Gordon, Democrat from Georgia; and Robert Withers, Democrat from Virginia were appointed to work on the Bruce Committee from May 1879 until March 1880 in order to complete the investigation surrounding the bank's activities.[14]

In order to thoroughly review bank documents, as well as conduct hearings and interviews with former employees of the bank and its many branches, Bruce hired a staff that included accountants and office personnel. Since the bank had operated from March 3, 1865, until June 28, 1874, there were volumes of information to review, and the senator did not miss a single hearing as he collected data for his Senate report.

In the end, when Bruce's Senate committee filed their report, a well-researched and appendixed document of more than five hundred pages, it was shown that the mismanagement had, indeed, predated Douglass's four-month involvement with the bank. In fact, records showed that bad management decisions had been rendered on a regular basis for the prior three years, and that Douglass had even attempted to use some of his own money to help the bank meet its obligations to the poor blacks who had relied on it.

Because Bruce realized that many of the black depositors incorrectly assumed that the federal government had guaranteed the bank's deposits, he felt that Congress should find some way to repay the losses that the blacks suffered. Furthermore, he believed it was unfair to penalize all of the depositors simply because of internal mismanagement and the bank's failure to properly secure the loans it was offering to borrowers. In a valiant but failed attempt, Bruce introduced a bill that would reimburse the depositors. He further arranged that the bank's main building in Washington be sold, thus making it possible for the bank to distribute sixty-two cents on the dollar to depositors. Although it took several years to accomplish this, Bruce's work to help the thousands of disappointed and bankrupt black depositors was eventually acknowledged by many. It was an act that helped restore his reputation as a champion for black Southerners, and it would later put him in a favorable position as future presidents considered him for appointments in their administrations.

CHAPTER TEN

c*∂©©∂>

1880–1888

Bruce Leaves the Senate, Joins the Treasury
Department, Then Enters Private Life

I am a Negro, and proud of my race.
—BLANCHE K. BRUCE
May 19, 1883

BY JANUARY 1880 — MIDWAY THROUGH THE FORTY-SIXTH CONGRESS —
Bruce began to feel at ease among his Senate colleagues. It was then
that he gained a true sense of a senator's power, even though it was now
severely impeded by those who belonged to the opposing party. With
the Democrats now controlling the Mississippi state legislature, he recognized that a second term would not be available to him or any other
Republican who desired his Senate seat. He knew that during the next
thirteen months, he would have his last opportunity to leave a mark
alongside the work of those legislators whom he admired in the Senate
Chamber.

As the Mississippi politician reflected on the past five years of his
term, he surveyed the room and recalled the men he had met there and
the impact they had made on his life and on his decisions. The ones he
respected most were all considerably wealthy Republicans who had
attended prestigious schools, supported liberal causes, established great
dynasties, and left important legacies. He wanted his own life, his

wife's and son's lives, to be the beginning of a meaningful legacy for their descendants.

Several of his Senate colleagues had left a strong impression. There was his first mentor, the liberal Roscoe Conkling from New York, who had displayed the courage to escort a black man to the front of the Senate. Considered combative and fiercely partisan, Conkling remained true to his liberal beliefs and never hesitated to confront his conservative colleagues. Only weeks after Bruce's term came to an end, the courageous Conkling would end up resigning from the Senate in June 1881 as a protest against federal appointments made by President Garfield.

His Republican Senate colleague who was seated next to him throughout the Forty-fifth Congress, George Hoar of Massachusetts, also represented a dynasty that Bruce hoped to emulate. He and Hoar had, together, openly opposed the discriminatory Chinese immigration policy in 1879. During that same year, on February 14, Hoar had aided Bruce in becoming the first black to preside over the Senate. George Hoar was the son of liberal U.S. congressman Samuel Hoar, and the brother of Ebenezer Hoar, a famous anti-slavery Whig who had served in the Massachusetts Senate, later became attorney general under President Grant, and then a U.S. representative while Bruce was still in the Senate. The Hoars, all graduates of Harvard, gave Bruce the idea of sending his son to that school as well as to Exeter, where George's nephew, Sherman, had attended.[1] In fact, Sherman Hoar graduated Exeter in 1878 and entered Harvard's class of 1882 while his uncle George and Senator Bruce were working together on several Senate bills. Years later, members of the Hoar family would write letters of recommendation for Senator Bruce's son, Roscoe, to support his applications to both schools.[2]

The New Jersey senator who was assigned a seat next to him for three years, seat number three in the chamber, was representative of another Republican dynasty that Bruce admired. Frederick Frelinghuysen was the son of Theodore Frelinghuysen, New Jersey's powerful state attorney and U.S. senator. His grandfather Frederick had been U.S. senator from 1793 to 1796. His nephew, Joseph, would later be elected to the U.S. Senate, and his great-grandson would be a Republican congressman from New Jersey, as would his great-great-grandson.

As Bruce looked at his own career and the future career of his young son, he, like many of his colleagues, thought of the success that he wished for his descendants. The question was how to create the opportunities for his son and these future generations when he had the modest background of a former slave and barely a generation of political connections. With several bank accounts, a large plantation, multiple rental properties, and an elegant wife with good credentials and an important presence in the community, he had, so far, proved his worth rather successfully. Now, he had to build a memorable legacy. He had no doubt decided sometime in late 1879, after Roscoe's birth, that he would use these last months to begin establishing a Senate legacy of opining on the controversial race issues that were important to liberals and blacks. He had begun it by introducing, in December 1879, a bill that was intended to aid several black colleges. The idea was that these colleges would be awarded any salary money that had not been claimed by deceased black Civil War soldiers. The next move for the normally reticent Bruce was to begin making demands for the starving black Kansas "exodusters," who had migrated from the South to avoid racial harassment. He had begun these public demands in the Senate in February 1880, and he continued them until the late winter of 1881, when he supported a Senate petition from his college schoolmate, George Cornelius Smith, that sought to give pensions to the heirs of colored soldiers in the same manner that heirs of white soldiers were receiving them.[3]

During this time, he also spoke in favor of the United States improving its treatment of both the Chinese in California and the Ute Indians in Colorado. On April 7, 1880, he told his Senate colleagues, "Our Indian policy and administration seem to have been inspired and controlled by a stern selfishness."[4] In the later months of 1880, he turned to the treatment of blacks and pushed his colleagues to investigate the rumors about the racial harassment of the injured black West Point cadet. And of course, the issue into which he put his greatest efforts involved his work in chairing the subcommittee that investigated the collapse of the all-black Freedman's Bank.

But even with the suddenly bold racial stands that Bruce was now taking, there was one character trait that he refused to relinquish: his almost single-minded obsession for maintaining favor with powerful whites. In this regard, he remained extremely successful. For example, although they represented opposing political viewpoints and differed dramatically on race issues, Mississippi Democratic Senator Lucius Lamar and Bruce became very close colleagues during this time.

While they both represented the same state, the mutual respect and friendship that developed between them was almost disconcerting, given their drastically different backgrounds. The powerful Lamar, who was clearly a beneficiary of the racial violence during the 1875 Mississippi elections, not only spoke of Bruce in complimentary tones in his presence but also advocated on his behalf in the company of white Democrats and Republicans. In January 1881, Lamar argued that Bruce should be considered for a position in President Garfield's cabinet.[5] Other Southern Democrats, like Congressmen Otho Singleton and Jonas Chalmers, agreed with Lamar in that they preferred Bruce to most any other Republican who was being considered for Garfield's cabinet. Although Garfield was an avowed Republican, he knew that he needed to curry favor with the Southern power brokers, and he was no doubt surprised to learn that Bruce—a black man—had become the Southern Republican who had met the Democrats' approval.

But while it was a surprise that Lamar, a segregationist, would have spoken so highly of Bruce, there was probably a logical explanation for why Bruce courted Lamar's support so aggressively. When James Alcorn left the Senate in 1877, and Rutherford Hayes became the new Republican president, Bruce naturally expected that, as the senior senator from Mississippi, he would have control over the patronage appointments handed out by the president in his state. Although this was a reasonable expectation, it was not to be fulfilled by Hayes, who instead chose to rely on white Mississippians—most of whom held no political office, and several of them Democrats—to advise him on who should receive federal jobs. Even though Bruce had reached out numerous times to Hayes—first in a June 25, 1876, letter to the presidential candidate, and then again in a private White House meeting between the two in late March 1877—Hayes refused to honor Bruce with an advisory role.

Understandably, Bruce was insulted by the racial slight, but he addressed it by building a stronger relationship with the junior Mississippi senator, Lucius Lamar. Even though Lamar was a Democrat, and even though Hayes had gone so far as giving plum jobs to some Mississippi Democrats in order to strengthen his white Southern base, the black senator knew that his own influence would be enhanced once he built alliances with multiple power brokers.

In addition to Lamar, the other important leaders who helped increase his influence while he was in the Senate included his friend John R. Lynch, the congressman from Mississippi. Lynch, who had been speaker of the House in the Mississippi legislature, was elected to the U.S. House of Representatives first in 1872, then again in the controversial 1875 elections, and then for a final term in 1880.

A savvy political strategist, Lynch had worked closely with Bruce to maintain the strength of the Republican vote in Mississippi so that white national leaders could not overlook that state's Republican electorate or its black Republican leaders. As two former slaves who understood the white power structure within both the Democratic and Republican parties, both Bruce and Lynch maintained control over the Mississippi Republicans throughout Bruce's Senate career and well into the late 1880s. They held on to this control with the assistance of a third black leader, James Hill, who had become Mississippi's secretary of state when the more liberal Adelbert Ames had been elected governor in 1873.

But as Bruce looked toward the end of his own term and considered his future with Josephine and Roscoe outside of the Senate, he must have contemplated his status in Washington as a former senator. He knew that in order to maintain his social and economic stature, he could not return to a Democrat-controlled Mississippi and settle permanently in an environment that was brimming with white supremacists who were still killing and harassing black residents.

In late May 1880, the Republicans prepared to gather for their national convention in Chicago. Before the convention opened on June 2, the leading candidate being discussed for the presidential nomination was former president Ulysses S. Grant. Despite a history of scandal and mismanagement during his presidency, Grant's image had recently been resurrected and made to seem more statesmanlike during his two-year post-presidency trip throughout Europe and Asia. During these months of 1878 and 1879, Grant's visits with Queen Victoria in England, Chancellor Bismarck in Germany, Prime Minister Disraeli in England, and Emperor Mutsuhito in Japan served to make him once again look like a revered world leader. Grant had the support of Roscoe Conkling, as well as Bruce's friend John Lynch. Another large group of Republican leaders was supporting liberal Maine senator James Blaine.

Confounding to many was Bruce's insistence on backing former Ohio senator John Sherman, who was currently serving as treasury secretary under President Hayes.

Always clever and calculating, Bruce no doubt had some strong reasons for supporting Sherman, an obvious long shot behind both Grant and Blaine. One explanation for his decision might have been that Bruce wanted to display loyalty to President Hayes, who was himself backing his fellow "Ohio son." In addition, Bruce had worked well with Sherman when he had joined the Forty-fourth Congress in 1875.

But a more likely explanation for Bruce's support is one fraught with expediency. It is quite possible that he was looking down the road at his own future and contemplating the political appointment that he wanted for himself after his Senate term expired in nine months. If he already knew that he wanted to serve as register of the U.S. Treasury, a substantial position and office that reported to the secretary of the Treasury, he could have been prescient enough to realize that a recommendation from the current secretary of the Treasury—John Sherman—would be beneficial.

By supporting Sherman, he could hedge his bets. If Sherman got the nomination for president and later won, Bruce would be rewarded with the job he wanted, because Sherman would simply give it to him. If, however, Sherman *lost* the nomination to another Republican who won the presidency, Sherman might be kept on as Treasury secretary and hire Bruce. If a Republican president did not keep Sherman in the job—the third scenario—Sherman still could recommend Bruce for the job of register of the Treasury. It was a calculated gamble, but the odds were in Bruce's favor.

In the end, after Bruce arrived for the opening of the June 2, 1880, convention with Lynch, Hill, and his Senate friends Conkling and Hoar, he discovered that Sherman stood no possibility of gaining the nomination. According to the convention's proceedings, Sherman was consistently behind both Grant and Blaine when the votes were tallied during the fourth day of the convention.

Surprising to many people was Grant's gradual loss of popularity among the delegates during the days of the convention. Bruce and others watched as his mentor, Roscoe Conkling, led the Grant delegates with a confidence bordering on arrogance. When a handful of West Virginia Republicans voted differently from Conkling on a technical matter, he attempted to have them thrown out of the convention. His intimidating airs managed to offend delegates who were originally undecided about Grant. The fact that Grant did not appear at the convention made Conkling's cause all the more difficult. By the sixth day of the convention, it became clear that Grant no longer held a wide margin over Senator Blaine.

Finally, former Ohio congressman James Garfield, who had been supporting Sherman's candidacy, was asked to become the compromise candidate. A former Civil War general, Garfield first protested against being considered, but after some gentle persuasion and an additional vote, he easily won the Republican nomination.[6]

Born in Cuyahoga County, Ohio, in a log cabin in 1831, Garfield had worked his way through Williams College in western Massachusetts and was considered a highly ethical man. A former classics professor who had served as a college president before joining the Union Army, he was known for detesting the corrupt practices of political patronage—a fact that would later put him at odds with the powerful Roscoe Conkling.

Although Bruce had miscalculated and supported Grant in his final losing convention vote to Garfield—thereby putting himself in temporary disfavor with Garfield—the black senator did receive two flattering nods during the convention, which added to his stature. First, he had the opportunity to preside over the convention for a short period when convention chair George Hoar gave him control over the floor. In addition, Bruce was given a courtesy of being among those nominated to be Garfield's running mate. Although short-lived and never expected to be embraced by many convention delegates, Bruce's nomination as candidate for vice president of the United States concluded with surprisingly positive results. In a field of nine vice-presidential nominees, including James Alcorn and Chester A. Arthur, Bruce came out as the fifth highest vote-getter—just edging out Alcorn. Bruce and his closest Republican friends knew that he would never seriously seek the position of vice president, but the voting results particularly enhanced his prestige, since he attracted more support than Alcorn, the successful white Mississippi native who had already served as both U.S. senator and governor of the state. Bruce withdrew his name from consideration afterward. And in the end, with the strong

support of Roscoe Conkling, New York's Chester A. Arthur was chosen as the vice-presidential candidate to run with Garfield.

When James Garfield was finally elected president that fall, several
white Republicans, as well as the Southern Democratic senator Lamar
and other Mississippi Democrats, encouraged Garfield to appoint
Bruce to a cabinet position. Garfield refused to bestow that honor, even
in the face of a shockingly complimentary endorsement of Bruce by
Lamar. Lamar and his Democratic colleagues had a very short list of
Republicans that they would support for cabinet posts, and Bruce was
among them. In January 1881, Lamar said, "Mr. Bruce's conduct in the
Senate has been such as not to alienate himself from the Southern people. He is an intelligent man, and the best representative of his race in
public life."[7] Bruce was similarly supported by his longtime mentor
Roscoe Conkling, whose opinion normally carried great weight. Unfortunately for Bruce, Garfield found Conkling to be arrogant and controlling, and may have intentionally disregarded Bruce's qualifications
for a high position simply because he *was* a nominee of Conkling's.
Whether it was because of Bruce's race or Bruce's mentor, it would be
two months before Garfield finally offered him a job with the administration, and in the end, it would not be at the cabinet level. It would
take another eighty-four years before a black was appointed to a presidential cabinet.[8]

December 1880 was the beginning of Bruce's last session in Congress, and he knew the weeks would be slipping by him quickly. During the prior fall, the Democrats had elected his successor, the
Democratic Mississippi state chair James Z. George, a bitterly racist
man who had been responsible for inciting much of the violent activity
against blacks and white Republicans in the election of 1875. That the
state could send someone like George was a clear sign to Bruce that his
own future lay in Washington and not back home in Mississippi. He
would, of course, maintain his plantation there and keep a stake in the
Southern state for political party purposes. But it was more essential to
stay in Washington with a meaningful political appointment, while also
keeping an active hand in the Republican Party.

In terms of policy making—or, at least, advancing a coherent political ideology—Bruce's last year in the Senate was his finest. Despite the
fact that the Democrats exerted enormous control over the entire gov-

ernment by 1880, controlling both the Senate and the House, Bruce had finally gained the confidence and self-esteem that allowed him to address subjects about which he honestly cared. Learning from those few remaining white liberal senators, like New York's Roscoe Conkling and Massachusetts's George Hoar, he developed a fortitude for speaking out on race-related issues—issues that he'd spent most of this Senate term avoiding.

Bruce made his boldest statements and the greatest gestures toward assisting the nation's deprived race from February 1880 until he left on March 3, 1881, including his support of assistance for the "heirs of colored soldiers."

During his last few weeks in the Senate, Bruce presented a petition that had been brought to him by his old Oberlin schoolmate and friend George Cornelius Smith. As Bruce's presentation described it, the petition was in support of a House bill titled "An Act for the Relief of the Heirs of Colored Soldiers." Bruce wanted to provide financial aid to widows and children of black men who served in the Civil War and further said that it was "an act to place colored persons who enlisted in the army on the same footing as other soldiers as to bounty and pensions."[9] Opportunities that gave the senator a chance to advocate for black citizens had been rare and almost nonexistent during his first four years in office, but Bruce finally seemed to be comfortable with the presentation of these issues by his last two or three sessions in the Senate.

During the remaining four weeks of this third and final Congress of his career, Bruce organized his Senate papers and files from the last six years. He also spent time trying to lobby the various advisers to President Garfield, hoping that there would be a job for him as soon as the new administration began its work. He found himself working on this up until the eve of Congress's last day in session.

On Wednesday, March 2, 1881, he had not gotten home until almost ten o'clock at night. It had been an extraordinarily long day in the chamber; the senators finally adjourned at 8:33 in the evening, as everyone had expressed an urgency to get through as much business as possible.[10] Since Bruce knew that Thursday, March 3, was to be his last day in the Senate, he, too, had been anxious to accomplish as much as possible in those final hours the night before.

On March 3, after Senate Chaplain Reverend J. J. Bullock offered the morning prayer, Bruce looked at his watch and noted that it was just a few minutes after eleven a.m. He knew that twenty-four hours from then, he would be entering a new phase in his life. He would be a former U.S. senator—a man without a job. He also knew that in the next session of Congress, only two black members would be present, both of them in the House of Representatives. And he knew that his home state would be represented by two Democratic senators, Lucius Lamar and James George, a sign of what the South had been able to reclaim for itself.

After a morning of pushing through final pieces of legislation, the last minutes of the Forty-sixth Congress were spent on swearing in Vice President–elect Chester A. Arthur into the position as the Senate's presiding officer. Vice President William A. Wheeler then thanked the senators for their patience and leniency as he performed his job as Senate president. With those words, Blanche knew that the day was over. The Mississippi senator packed up his papers and placed them into his leather satchel. He looked up to see the afternoon sunlight shining through the glass panels above the large room, and then he walked out of the Senate Chamber and across the hallway's brightly colored Minton tile floors for the last time.

Like many of his Republican friends, Bruce was concerned that James Garfield did not appreciate the importance of rewarding party leaders with plum appointments, and might drag his feet in giving him a position with the administration. He feared that Garfield, a former army general who rose out of Ohio politics, was going to be just as stubborn as the Ohio-born president that had preceded him. In fact, when Rutherford B. Hayes had made his major appointments four years earlier, he offended old-line Republicans, who had remained loyal to the Union, by naming former senator David Key of Chattanooga, Tennessee, to the powerful position of postmaster general. An avowed Democrat, Key had been an officer in the Confederate Army. Hayes had also disturbed Bruce and other party leaders by making it illegal for men holding federal offices to serve as party officials. Given the fact that Hayes had gotten the presidency through party-leader negotiations—and not by winning the popular vote—it was ironic that he came to embrace such seemingly ethical and non-partisan practices.

Bruce hoped that Garfield had a better appreciation of the factions that had brought him to power, and how they should be rewarded. While many of Bruce's friends thought that there was a possibility that he could be the first black member of a presidential cabinet, he was more of a realist. He knew that he was popular among the Republicans, as well as some of the Southern Democrats, such as his former Senate colleague from Mississippi, Lucius Lamar, but Bruce sensed that no amount of popularity would bring a black man into Garfield's cabinet.

The fact that Bruce had not been an early supporter of President Garfield was another strike against his position as a future cabinet member. Another factor that weighed against Bruce was his friendship with Senator Conkling, who had quickly become a thorn in Garfield's side. Haughty and uncompromising, Conkling had grown accustomed to wielding complete power in all matters involving his home state of New York—even when federal issues came into play. When Garfield challenged Conkling's control of the port of New York—specifically, the New York Custom House, an important financial and political institution in Conkling's state—the senator spoke out against Garfield and encouraged other Republicans to do the same. Conkling believed that the Custom House was an important cog in his wheel of patronage, and he did not want the president involved with it. Garfield made it clear that ports and customs were a federal issue and that he was not going to allow Conkling to control it as if it were a local favor bank.

With Bruce's past and present career closely tied to Conkling's, it is likely that Garfield was not inclined to do Bruce any favors. Nevertheless, Bruce pinned his hopes on an appointment to serve either as a foreign minister or as register of the Treasury; the latter ran a sizeable department of at least 150 employees and reported to the Treasury secretary.

After hearing rumors that Garfield would be appointing Bruce's friend Frederick Douglass to the position of Washington's recorder of deeds, the senator approached Garfield's advisers about the Treasury job. Garfield responded by proposing two positions to Bruce: foreign minister to Brazil or assistant to the postmaster general.

Bruce was unimpressed. To his closest friends, he revealed that he was rather insulted. He declined both offers. The job as the postmaster general's assistant did not seem sufficiently lofty for a former senator, and he felt it would not be appropriate for him or any other black man to serve as foreign minister to a country that still practiced slavery.

But in actuality, there were more pressing reasons for turning down the Brazil post. First of all, he knew that his wife, who maintained close relations with her parents and her sisters, would never consent to moving their home and their two-year-old son outside the country. Second, Bruce knew that he would not be able to monitor his plantation and other rental properties in Mississippi, or remain active in the Republican Party, if he relocated outside of the United States for the four-year appointment. His third and final reason for turning down the Brazil position was its relative prestige. Bruce relished the idea of breaking barriers. Foreign-minister positions had been handed out by past presidents to respected blacks like John Langston and Ebenezer Bassett. These men had both served in Haiti, and attorney James Turner had served as minister to Liberia. As a former senator, Bruce wanted a position that would eclipse them all and that would underscore his importance over and beyond any other black who had received a presidential appointment in the past. In his mind, that position could only be register of the U.S. Treasury—a post that would place his name on U.S. currency and which was ranked higher than any previous job given to a black presidential appointee. The post was not in the cabinet, but it would be held in high regard in political and social circles.

When Bruce proposed the idea to Garfield's representatives, it was met with immediate resistance. At first, Garfield's people stalled the nomination, claiming that it would be too awkward to have great numbers of white women working for Bruce's department. Bruce and his closest advisers suspected that one reason Garfield was dragging his feet on the position was because he and his advisers worried that if Bruce were given the position, his name and signature would have to be printed on all U.S. paper currency, alongside that of the U.S. treasurer and the secretary of the Treasury. The idea of having a black man's name on U.S. money was attractive to Bruce but confounding to Garfield's advisers.[11] Garfield's people were simultaneously expressing their annoyance with Bruce's biggest supporter, Roscoe Conkling, who was about to resign from the Senate out of protest against the other appointments that Garfield had made without Conkling's input.

Nevertheless, Garfield finally caved to pressure from Republicans as well as from Mississippi Senator Lamar, and nominated Bruce to the position of register of the Treasury on May 19, 1881. Bruce was enthusiastically supported by Garfield's Treasury secretary, William Windom, and quickly confirmed by the Senate. In his new position, Bruce reported to Windom, with whom he had worked for six years when Windom had served as a U.S. senator from Minnesota. A respected politician with his own large following, Windom had been a serious contender for the Republican presidential nomination at the Chicago convention that prior June.

As register of the Treasury, Bruce was responsible for maintaining records of all debts owed by or to the United States government and for tracking all federal money being spent. His office issued and transferred all government bonds and maintained records of gold certificates, interest notes, interest checks, and currency. Describing himself as the "bookkeeper" for the federal government, Bruce maintained an office staff of more than 150 full-time people. It was supplemented by an additional 45 part-time and temporary workers. Reporting to him were five division heads who ran departments focused on currency, notes, loans, tonnage, and expenditures. Despite President Garfield's concern regarding white women having to work for a government agency run by a black man, nearly half of the full-time staff were female.

In fact, although Bruce hired his black friend from Oberlin, George Cornelius Smith, and a few other blacks, he made little effort to improve the racial diversity of the office staff. Rather than facing criticism from the white community, Bruce actually heard more complaints from the black Washington community who argued that he chose white female workers in favor of black workers of both genders.

While his position was heavily administrative and consumed as much time as his former position in the Senate, it paid only $4,000 per year—about $72,000 in today's dollars. The modest salary made it essential that he maintain his rental properties and his thriving Mississippi plantation in order for him and Josephine to continue the lavish lifestyle that they had established in Washington several years earlier. Because he lacked an accounting background, his first months in the job were particularly challenging. He would arrive each day at his office in the massive Treasury Building, next door to the White House, before virtually anyone else. He studied hard to learn the inner workings of the office, and he relied heavily on his deputy, William Titcomb, who had been with the department for the past sixteen years. In his typical fashion of keeping long hours to compensate for his early lack of efficiency, Bruce soon impressed his top staffers, as well as the leading officials working with Treasury Secretary Windom.

On July 2, 1881, only four months into his appointment at the Treasury Department, Bruce and his colleagues learned that President Garfield had been shot in a Washington, DC, train station. The president had been waiting for a train to take him to a college reunion in Massachusetts when Charles Guiteau, a disgruntled political operative, approached Garfield with a revolver and, at close range, fired a bullet into his back. A small-claims lawyer who reportedly was disappointed by not receiving a position working for the U.S. consulate in Paris, Guiteau was perceived by many to be mentally deranged. Garfield lay ill for several weeks. Because of infection brought on by doctors who failed to sterilize their medical instruments, he finally died on September 19, and his vice president, Chester A. Arthur, was sworn in as the twenty-first president. The son of an abolitionist minister, Arthur had an impressive background in civil rights law, which he had practiced in a large New York City firm. Although he would later severely limit the rights of Chinese to immigrate to the United States, he believed strongly in the civil rights of black Americans. With this background, it was not surprising that Arthur was to let Bruce maintain his Treasury position throughout his term.

During the next two years, as Bruce worked as register, he and his Republican friends sought to continue building the party in the South. To their disappointment, they faced ongoing political and economic setbacks that undermined the black community. One of the greatest hurdles for Bruce and his friend John Lynch was an October 15, 1883, Supreme Court ruling that declared the Civil Rights Act of 1875 unconstitutional. The legislation, which Lynch, in particular, had worked so hard to pass eight years earlier, had prohibited discrimination in hotels, restaurants, theaters, and other public accommodations. The act punished violators by fining them $500, which they had to pay to the discrimination victim. When the act was struck down, it suddenly gave new permission to whites who had been looking for ways to further exclude blacks from public life.

Another loss for Bruce was more personal in nature, but it was caused directly by the very public setbacks that resulted from the dismantling of Reconstruction. In 1882 and 1883, he lost two helpful black colleagues who had served as role models and advisers in his own career as a Reconstruction-era politician. Alonzo Ransier of Charleston, South Carolina, had been elected lieutenant governor of South Carolina in 1870 and then served in the U.S. House of Representatives for a single term until 1874. Despite his successful political career, the end of Reconstruction brought on severe anti-black treatment, and the subsequent discrimination in employment left Ransier unemployable. He finally resorted to working as a street sweeper and a security guard in the Charleston Custom House. When he died in 1882, he was financially destitute. The following year, a similar end came to the career of Congressman James Rapier, who was first a successful black Alabama newspaper publisher and cotton planter, before being elected to Congress in 1872. Despite his wealth and his generous philanthropy toward black colleges, he also was unable to find work, and died penniless a decade later, in 1883.

These setbacks in the black community affected Bruce privately, but he was determined not to let them alter his public face. In fact, at times, his public stoicism gave him the appearance of seeming unmoved by the losses in the black community. His appointment as register of the Treasury might have prevented him from being able to serve as an officer in the Republican Party, because of an executive order signed by Garfield; nevertheless, he traveled extensively to give speeches on politics and race to church and political groups around the nation. In addition to maintaining his stature as an important political figure, these lectures allowed him to gain a sense of the national mood of the electorate—thus making him more effective as he strategized with his Mississippi friends John Lynch and James Hill. These national trips often elicited favorable articles about him from newspapers around the country, raising his national profile.

Bruce's influence and stature would have been far greater had two factors not been in play. One important factor that had managed to diminish his influence was the almost complete dismantling of his party in Mississippi. The White Leaguers and Mississippi Democrats had so terrified the remaining Republican carpetbaggers and scalawags in his home state that by 1883, most of them had left political life and either entered the practice of law or farming in the South, or had simply abandoned the state altogether for political activity in the North, moving to states as far as Illinois or even Colorado. One of Bruce's first mentors, former Mississippi governor Adelbert Ames, had left the state and settled into the flour-mill industry in New Jersey four years earlier. The South's "Redemption" period had frightened many other white former state Republican leaders into less controversial roles as small-business owners and merchants. Black Republican activists did not enjoy such easy transitions to private life. In the South, they now had to resume their previous second-class citizenship and work as laborers on plantations or move to urban areas in the North, where they also were resigned to work in low-level jobs reserved for blacks. With his home state lacking a meaningful Republican Party organization, Bruce had little to back him.

Another factor that weakened Bruce's status was President Chester Arthur's approach to the presidency and the Republican Party. Since Arthur had come to the presidency only upon Garfield's assassination, he had never positioned himself as a party unifier or even as a leader of the party. Even though he had been a longtime beneficiary of the New York State Republican Party spoils system when running the Custom House in New York, he immediately declared himself to be an independent thinker and spoke out against the system of party favors. Arthur quickly distinguished himself as a champion of the civil servant and supported legislation that made the awarding of government jobs more evenhanded. While Arthur won points with the civil-service community and brought greater integrity to the presidency, he further weakened the Republican Party's control of appointments. Bruce felt this weakened position in both his Mississippi and Washington activities.

On August 28, 1883, Bruce opened his mail to find a shocking piece of correspondence. It was a letter from his friend Frederick Douglass, but its tone was unlike any of the prior letters he had received over the years from this close adviser. In the letter, Douglass accused Bruce of making critical remarks about him behind his back. For a man who spent so much of his time crafting a positive image of himself as a discreet and faithful friend to the black and white elite, this accusation was a major disappointment to Bruce. The letter from Douglass mentioned that unnamed people in Washington were saying that Bruce was pleased to hear of Richard Greener's attacks on Douglass regarding the

Liberian immigration issue and other topics affecting black people. "You are reported as saying you hate me as much as Mr. Greener does," wrote Douglass. "But you keep in with me simply because you can use me."[12] The first black man to graduate from Harvard College (class of 1870), Greener had served as dean of Howard Law School, and had been a longtime advocate for black migration out of the South, to both Kansas and Liberia. Because Douglass had opposed migration, Greener had been a frequent critic of the famous abolitionist.

In the four-page letter, Douglass demanded that Bruce prove his friendship by putting a denial in writing and sending it to him. Douglass wrote, "May I ask you to send me a note in your own handwriting contradicting in positive language a statement . . ." It is not clear that Douglass had positive proof of Bruce's negative comments, but Douglass felt fairly sure that Bruce had been using him while also competing with him on a professional level. Douglass clearly used this opportunity to surreptitiously offer his own thinly veiled, backhanded criticisms of Bruce when he wrote that these rumors were probably being spread by the same enemies who "belittled your ability, denounced you as a failure in the Senate and affected to be ashamed of your political career."

Although the two men often competed against each other for the few political spoils that the white Republicans were willing to share with a handful of black men, the rift between Bruce and Douglass was never deep or permanent, because they often ended up socializing with each other and including each other in political strategy sessions. In fact, when Douglass married for the second time, in 1884, he asked Blanche and Josephine to serve as witnesses at his wedding. What was so newsworthy about this event was not just that it included two of the most influential black men in the nation at the time, but that Douglass's bride was a white woman. Having portrayed himself, and long been accepted as, an outspoken representative of black people's struggle for equality, Douglass was criticized widely for his decision to marry Helen Pitts, who was not only white but twenty years younger than he. Pitts, an outspoken feminist, was a graduate of Mount Holyoke College and had worked as Douglass's secretary and clerk when he was recorder of deeds for Washington, DC. Although her father, Gideon Pitts, was a white abolitionist from New York, he joined other whites and blacks in opposing this interracial marriage.

The fact that Senator and Mrs. Bruce participated in the event elicited further criticism from the black community, which had already accused the elite couple of preferring white social circles to the company of less affluent blacks.

In June of 1884, while still serving as register of the Treasury, Bruce was asked by President Arthur to serve as the director of the colored exhibits at the World's Industrial and Cotton Centennial Exposition, which was being held during 1884 and 1885 in New Orleans. Although segregated from the other elaborate displays at this national gathering, the exhibits under Bruce's control would represent each of twenty-three states and would emphasize the inventions, artworks, and other contributions black Americans had made to the nation. Although the assignment paid only modestly, it was a prestigious project that would attract international media attention to Bruce. The additional benefit was that the post would allow him all-expense-paid trips to the South, which would permit him to make stopovers at his Mississippi plantation.

As the summer approached, Bruce and his friends braced themselves for the coming fall 1884 presidential campaign. Having been diagnosed two years earlier with a fatal kidney ailment known as Bright's disease, President Arthur had little interest in running for reelection. Since he had also been recently widowed, it was clear that he lacked both the physical and emotional strength to launch a serious campaign even if he had been persuaded to push forward.

Still working with Mississippi's John Lynch and James Hill, Bruce attended the Republican National Convention in Chicago and got Lynch selected as temporary chair of the convention, where Lynch delivered the keynote address.[13] During the convention, the Republicans chose former Maine senator James Blaine as their candidate to challenge Democratic candidate Grover Cleveland. With an ailing president in the White House—one who was unwilling to run and unable to campaign very much for his own party—the Republicans were at a severe disadvantage.

Cleveland, an unmarried New York politician who had fathered a son out of wedlock, was the beneficiary of the Republicans' disorganization. Born into a poor family in Caldwell, New Jersey, Cleveland never attended college and had little formal education. He had served as mayor of Buffalo for only one year when he was elected governor of New York in 1882. During a long-term affair with a woman named

Maria Halpin, in 1874 he fathered an illegitimate child, whom he later acknowledged. Despite his obvious intellectual and moral failings, conservatives in the North saw him as the ideal candidate to represent the Democratic Party and unify it with their equally conservative brethren in the South. Because of Cleveland's anti-black views, his support of segregated schools in New York, and his belief in white supremacy, Southern Democrats immediately embraced him as a unifier of Northern and Southern conservatism. As a former governor of New York, he was almost certain to carry his home state, and as one who spoke of reducing the rights of blacks and openly complimented Confederate leaders, he was considered a great draw for the Southern vote. In the end, he won the presidency by winning New York State by a margin of less than 1,200 votes.

Like Blaine, Bruce was devastated by the loss. They both had expected the large black population in the South to have voted the Republican line and overcompensated for the large white Democratic turnout there. Infuriated by the large loss in the South, Blaine immediately accused racist Democrats in the South of suppressing the black vote—a believable and accurate assessment, given the white Southern practice of terrorizing black voters and creating poll taxes and other discriminating policies. But shockingly, possibly as a means of currying favor with the now-victorious Democrats, Bruce immediately and publicly turned on Blaine by announcing that Blaine was unfair to criticize the white Southerners of foul play. Bruce made the incredible and untrue statement to the *New York Times* that "The greatest of harmony has existed between the white and colored population and Mr. Blaine's charges of violence and intimidation at the polls are altogether false."[14] In the end, the remark did very little to help Bruce's case with the Democrats and only angered blacks and Republicans, who saw this as an example of the black senator's cynicism and hypocrisy.

With the Democratic president Grover Cleveland in office, Blanche knew that he had no hope of receiving any future political appointments. In fact, as the Democrats moved into every phase of public life in the nation's capital, Washington became an inhospitable city for most Republicans. And while retiring Republican officials were able to land positions in the private sector, Blanche knew that no such option was available to a black man. Despite his past influence, both the hate organi-

zations and white conservatives made it impossible for him to consider settling and raising his family in his home state of Mississippi.

He was able to keep his Treasury appointment for several months
into President Cleveland's term. At the beginning of the year, he traveled to New Orleans with Josephine and five-year-old Roscoe to continue his work as chief of the Department of Colored Exhibits at the
World's Industrial and Cotton Centennial Exposition. With displays
from twenty-three states, the colored exhibits showed everything from
patented products built by black engineers to elaborate dresses designed
and made by black seamstresses to literature written by black intellectuals and novelists.

While in New Orleans, he networked with several prominent families whom he had met through the black New Orleans newspaper
publisher and former lieutenant governor P. B. S. Pinchback. According to the personal date book that Bruce maintained at that time, he
attended the Creole Ball on January 1 and was entertained by several
prominent New Orleans families, including the Martinets, the Par-
rishes, and the Kennedys.[15]

He finally returned to Washington on January 7, leaving Josephine
and Roscoe in New Orleans for another six weeks, until February 18.[16]
Within days of his departure, it became immediately obvious that
accepting his role as chief of the Department of Colored Exhibits at the
World's Exposition had been a wise move, because it introduced him to
a whole network of representatives from different states around the
nation. In fact, what had really empowered Blanche was his authority
to appoint the black exhibit managers—one from each of twenty-three
states. So, almost as in government patronage jobs, Blanche was able to
reward certain allies in some states, honor one or two relatives in other
states, and build new friendships in states where he previously had no
contacts. For example, he appointed his brother James Bruce of
Brunswick as the Missouri representative. In Tennessee, he appointed
the wealthy Republican banker James C. Napier, who was also a close
friend of Bruce's Memphis friend Robert Church. In North Carolina,
he selected John Leary, a member of that state's best-known black families who had been free people of color. By using his power under the
exposition position and picking wealthy businessmen, socially important people, and well-connected Republicans, Blanche enhanced his
influence exponentially.

But along with this network came requests for assistance from people around the nation who sometimes did little or nothing for him in return. According to a reporter writing for the *Washington Bee*, "I really pitied Mr. Bruce, when here, as he was constantly in demand to adjust some petty annoyance brought on by the would be great men temporarily clothed with a little authority . . . but [Bruce] is so even in temper and gentle in manner."[17] Only two days after leaving New Orleans, he received a letter from the New York state commissioner for the Colored Exhibits, in which a Mr. P. W. Ray asked him for assistance in finding employment.[18] Even though Bruce had no ties to New York, the presumption for many people was that Senator Bruce was a powerful and influential black man who could help blacks in any part of the country.

One of the largest headaches to come out of the New Orleans exhibition was Blanche's rather public conflict with Archibald Grimké, a black 1874 graduate of Harvard Law School and popular civic leader among upper-class blacks at the time. Not long after Bruce had appointed Grimké as the Massachusetts representative, Grimké argued that it seemed discriminatory for the exposition to separate black exhibits from the rest of the exhibits. He felt that separating the accomplishments of blacks was to suggest that they were not on par with the achievements of whites which were displayed in the main part of the exposition. Blanche was forced to address the issue once Grimke resigned his position and the press demanded an explanation from the former senator. He defended the colored exhibits when he said, "This is the first and doubtless will be the last time that the colored people will want or have such an opportunity to show their advancement and deny the assertion . . . that freedom has not developed in them the higher aims . . . showing to the world what they have been able to do in less than twenty years of freedom."[19]

Just before the conclusion of the New Orleans exposition, Blanche wrote a resignation letter to the new Treasury secretary, Daniel Manning, informing him that he would be stepping down, as the new Democratic administration had requested of appointed officials from the Chester Arthur administration. Finally, on June 8, 1885, he ended his term as register of the U.S. Treasury. For several weeks, he had known that his position was being given to a Democratic congressman, William Starke Rosecrans, an appointee of Cleveland. A class of 1842 graduate of West Point, Rosecrans had been a Civil War general under Ulysses Grant. He had earlier served as minister to Mexico under President Andrew Johnson, and then as U.S. congressman from California for two terms. Noting the act carefully in his 1885 personal date book, Bruce turned his keys and documents over to Rosecrans at eleven o'clock in the morning on June 8 and went home to his wife and son.

Without a political position or the possibility of earning income through the private sector in Washington, Blanche relied on the income from occasional speeches and from his landholdings in Bolivar County. The cotton plantation and the rental properties that he owned there yielded enough to provide a comfortable life for himself, Josephine, and Roscoe.

Since he was not as occupied with political activities, he used this time to finally reconnect with his relatives who remained in the Midwest. It was now possible to accept one of the many family invitations that had been extended to him since his Senate term had ended in 1880. With his term as register of the Treasury concluded, Blanche could offer no excuse for missing the many family gatherings that had been arranged in Kansas and Missouri. Three months after he left his job, in early September 1885, he and six-year-old Roscoe boarded a train to visit his relatives in Leavenworth and Atchison, Kansas. Since his departure from the Missouri and Kansas area twenty years earlier, most of his family members had remained either in Brunswick with his brother James, or in Leavenworth, with his mother, Polly, and his two sisters.

Going home to his relations was a rare occasion for Blanche, but his siblings and cousins held no resentment for the prodigal son who had made good. Interestingly, there seems to be no record of Josephine's ever joining her husband on his visits home, even on those rare ones when he brought Roscoe. Despite the interest expressed by the Bruce relatives, Josephine made no effort to correspond or visit with his family members. She had not invited them to the wedding hosted by her parents in Cleveland, and many had still not met her ten years later.

Possibly feeling that her social class justified her lack of interest in his poor relatives, Blanche no doubt acquiesced to her snobbery and never insisted that she engage with his family members. Knowing that her own family included educated and well-to-do siblings, parents, and grandparents—none of whom had been slaves, like his family members—it is likely that Blanche might have felt that his relatives would embarrass or be made to feel out of place by her near-white appearance and upper-class mannerisms. Whatever his reasons for not insisting that she bond with his family, he often made excuses for her in his personal correspondence with them, and in his reports back to her. In a letter while he visited his family with Roscoe in the fall of 1885, Bruce wrote,

> *My darling wife, . . .Granny met me here. Roscoe is greatly delighted. All are well and send much love. Folks are very sorry that you did not come also, but I have explained that you could not get ready on so short notice. Roscoe says his cousins are all very good. Your husband, Blanche.*[20]

Although Bruce made excuses for his wife, it is unlikely that many of his relatives believed she wanted to be there; it would have been difficult to believe that Josephine would be unable to travel with her husband and son to Kansas when it had already been well publicized in the national press that she had traveled with him in the past to Europe, New Orleans, Mississippi, Indianapolis, and other distant locations. She had servants that took care of their home and her personal needs. She had only one small child, no job, and at this point was not yet active in her women's club affairs. Furthermore, she had no other family or responsibilities in Washington that should have occupied her time to such an extent that she could not have accompanied her son and husband on a trip planned well in advance of his resignation from his Treasury job. Except for her noted antipathy toward poor people, there was no reason why she should not have accompanied her husband on some of these visits to see his relatives.

Because Blanche continued to give political lectures on behalf of the Republican Party throughout the nation during his absence from political office, Josephine decided that she would temporarily relocate herself and Roscoe to Indianapolis, where her parents and two of her sisters, Mary and Victoria, were living.[21] Her parents had recently moved there from Cleveland, because her father had retired from his dental practice. As of late summer of 1886, Josephine's address was 449 College Avenue in Indianapolis, where Blanche also lived in between his lecture engagements. The nation's capital had become so inhospitable to Republicans, with Democrats controlling every branch of government, Blanche was glad to find an excuse to be away from Washington. Besides, the highly calculating Bruce might have recognized that a rising star in the Republican Party—Senator Benjamin Harrison, the nation's next president—was also a highly prominent attorney from Indianapolis. During their eighteen-month residence in Indianapolis, Blanche and Josephine grew closer to her parents and sisters, Mary and Victoria, who were well-established elementary-school teachers in the city. In addition to lecturing for the Republican Party, Blanche also began to lecture to nonpolitical audiences in Iowa, Ohio, Wisconsin, and Michigan through the Northern Lecture Bureau, a private agency that paid him $150 per speech.

In Indianapolis, Josephine and Blanche carved out a social life that was even more rarefied, in racial terms, than the life they had led in Washington. Here, they made even less of an attempt to socialize with the larger black community than they had in the capital. No longer surrounded by a circle of black upper-class friends, they retreated into a mostly white world. In their neighborhood and their activities, they represented the rare face of color. Like Josephine's parents, the young couple joined the city's all-white Saint Paul's Episcopal Church.

At around the same time, Josephine's renewed bonds with her family made her better acquainted with her brother's adult life. Several years older than she, Leonidas Willson had never been very close to Josephine or his other sisters after graduating from high school. By the time Josephine and Blanche had moved to Indianapolis, the divorced Leonidas was practicing law in a white firm in Cleveland. Neither Josephine nor her parents and sisters had ever used their light complexions as a means to pass into the white community, but Josephine suspected that once Leonidas married his second wife, Anna Foote, a very light-complexioned schoolteacher, he made the ultimate decision to cut off family relations, and begin to practice law only alongside whites, and cease socializing with blacks altogether. Although Josephine refers to her parents and sisters in many letters throughout her life, she makes no reference to Leonidas, which suggests that he had cut off any involvement in her or her family's lives by the time of his second marriage.[22]

Walking the line between black and white remained a delicate balancing act for most members of the Bruce family. Even once the senator was out of office, he was still quite circumspect in his rhetoric when he feared that it might carry racial implications. Although the press spoke of him as bold and outspoken, he was curiously cautious in his speeches, particularly when addressing the white media. He made points that might have seemed, at that time, progressive to whites, but he phrased his arguments in a peaceful, almost obsequious manner that sought to avoid offending, if not flatter, the white audience. Unlike Booker T. Washington, who insisted that blacks should be responsible for their own uplifting, Blanche pointed out that white people and the government had a responsibility for helping blacks, since it was their laws of slavery and discrimination that put blacks in their unfortunate situation. However, Blanche always tried to avoid using such words as "slavery," "discrimination," or other terms that might make white audiences feel responsible or uncomfortable.

In early 1887, he was lecturing in Philadelphia, and he gave an interview to the *Philadelphia Times* on the current state of blacks in America. When the interviewer asked him if Negroes in the South could meet their own educational needs without assistance, Blanche responded,

> No, they cannot . . . There are emergencies in the lives of com-
> munities as in those of individuals, which their strength will
> not meet, and after their best energies have been expended
> auxiliary aid is absolutely required. This is the condition . . . of
> the colored race in the South . . . The period has been reached
> when the national authority should intervene in the interest of
> this people. The power that gave them freedom should afford
> them such educational facilities as will render that gift valu-
> able.[23]

The former senator went on to explain that better elementary education, increased expenditure in technical training, and better-quality educational facilities were the responsibility of the federal government, and that blacks would not be able to improve their lives until the government assumed this role.

After spending eighteen months in Indianapolis, Blanche, Josephine, and Roscoe finally returned to Washington in March 1888. Bruce and other Republicans had grown more confident that they could take the city back from the Democrats. The Bruces bought an elegant town house, just off Dupont Circle, at 2010 R Street NW for $10,250, and picked up their Washington life where they had left off in 1886.

As the summer approached, Bruce once again made plans with Lynch to organize Mississippi Republicans. By the time they reached the Republican convention, they were optimistic that Benjamin Harrison might be able to take the White House from Grover Cleveland and the Democrats. Although he wasn't a dynamic personality or a physically impressive figure at five feet six inches, Benjamin Harrison was an easy candidate for Bruce to get behind. The grandson of former president William Henry Harrison, well educated and raised amid considerable wealth, Benjamin was a former Civil War general who had rather liberal views about blacks. Bruce was happy to support the Indiana senator's candidacy. Things looked ever more promising for the fall elections, because it appeared that the Republicans would reclaim the Senate and the House for the first time in twelve years.

The election of Benjamin Harrison in 1888 was a triumph for black Republicans, who had endured four years of Grover Cleveland's Democratic regime of discouraging the federal government from protecting the poor and underprivileged. Blanche traveled the nation, promoting the party platform and president-elect Harrison's candidacy, and fully expected that his hard work would be rewarded with a Washington job. This election year brought two new black members to the House of Representatives: John Langston of Virginia, who had earned a master's degree from Oberlin before serving as minister to Haiti under President Hayes, and Henry P. Cheatham of North Carolina, who had graduated from Shaw University and would later be appointed Washington, DC, recorder of deeds by President William McKinley. This was a great improvement over the prior term, which had no black members in Congress.

Because of his party loyalty, Bruce was confident that he would be able to return to Washington with a new political appointment. Since he had already served as senator and register of the Treasury, he hoped to return to Treasury or possibly to be considered for a cabinet post.

But even if Blanche had felt that his own fortunes were improving, he must have found them bittersweet as he saw opportunities for blacks falling farther behind, especially throughout the South. Not only was lynching on a rise—with the 1882–1888 period reflecting the highest number on record—but there was increasing anti-black backlash that resulted in additional discriminatory laws. Particularly disheartening was what seemed to be happening with greater frequency in his own home state: just months before President Harrison finally offered him a position, he saw that the South was continuing to regress in its treatment of black citizens. In its ongoing efforts to stigmatize blacks, Mississippi passed additional legislation to segregate the races in public waiting rooms and other facilities. With each advance Bruce seemed to make for himself, he found the rest of black America either slipping backward or exhausting itself trying to maintain gains from prior years.

CHAPTER ELEVEN

ᴄᴙᎾᏀᎠᴐ

1889–1895

Bruce Persuades President Harrison to Give Him a Job and His Wife Gains Her Independence

BLANCHE HAD ALWAYS MAINTAINED SUFFICIENT EMOTIONAL DIS-
tance from his family that he was able to avoid being drawn into
their personal dramas. On occasion, he received requests for money or
gifts, but their correspondence rarely revealed many specific details of
their problems. Because Josephine had a considerably closer relationship with her parents and sisters, she was more involved in their life
experiences—whether everyday concerns or more emotional episodes,
like those described in a letter she received from her father, Joseph
Willson.

Dr. Willson was a reserved man who generally showed little emotion, but he was clearly incensed by what had recently transpired in his
son Leonidas's home—and he wasted no time apprising his daughter of
the disappointing situation. Although Josephine had not maintained
close communication with her brother, a prosperous lawyer, since she
had left home ten years earlier, it seemed inconceivable to her that she
could have been so unaware of how unhappy his one-year-old marriage
to Anna Foote, a former schoolteacher had become. Even though they
had not corresponded, she had sufficient family members and friends
in Cleveland, where Leonidas lived, who should have called her attention to the discord before it became so public.

On August 28, 1889, Joseph Willson had written her a letter

explaining that Leon's wife had just deserted him and had done so secretly, by emptying their three-bedroom Cleveland home of all its furnishings and their personal effects while he was in a meeting with clients at work. Although Leon's housekeeper was able to save a few of his smaller possessions by quietly ferrying them over to a neighbor's house for safe storage, Anna had managed to hire a horse and wagon and transport virtually all the contents of the house across state lines.

Now living in Indianapolis, too far away to offer his son a safe haven, Joseph wrote to his daughter about her brother's dire situation. Evidently, Leon had also confided in his other sisters, Mary and Victoria, even forwarding them copies of the letters that had been left by Anna on the day she left their Cleveland home. Joseph's August 28 letter to Josephine said,

> *My Dear Daughter, You are acquainted with the leading*
> *fact of Anna's disappearance from Cleveland . . . You will*
> *be still more surprised when you read the enclosed letters.*
> *One of these letters was sent from Anna's mother to Anna. The*
> *pious old lady tells Anna that if she "could get away with some*
> *money," she need not "care for the things."*
> *   The other letter is from Anna to Leon and was left on his desk*
> *at the time of her departure . . . Leon seems ashamed that the world*
> *should know that Anna has left him, but it is a blessing for she has*
> *impoverished him. She has taken everything out of the house—*
> *the piano, beds, sheets, pillow cases, dishes, glasses, knives and*
> *spoons . . . The servant, seeing what was going on, took some lace*
> *curtains and a quilt to hide them with a neighbor . . .*[1]

Since Josephine had not been living in Cleveland for the past ten years, and since her parents had moved to Indianapolis in 1886 to be closer to their unmarried daughters, Mary and Victoria, Leon's life was rather a mystery to Josephine. Even though he would die rather early—in 1901—Leonidas had raised two daughters with his first wife. But neither he nor his children played a role in Josephine's adult life. In his early letters to Josephine during their courtship, Blanche asked about her sisters and parents but never inquired about her brother. Similarly, when addressing family affairs in her letters to Blanche, she never even mentions her brother's name.

This detached relationship between Josephine and Leonidas continued for almost her entire adult life. In fact, although her personal papers revealed correspondence to and from her three sisters and her parents throughout her later life, there are no records of correspondence between her and her brother—or any statements that include him or his two daughters—at any time between her marriage and her death in 1923.[2] The only records that address the relationship that she maintained with Leon are 1878 newspaper accounts that mention his wedding gifts and his involvement in Josephine's 1878 Cleveland wedding to Senator Bruce. Otherwise, he is the only family member that was specifically *not* referenced in Josephine's papers.

According to Joseph Willson, Leon's wife, Anna, had never been a good homemaker and had succeeded only in spending most of his son's money. It is possible that Anna's departure was related to the overwhelming responsibilities he had placed on her. Newly married, she was suddenly responsible for raising the two girls he had reared with his now deceased first wife—a white woman whose family were not very accepting of their black relations. It is not clear if the two daughters—Laverne and Leona—stayed with Leonidas or lived with another relative, but it is apparent that Anna and Leonidas did not remain married. Less than a year after Anna's departure, the couple were divorced. Interestingly, when he executed a will several years later, he would apologize to her for not being a better husband. Leon did, however, continue his legal practice in Cleveland.

In the midst of Josephine's family drama, Blanche was dealing with his own family crisis: the death of his mother, Polly. As the strong matriarch of the family, Polly had survived slavery and raised her own children as well as the children of four different families who had probably owned her. In what seemed like a complicated relationship not only between mother and son but also between the son and his siblings, Blanche had long ago established an arm's-length relationship with most of his relatives, who still lived in Kansas and Missouri. Perhaps because all of them had been slaves and most of them were, by now, poorly educated farmers—with the exception of his brothers Henry and James—Blanche did not maintain strong ties with them during his adulthood. Blanche did help Henry find government employment in Washington in the early 1880s, and he helped James by appointing him to a position to represent the state of Missouri in the colored exhibits at the World's Industrial and Cotton Centennial Exposition in 1884.

Henry also entered politics in the state of Kansas. While he never found the political or monetary success of his brother, he did attract moderate attention within state political circles. Henry was nominated by the Republican Party to run in the 1880 Kansas state legislature race. It was a close race; he lost to his Democratic opponent by only twenty-five votes. Because of his strong showing, party leaders rewarded him with the job of doorkeeper of the Kansas state Senate. When that position concluded, he found himself punished by local Democrats, who were seizing any gains that had been made by blacks in local political and business circles. Henry was unable to find work, and he ended up accepting a dangerous, low-paying job as a construction foreman on a project that involved laying railroad track between Kansas and Nebraska. He finally turned to Blanche for help. According to Henry, in his 1895 autobiography, *The New Man: Twenty-nine Years a Slave and Twenty-nine Years a Free Man*, Blanche told him that while he couldn't help him in Kansas, he could find him employment in Washington. Henry says that, in August 1881, "my brother, who was then Register of the U.S. Treasury, telegraphed that he could get me a position in the Post Office Department, at Washington, at a salary of seven hundred and twenty dollars per annum . . . and I accepted it and came to Washington."[3] A year later, Blanche found a position for Henry again. This time, it was an entry-level job in the United States Pension Department. This seemed to be the extent of Blanche's contact with his siblings during his years in Washington.

The only other family member Blanche remained in touch with was his mother, Polly. On at least two occasions, he brought his son, Roscoe, on Midwest excursions to visit with her. During his many lecture tours through the Midwest, he also visited her on his own, stopping in to see her after she moved from Brunswick, Missouri—where the family had resided at the end of the Civil War—to Leavenworth, Kansas. She had moved to Leavenworth to live with one of Blanche's sisters during the early 1880s, and had remained there until her death.

Because he was both secretive about his private life that preceded his marriage and stoic in dealing with personal setbacks, it was hard to know how Polly's death—and the years that preceded it—affected Blanche. Except for acknowledging that he had been born into slavery and raised by his mother, he never offered the press many details about his family's early background. This was presumably because it worked against the prosperous image that he had worked so hard to cultivate for the public. When his mother died, he did travel to Leavenworth, but it was an abbreviated trip. Of course, one might excuse his lack of filial dedication, because Polly's death also took place at a time when he was unemployed and fully preoccupied with the task of finding a position in the new administration.

Both Josephine and Blanche seemed able to suppress family members' personal crises and needs so that they could better focus on their own ambitions.

One of Blanche's ambitions was to convince President Benjamin Harrison's advisers to offer him an appointment—an appointment, in fact, that he had many reasons to feel he deserved. Since Blanche's temporary relocation to Harrison's home state of Indiana in 1886, he had been positioning himself as a "hometown" supporter of the former senator. Although Blanche had, in the past, claimed to be a native of Mississippi, or of Virginia, or of Missouri, this Washington resident was quick to claim his ties to Indiana—a state where he spent less than two years—when Indiana sent a native son to the White House.

Blanche knew that in order to gain credibility with President Harrison's people, he had to make it clear that he had been a longtime, "hometown" supporter of the president-elect—not just a new arrival to a winning campaign. And although Harrison was not a radical Republican, Blanche rightfully concluded that Harrison's prior pro–Native American and pro-Reconstruction policies were an indicator of his fairly liberal views about blacks in government. Prior to his election as president and during the first few months of his presidency, Harrison did, indeed, appear to embrace positive views about blacks. Soon after, in an attempt to mollify Southern Democrats, he began to advance a more conservative agenda and to support views that discriminated against blacks.

Blanche remained optimistic about getting a position from Harrison—even though he knew he was not being discussed as a cabinet candidate, as he had been after President Garfield's election. He simply hoped for a job that would allow him to retain some of the stature he had enjoyed while living in the city as senator and then as register of the Treasury. Gaining a prestigious job was necessary to him for two reasons. First, it assured him respectability among Washington's elite. And second, it allowed him to maintain his position as the leading black Republican in the small but still active state Republican Party organization back home in Mississippi. After all, that was still his long-term power base.

Within the black community at the time, it was believed that the best job any black man could get from Harrison would be recorder of deeds for Washington, DC, a job that was not nearly as prestigious as a national appointment or as a foreign minister. While the position was appointed by the president, and carried a good income and an impressive number of staff members, it was not at all what Blanche had in mind. He felt he deserved a much loftier position, but others told him not to hold much confidence in Harrison's ability to reward Bruce or any black man with a high-level post.

Bruce's optimism regarding a good job, however, was not completely unfounded: the last year had brought his family good fortune, and he had no reason to believe it was about to end. The Bruces had returned to Washington in the spring of 1888, after an eighteen-month stay in Indianapolis. Blanche and Josephine were enjoying life in their spacious Washington town house at 2010 R Street NW, where they entertained frequently and had plenty of space to raise ten-year-old, Roscoe. Both high-profile blacks and whites in the city dined and socialized in their home on numerous occasions. They continued to be the subject of flattering profiles in both black and white newspapers.

In June 1888, when the Republicans gathered in Chicago for their national convention, Bruce was once again considered among the nominees to run for vice president. Although the nomination would ultimately be given to New York's Levi Morton, Bruce's high status in the Republican party was confirmed, even in the absence of a Republican president. When former Indiana senator Benjamin Harrison was finally nominated by the Republicans, Bruce began campaigning aggressively throughout the Midwestern states of Indiana, Wisconsin, and Michigan on Harrison's behalf.

But despite Bruce's work, the newly elected president was slow to reward the former senator or any other blacks who had supported his campaign. In fact, although Blanche and Josephine assumed that Harrison would at least reappoint him to the position of register of the Treasury, by the summer of 1889, many blacks in the Republican Party had begun to realize that the tide had changed considerably. Because Harrison had not actually won the popular vote in the presidential elections (Grover Cleveland had gotten 5,540,309 votes as compared to Harrison's 5,439,853) but had won the office only by beating Cleveland's electoral college total by 66 votes, Harrison's advisers felt he had not earned sufficient political capital to antagonize the Democrats over issues the conservatives embraced dearly. In keeping with this view, Harrison quickly demonstrated a skill in pandering to those white Southern Democrats who were still upset that their more popular and more flamboyant candidate had lost on what some considered a "technicality."

In order to assure white Southerners he was still respectful of them, Harrison offered a statement that outlined how much he sympathized with whites who did not want to have political or professional contact with blacks. He said, "Personal contact with an alien race in social, political, and professional life would not be agreeable to me. I would not like to see a Negro Mayor or Postmaster of Indianapolis . . . It would not be agreeable to me to practice my profession before a colored Federal judge or to meet a Negro at the Federal bar."[4]

As a part of that same racially pandering statement, Harrison said he would never put the nation's fiscal power or authority in a "Negro" person's hands. This should have been a strong indication to Blanche that he would never be renamed to the register position, but several months later, still without any offer from the administration, Blanche held out hope that the new president would give him the job for which he had been well suited. He felt even more confident about this because his old Treasury secretary boss, William Windom, was back in the cabinet job after being absent from the Grover Cleveland administration.

Unfortunately, Bruce had miscalculated Harrison's ability to overcome his advisers' own race prejudice. Determined to draw racial lines around the important presidential appointments, Harrison refused to

offer any blacks—even those who campaigned for him—any significant jobs. When Harrison reappointed William Rosecrans—a Democrat from Grover Cleveland's administration—to the job of register of
the Treasury, there began a significant groundswell of complaints from
the larger black communities and newspapers from across the country.
Many of them had concluded that Harrison's bigotry was particularly
reprehensible, given that the Southern Democrats were not even controlling the House or the Senate anymore. His bigoted gestures were, to
them, willful and gratuitous.

Many of these black newspaper editors and politicians also accused
the president of standing by quietly as illegal discrimination against
black citizens was being carried on by others. But despite these complaints, the ever-calculating Bruce was steadfastly speaking in support
of Harrison.

In the fall of 1889, almost a year after Bruce had gone without any
appointment, and only three months after Harrison had stated that a
Negro was not fit to serve on the federal bench and that it would not be
"agreeable" to him to have "personal contact with an alien race," the
unemployed former senator defended the president in a *New York Age*
editorial. Blanche said, "The President has faithfully executed all existing laws and however much he may execrate Southern outrages against
the colored race, he is powerless to do more. I fully appreciate the
deplorable condition of the colored people in the Southern states. There
is but one course left to us: . . . We will appeal to the just and enlightened sentiment of the nation."[5] Other than his own self-interest, there
was no cause to advance when Bruce blatantly misled the black public
about Harrison's commitment to them. It is likely that he was so desperate for an appointment of any type, Bruce thought it would only
hurt his opportunities if he agreed with the chorus of black people who
argued that Harrison was just as insensitive to anti-black treatment as
past Democratic leaders had been.

It must also have occurred to him that he was quickly losing
ground with his former white Senate colleagues, who had either
become senior senators with enhanced tenure and power or had gone
on to receive other important government positions. For example, virulent segregationist Lucius Lamar, who had been the junior senator
from Mississippi when he joined Bruce in Congress in 1876, was now
sitting on the U.S. Supreme Court, appointed by Grover Cleveland.

Lamar had also enjoyed a three-year stint as secretary of the interior, from 1885 to 1888.

James Blaine, who had joined the Senate two years after Blanche had been elected, was deeply ensconced in Harrison's cabinet, serving as secretary of state—a position he had also previously been given in President Garfield's administration. And Frederick Frelinghuysen, the New Jersey senator who sat alongside him during two years of their overlapping Senate terms, had gone on to serve as secretary of state in President Arthur's administration. It seemed that men who were considered his peers were having no problem gaining positions of power and influence. This made Blanche more determined to do whatever it took to gain favor—even if it meant defending President Harrison in the face of the man's blatantly bigoted statements about black people.

Toward the end of 1889, a full year into his administration, the president finally appointed a black: Frederick Douglass was given the position of U.S. minister to the Republic of Haiti. Although it was not a job that Bruce would have wanted, it made him uneasy that Douglass had been offered an appointment and he hadn't. While Blanche and Douglass considered themselves friends, they were also rivals, and each vied for being seen the preeminent black leader of the period. Twenty-four years older than Blanche, Douglass had come to national prominence with the abolitionist movement in the 1840s, when he published his slave biography and traveled to Europe to speak about the rights of blacks and of women.

While it was acknowledged by both men that Douglass was the more nationally famous of the two, Bruce felt that he outranked his friend vis-à-vis social status, personal wealth, and political party stature. Finally, in December, after more than a year of waiting, Bruce was told that the president would be naming him recorder of deeds for Washington, DC, a job that Douglass had held from 1881 to 1886. Bruce's appointment was announced on January 30, 1890, and the Senate confirmation was made on February 6. Although he was glad to have the job, and grateful to be earning a salary to supplement his real estate income from his Mississippi properties, it no doubt bothered Bruce that not only had he been appointed to a job *after* Douglass, but also that the position he was given was one that Douglass had already held in a prior administration.

It was not evident to most people at the time, but the recorder of deeds was able to earn nearly $20,000 annually (worth approximately $350,000 in today's dollars), an extraordinary salary that exceeded many of the presidential appointees' annual incomes. The office, which was originally created by Congress in 1863, consisted of about thirty employees. It was charged with recording deeds and official papers related to any residential, commercial, or governmental properties within the District of Columbia.

As soon as Bruce received the appointment, he hired his longtime friend George Cornelius Smith as his private secretary. By this time, Smith had become a fixture in Bruce's "kitchen cabinet" of advisers and confidants. Ever since their days at Oberlin together, when he had first encouraged Bruce to travel to Mississippi and take advantage of Reconstruction opportunities in 1869, Smith had stayed close to Bruce and had served as a behind-the-scenes researcher, publicist, and adviser for the politician. Over the years, Smith wrote both anonymous and signed letters to newspapers, extolling the positive attributes and contributions of his friend. Bruce made some additional hires, but for the most part, he maintained the division heads and clerks that were already employed in the office when he took over.

It did not take long, however, before Bruce was being accused by the black community of not hiring a sufficient number of blacks for the recorder's office. Disturbed that his first appointment, that of his deputy, had gone to George Schayer, a Jewish man who had no standing in the black, Republican, or Mississippi communities, black Republicans in Mississippi soon criticized Bruce for not rewarding his primary supporters with positions.

The office of the recorder of deeds had an interesting history that would later prove ironic for the Bruce family. Not only had Frederick Douglass held the position beginning in 1881; the job had also been held by another black prior to Bruce's appointment. During Grover Cleveland's administration, the position was held by James Monroe Trotter, who served from 1887 until the Democratic president left office. Trotter, the patriarch of an elite black Boston family, was at the center of a group of black upper-class Bostonians who would interact with the Bruce family for two generations. James's son, William Monroe Trotter, a Phi Beta Kappa Harvard graduate, would finish Harvard the year before Bruce's son, Roscoe, began.

While still in college, Roscoe would be hired by Booker T. Washington to spy on William, who by then was publishing a well-regarded liberal newspaper that criticized the accommodationist practices of Washington and his university employees, who came to be known as his "Tuskegee machine."[6] It would be Roscoe's job to collect data on those opposing the Tuskegee leader's efforts and to clip William Trotter's negative articles about Booker T. Washington. Even before his appointment to the recorder's office, James Trotter was also close friends with Boston's George and Josephine Ruffin, who also socialized with the Bruces. George, a Harvard graduate, was a judge, and his wife, Josephine, later worked with Josephine Bruce and Booker T. Washington's wife, Margaret, in leading the National Association of Colored Women. So, despite political-party disagreements and differing geographical and intellectual backgrounds, members of the black elite almost always had more in common with each other than outsiders ever would have anticipated.

By this time, after his extended absence from government work, Blanche and Josephine had firmly reestablished themselves among the small black elite community. Again, they became prominent socialites and entertained at their elegant town house off Dupont Circle.

When Blanche's position as recorder of deeds was announced in newspapers in 1890, it was clear that Blanche had refashioned his image into that of an old Washingtonian. It was consistently noted in the many articles written that Bruce was a resident of Washington—*not* Mississippi. The *New York Times*, on January 30, 1890, reported, "The President today nominated ex-Senator Bruce, formerly of Mississippi, now of the District of Columbia, to be Recorder of Deeds for the District."[7] The characterization of Bruce as no longer being a resident of Mississippi no doubt fed the growing animosity of his Mississippi Republican party colleague, James Hill, as he watched the former senator plow deeper into DC society while benefiting from the Mississippi Republican power structure that Hill and John Lynch were holding in place. This might explain why, by early 1892, relations between Bruce and Hill were eroding in the public eye. The *Washington Bee* reported, "For some time, James Hill, aided by someone behind the screen, has been making a fight against Messrs. Bruce and Lynch. The burden laid at Mr. Bruce's door is that he is not a resident of the State [of Mississippi]."[8]

Conflicts around Blanche Bruce could have been seen brewing among more than just Lynch and the black Mississippi community by early 1890. Republican newspapers in several cities reported the criticisms aimed at the former senator on their front pages within only weeks of the new appointment. For example, the editor's column running on the front page of the February 1, 1890, *Washington Bee* remarked, "I want to state to those gentlemen who are abusing ex-Register Bruce that he has never . . . attempted to be the mouth-piece of this Administration. The masses of the American people honor and respect Mr. Bruce, and it is only the pot-house politicians who abuse and try to traduce him."[9]

Since Bruce and his loyal friend George Cornelius Smith worked very hard to cultivate friendships among the editors of various newspapers, it is likely that one of them had a hand in getting the press to run editorials that flattered him, yet were not tied to any particular anniversary or news event.

That fall, Bruce was pleased when the Washington, DC's schools—which were segregated and maintained an all-white school system and an all-black school system—asked him to join the board of trustees for what they called their "Colored Schools." The invitation bolstered his reputation in the black community and helped undermine the accusation that he had little to do with the concerns or institutions of ordinary black people. The DC schools became a family occupation. The senator's son, Roscoe C. Bruce, would later head the city's Colored Schools as assistant superintendent, from 1907 until 1921.

At the time that Blanche joined the schools' board of trustees, the Colored Schools' most prized institution, their high school, was enjoying its first successful years. Later known as M Street High School and Dunbar High School, the school was then known as the Charles Sumner High School (named for the outspoken liberal Massachusetts senator), and was run by its popular black principal, Francis L. Cardozo. Accomplished and widely respected, Cardozo remained in that position for twelve years and saw to it that graduates gained admission to the best black and white colleges in the country. Bruce's son, Roscoe, as well as his daughter-in-law, grandson, and granddaughter would all attend that high school for a period before entering Harvard and Radcliffe.

Although Blanche was disturbed that President Harrison had dragged his feet in giving him an appointment at the beginning of his administration, like most blacks, Blanche was encouraged by Harrison's attempt to pass legislation that advanced the rights of blacks. For example, Harrison supported Senator Henry Cabot Lodge's Force Bill, which would have brought federal supervision over congressional elections, which had been disenfranchising black voters in the Southern states. He also lobbied for Senator Henry Blair's education bill, which would have increased federal aid for blacks' education in the South. The fact that he was unable to push these bills through was further evidence that any remaining liberal agenda for black Americans was quickly vanishing. And this became more evident when Harrison entered the 1892 election season looking weak and vulnerable next to the reenergized Grover Cleveland, who was ready to face Harrison once again for the presidential race.

With negative fallout from his support of the Sherman Silver Purchase Act of 1890 and the McKinley Tariff of the same year, things were made worse for Harrison as his ailing wife became more ill from tuberculosis. These factors made the year seem glum for both Harrison and his fellow Republicans. In the end, the 1892 election caused the Republicans to lose not only the White House but also the Senate and the House of Representatives.

Beginning around 1892, cracks started to form in the armor of the black Mississippi Republican organization. Until that time, Blanche Bruce, John Lynch, and James Hill had effectively organized and controlled the organization to the extent that they could dictate which national Republican candidates would receive support from the Mississippi Republican Party. In the past, they had succeeded in directing the vote in both the black Republican and the white Republican communities.

But in the early 1890s, it became evident to James Hill, the least known of the triumvirate, that he was not receiving rewards or stature equal to what was being given to Bruce and Lynch. By this time, Bruce had enjoyed a six-year Senate term, two presidential appointments, and two vice presidential nominations. Lynch had received many plums as well, including a seat in the U.S. House of Representatives, the chance to be the first black to deliver the keynote address at the Republican

National Convention, a position on the Republican National Committee, and a presidential appointment as treasury auditor for the U.S. Navy. Hill was, no doubt, frustrated that while his two friends had won Senate and House elections, as well as federal appointments that kept them in Washington, he was still stuck in Mississippi, running the state party machine.

Part of Hill's frustration arose from the fact that while it was necessary for all of them to maintain their Mississippi ties, he was the only one of the three who was actually residing in the state on a full-time basis. There must also have been some resentment that the highest elected position he ever reached was that of Mississippi's secretary of state, which limited his celebrity to a regional status, while the other two used the triumvirate's combined power as leverage to operate on a national scale. Hill's life was distinctly unglamorous. Even when he received a federal appointment as a postmaster, the position was located in Vicksburg, Mississippi, a city that was completely run by racist white Democrats. Hill was rendered so powerless in his new position that he had to appoint a white Democrat as his deputy—a man who would be permitted to set more policies than Hill himself. The *Washington Bee* made note of this situation in a February 27, 1892, article: "When he was appointed postmaster at Vicksburg, it became known that it was not safe for him to attempt to administer the duties of office in person; in fact the only condition on which he could hold the office was that he would appoint a deputy selected by local Democrats."[10]

Hill's resentment toward Bruce must have been further exacerbated when, in late January 1893, Bruce offered a tribute to the recently deceased Democratic Senator Lucius Lamar. Lamar had been considered anathema to black Republicans, and black Mississippi Republicans in particular, yet Bruce gave overwhelmingly laudatory comments about him. This shocked and disturbed many blacks, who rightfully believed that Lamar had done more damage to Mississippi blacks' civil rights than virtually any other political leader. Lamar, who had grown up wealthy in Georgia, attended Emory University, then married the college president's daughter, had long been viewed by black political figures in Mississippi as a clever and ambitious racist whose principal goals were advancing white people and himself at the expense of the state's black residents.

Hill and other blacks toiling away in the state Republican Party organization had been battling against Lamar's statewide power for years, and they no doubt took it as a personal affront when Bruce, supposedly one of their own, told the press that Lamar "was always my friend" and called him "a profound scholar," "large-souled," "kindhearted," and "generous."[11] These must have been pretty difficult words for the black leaders and black citizens of Mississippi to swallow, after having been oppressed for two decades by Lamar's anti-black policies and programs.

It is likely that Bruce, always calculating his next career move, was making these statements about the opposition for only one reason: personal gain. Since Democrat Grover Cleveland was now in the White House, it is possible that Bruce was trying to gain favor with Cleveland by complimenting an important figure in the president's party. Whatever the reason, it not only failed to win him a job in the Democrat's administration but also antagonized Hill and other black Republicans from Mississippi.

Only a few short months later, Hill was incensed again when Bruce received an additional bit of attention from the nation's leading black institution—offering the former senator yet another honor that had not been bestowed on the hardworking Hill. Howard University, in its twenty-sixth year, asked Bruce if it could give him an honorary degree.

But there were more urgent challenges facing Hill and Bruce, and these challenges were far more pressing than their state's party politics. After Harrison lost his reelection bid in 1892 to the returning Grover Cleveland, the black Republicans were once again in the minor party. Their black Southern brethren were worse off for more than just political reasons. Their livelihood was at stake: the nation's economy, which was shifting from an agrarian, rural-based one to an industrial, city-based one, was undermining the Southern farm and the farmworkers' way of life. The nation had changed dramatically in the 1890s in that for the first time, the majority of the nation's citizens no longer worked and lived on farms. And despite President Harrison's claim, weeks earlier in 1893, that "there has never been a time when work was so abundant or when wages were as high," in March 1893 President Cleveland took over a country that was headed for an economic collapse.

In the spring of that year, the bankruptcies of the Philadelphia and

Reading Railroad and the National Cordage Company led to a May 5 Wall Street collapse. This Panic of 1893, as it was soon called, created an economic downturn that left more than 20 percent of the American workforce unemployed. The economic depression had hurt farmers and railroad employees as well as urban workers. It also struck close to home for Blanche's friends in Washington. James T. Wormley, the son of the wealthy black Washington entrepreneur James Wormley, was so badly in need of cash that he was forced to sell the Wormley Hotel, the famous establishment on the corner of H and 15th Streets NW. The hotel had been the site of the infamous Compromise of 1877, which had ended Reconstruction. The Wormley family, who had been successful caterers and restaurateurs before buying the hotel in 1871, had been an important fixture in Blanche and Josephine's black Washington social circles.

By June of 1893, Blanche was feeling that even if Hill and other Mississippi blacks were upset with him, he was now so deeply entrenched with Washington's black and white elite that nothing could derail his local popularity in the capital. Not only had he spent the last three years on the city's school board and received Howard's honorary degree, he was also preparing to join the board of trustees at Howard University. Now that Congress's black representation had dwindled down to just one man, Bruce and his legacy seemed all the more remarkable.[12] His status in Washington was now unimpeachable.

But even with all of these accomplishments, Bruce was not sitting on top of the black DC social pyramid by himself. In fact, in early 1893, as he passed by the Chinese Embassy, he could hardly contain his envy as he watched the six-bedroom brick mansion being completed on Bacon Street for the newest black-elite family that was moving to Washington. The house had already dwarfed his home on R Street, making him look less like the "king of the Washington Negroes" as each new brick was put in place at the ornate structure. Bruce stood across the street and shook his head in disbelief.

The home he stared at was being built by his friend Pinckney Benton Stewart Pinchback, who was relocating his family from New Orleans. A large, light-complexioned black man, the outspoken Pinchback had made his fortune in New Orleans as a businessman, newspaper publisher, lieutenant governor, and interim governor of Louisiana. He was just four years older than Bruce. Having benefited as much as was possible during the Reconstruction period in Louisiana, he left his home state and was coming north to Washington as a new "star" among the city's black aristocracy. Still annoyed with the Louisiana officials who had refused to seat him several years earlier when he had been elected to the U.S. Senate, Pinchback was happy to move north.

Already well connected among liberal white and black political figures, Pinchback and his wife had no difficulty reaching into the black society circle and inserting themselves next to Blanche and Josephine. In fact, they were ranked by the *Washington Bee* as the fourth richest black family in Washington in the 1890s—just behind the John Cooks, the Bruces, and the large Wormley family, who owned a great deal of real estate in the capital.

Although Bruce and Pinchback had previously been allies who worked together in building the Republican Party and each other's careers, they now sometimes competed with each other on a social level. It was evident to Bruce that his friend had more esteemed beginnings than his own past as a slave had given him. Pinchback had always been a free black man. Although born in Macon, Georgia, in 1837, Pinchback had been born free, because his mother had been emancipated just prior to his birth. The years that followed for Pinchback were also more advantaged in that he was reared in the more progressive state of Ohio, where he was educated from childhood.

Considerably more worldly, sophisticated, and ostentatious than the reticent Bruce, Pinchback and his extravagant lifestyle with his wife and four children quickly became the center of attention in the black-elite social circle. In addition to New Orleans, Pinchback had also lived in New York before finally settling in Washington. His flamboyant reputation continued for several years, as his children attended the nation's best schools, as he entertained generously in his elegant home, and as he later made the controversial decision to abandon the Republican Party and join the Democrats because he began to believe that the Republicans were taking black voters for granted.

As Josephine juggled her responsibilities as hostess for her husband's political gatherings and as mother of an adolescent, she still found time to pursue her own social activities with other affluent black women in

Washington. By 1894, she was spending much of her time with the
Colored Woman's League, an organization that she, Mary Church Terrell, and Helen Appo Cook had started two years earlier. It was a group
that collected money, clothing, food, and other items for the benefit of
less privileged blacks. At their gatherings, they also discussed political
and social issues affecting black women and the black family. Although
the group would later be consolidated with the Federation of Afro-
American Women, an organization that had been founded by
Josephine's Boston friend Josephine Ruffin, it was well respected in
Washington. It brought Josephine Bruce in closer contact with those
affluent black women and families that she otherwise would not have
met in Washington and other cities. Because she had considerable
household help by this time—to raise Roscoe as well as maintain their
home in Washington, their plantation in Mississippi, and a larger house
that sat on their Maryland farm in Prince George's County—Josephine
suddenly had the freedom to move about and become more active in
these black women's civic groups.

While Josephine became more consumed with her community
activities, she and Blanche were also becoming more involved in a new
church that they had recently helped found in Washington. The University Park Congregational Church was a mostly white Congregational church located in the city's northwest quadrant. Since Josephine
and her parents had long been members of the Episcopalian faith, it
appeared that Blanche was the likely impetus for their sudden ties to
the Congregational Church, possibly because of that faith's emphasis on
higher education. Whatever the reason for the change in denomination,
it is clear that this was a period when Blanche became more involved in
religious and educational issues than ever before. In fact, the more time
Blanche spent on the academic issues that were now facing him as a
member of the DC schools' board of trustees and of the Howard board,
the more anxious he became about his own son's academic future. Part
of his plan for building an elite dynasty was making sure that Roscoe
attended the best schools available. That, of course, meant sending the
boy north for his last two years of high school.

Josephine was not thrilled by the idea of sending her sixteen-year-
old son hundreds of miles away to boarding school, but having been
educated in the north herself, she knew it was best for his future.

Before she surrendered to the idea too quickly, she mentioned to Blanche that Roscoe's current school, M Street High School, had been sending colored boys and girls to the best colleges in the north for more than three decades. Amherst, Dartmouth, Wellesley, Smith, and Harvard had been popular destinations for graduates of their black high school. So perhaps he could still gain admission to one of those colleges from the local public high school.

Bruce knew that there was no black high school in the nation that compared to the prestigious M Street High School, which had been founded in 1870 as the Preparatory High School for Colored Youth. Established by their friends William Wormley and William Syphax, the school had a curriculum driven by George Cook—another friend of the Bruces—who had, in 1871, become the city's first superintendent for DC's Colored Schools.

But there were factors that bothered Blanche about having his son continue at M Street. First, he wanted Roscoe to learn how to compete with whites, and he did not like the idea of his son having to wait until he was a college freshman—already eighteen years old—before he had his first interactions with white students and white faculty. He wanted him to be better prepared for that experience. And attending an all-black, segregated high school in Washington would not help him get ready for that. His second reason for wanting Roscoe out of M Street was that he wanted his son and, thereby, his family, to enjoy the clout that came along with forming ties with a prestigious white New England boarding school, like Phillips Exeter in New Hampshire or Phillips Andover in Massachusetts.

For four years, as he had worked in the Senate alongside Massachusetts' George Hoar, he had heard stories of the New England boarding schools. Many of George's family members, including his nephew, Sherman, had attended Exeter. This was, after all, one of the family dynasties that Blanche had emulated. By collecting such credentials, Roscoe and the Bruce family could possibly gain a similar type of family prestige. And furthermore, while it was true that black students from M Street High School had gone on to great white colleges in the North, a degree from Exeter was a guarantee that his son would attend an Ivy League university.

Early in 1895, while Blanche and Josephine researched the various prep schools, they and the national black community were rocked by the death of their close friend—abolitionist and political leader Frederick Douglass. He died after a short illness, on February 20, 1895. During his seventy-eight years, he had accomplished far more for black Southerners than his longtime friend and occasional rival, Blanche Bruce. As a courageous and outspoken leader for civil rights, Douglass had captured the attention and support of more blacks and liberal whites than Bruce would attract, which made him a national leader with a larger legacy. Douglass's family had also been distinguished by the accomplishments of two of his sons. One son, Lewis Douglass, had served as a sergeant in the Union Army's Fifty-fourth Massachusetts Infantry before marrying Amelia Loquen, the daughter of an AME Church bishop. Amelia's sister, Sarah Marinda Loquen, graduated from Syracuse University School of Medicine in 1876 and became the first black woman physician in New York State. Another son, Charles Douglass, had served as a major in the Union Army, and then later was credited with founding the Highland Beach resort, just outside of Washington, when he purchased the first acreage for a summer beach community for the black upper class along the western shore of the Chesapeake Bay. For generations to come, Highland Beach would remain a popular place for wealthy black Washingtonians to build their summer cottages.

At his death, most of black and white America perceived Frederick Douglass as a champion for the disenfranchised and less privileged. Interestingly, many among the black *elite* saw Douglass as a champion, but one who was possibly as elitist and as color-conscious within the black community as they were. His marriage to a white woman and his decision to limit most of his social ties to upper-class black families and certain liberal whites in his later years were factors that caused certain black Washingtonians to form mixed feelings about the greatest black leader of the nineteenth century, even at his death.

Following Douglass's death, Bruce was suddenly looked upon as the preeminent voice in the black community. Although it was by default, Bruce no doubt reveled in finally being acknowledged as the black leader without equal. It was an honor that he had not enjoyed even when first elected to the Senate in 1874, because Douglass had already achieved national fame through his abolitionist speeches in the

1860s and political positions in the early 1870s. But unfortunately for Bruce, his own reign as the "most famous" black leader was short-lived. During the year of Douglass's death, there quickly emerged a figure who ultimately became more renowned and more powerful than both men.

CHAPTER TWELVE

1895–1898

The Senator Gets Appointed
by President McKinley
as His Son Breaks Barriers
at Phillips Exeter; the Senator Dies

ON SEPTEMBER 18, 1895, BOOKER T. WASHINGTON, THE FOUNDER AND president of Tuskegee Institute, a small black college in Alabama, gave a speech that would alter the power structure in the black community for the next twenty years. It was in Atlanta, at the Cotton States and International Exposition, that Washington spoke in front of hundreds of white men and told them of the need for black Americans to cease asking for equality in employment, education, and social settings, and instead to focus on self-help measures for the black community.

Few people had heard of Washington before 1895. He was born a slave in Franklin County, Virginia, in April 1856. His mother was a plantation cook and his father an unknown white man who lived in a nearby community. For the first few years of his life, like most slaves, he had no last name. He chose the last name "Washington" out of reverence for the nation's first president and because it was the first name of his mother's new husband. After the Civil War, his mother and he moved to West Virginia, where he worked first in the local coal mines, and then as a house servant for a wealthy white family in Malden, West Virginia, who gave him occasional tutoring in math and English. That family, the Ruffners, was headed by a retired Confederate general and his wife, who had been raised in New England. Mrs. Ruffner had long perceived Washington as having the skills and ambition to be a good and loyal house servant. He would later credit her as his first mentor.

When Washington was fifteen, he entered Hampton Institute, where he found his most important mentor, Hampton's white principal, General Samuel Chapman Armstrong. Armstrong had been a general in the Civil War and had been in charge of an all-black troop. Although eager to aid poor, uneducated blacks, Armstrong perceived them as having less innate intelligence than whites—and believed they should assume a role subservient to that of white people. Like other black students at Hampton, Washington followed the "industrial" curriculum that taught practical work skills rather than intellectual material, such as history or literature. Like the other students, he utilized the practical labor skills he learned at Hampton, including carpentry, painting, and plumbing.

Armstrong believed that blacks would succeed in America if they embraced trade skills rather than the traditional liberal arts education offered to white students. Washington graduated from Hampton in 1875 and then vowed to live his life as a teacher in the way that his mentor, General Armstrong, had advised him. He moved back to West Virginia and took up teaching. He then spent a year teaching in Washington, DC, at Wayland Seminary, a school that taught liberal arts to black students. Having fully embraced Armstrong's belief that it was pointless for blacks to study the traditional subjects that white students studied in college, Washington left Wayland and returned to a two-year teaching position at Hampton Institute. There, he directed a division of the school that educated part-time students who worked during the day and attended classes at night.

In 1881, Washington was able to follow his mentor's example and began his own school with thirty students that September in Tuskegee, Alabama. By this time, several other black colleges were thriving, but virtually all of them, including such well-regarded ones as Howard, Fisk, and Atlanta University, advanced the idea of teaching the same college subjects to blacks as other colleges were presenting to white students.

During the next several years, white philanthropists learned of Washington's approach to teaching blacks vocational skills and getting blacks to accept a subservient role in American society. This notion appealed to conservative and wealthy whites, and became so popular among their circles that many of them ended their support of black colleges and began financing the growth of Tuskegee Institute and Booker T. Washington's accommodationist agenda.

By the time the thirty-nine-year-old educator was asked to address the Cotton States Exposition on September 18, 1895, the white public was ready for his conservative views and speech, which quickly came to be known as the Atlanta Compromise speech. It launched Washington into a powerful position with white philanthropists and officials around the nation. Eclipsing both Blanche Bruce and Frederick Douglass as black leaders who had the ears of powerful whites, Washington suddenly was able to meet with and win financial support and advice from such white industrialists and philanthropists as Andrew Carnegie, August Belmont, Jacob Schiff, and J. Pierpont Morgan—all people who had barely even known of Blanche Bruce's political career.

In fact, so meteoric was the rise of Booker T. Washington that his advice and involvement were being sought out by liberal white institutions and individuals who believed that his voice and presence were a proxy for all of black America. This became clear to many black and white citizens later, in 1896, when Harvard University decided to bestow one of its honorary degrees on Washington the same year it gave one to the inventor of the telephone, Alexander Graham Bell.

During the fall of 1895, Blanche Bruce saw his own importance eclipsed by that of Booker T. Washington. At that time, he was also frustrated by the environment to which his son was being exposed. He did not like the idea of raising Roscoe in a city where blacks so clearly had a second-tier status—making it more of a necessity to explore New England boarding schools. Added to all of this was the apparent agony his wife was experiencing as she worried about the quickly declining health of her father.

Joseph Willson had complained in his letters of blood circulation problems and aching joints for more than two years, because of his diabetic condition. During that time, Josephine visited him several times and did her best to assist her two sisters with his ongoing care. He had long ago retired from his dental practice and spent most of each day inside as an invalid in his Indianapolis home. Dr. Joseph Willson finally died at his home in Indianapolis on Monday morning, September 2, 1895. He was seventy-eight. An aristocratic man who was held in high regard by his neighbors, he had lived a full life that carried him from the South to the Northeast and to the Midwest. Although born in Georgia to a freeborn black woman and a white cofounder of the Bank of Augusta, Willson spent most of his life in the North and identified mostly with educated Northern blacks living in integrated or mostly white communities. Although he had sparked great controversy when he published, in 1841, his book about the black upper class in Philadelphia, Dr. Willson had generally lived a rather quiet life during the years that he and his wife, Elizabeth, spent in Cleveland and then in Indianapolis.

The year 1896 did not show much improvement for Blanche's political fortunes. Although Democratic president Grover Cleveland had long ago lost his popularity and would not be running again in the fall elections, the Democrats continued to maintain a strong presence in the South, making it difficult for Blanche and his Mississippi Republican Party colleagues to exert much control. What also was creating problems for Blanche was his financial situation. Although he was a large landowner in Mississippi and Maryland, the nation's economy was in such a deep depression that the dollar was worth very little. The chickens and produce that he was raising on his Maryland farm and the cotton that he was growing on the Mississippi plantation in Bolivar were not providing the income that he had earned in the past.

Furthermore, Josephine had finally relented and Roscoe had been accepted at the rather costly Phillips Exeter Academy boarding school in New Hampshire, a school for the boys from affluent families. While this pleased Bruce, it also meant he was facing greater expenses. There was no scholarship assistance or aid to help Roscoe, so Blanche knew that the next several years of boarding-school expenses and college would require that he eventually find another government appointment. And with conservative attitudes sweeping the country, the opportunities for black men were shrinking quickly.

That spring, there was even less reason for blacks to believe that their fortunes would improve. In May of 1896, the Supreme Court finally ruled on a case that would have great consequences for blacks in the country. It would serve to solidify and legalize the discriminatory attitudes and policies that various states and municipalities had already put into place with the wide-spreading Jim Crow laws. The suit involved a thirty-four-year-old white-looking man named Homer A. Plessy of New Orleans. A light-complexioned "Negro" who was actually only one-eighth black, Plessy was arrested after he purchased a first-class ticket on the segregated East Louisiana Railway train on June 7, 1892. Although there were separate railcars for blacks and whites, Plessy wanted to sit in a first-class section, but the rail company permitted only whites in first class.

A member of a well-to-do black family in New Orleans, Plessy and other black and Creole families in the city had recently been speaking out against a discriminatory law known as the Louisiana Separate Car Act, which required blacks and whites to travel in different train cars. After his arrest, Plessy sued to overturn the law, arguing that it violated his Thirteenth and Fourteenth Amendment rights. When the Supreme Court's majority opinion ruled that the Constitution did not prevent states from passing laws that prevented the "commingling of the two races," blacks throughout the nation were devastated. Not surprisingly, this 1896 ruling had enormous and immediate impact on the South as well as the North, as it allowed and encouraged further segregation of the races through Jim Crow Laws that discriminated against blacks in every facet of daily life. Within weeks, officials began to ensure not only that their schools and trains were segregated, but also that blacks were removed from restaurants, stores, public parks, theaters, restrooms, waiting rooms, hotels, and even churches.

Immediately after learning of Justice John Marshall Harlan's dissent in the *Plessy* case, Blanche Bruce wrote him a supportive note in which he pointed out the dangers of laws that perpetuated discrimination and the humiliation of the black race. He wrote, "I have read your dissenting opinion . . . I was impressed . . . with your conclusions relative to the validity of the Louisiana statute. The motives that suggested it and the conditions under which it could be administered constitute a substantial invasion of the civil rights of the colored race. In operation, it will carry both humiliation and inconvenience."[1]

A few weeks later, Bruce traveled to St. Louis for the Republican National Convention, where it became evident that the black Mississippi Republican power structure no longer had the clout that it had enjoyed in prior years. By now, Hill was openly resentful of Bruce, and Lynch was more focused on his future legal career—a pursuit that caused him to spend far more time in Washington than in Mississippi.

At the convention, it was another Ohioan who received the nomination for president. This time it was a former congressman and governor named William McKinley. Although not a charismatic man, McKinley had risen through the ranks of the party as a protégé of Rutherford B. Hayes. He had served in Hayes's Civil War regiment, and then later received guidance from President Hayes as McKinley moved through Ohio political circles.

Backed by major financial and industrial interests, and aided by the public's anger with the weak Democratic response to the economic depression, McKinley easily won the presidency over his Democratic opponent, William Jennings Bryan of Nebraska.

Following the convention, Blanche and Josephine got ready to see their son, Roscoe, off to boarding school. His entire life had been spent in the all-black schools of Washington, DC, with the last two years at the city's premier black high school, M Street High. Roscoe's future of living at Phillips Exeter Academy, in New Hampshire, would be a dramatic change for him and his parents.

A bright and conscientious student during his grammar school and early high school years, Roscoe was just the type of student who would thrive at an academically rigorous school like Exeter. The four-year institution had approximately 250 boys—mostly coming from the East Coast and generally representing upper-class or upper-middle-class white Anglo-Saxon families. Most families sent their sons to the school because the academic curriculum was suited to preparing them for Ivy League colleges in the Northeast. Although the school also emphasized athletic activities—an area that captured little of Roscoe's interest—it otherwise seemed like the ideal institution for an ambitious and intellectually curious student. Blanche was particularly enamored by Exeter because it was where President Lincoln's son had studied before entering Harvard College.

After Roscoe was admitted, but just prior to the fall 1896 semester, Blanche made inquiries regarding his son's housing choices on the Exeter campus. With the newfound, growing popularity of segregated institutions and facilities, it was likely that Blanche and Josephine were concerned about the school's boarding policies for their few black students. Blanche's query elicited a letter from the school secretary, Y. A. Tufts, that offended the former senator. This initial letter from Tufts argued that Roscoe should live alone, and its immediate effect on

Blanche was to make him consider not sending Roscoe to Exeter but to enroll him at another boarding school or to leave him in his public school in Washington. But on August 14, 1896, Tufts sent a rather apologetic but frank letter to Blanche, which said, "I am sorry there should be any doubt about your son's coming. What I wrote about his rooming alone, it was simply a suggestion made because I think it somewhat risky for a boy to room with a stranger. Still, if you prefer to have your son take a chum, he can make his room selection after he arrives. There will be others looking for chums."[2]

Since many of the students arriving for their first year were living with students who were strangers from another part of the country, Tufts's explanation for suggesting that Roscoe live alone falls flat. It is likely that he did not want to explicitly put in writing that the black students did not live in any of the Exeter dormitories. Although Exeter had two or three black students in each of its four class grades, none of the school's three red-brick dormitories—Peabody, Soule, and Abbot Halls—housed a black student. And while many of the students lived in nearby Exeter-approved boardinghouses, those also housed only white students. There were only three or four private homes or boardinghouses in the town that permitted black students. In other words, although both the school and the town were liberal and fairly welcoming to the few black students on campus, there was virtually no race-mixing in the campus dormitories or the school-approved boardinghouses.

In September 1896, Roscoe finally left for Exeter. It would be the first time he would be living away from home, and also the first time that he would be attending school with white students and faculty. A rural, white New England town and campus that had less than a dozen black students must have been a culture shock to the seventeen-year-old.

The student population of the 115-year-old New Hampshire school stood at approximately 250 boys spread out over four class grades. Rather than using the labels ninth, tenth, eleventh, and twelfth grade that other high schools used, Exeter referred to the grades as junior class, lower middle class, upper middle class, and senior class. Roscoe entered as one of eighty students in the upper middle class grade, which was considered a popular entry point for parents who wanted to be sure their sons benefited from the Academy's reputation for getting its graduates into Ivy League colleges. There were some families who enrolled their sons earlier, because of the parents' busy home life. Those with careers or social lives that required constant travel were particularly supportive of a school that not only boarded their children but also kept them on busy schedules and gave them adult-like responsibilities. Whatever reason a family had for sending their sons, it was widely known that Exeter had built a reputation of turning bright, well-mannered boys from the best WASP families into sophisticated young men who would eventually take leadership roles in business, government, academia, and other institutions that their family dynasties had begun. By the late 1890s, the academy's students were coming from thirty-two different states plus Canada and England, and the expectation was that most would end up at Harvard, Yale, or Princeton.[3] It was a school that imposed rigor, discipline, and scholarship on its students, but it rewarded its graduates with assistance from a powerful network of loyal alumni that included Wall Street millionaires and American presidents.

Blanche was unapologetic about sending his son away, perhaps rationalizing it as a good thing so as to assuage his own guilt for being on the road for political trips so often. In October 1897, he sent his son a letter that addressed this very situation. It began,

My Dear Son,
We miss you very much, but of course your absence at school is a necessity to your development and your life equipment. We are proud to learn of the high compliment paid you by one of the professors . . . Mama wants to know if you had your hair cut since you have been away . . .[4]

Blanche increased his travel schedule once Roscoe began Exeter. Within the first few months of Roscoe's first year at the New Hampshire school, Blanche found himself lecturing on behalf of the Republicans throughout Ohio, New York, New Jersey, Indiana, and Missouri, often writing back to his wife and son—in separate letters—on hotel stationery. With the newfound responsibility of negotiating with his landlady over rent charges, shopping for his own clothes, and self-monitoring his own nighttime study habits, Roscoe's life away required a great deal of self-discipline and maturity. In a letter to his father, during his first year, Roscoe wrote, "There is nothing new up here. Grind,

grind, grind is still the order of the day . . . I received Mother's letter
and Mrs. Field [Roscoe's landlady] spoke to me about my room rent.
She hemmed and hawed a good deal but at last consented to reduce it."[5]

Roscoe developed fast friendships with three or four of the other
black students at the school. Because none of them were housed in the
conveniently situated red-brick dormitory buildings on the sprawling
campus, between classes he often found himself walking along the
fieldstone sidewalks lining Spring Street or the busier Front Street,
which took him across the front of the school and past Peabody and
Abbot Halls. One of his closest friends, whom he referred to as "Shaw"
in his many letters home, was George Shaw from Charleston, South
Carolina. Like most of the other black students at the school, he had
been raised in the South, where racial segregation was the norm. It was
no surprise to him that he and the other black boys would not be fully
accepted into the fabric of the school.

His father paid little mind to that. An October 19, 1896, letter that
Blanche wrote to his wife while visiting Roscoe at Exeter speaks with
the proud, almost aristocratic formality he had used when addressing
his political colleagues. His self-confidence and pride regarding the
family possessions and finances are reflected in his own words and the
recounted words previously spoken to him by his son.

> *My dear wife,*
>   *Mr. R. C. Bruce wishes me to "tell you that I saw him and that
> he was looking well." On my return from New York Saturday
> night where I had spoken to an immense audience, I made up my
> mind suddenly to visit Ros . . . go to New Hampshire to see my son.
> I arrived here this morning and went at once to the Hotel . . . and
> after changing my clothing I strolled to the Field House.*
>   *Ros knew nothing of my arriving. He and I will take a stroll
> over the Town after dinner and tonight I shall call on Amen,
> Schillar and Tufts[6] . . . Roscoe is as fat and rosy as you please. He is
> in fine condition in every way. He is delighted with this place and
> is, I am sure, making great progress in his studies. But of this I shall
> learn more when I see the professors . . .*
>   *He showed me his new suit. It is elegant and quite in style. He
> does not wear it except when he wants to "lord it." He had, he says,
> written me for money . . . I shall stop at the Hoffman [Hotel in*

New York City] on my return . . . Things look hopeful for
[presidential candidate] McKinley and I believe he will be elected.
    By the way, Rosco . . . was informed that [scholarships] were
only given to boys who could not get through without them. He at
once informed Amen that he was quite able to get through without
aid from any source.[7]

There was a pride shared by Blanche and Roscoe that made it important, almost necessary, to let others know that they were Negroes with a
unique background and that they did not need financial, emotional, or
any other type of assistance from outsiders. In the senator, this attitude of
self-reliance derived from the success he accomplished through his own
hard work. In Roscoe, at this young age, it derived from his naive belief
that because his family was wealthy, respected, and powerful, they were
inherently superior to most whites, and all blacks.

Along with Shaw, Roscoe made friends with the half dozen other
black boys, like Bruce Green, who would later attend Brown University, T. John Syphax, who would attend Columbia, as well as Ed
Wellington Lewis, Paul Pinn, and Thomas Williams, who'd all go to
Harvard.[8] All of the boys, as Blanche had predicted, were expected to
live off-campus, away from the white students. Exeter was, nevertheless, one of the most liberal prep schools when admitting blacks. Other
New England boarding schools made no efforts to admit gifted black
students. Black Exeter students of this period simply had to accept the
fact that their housing choices would not be listed on the official
Phillips Exeter Academy map.[9] They were, instead, expected to live
with one of the few local black families or rent a room in a boardinghouse that was designated as a "Negro" boardinghouse. Since Shaw
and many of the other black students had come from segregated cities,
they were probably not devastated or surprised by having to live apart
from the white students and being relegated to either Mr. Proctor's
house or Mr. J. W. Field's house several blocks away from the school.
But slights like these, no doubt, bothered Roscoe. Even as a teenager, he
was a young man who kept score of where he ranked with others—
socially, intellectually, and otherwise.

He felt that he deserved greater respect. Not only was his father a
wealthy man and a U.S. senator, but, as he told his classmates, his
great-grandfather had helped found the Bank of Augusta, his maternal

grandfather had authored a well-known 1841 book about the black upper class,[10] and his uncle Leonidas was then a respected Philadelphia lawyer. His mother's own status was equally appealing, as his mother was a founder of the National Association of Colored Women and a socialite who, twenty years earlier, had been profiled in the *Washington Post* and the *New York Times*.[11] And, as Roscoe would point out to many during his time at the boarding school, his father, as register of the U.S. Treasury, was the first Negro ever to have his name and signature printed on U.S. currency.

As Roscoe's letters would reveal for years to come, almost everyone was a potential target for his derision—even "educated Negroes," who, he would say, "have no common sense."[12]

Thinking himself a "man of culture"—a phrase he often used—Roscoe felt no compunction about mocking even those young men he considered his friends.[13] At times, he dismissed Shaw's ambition to become a dentist—a distinctly middle-class aspiration. And when he did offer compliments, they could be backhanded and bigoted, as when he made the blatantly anti-Semitic remark about the non-Jewish George Shaw when writing to his mother from Exeter. "I bought a fine pair of college shoes in Boston," he wrote. "They are six dollar shoes but I got them—thanks to Shaw's Jewish propensities—for five dollars."[14]

Dismissing the popular athletic and musical pursuits at the school, Roscoe chose to follow a more intellectual route, which included writing for the school's *Literary Monthly* and *The Exonian*, where he became an editor. Also on the *Literary Monthly* was his friend Theophilus John Minton Syphax, another boy from a prominent and fairly wealthy black family. Roscoe and his family had known Syphax's family for many years because they, too, had lived in Washington. By the time they started at Exeter, the boy's family had moved to Philadelphia.

Although Roscoe considered Syphax a friend, he did not hesitate to write to his father when Syphax's family could no longer afford to pay the school's tuition. In January 1897, eighteen-year-old Roscoe wrote to his father from Exeter:

> *Mon cher pere,*
>   *I have been busy putting my room in order and grinding for the past two or three days. My room seems very bright and inviting. I have arranged the pictures as tastfully [sic] as I could ... There*

are three or four new boys here now. They are unanimous in
pronouncing Phillips Exeter Academy as a "mighty hard place to
get through" . . .
 Syphax is relying entirely upon charity to get through this
school. His tuition and board cost him nothing. I envy him his
freedom from bills. My term bill came to me today. I enclose it.
 With much love for you and Mother, I am Your boy, Rock[15]

Although "Syphax" was the scion of a respected old black family
distantly related to First Lady Martha Washington, and the family was
the owner of Virginia acreage that was eventually sold to the federal
government to help enlarge Arlington National Cemetery, in 1898,
young T. John Syphax's parents did not have access to his relatives'
wealth.[16] And that fact was not missed by young Roscoe or his parents,
who were, by this time, the richest black family in Washington.[17]

 Like the Bruce family's, the illustrious history of the Syphax family
was virtually invisible to the white students at the prep school. Both
Roscoe and T. John Syphax, who was in the class behind Roscoe,
worked together on the *Literary Monthly* during Roscoe's last year at
Exeter. But despite their friendship at the school and during their college years, Roscoe felt a need to constantly measure himself against
Syphax to reassure himself that he was the most accomplished young
black in their circle of friends. It bothered him greatly that Syphax's
deep roots among black society in both Philadelphia and Washington
could eclipse his own.

 Syphax had a lineage that included millionaires, Civil War heroes,
and links to the most prominent black families in the nation. His
grandfather was Colonel John McKee, who, in the 1840s, had married
the daughter of James Prosser, one of the most successful black caterers
in Philadelphia. McKee, a light-complexioned black man who had
grown up in Virginia, helped grow his father-in-law's catering and
restaurant business even more and eventually moved into the real estate
business as well. During the Civil War, McKee enlisted and fought
with the Union Army in a Pennsylvania regiment.

 McKee and his wife had two daughters, Martha and Abbie.
Martha married Theophilus Minton, who was the descendant of Henry
Minton, another wealthy caterer in Philadelphia. Martha and
Theophilus Minton had a son named Dr. Henry McKee Minton, and

Henry later married into a famously wealthy black Washington family when he married Edith Wormley. The Bruces had been close friends of the Wormleys, who owned a large Washington hotel. The second daughter of John McKee, Abbie, married Douglas Syphax of Virginia, whose family owned some of the acreage that helped create Arlington National Cemetery. It was one of Abbie and Douglas Syphax's sons, Theophilus John Minton Syphax ("T. John"), who was Roscoe's Exeter classmate.

By the time T. John was in prep school, his elderly grandfather Colonel John McKee was worth almost three million dollars, but that would not have an impact on T. John's life for another four decades. In fact, just a few years following their time in prep school, in 1902, when Roscoe was at Harvard and T. John at Trinity College, T. John's grandfather died, leaving an estate worth more than $2 million.[18] In today's dollars, the fortune would be worth $35 million. But his wishes, as recorded in his last will and testament, were that most of the $2 million be given to the Catholic Church, with the orders that it should one day be used to open an orphanage for both black and white children. The grandfather made minimal provisions for T. John's mother, leaving her less than $10,000 and giving T. John only $50 per year (worth, respectively, $170,000 and $850 in today's dollars). These small sums did little to assist T. John's tuition and expenses at Exeter.

Although Roscoe and his future wife would count T. John among their closest friends, they would quickly fall out of contact with T. John when he changed his name from Theophilus John Minton Syphax to T. John McKee and used his light complexion to begin passing as a white man. After graduating from Columbia University Law School, he married a white woman, fathered two children, severed relations with his black brothers and other relatives, and never acknowledged his black friends or black identity until the 1940s, when he discovered that his siblings and first cousins had all died, thus allowing him to sue and contest his grandfather's will and the portion of the original $2 million estate that had not yet been distributed.

Roscoe's comfortable and insular world was well populated with affluent blacks whose past business or family connections tied them together in surprising ways. Like many children born into families that already had great wealth, he had no real sense for what it would be like to live without financial advantages. As revealed in many of his letters to his parents, his primary concern was maintaining the family's stature—hence his regular requests for money and queries regarding his father's future appointments and positions.[19]

In addition to gaining new responsibilities, Roscoe was also becoming more sociable with girls. During this time, he dated some in the Boston area, and some while he was at home during the summers in Washington. All of these girls were affluent, well-educated, light-complexioned children of respected black families. At times, his letters suggested that he was as credentials-obsessed as his parents when it came to evaluating his relationships. Having befriended the bright and ambitious Clara Burrill while they were still students in the DC schools, Roscoe continued to correspond with her after he left for Exeter and she remained at M Street High School. When he wrote to Clara in October 1896, on Exeter letterhead, calling her "Carrie"—as he often did later in life—it does not appear that they were yet romantically attached. But some of his words suggest a strong flirtation on his part. He wrote,

> My dear Carrie—
>   Perhaps you have wondered why I have not written to you before. Indeed, you may possibly have imagined that I had banished your sweet face from my thoughts. But, I assure you that this has, by no means, been the case . . . But I shall try to write to you (if you do not object) as often as possible.[20]

It was not long, however, before Roscoe also began relationships with two girls from prominent black Boston families—the Lewises and the Lees. Mamie Lewis was the daughter of John Lewis, a well-known Bostonian who owned a successful tailoring business as well as his own horses that he raced at Boston's Mystic Park. Tessa Lee's family owned a large catering company in Boston and socialized with many prominent black families in New England. Roscoe's remarks about Tessa and Mamie sounded very much like an adult's assessment when he wrote about the girls to his mother in a January 1897 letter. He wrote, "My darling mother, I am wearing a ring of Tessa Lee's now. She is a very sweet girl. I am sure that you would like her. She is a great deal prettier and much more 'college' than Mamie Lewis."[21] Although he was only sixteen at the time, he understood that his mother and father would appreciate the fact that a girl who was "college material" would be far superior to one who was not.

In a later letter to Clara, Roscoe appeared to flirt with her more aggressively, and even went so far as to flatter her, then casually mention toward the end of the letter that he might visit Mamie Lewis—a potential date—before he returned home for Christmas vacation. He wrote,

> *Ma Chere,*
>
> *I have not heard from you for a century. Have you forgotten my address? Or, are you so well-entertained by Mr. Walton, Mr. Wormley, etc. that you don't care to write to me?*
>
> *I heard something very nice about you . . . Syphax said that of all the girls in Washington, you were most nearly his ideal of what a girl should be. For once in his life, Si was right. Don't think I am trying to flatter you for I am only telling you what Si said . . . I shall probably see Miss Mamie Lewis who was in Washington last summer.*[22]

Once Roscoe had left for boarding school, the family dynamics in the Bruce household changed significantly for his mother. Blanche continued to travel to the North and Midwest to lecture on behalf of McKinley and the Republican Party. In New York, staying at the opulent Grand Union Hotel or the New Hoffman House Hotel on Madison Square, he would stop by McKinley campaign headquarters and get his orders for upcoming lectures.[23] This traveling lecture schedule continued throughout the fall, and now, for the first time since they were married, Josephine was no longer tied to her husband's career and her son's daily schedule.

In the past, when Blanche was home, Josephine acted as hostess, mother, and supportive wife. Whenever Blanche went on the road for lectures or to oversee his Mississippi plantation and other properties, Josephine was left at home with her son and their servants. But now that her son was in boarding school, and the Republicans were out of the White House, and Blanche was out of a job and simply on the road giving speeches on behalf of William McKinley and the Republican Party, Josephine had the opportunity to pursue her own interests.

It was during the autumn of 1896 that Josephine began to work aggressively with civic organizations that catered to black upper-class women. Although there were no black sororities at the time,[24] the powerful National Association of Colored Women (NACW) had been created that summer in Washington, by the merger of her own group, the Colored Woman's League, with the National Federation of Afro-American Women. The NACW lobbied for legislation that addressed political, economic, and social needs of the black community. It also became involved in international reform movements. With Mary Church Terrell as the group's first president, the NACW also spoke out against the widespread practice of lynching; and they proposed responses to the continued disenfranchisement of black citizens.

As a part of her role in the NACW, Josephine gave lectures, like many of the other active NACW cofounders. She traveled and attracted attention for herself and for the social, political, and educational issues targeted by the NACW. During the year, she was invited by Booker T. Washington to visit Tuskegee, where she gave a speech to the students and faculty. Coming at a time when the Tuskegee Institute president was becoming nationally famous on the heels of his controversial 1895 Atlanta Compromise speech, this invitation helped Josephine recognize that she had ambition and talents of her own. Her husband encouraged the friendship while simultaneously imposing on Washington to use his considerable influence as McKinley selected the new members of his administration. Three years later, in 1899, after Blanche's death, Josephine would be invited by Booker T. Washington to return to the Alabama school, where she would assume the role of lady principal.

Given the support Bruce eventually received from Booker T. Washington and others, it is hard to understand why it took so long for the former senator to receive an appointment in the McKinley administration. Although Bruce had been a loyal foot soldier in campaigning for McKinley, it is possible that the president's advisers were uneasy about Bruce because of the new segregationist mood that was quickly sweeping through the country. Since the Supreme Court ruling in the *Plessy* case, there was increased interest in creating ways to segregate and stigmatize black people in both the North and the South. With the proliferation of new Jim Crow laws, and the enthusiasm that whites showed for them, it is possible that McKinley feared giving a meaningful job to a black man at this time.

What is clear, though, is the Herculean effort that Bruce made in order to win a job from the administration. From the time of McKinley's election in 1896 until the end of 1897, Bruce enlisted friends and supporters to help him lobby for his old position as register of the Treasury. A longtime supporter of Bruce's, the *Indianapolis Freeman* newspaper remarked that Bruce was the most popular candidate for the job. In July 1897, the paper remarked, "He should be made Register of the Treasury—or something better. He is supported by the strongest white journals. He is the unanimous choice of the Negro press, and his merits are extolled by the ablest writers . . . He is endorsed by the weightiest party leaders."[25]

Given the fact that several members of the black press and white press, such as the *Washington Post*, were suggesting that McKinley appoint Bruce to a cabinet level position, Bruce probably believed that his request for the Treasury appointment was well within his reach. In fact, for several weeks, at the close of 1896 and beginning of 1897, the *Washington Bee* ran articles encouraging McKinley to put Bruce in his cabinet. At the time, the presidential cabinet consisted of a very small group of positions. In addition to the attorney general and postmaster general, there were only six other cabinet positions: secretaries of agriculture, treasury, interior, war, navy, and state. The latter position, secretary of state, was being awarded to Blanche's former Senate colleague John Sherman. Some of his black colleagues honestly believed that the public might accept a black postmaster general, particularly since there was no high-profile person being mentioned for the job. But Blanche was not so hopeful. He thought it made more sense to aim for a second-tier position.

Blanche focused his attention on ways to convince both the president and the new Treasury secretary, Lyman J. Gage, that his past experience as register of the Treasury would make him the ideal candidate for the job. A shrewd businessman, Gage had been a bank president in Chicago and a close friend and adviser to President Hayes. At the time of Hayes's presidency, Hayes had tried, unsuccessfully, to get Gage to leave the banking business and join his cabinet as Treasury secretary.

So aggressive was Bruce in his pursuit of the Treasury position that he imposed on Booker T. Washington, as well as several members of Congress and other politically powerful individuals, to write on his behalf. Each morning, he would take a carriage over to his office at the

Ohio National Bank Building on the corner of 12th and G Streets NW, where he leased space for his company, the B. K. Bruce General Claim Agency. From his office, he would send out letters and telegrams to friends. In fact, by the time he had completed his job campaign, he had gotten more than fifty people to write to the president or Treasury Secretary Gage, regarding his suitability for the job.

In April 1897, Bruce wrote to thank Booker T. Washington for his many months of assistance in trying to get McKinley to appoint Bruce to the job of register of the Treasury. His letter said,

> My dear Mr. Washington,
>   Many thanks for your letter to the President. It comes at the right time—just when the Senate is making strong efforts for me. Information just received is to the effect that my appointment has been determined upon . . . My wife sends her best wishes.[26]

But, still, Bruce was not without his critics. It seemed that not only were there representatives from black civil rights groups who opposed his appointment, but also there was intense dissatisfaction coming from black political leaders both inside and outside his home state of Mississippi.

One black Republican club in upstate New York passed a resolution opposing Bruce's nomination to the register position on the basis of its belief that he did not care about black citizens or their plight. The organization, based in Albany, New York, mailed the resolution to Treasury Secretary Lyman Gage. Sent with a letter dated June 23, 1897, the resolution said, "this club earnestly protests the appointment of Mr. B.K. Bruce as Register of the Treasury since he is not in touch or sympathy with the Negroes of this State and has no influence with the colored voters of this Country."[27]

Also joining in this negative chorus was T. Thomas Fortune, editor of the black weekly New York Age. Given Fortune's close relationship with Booker T. Washington, it was surprising that Fortune had become so critical of Bruce. For years, there had been quiet criticism regarding Bruce's lack of involvement with average blacks and their concerns. Now, these widespread feelings threatened to sink his stature within the white power structure. But despite all these critics, nothing seemed to dampen Blanche's enthusiasm when he saw his son's pride, and received letters from Roscoe, who constantly encouraged his father in his pursuit of a federal post. Even at age sixteen, Roscoe was fully engaged in his father's career and future legacy. In a January 1897 letter to his father, Roscoe wrote, "Is the Cabinet still being formed? I hope so, for [President] McKinley[28] can't fail to see to whom one of his plums should go."[29]

Another factor that complicated Blanche's chances for getting a position was the tenuous position he held as a "vote deliverer" of black Southerners for the Republican party. This was because Southern states were creating new laws that limited the legal right of blacks to register to vote. In 1897, Louisiana was the first state to amend its constitution with a new grandfather clause that stated that the only persons who could vote were those who had a father or grandfather who had been eligible to vote on January 1, 1867. Since almost every black man's father or grandfather had been ineligible to vote on that date, this craftily worded law—which was adopted by other states in the South—kept virtually all Southern blacks from legally registering to vote. With the adoption of these voter registration laws, the black vote would mean less and less to political figures like President McKinley, and Blanche feared that it would make his own candidacy less attractive to the president and his White House advisers.

Despite the barriers that stood in Blanche's way, his prayers were finally answered in December, when McKinley announced his plans to name Bruce to his former position as register of the U.S. Treasury. Blanche wrote to Josephine, who was in Indianapolis at the time, visiting her ailing mother. In his letter, he mentioned that Roscoe, away at school, had just sent a special delivery congratulatory letter. Blanche continued, remarking that congratulations were coming from all over the country, "Dear, I am overwhelmed with visits both at the house and at the office. You never saw anything like it. Yesterday I mailed 49 replies to letters and telegrams of congratulation and have more than a hundred yet to answer."[30]

When Blanche was finally sworn in to the job in mid-December 1897, Josephine had still not returned to town. Still on a visit with her sisters and mother, she had remained in Indianapolis. It was clear to them both that she was no longer dropping her own activities in favor of his changing schedule. In his letter to Josephine, Blanche implied that many people were happy for him, but some were not. He noted that Booker T. Washington was coming to town that evening, that he had just thanked McKinley's powerful benefactor Marcus Hanna, and that he had still received no congratulatory message from their supposed friend P. B. S. Pinchback. Blanche wrote, "My Darling, Enclosed you will find notice of my appointment from NY papers. The *Times* of this city has a fine sketch of me. I was sworn in this morning and took charge of the office. I am simply overwhelmed with letters of congratulations. Not a word from Pinch. He is dead in his shell . . . I wired my thanks to Hanna."[31] In the same letter, possibly as a reminder of her duties back home, he let Josephine know that their maid was doing well and was going to be giving the household receipts to Josephine upon her return.

On December 9, 1897, Robert Terrell wrote an unabashedly flattering profile of Bruce for the *New York Age* to celebrate Bruce's appointment as the register of the Treasury. The article was generously sprinkled with laudatory comments about the president and mentions of the gratitude that black people felt for his acknowledging Bruce, its tone suggesting that Terrell was trying to curry favor not only with Bruce but also with the McKinley administration.[32] Several months later, Terrell, who had graduated from Harvard in the 1880s, would write a letter of recommendation on behalf of Roscoe when the boy applied to Harvard College.

Preparing to return to the federal payroll, Blanche immediately wound up his affairs in his firm at the Ohio National Bank Building. The office, which handled the purchase and sale of real estate, was also still used as his private office for personal records and the business files related to the plantation and the other rental properties owned by the family.[33]

Once he returned to his job as register of the Treasury, Bruce came to a position that was not nearly as demanding as it had been when he had worked there during the Garfield administration. The staff had become smaller since some of the duties had been switched to the office of the Treasury Secretary. Nevertheless, from the time that he assumed the job in December 1897, he remained busy with his duties of the office. But it wouldn't be long before the fifty-seven-year-old politician would begin to feel his health deteriorate.

Weighing over 250 pounds, Blanche Bruce had long lived with an unhealthy diet of pastries, breads, sweets, heavy meats, and highly salted foods. With a typical daily breakfast of ham, sausage, fried eggs, toast, and grape jam, he believed in enjoying meals as a part of his social schedule. His diary entries from later years were filled with dinner appointments, dinner meetings, and dinner parties.[34] Furthermore, Josephine was spending greater amounts of time away from home, visiting with her sisters in Indianapolis. Neither one of them was taking notice of any negative changes to his health.

Although the Spanish-American War did not officially begin until April 1898, President McKinley and Congress were using all their efforts in negotiating with representatives in Spain and in Cuba in order to resolve the conflicts between the two. In January, McKinley decided that the United States' investments in Cuba were in jeopardy because of Cuba's conflicts with Spain, and gave the U.S. Navy permission to send one of its second-class battleships, the USS *Maine*, to sit in the Havana Harbor. Several weeks later, on February 15, the battleship exploded, and although it could not be proved that the Spanish blew up the boat, U.S. newspapers pointed the finger at Spain.

Only a week later, Blanche and his fellow black colleagues learned that the attacks on blacks holding federal appointments were escalating. On February 22, the black postmaster in Lake City, South Carolina, was killed alongside his infant child by white residents who burned down his house and shot him, his wife, and four other children. Like white residents in many Southern communities, this mob objected to the federal government's decision to give positions to local blacks.

The violence that was erupting throughout the South against blacks, and the conflict that was growing between the United States and Spain, had created an atmosphere of anxiety for Republican politicians in Washington. Even if they could ignore the racial unrest going on at home, they were pulled deeper into the conflict abroad with Spain going into Cuba and the Philippines. Many of the black newspapers argued that the president should not ignore the atrocities being committed against black Americans on their own soil, but they knew that ultimately the United States was going to focus its efforts where its economic interests lay—and that was going to be in Cuba.

The stress that Blanche felt from both Washington and Mississippi black citizens, as well as that from his new job, took its toll. Having lost, through death or political infighting, many of his advisers, including Frederick Douglass, James Wormley, P. B. S. Pinchback, James Hill, and John Lynch, Blanche had trouble maintaining his erstwhile enthusiasm and vitality.

After an early March 4 morning meeting with Washington attorney John P. Green, who was an appointee with the Stamp Bureau, Blanche went for a large noon lunch not far from his office. After getting home, he complained of symptoms that he and Josephine believed were indicative of severe indigestion. Unfortunately, his stomach pains were soon discovered to be complications with his kidneys. By March 15, it became clear that the senator's situation was life-threatening. Dr. John R. Francis, a young, well-regarded black physician who had graduated from University of Michigan Medical School and served many among Washington's black elite, realized that there was nothing he could do to reverse Blanche's kidney failure. On March 12, Josephine had already publicly announced to the *New York Times* and other major papers that her husband was critically ill.[35] Three days later, Josephine sent a telegram to Roscoe at Exeter, telling him to take the next train to Washington.[36] She had seen these signs before, when her father's kidneys failed as a result of his severe diabetes. Only a day after Roscoe reached Washington, on March 17, 1898, Blanche passed away at their R Street home. On the death certificate, Dr. Francis listed the primary cause of death as diabetes and chronic nephritis.

Since Bruce had already executed a last will and testament, leaving his entire estate to Josephine, he had, no doubt, also discussed the details of his funeral and burial. Josephine employed James W. Dabney as undertaker and planned the funeral for March 21, with an interment to follow at Woodlawn Cemetery in Washington.

Although he was not a congregant there, Bruce's funeral was held at the Metropolitan African Methodist Episcopal (AME) Church at 1518 M Street NW. Completed in 1886, the handsome red-brick Gothic structure was an important landmark church that hosted large concerts and gatherings related to Howard University and other black institutions. In some ways, it was an odd choice of venue for the Bruce family. It was not of the Episcopal or Congregational denominations, which were followed by the Bruces. With the exception of Frederick Douglass and a few other families, it was not an overwhelmingly popular church among the black elite community. Knowing the Bruces to prefer most white institutions over black, many blacks in Washington were pleasantly surprised that, at his death, Blanche Bruce had returned to the people they believed he had snubbed for so many years. Although the church soon became very popular among the black professional community, at the time, many had assumed that a more likely choice for Josephine would have been a church with a large white congregation, particularly since she knew that the attendees, pallbearers, and speakers at her husband's funeral would include both blacks and whites. But the white churches in Washington had become extensively segregated by that time and would not have permitted a black funeral, even for the register of the Treasury.

At the funeral, there were thirty-two pallbearers—all men who represented the best-known black families. Among them were former congressmen, including John Lynch, George White, and Henry Cheatham; such powerful men as former Louisiana Lieutenant Governor P. B. S. Pinchback, *Washington Bee* publisher Calvin Chase, and Memphis millionaire Robert Church. Robert Terrell, who was married to Church's daughter, Mary Church Terrell, was the chief organizer for the funeral. Evident from news articles that reported on the funeral was that none of Blanche's siblings or relatives played a role in the ceremony. Josephine had not even listed them in the formal obituary. It seemed that right until the end, Blanche kept his family at arm's length.

With eulogies and speeches given by more than five ministers and a half-dozen political figures, the service gave a full presentation of the accomplishments and legacy of Bruce, who had risen from slave to the highest-ranking elected black official in the nation. In Washington, there seemed to be a unified response to Bruce's death: although he had always been cautious, he had gone farther in the political field than any other black man in history. At his death, even white Democrats praised his accomplishments and his contributions to the federal government. The Democratic South Carolina newspaper *Charleston News and Courier* remarked, "He was equal in ability to the average Cabinet officer and bore a higher character, personally and officially, than 90 percent of the candidates for prominent positions." For a black Republican who cared desperately about his acceptance by the white mainstream, this sentiment offered by a representative of the conservative white press would have been received with gratitude. It bore witness to the fact that he had represented his people with the type of dignity that he had always demanded of himself.

CHAPTER THIRTEEN

March 1898–June 1902

The Senator's Son Begins a Courtship at Harvard, and the Senator's Widow Carries Out a Legacy

BY THE TIME OF SENATOR BRUCE'S DEATH, A DRAMATIC CHANGE HAD taken place in the makeup of the United States Congress. Although the Republicans were back in control of both the Senate and the House of Representatives, there was only one black elected official in the two houses. Furthermore, as the rise in lynchings occurred throughout the nation, blacks in the capital saw their position in the nation backsliding quickly. Many black Washingtonians found themselves living in an increasingly segregated city. The conservative Democratic regime of Grover Cleveland had moved many blacks out of government employment, and those few who were still working were made to feel out of place in a city that had once been quite hospitable to them.

At 86,700 people, the DC black community was larger than any other city's black population at the time, but it was a mostly destitute population. Although a Republican, William McKinley, was now in the White House, the devastation of the 1893 depression had upset the economic opportunities with sufficiently dramatic consequences that even the policies and attitudes of a more progressive administration were not enough to put black citizens back on their feet.

With his father now gone, Roscoe returned to Exeter at the end of March. His father's illness had advanced so rapidly that Roscoe had been given only a day to prepare for his death, and only a few days to mourn before he had to return to the school's New Hampshire campus. Josephine told him it was important for him to successfully complete his senior year, and to complete the Harvard College application that he had begun that February.

When he arrived on the campus, he focused on his application with the same single-mindedness that his father had exhibited when going after a presidential appointment. He called on his father's Senate colleague George F. Hoar of Massachusetts, who had attended Harvard and had sat on the university's board of overseers. Hoar arranged for Roscoe to receive a recommendation from George's son, Rockwood Hoar, and his nephew, Sherman Hoar, both of whom had attended Harvard and were politically connected with the Republicans as well as the Democrats in Massachusetts.[1]

It is not likely that Roscoe really needed such powerful connections in order to gain admission to one of the Ivy League colleges. Although Princeton University still did not admit blacks at the time, the fact that Roscoe ranked among the top seven students at Exeter assured him that he could have his choice among Harvard, Yale, Brown, Dartmouth, or Columbia. The 1897–98 Phillips Exeter catalog listed him as an "Honor Man" for having received only As or Bs during the prior year.[2] Such grades were rare for Exeter students.

With his mother's assistance, Roscoe also contacted Booker T. Washington in order to solicit help for his Harvard application. So impressed was Washington that he sent the university the following letter that spring, on Tuskegee Institute letterhead:

April 25, 1898

To the Faculty of Harvard University:
 It gives me pleasure to recommend to you for admission to the University, Roscoe Conkling Bruce, the son of the late Hon. B.K. Bruce, who was one of the most eminent and useful men that our race has ever produced. Mr. Roscoe Conkling Bruce is a young man of the highest character and is in every way worthy and earnest. In thoroughness, application, and scholarship he stands high as his record at Exeter Academy abundantly proves.
 Yours respectfully,
 Booker T. Washington[3]

At the same time, Dr. Harlan P. Amen, Exeter's headmaster, wrote a strong letter on Roscoe's behalf to Harvard's dean Briggs. Written on April 25, 1898, it stated, in part,

> *My Dear Mr. Briggs,*
>   *Mr. Bruce, Register of the U.S. Treasury and former U.S. Senator from Mississippi has lately died. He left a widow and the son now in our Senior Class. The death of the father has completely upset the son, who is an excellent boy, a good scholar, and the best specimen of his race that we have had. His father was prosperous, paying all bills . . .*[4]

The fact that Roscoe's parents had been paying the full annual $100 tuition,[5] plus his room-and-board costs,[6] resulting in expenses of almost $500 for the year—a truly astronomical sum in 1897—was yet another means by which Roscoe was distinguished from other applicants.

As Roscoe waited to hear from Harvard, he spent the rest of the school year with his other black friends at the school: Bruce Green, John Syphax, Ed Wellington Lewis, Paul Pinn, and Thomas Williams. Most of his time he spent with his closest friend, George Shaw, who was from Charleston, South Carolina, and who would later attend college at Tufts University, just a few miles away from his own Harvard College Campus.[7]

When the school year ended, he returned home to Washington and spent the summer with his mother.

With her husband gone, Josephine expressed mixed feelings to her friends about seeing her only child leave town for college. Although nearby Howard University was considered the nation's finest black university—a school her own husband supported for several years as a financial contributor and as a board member—Josephine and Blanche had decided years before that it would never be good enough for their son. She knew that there was much greater promise for Roscoe if she could move him out of this increasingly racially divided city and into an environment that embraced a liberal view of racial equality.

When Roscoe finally boarded the train from Washington to Boston in the fall, his father had only been dead for six months. It might seem inconceivable that a black teenager would be able to leave home, enter a new all-white, racially segregated environment, and thrive with rigorous coursework in the wake of his father's death, but Roscoe had been raised to be stoic. Following the example of his very public parents, he had been taught to conceal his emotions from a public that scrutinized his actions. As proud as Blanche was of his son, he had never been warm or openly affectionate, and because of his political activities in Washington and his constant traveling around the country, he remained both physically and emotionally distant from his son.

When Roscoe was growing up, the family was constantly on the move, as they shuttled between Washington, Indianapolis, and Mississippi—or as Josephine and Roscoe were left in one place while Blanche traveled the country to bolster his national reputation. By the time Roscoe was finally of an age when he could have bonded intellectually with his father, Blanche was deeply ensconced in a busy government position and involved with his board responsibilities for the Washington, DC, schools and Howard University. Even if Roscoe could have engaged his father's attention at that time, the point immediately became moot when his parents sent him away to boarding school. So, despite their mutual respect, Roscoe and Blanche had grown accustomed to living apart from each other. The correspondence between them demonstrated Roscoe's desire always to flatter his father and gain his respect, while the letters from Blanche revealed his own inability to connect on an emotional level. Rather than ask Roscoe about his feelings, his friendships, or his happiness, Blanche used his letters to expound on his own political agenda and activities. It was only on the rarest occasion that Blanche would even mention the name of one of Roscoe's friends at school. Hence, it is not surprising that Roscoe's loss of his father lacked the emotional impact that a child would normally experience when losing a fully engaged parent. It was true, however, that one sure outcome of this loss was Roscoe's seemingly lifelong search for a male mentor who could advise him on personal matters.

But as the nineteen-year-old student rode along in the steam train headed North, he thumbed through a folder full of pages on which he had mounted clippings from newspapers that had profiled his father at the time of his death. Papers from every corner of the country were represented: New York, Indianapolis, Baltimore, Chicago, St. Louis,

Boston, Jacksonville, Washington. The *Washington Post* piece read, "The death of the Hon. Blanche K. Bruce, Register of the Treasury, may be a calamity to the whole Negro race in this country."[8] And a clipping from the *Indianapolis Star* read, "He was a man of dignified bearing, calm and steady of purpose and gave good advice to his race."[9]

And yet another article—this one from the *Colored American*—complimented his father, saying, "Mr. Bruce was great as a politician, great as a strategist and tactician."[10] Roscoe had read all the articles at least four or five times since leaving home. At that moment, they may have felt like the closest ties he had to his father and his father's legacy. He had gotten his mother to promise to send others once they arrived at her house. And those he'd also read again and again, after they had been carefully cut out and glued onto paper.

He must have wondered how he would ever live up to the accomplishments of his father—the great man to whom he never grew close enough to really know beyond what the newspapers said about him. He had boxes full of letters that his father had written to him over the years—many on the letterheads of hotels in the cities where Blanche had been traveling during his political career. These, too, were moving North with him on that train.

When Roscoe arrived in Cambridge to begin his freshman year at Harvard, most of black America was living below the poverty line in segregated communities south of Washington. What meager economic gains they had realized during the Reconstruction years had been almost fully erased by the policies of Southern "Redemption." And with the death of Frederick Douglass, the rise of Booker T. Washington, and the legalization of widespread segregation through the 1896 *Plessy v. Ferguson* Supreme Court ruling, blacks were losing ground precipitously.

Black activists like Douglass and black Republican elected officials like his father had been replaced by white Southern Democrats bent on revenge. Lynching, house-burning, and Ku Klux Klan rallies had become a popular way of keeping blacks in line. In the fifteen years from 1883 to 1898, nearly three thousand people had been lynched throughout the South. There was only one black left in Congress by this time, because of the Southern states' implementation of new grandfather clauses, poll taxes, and other methods to subdue black voting.

With black political clout fully suppressed, it was not a surprise when that void was filled by Booker T. Washington. In 1895, he was anointed by powerful whites who supported segregation and discrimination against blacks.

As black America was dropping further and further into disenfranchisement and segregation, Roscoe's entrance into Harvard made him seem even more removed from the common black experience of his day. When he arrived on campus, the school was in its 265th year. It was by far the richest university in the nation; its endowment stood at $12 million.[11] The undergraduate school—the college—had 1,851 young men on campus.[12] Its sister school, Radcliffe, also located in Cambridge, just four blocks away, had fewer than 450 women enrolled in its graduate and undergraduate programs.[13]

Although Harvard was internationally known and respected and had attracted some of the greatest scholars from throughout the U.S. and Europe, the makeup of the student body at that time was surprisingly homogeneous. Not only was it primarily white, Anglo-Saxon, and Protestant, with almost no Irish, Jews, or Italians, but it was also surprisingly geographically homogeneous. Wealthy young men from old, respected New England families were the typical students in each class. More than half of the 471 boys in Roscoe's entering class came from the Northeast and had been educated at boarding schools like Exeter, Andover, or Groton, or had come from private day schools in Northeastern communities.[14] More than 30 of them had been his classmates at Phillips Exeter, and less than one-third had graduated from public schools. With so many of them coming from wealthy families, the annual tuition of $150 was not much of a hardship for these students.

Also notable about the school at that time was that the junior and senior classes each had at least 100 fewer students than did the freshman and sophomore class, because of the high number of students who either had to repeat an earlier year or leave the school because of its high academic demands. By the end of Roscoe's freshman year, it was evident that 80 of his classmates were either leaving the college or being forced to repeat the school year, and in the following year, another 115 of his classmates either dropped out or were required to repeat the year.[15] Not only was the subject matter intellectually challenging, but also the school was rigorous in its attendance demands. The college employed two individuals—a recorder and an assistant recorder—to keep track of students' absences in each class.

From a racial standpoint, things were not too different at Harvard than they had been in boarding school. While the college had been accepting blacks since 1865, when Richard T. Greener, a young black man from Philadelphia, first entered, there were never more than two blacks in each class. And in several of the years, between Greener's freshman year of 1865 until 1899, there were no black students in the entering freshman class.[16] At neighboring Radcliffe, blacks were even less evident, as the first black student did not graduate until 1898.[17] Roscoe's class of 1902 had four students who identified themselves as Negro.

Roscoe was attending Harvard at an important time in the school's history. Charles W. Eliot was the current president—a position he had held since 1869.[18] Considered to be somewhat liberal on class and race issues, he made national headlines two years earlier, in 1896, when he had the university award Booker T. Washington an honorary degree—the first ever given to a black man. Eliot was also credited with keeping the tuition low so that the school could attract middle-class and working-class students who had excelled in public schools. Around this time, Eliot had said, "I want to have the College open equally to men with much money, little money, or no money . . . I care for the young men whose families have so little money . . . they constitute the very best part of Harvard College."[19]

Despite Eliot's attempt to make the school more diverse from a social class perspective, throughout his four years, Roscoe's schoolmates were primarily from wealthy families who had deep ties to the school. Future president Franklin D. Roosevelt started his freshman year in 1900, when Roscoe was a junior. That same year, Theodore Roosevelt (Harvard class of 1880) ended his term on Harvard's board of overseers and was elected president of the United States.

While intimidating to many, the school should not have been so off-putting to Roscoe in that it was not very different from Exeter in its racial makeup and its intellectual demands on students. And furthermore, just as he had known children of black elite families at Exeter, he also knew them at Harvard. At least three other black friends from prep school attended college with him. Robert Terrell, a Washington friend of his parents, had graduated from the school in 1884. Then a lawyer, and the husband of the very wealthy and socially connected Mary Church, Terrell had even written a letter of recommendation for Roscoe's Harvard application.[20] Furthermore, Roscoe had come to the school under the recommendation of some of the most powerful people in the country. Among his recommenders was U.S. Senator George Hoar. The Hoar family had important ties to Harvard since Senator Hoar's brother, Rockwood Hoar—former U.S. attorney general under President Grant—had sat on Harvard's board of overseers. A Hoar ancestor, Leonard Hoar (Harvard class of 1650) had been named president of the school in 1672.[21]

In an April 26, 1898, application letter to Harvard's Richard Cobb, Roscoe had mentioned some of the individuals who were writing on his behalf. The letter read, in part:

> *Dear Sir,*
> *. . . Professor H.P. Amen and Professor B.L. Alley of Phillips Exeter Academy have very kindly written letters recommending me to Dean Briggs. Senator Hoar sometime ago wrote to President Eliot in my behalf, and I enclose another letter to President Eliot from Doctor Rankin of Howard University. In a few days I shall send you one or two more recommendations . . . I am truly yours,*
> *R.C. Bruce*[22]

But even with connections to people who wanted to support this bright black student, the Harvard campus was not quite the liberal bastion that Roscoe had imagined it to be. Harvard Yard dormitories were heavily populated by young white men whose fathers and grandfathers had attended the school, and the black and white students rarely mixed. While students of both races took classes together and studied together in the handsome red-brick buildings that were dotted between large elm trees, their social lives were completely separate. In fact, there was a great contrast between the campus and the surrounding town of Cambridge, because while the campus offered virtually no black presence, the town had several dozen black families with deep ties to Cambridge and Boston.

Roscoe lived in a three-story boardinghouse at 55 Frost Street, just a few blocks from the campus. A relatively new row house–style building built in 1882, it offered comfortable but small quarters for several black Harvard students. Room and board cost him $54 for each term.[23]

Living off-campus and having few black friends on campus during his first year, Roscoe dedicated himself to his schoolwork and his extracurricular debating activities. He probably knew that with his father gone, his mother might ask him to apply for a partial scholarship, which would necessitate his maintaining a high grade-point average. This was exactly what happened during the spring of his freshman year. In May of 1899, Roscoe applied for a scholarship, stating that although Josephine could pay for his complete tuition, he might need assistance with his room and board. He wrote in the four-page application, "The death of my father and the depression in the cotton market have placed [my] mother and me in unusual circumstances. A large part of the crop of 1898 is yet unsold, and consequently it is impossible to say what income we shall get this year."[24]

The plantation was not being operated as efficiently or as profitably as it had been during Blanche's life, but Roscoe's mother still owned rental properties in Mississippi, homes in Washington, and a farm in Maryland. Her available cash was probably limited, because she was helping to take care of her widowed mother and spending a great deal to pay her staff of workers at the different properties while also maintaining her social life and women's club activities, but it is unlikely that she was a truly needy case. Nevertheless, Roscoe applied for assistance.

As a freshman, Roscoe was an extremely serious student, eager to prove to his mother and others that sending him to the school was worth any sacrifices she endured. In a letter written during his first semester, he told his Washington friend Clara Burrill about the demands of his schoolwork:

> *Ma Mignonne, At last my long silence is broken. I hope, dear, that in your thoughts you have not wronged me for it though. [I am] taking English 22, where I am writing in the narrative mood, the descriptive mood, the argumentative mood, the critical mood and also taking Medieval History, Constitutional Government, French, German and English 28 . . . Here at Harvard, I am seriously attempting to equip myself for the bat-*

tle of life. I am trying to learn how to wield that weapon of the gods: the mind.[25]

Despite his recent success at Exeter, in these early months Roscoe was overwhelmed with the work assigned to the freshmen and wrote home often, telling how he was "grinding away" at all hours of the night in order to stay ahead. Clara, who had not yet decided to attend Radcliffe, was making plans to attend Howard University or a teachers college in the Northeast. In her letters to Roscoe, she expressed sympathy for his heavy course load, but believed he would succeed.

By the time the spring semester of 1899 arrived, Roscoe was proving to the Harvard administrators that he was as gifted as the most talented white student on campus. In early 1899, he was asked to compete for the Pasteur Medal, a prize offered in a debating contest on campus. According to the May 6, 1899, edition of the *Colored American* of Washington, the question Roscoe had to answer in this oratory contest, which included freshmen and sophomores, was "whether the form of government of the Second Empire or that of the present republic was best fitted to the needs of the French people."[26] Still a freshman, he took on a sophomore team during the debate, and managed to beat his opponents and win the prize for Harvard's top orator.

During his sophomore year, Roscoe would move onto campus, which was when he would first develop a social life with his classmates. Prior to that time, he had found himself stuck in the middle: the wealthy white students lived in upscale residential buildings on nearby Mount Auburn Street, and the middle-income white students resided at the dormitories in Harvard Yard. For a black student living in an off-campus boardinghouse, there were few social ties to be found.

There were a few well-to-do black families in Cambridge who would host the young black Harvard men in their homes for teas and weekend dinners. One of these families was the Hemmings, who had a teenage daughter named Anita. Anita would eventually become a close friend to Roscoe and then to Clara, when the latter moved to Cambridge to enter Radcliffe College.

Several other blacks who attended Harvard around the same time as Roscoe endured this separation between blacks and whites. Scholar W. E. B. DuBois, journalist William Monroe Trotter, and future college president Leslie Pinckney Hill were among them.[27] In fact, DuBois spoke very adamantly of how far removed Harvard's white world was from his life there as a student in the class of 1890. He wrote:

> When I arrived at Harvard, the question of board and lodging was of first importance . . . I tried to find a colored home, and finally at 20 Flagg Street I came upon the neat home of a colored woman . . . I sought no friendships among my white fellow students . . . I doubt if I knew a dozen of them . . . I was happy at Harvard, but for unusual reasons. One of these was my acceptance of racial segregation. I escorted colored girls to various gatherings. Naturally we attracted attention . . . Sometimes the shadow of insult fell, as when at one reception a white woman seemed determined to mistake me for a waiter . . .
>
> In general, I was encased in a completely colored world, self-sufficient and provincial, and ignoring just as far as possible the white world which conditioned it . . . I was in Harvard, but not of it . . . With my colored friends I carried on lively social intercourse . . . I called at their homes and ate at their tables.[28]

The racially segregated experiences that DuBois described at Harvard were similar to those seen by other blacks who attended the college at the end of the nineteenth century. Since there were only about ten college dormitories—enough to accommodate about five hundred of the two thousand students, most of the students lived off the main campus.

Although Roscoe boarded off-campus that freshman year, he was determined not to lead the completely segregated Harvard life that DuBois and other black students faced. During his second year, he moved onto campus in Holyoke House, a five-story dormitory situated close to Gore Library, and met more of the white students. More important, he became involved with the black student population, which had grown since his freshman year. By then, he was able to socialize with his two black Exeter friends who were now on campus: Edward Wellington, also from Washington, DC, who had started Exeter at the same time as Roscoe; and Paul Calvin Pinn, who had entered Exeter a year after Roscoe. The following year they would be

joined by Thomas Calvin Williams of South Carolina, who had graduated from Exeter the same year as Roscoe.

While none of the social clubs on campus—known as finals
clubs—were open to blacks, he was able to join the debate team and the
Harvard Republican Club. He also spent several hours each week
studying in the school's Gore Library, a large ornate Gothic building
built in 1841 in the southeast corner of the Yard. Although he would
see some of his fellow classmates while taking his meals in Memorial
Hall, a mammoth building at the north end of the Yard, or in the
newly built Randall Hall that had opened a few months earlier, the
school's caste system was already obvious to him. He knew that his
wealthier classmates spent little time in the Yard and, instead, returned
to the five-story residential buildings that sat along Mount Auburn
Street in Cambridge. Since the college had done away with compulsory
daily chapel services twelve years earlier, there were even fewer opportunities that drew students together outside the classroom.

Roscoe remained in Holyoke House for his last three years at the
school. Since the dormitory, which was built in the 1870s, stood at the
southwestern edge of Harvard Yard, he was closer to the school's
pulse in his upper-class years. This building was very similar to the
other freshman dormitories—Hollis, Grays, and Weld Halls—but
was the newest of the four. It was definitely not as grand as the "off-
campus" residence buildings, such as the Westmorly Court, Claverly
Hall, Apley, or Fairfax, but it was still considered to provide nice
quarters for a young student.[29] More important, it gave him the
chance to interact with a few of the students that he came to know in
the Republican club and debate team on campus. Each day, as he left
Holyoke House, he would meet up with his friends and walk past the
austere granite Boylston Hall and toward Sever Hall, where he took
several of his classes.

While Roscoe did make an effort to become as much a part of
Harvard's mainstream as was possible for a nonwhite student, he also
maintained close contact with his black friends from Washington. Chief
among that group was nineteen-year-old Clara Burrill, who was then a
senior at M Street High School, his former school in Washington.
Although they had not been dating before this time, Roscoe had corresponded regularly with Clara while he was at Exeter. But now that he was
at Harvard, his letters became more frequent and more personal.

During his junior year, he wrote to her about the Christmas cotillions and parties he was attending. "Dear Carrie, For Christmas Day, my roommate and I spent time at the Hemmings. We had a fine time. George Ruffin, Miss Theresa Stubbs, Miss Elizabeth Hemmings, and 'the fair Anita' herself sang and played for us . . . I am delighted to know you are having so delightful a time with parties, balls, and assemblies galore! I certainly wish I could be in Washington if only for two or three days."[30] Roscoe and Clara would remain in weekly contact through their letters right until Clara arrived at Radcliffe College in September 1901 — the beginning of his senior year.

During the summer after his freshman year, Roscoe stayed at his grandparents' Indianapolis home with his mother, at 1639 College Avenue. Following Blanche's death the prior year, Josephine sought the companionship of her widowed mother and her two sisters, Mary and Victoria, who were still teaching in the Indianapolis public schools. There, Roscoe spent several weeks working in a summer job selling books for the K. R. Publishing Company. At the end of the summer, as he prepared to return to Harvard, his mother was suddenly faced with an opportunity that kept her from returning home to Washington. Booker T. Washington made her an offer to come to Alabama and join Tuskegee Institute as a school administrator.

Josephine abhorred the idea of returning to her empty town house without her husband, especially since Roscoe was in college five hundred miles from home. She also missed her prior work as a teacher, and so she accepted Washington's offer. The Tuskegee educator was now a very important figure in political and academic circles.

While held in high esteem among many in the black community and the few whites in the North who learned of his trade school through his lectures or the visits of Tuskegee's chief fund-raiser, Olivia Davidson—a woman he would eventually marry—Washington was not considered a nationally recognized man until his famous 1895 speech.

It was a speech that would transform his name and reputation into one of power and influence. Aiming primarily at a white audience, Washington outlined a policy that basically told whites that blacks should accept segregation, discrimination, and second-class status in an effort to advance themselves in the jobs for which whites were willing to hire them. He argued that self-reliance should be the focus of black citizens and that they should not demand equality.

The most famous line from his speech to the two thousand listeners was one that gave great comfort to white Southerners whose primary concern was getting blacks to accept segregation. Washington made it clear that he could get blacks to fall in line with the idea that "in all things that are purely social we can be as separate as the fingers, yet one as the hand in all things essential to mutual progress."[31] His speech made it clear to whites in the North that Southern blacks would refrain from traveling to their cities—a fear that many of them had embraced. His message that blacks could be patient with their slow economic advancement and not attempt to rise beyond jobs that focused on physical labor gave white Southerners great comfort.

The address made him an instant star among whites who liked his views of appeasement. Wealthy whites in the North and South began sending him money, inviting him to lecture to other white audiences, and encouraging his work. He was suddenly considered the spokesman for black America; his name began to be mentioned in the same breath as top leaders like Blanche Bruce. And with the February 20, 1895, death of Frederick Douglass, there was no question that the nation was ready to accept the crowning of a new black leader.

By 1896, Washington's name was riding a crest of popularity throughout the nation. That was the year that he had first invited Josephine Bruce to visit his school and address his students on the role that she and her family were playing in the nation's capital. She had remained in touch with Washington; he was one of the first out-of-town people that Josephine contacted when her husband fell ill in March of 1898.[32] Several months after the senator died, Washington told Josephine that his own wife wanted to step down from her role as lady principal (dean of women) of Tuskegee Institute, and wanted to know if she would accept the position herself, beginning in the fall of 1899. Since Josephine was living alone in Washington and having to manage the family's Mississippi plantation from such a great distance, she saw that a move to Alabama would cure her loneliness and bring her closer in touch with the activities on her plantation. After all, by that time, her son, Roscoe, would be fully occupied at college.

During the summer before her tenure was to begin, Booker and

Josephine negotiated over her salary, which she wanted to be set at $90 a month and to include her board and all expenses. She sent him several letters, but they went unanswered. Finally, Washington responded, giving her only a few days' notice before she was to arrive on campus. In his inimitable style of controlling his staff and controlling his public image, he issued a press release about her new position at the school, without even showing it to her first. He finally wrote her a letter on September 6, 1899, which began:

> *My Dear Mrs. Bruce: Please excuse me for my long delay in answering your letter of August 25th; I did not reach home until early this week and have scarcely had a minute to write since coming home. Mrs. Washington, however, tells me that she wrote you several days ago. I have just sent you a telegram saying that we expect you next week.*
>
> *Anticipating newspaper announcements in regard to your coming here I have prepared a short reference to the matter which I have sent out to some of the leading white and colored papers. I have placed it in a form which I feel quite sure will not be objectionable to you. Had the matter been left for the newspapers to get hold of the best way they could to make their announcements I fear the announcements would not have been so satisfactory.*
>
> *Suppose for the present we place the salary at $80 per month and board, board to include all expenses except traveling. If later on I can see my way clear to make it a larger figure.*[33]

Getting Josephine to accept a position with Tuskegee was a tremendous coup for Washington. Having a U.S. senator's widow as the school's lady principal brought the type of immediate prestige that Washington sought as he worked to present his school as the gold standard for Negro education. But his letter to her revealed him to be a genius at manipulation. Despite the fact that they had not yet agreed on her salary terms, Washington sent out a release announcing her employment there. Despite his claims to the contrary, he should have had time to show her the release before sending it to the newspapers. Since Washington was always very deliberate, and since much of his correspondence with individuals and with the press was drafted—and often signed—by Emmett Jay Scott, his secretary, it is unlikely that

Washington's claim that he "scarcely had a minute to write" was the true reason for his timing of the release and this letter. For a position as significant as the school's lady principal, it is unlikely that he would have left so many matters unsettled.

It is more credible that he was determined to phrase the press release in terms that were most favorable to himself, without any changes. Furthermore, he knew that a late response to Josephine could also force her to accept his lower salary figure, because her travel plans would already have been settled and the announcement of her arrival on campus would already be on the desks of the newspaper editors. Washington knew that he had forced her hand on both counts.

When Josephine arrived on campus to assume her role as lady principal, she found that Washington had a tight circle of advisers who guarded their turf and their nationally known leader with a devotion bordering on fanaticism. Emmett Jay Scott, who would eventually become the most powerful adviser to Washington, was the personal secretary who had arrived two years earlier from Houston, Texas. A slightly built, pale-complexioned black man, Scott was a great strategist on race issues, and an astute writer and speaker who knew how to draft persuasive letters and speeches. The scientist George Washington Carver had joined the faculty three years earlier. Although he was not a poised or sophisticated man, Carver's research and scientific developments with the peanut and other projects brought serious attention to the school.

Another highly valued lieutenant to Booker was Warren Logan, the school's treasurer, who had arrived at the school fourteen years earlier as an instructor in bookkeeping. Logan was deemed to be in charge of the school whenever Washington was out of town—which proved to be a common occurrence. In fact, that very year, Booker and his wife, Margaret, had left the country for a three-month European trip, during which they visited world leaders, philanthropists, and royal family members in England, France, and other countries. Mr. and Mrs. Washington returned a few weeks before Josephine's arrival, and numerous articles and accounts were published thereafter to describe Booker's European activities.[34] As Josephine read of them, the contrast made Alabama seem all the more dismal to her.

Having lived her entire life in such relatively cosmopolitan cities as Cleveland, Philadelphia, and Washington, DC, Josephine must have been unprepared for what she found in Tuskegee. Not only was it a rural environment with little culture to recommend it, but the school was also lacking any black elite community that could welcome her and make her feel at home even outside of her work. Despite the fact that thousands of dollars were being donated to the school, and handsome brick buildings were being erected on the campus, the institute was still in the middle of a farm community, with no large city to support it.

It was also a challenge for Josephine that the students at Tuskegee were not like the ones she had encountered in her home community of Washington, DC. They were not the well-poised, intellectually curious, elite children that she knew at Howard University, or others she had met in Washington, who had attended schools like Fisk in Nashville or Morehouse and Spelman in Atlanta. These students were largely from poor, uneducated families that lived in what many called the "Black Belt"—the Deep South, where their lives had been spent mostly on plantations and farms.

Never having lived in the rural South, except for occasional short visits to manage their Mississippi plantation properties, Josephine felt immediately overwhelmed by the tasks facing her as lady principal. Back in Washington, she has always been aided by servants—maids, secretaries, cooks, drivers, and others who were well-trained at assisting a "club woman" in her duties as hostess or community volunteer. But such helpers were a rare luxury on a campus as stark and simple as Tuskegee Institute. Still, she dug right into her duties during those first months. Because it was a coed school that offered separate curricula for men and women, her job was to focus on "all that pertains to the life of the girls at the school."[35] She reviewed the curriculum and made sure that the young women were being offered a wide range of courses that supported Washington's industrial trade-skills approach: cooking, sewing, housekeeping, child care, and horticulture. Drawing on her background as a schoolteacher, she attempted to inject some culture and classical lessons into the practical coursework. Josephine was also a member of Tuskegee's executive council that met twice each week to discuss the nine departments of the school.

What was impressive to Josephine was the influence that Washington wielded with both blacks and whites beyond the confines of the campus. It must have reminded her of her life with Blanche when she saw Booker organize meetings with blacks and powerful whites who respected him. On December 4, 1899, just three months after her arrival, Washington arranged such a gathering when he scheduled an endowment meeting in New York's Madison Square Garden with two thousand people, including such white supporters as J. Pierpont Morgan and John D. Rockefeller, who wanted to discuss how to raise more money for Tuskegee Institute and Washington's work of persuading blacks to embrace self-reliance rather than to demand social equality or an end to segregation.

But, of course, Josephine noticed that there were many detractors—people who felt that while Tuskegee was doing a marvelous job teaching trade skills, Washington's policies and messages served only to undermine the black man's fight for equal rights. Many of these critics were based in Washington, DC, and Atlanta, and included people like the scholar W. E. B. DuBois and the church pastor Francis Grimké. But the most aggressive group of anti-Bookerites was located in Boston and had ties to Harvard. They included William Monroe Trotter, editor of the weekly paper *Boston Guardian*, as well as his colleague George Forbes. Napoleon Marshall and Clement Morgan were two other Bostonians who openly disagreed with Washington. All four of these black men had attended Harvard College or Harvard Law School and resented the anti-intellectual, white-appeasement arguments made by Booker.[36] They wrote articles, gave speeches, and expended great efforts to show how dangerous Booker was to the struggle for equal rights. They pointed out that his policy of appeasement was demeaning to blacks and that it played into the hands of white bigots who were happy to give money to a black spokesman who would keep the black people in their place and prevent them from demanding an end to discrimination.

By the time Washington finished writing his autobiography, *Up from Slavery*, he was able to highlight the fact that the widow of Senator Bruce was a member of his school's faculty. And, in fact, it was around that time that it occurred to him that the Bruce family connection could assist him in another way. By 1900, Josephine's son, Roscoe, was in his junior year at Harvard, right at the epicenter of Booker's problems in the North. It occurred to him that Roscoe could aid him and his lieutenants by keeping an eye on Trotter, Forbes, and other Boston blacks who opposed Washington. So, Roscoe was enlisted to conduct whatever espionage he could so that Washington and Scott could protect themselves against their detractors.

During this time, Roscoe would clip articles from the local Boston papers and try to identify the local blacks who were posing the greatest threat to Washington. He would then report back to Washington's trusted assistant, Emmett Jay Scott. Roscoe even attended speeches given by Trotter or Forbes and attempted to meet with Forbes's boss in the Boston Public Library to see if Forbes could be silenced by a threat to his employment. A twenty-one-year-old Roscoe, still in his senior year at Harvard, wrote the following letter to Washington in February 1902:

> *My dear Doctor Washington—I enclose a significant "cutting" from the* Guardian. *I really fear the paper is doing harm—it serves to organize the malcontents and to intimidate the weak. Moreover, there seems to be no immediate or even remote prospect that the paper's resources will dry up; it is supported by the . . . rather large lower middle class of Negroes who yearn for a lively race paper in Boston. Forbes & Trotter, therefore, aren't likely to be losing money . . . Trotter writes, I have reason to believe, very little for the paper. He is a man with the persistent audacity of a fanatic. Forbes delights in writing the editorials . . . Just one word from the Librarian would in my opinion shut Forbes's mouth. Trotter can't carry on the paper alone . . .*
>
> *If something is not done, the* Guardian *may exert some slight influence over the white people here—that of course is the hope of Forbes & Trotter. Several white men of eminence have asked me how to account for the attacks upon Tuskegee of Boston Negroes . . .*
> *Faithfully, Roscoe C. Bruce*[37]

As both a spy and a strategist, Roscoe was suggesting that Washington should try to shut down the newspaper that was undermining Washington's reputation. Although the anti-Bookerites were voicing what many educated blacks also believed, and they were exercising their right to free speech without relying on slander or libel, Roscoe suggested an aggressive means of quieting the paper and its supporters. His suggestion was for Washington to contact Forbes's boss at the Boston Public Library and threaten the loss of his day job if he did not cease writing anti-Booker articles in an outside paper. Roscoe seemed well prepared to take on the task for which he had been hired.

Two weeks later, Roscoe revealed that he had actually begun to execute the threatened action that he had suggested to Washington. Determined to please his new mentor and role model, he did, indeed, seek out George Forbes's employer at the public library in Boston. He reported the following to Booker T. Washington in a letter dated February 22, 1902:

> My dear Mr. Washington—I sent you a copy of the Boston Globe containing a report of a speech I delivered at the Middlesex Club. I tried to make such a speech as would please both north & south & emphasize the educational needs of the Negro. In the Guardian was printed a mud-flinging attack upon speech and speaker. Of course I paid no attention publicly to the Guardian; privately I consulted Doctor James L. Whitney, Forbes' chief. Doctor Whitney is of course enthusiastic in his admiration for you & Tuskegee. I let him understand the situation created by the Guardian . . . He promised to do whatever he could to shut Forbes' mouth. Under the Civil Service rules it would hardly be possible to dismiss Forbes.
>
> . . . With Forbes in the Library, we have a constantly effective check upon his audacities. As for Trotter I see no remedy except his own ill judgment and fanaticism. If we give him rope enough, he is sure to hang himself. He has already lost character in the eyes of the few white men who have heard him . . .
>
> Faithfully, Roscoe C. Bruce[38]

The relationship continued and was fruitful for both, in that Washington maintained control over what happened in Boston, and Roscoe developed a mentor-protégé relationship with the most powerful black man in America. At one point, early in 1902, Washington even advised Roscoe on his area of concentration at Harvard. He told him that rather than majoring in humanities he should major in education. Washington also added that he would consider bringing Roscoe to Tuskegee to aid the school's academic curriculum.[39]

Much of this must have seemed rather contradictory to anyone who knew Roscoe and understood his long pursuit of scholarship. Much of his life had been spent in the purely academic settings of Exeter and Harvard, yet here he was, suddenly agreeing with a man who argued that blacks should forgo higher academic education in favor of training at industrial trade schools where they could learn to work with their hands. Roscoe either failed to see the contradictions because he felt that an upper-class black like himself was exempt from the policies that guided other blacks, or simply recognized that he could benefit more by ignoring the obvious hypocrisy of his actions since his greater goal was to befriend the influential Booker T. Washington.

At the time, Roscoe was living almost a dual life in that he was still very involved in such Harvard student organizations as the University Debating Council, where he served as president, and also served as editor in chief of the *Harvard Illustrated Magazine*. It appears that he never informed his friends or student organization colleagues that he was simultaneously working as a spy for the influential "Wizard of Tuskegee."

Roscoe's life was made even more challenging by the fact that his girlfriend, Clara Burrill, entered Radcliffe in September 1901. Living only a few blocks apart in Cambridge, Clara and he met and spoke often about his work of observing and reporting on the anti-Bookerites at Harvard and in Boston. There is evidence from their early letters that Clara was not so infatuated with Washington's views. In the end, while Roscoe would remain loyal to Washington, he resisted the advice about completely changing his course concentration from political science and philosophy to that of education.

About that same time, in July 1901, Josephine found herself trying to realize her own political ambitions for the first time when she decided to run for president of the National Association of Colored Women. As the lady principal of Tuskegee for the prior two years, she had drawn the attention and admiration of black men and women around the country. The convention where she would announce her candidacy was in Buffalo, New York.

What complicated her ambitions in the organization was the fact that another candidate for the office was Margaret Washington, the wife of Josephine's boss, Booker T. Washington. In the end, both women would lose the election to a woman from Kansas City, because both Josephine and Margaret ended up making a blunder that insulted many of the members. In their efforts to appease a local Buffalo organization of white women who had invited the two famous black women to a white reception, both Josephine and Margaret failed to attend the primary reception being held by the black female members, who were hosting the annual convention. Needless to say, the idea of Bruce and Washington snubbing their own black colleagues in favor of an organization of white women—who were strangers—infuriated the members who were attending the convention. As reported in many black newspapers around the country, both candidates were punished by defeat in the election.[40]

While his mother was pursuing her career and social activities in both Tuskegee and Washington, Roscoe was continuing to enjoy his last semesters at Harvard. He was performing well in his coursework, especially in French history, philosophy, and government studies. He spent his weekend evenings escorting young women to parties and balls that were hosted by local black families and black organizations. Although he and Clara continued to maintain their own relationship, they both openly discussed the cotillions and parties that they attended with other friends. It was a few months into his senior year at Harvard and her first year at Radcliffe that they became more serious about each other. Because Clara's school, in particular, frowned upon serious dating and unescorted visits for its female students, their "dates" were short and rather public—consisting of walks around the two Cambridge campuses and conversations in Radcliffe Yard.

By senior year, he reported to her that he would be graduating Phi Beta Kappa and magna cum laude but that his primary focus was on finding a job to follow his graduation. Even though he had been receiving a small stipend for his work for Tuskegee, it certainly did not amount to a full-time job.

Although Josephine had no doubt annoyed Booker T. Washington when she had decided to oppose his wife, Margaret, in the failed 1901 bid for the National Association of Colored Women presidency, it must not have created too many ill feelings, because Washington continued to maintain contact with her son and offer him career advice. He would eventually offer Roscoe a job at Tuskegee several months prior to his Harvard graduation—no doubt a move to solidify the prestige that the Bruce family bestowed upon Washington's school with their positions on staff.[41]

At his June 1902 graduation, Roscoe was one of 308 seniors to receive a bachelor's degree. His Phi Beta Kappa degree must have seemed all the more incredible to Josephine once it occurred to her how many of his classmates had fallen by the wayside since he started four years earlier: his freshman class had consisted of 471 students, but by his senior year, one-third of the class had dropped out.

Despite the rigors of attaining a Harvard degree, and his stellar record at the school, the racial situation in America made Roscoe's accomplishments seem almost worthless when it came to finding employment. While Roscoe's white classmates were going off to white-collar jobs in banks, insurance firms, and prestigious companies, the only jobs open to black graduates in the North were entry-level clerk positions in the post office, or custodians, or elevator operators in hotels and department stores. As was clear to everyone, including the university's president, the only respectable jobs available to a black Harvard graduate at the time were in the South, and they were limited to teaching at a segregated black school or college.[42] Roscoe was, therefore, grateful to once again rely on his family's connections—this time, connections that would take him South, closer to his father's family roots.

CHAPTER FOURTEEN

ოⴢⵇ

1902

Roscoe Builds an Alliance
with Booker T. Washington

I hoped that you'd sell the old plantation—beautiful and full of promise though it be . . . Well, of the plantation, I can hear the cheery "Christmas' gif'" from the little ones and the big ones crowding the steps Christmas morning. They are a humble folk— those poor colored people—but a sweet voiced, gentle folk. On the Bruce Plantation, they receive recognition of their essential worth as human beings, and that is gratifying."[1]

SO WROTE ROSCOE IN A LETTER TO HIS MOTHER, SOON AFTER HE HAD graduated from college and established himself in Tuskegee campus.

By the time he was in his early twenties, Roscoe Bruce was displaying a strong resemblance to the pampered and pretentious classmates that he met while a student at Harvard. The manner in which he referred to working people—particularly black ones—in his letters from boarding school, college, and Tuskegee, was often brimming with condescension. When referring to the workers on his mother's Mississippi plantation, he often sounded as racist and emotionally distant as a wealthy white plantation "master" from another period. Even worse was the fact that he was most concerned about the potential cash that he would receive if and when his mother sold the sprawling property that his father had established two decades earlier.

Because so much was being given to him by his mother and by those who were happy to do favors for him on her behalf, there was little for which Roscoe had to struggle. And he seemed to find it difficult to identify with those who did have to struggle for what they received. He had gotten the job working at Tuskegee Institute through his parents' prior friendship with Booker T. Washington. Despite earning his own salary, he still allowed his mother to pay for many of his expenses.[2]

By this time, Roscoe must have known that he was failing to face the challenges of the real world, because, only a few months later, he wrote, "My Darling Mother . . . I sometimes think that Papa is far away in some higher and better world, looking down upon me with a certain disappointment."[3]

Roscoe must have recognized the stark contrasts between his father's and his own life experiences. By this age, his father had long been on his own, with no emotional or financial support from his parents or family. Roscoe, on the other hand, desperately relied on the money, business contacts, and social connections that his family still provided for him. Roscoe knew it was not something that his father would have been proud of, but the boy lacked the independence and maturity that would have allowed him to do for himself and possibly even give back to his mother.

Although he was a complicated young man who, at twenty-three, was still trying to identify a role for himself that would define his potential, he was not totally to blame for his predicament. He had been raised by two busy, high-profile parents who had conducted their lives in the public eye. Much of his early life had been dictated to him and laid out without regard to his individual wants or needs. His father had been the sole decision-maker in choosing to send him to Exeter because other congressmen sent their sons to the school. His parents had long ago decided he would go to Harvard because they liked its reputation for educating boys from accomplished families. Neither of his parents had encouraged his friendships with other young boys or with his young relatives. Unlike his parents, he was raised an only child, with few playmates or confidantes. His mother, now a widow, had never bothered to renew a bond with her son even after the almost simultaneous occurrence of Blanche's death and Roscoe's graduation from prep school. She had, instead, packed her bags and moved even farther away when she took the principal's position at Tuskegee.

Despite all that his parents had accomplished, Roscoe seemed unable to embrace their pragmatic approach to life. Perhaps this was because his father had always been on the public stage rather than at home. The emotional and physical distance that Blanche mantained between parent and child made it difficult for Roscoe to have learned a great deal from his father. Since Roscoe's birth, his father had kept a schedule requiring him to be away campaigning or giving speeches on behalf of the Republican Party. When he visited his son at Exeter, it was always without notice, simply because a speech or meeting had suddenly brought him to the Northeast—and thus, the stay was inevitably brief.[4] In many of Roscoe's letters, he expressed his desire to be at home or to at least spend more time with his parents. Even at age eighteen he wrote from boarding school, saying, "There are moments when I feel like 'a silly baby' lost in an unfriendly world far away from home. I wish that I could be with you and mother at home. But my jail-sentence doesn't expire for ten weeks—ten, long, dreary weeks."[5] Roscoe's yearning for his parents' company was palpable in many of the letters he wrote to them during his adolescence and young adulthood.

Blanche lacked the humor and lightheartedness that would have made him a playful and approachable father, so he most often related to Roscoe through formal political discourse and long didactic letters that he sent to him while traveling around the country. When Blanche was home, he and Josephine remained occupied with dinners and gatherings with his political colleagues or her friends from her social clubs. And for the last six years of his own life, Roscoe had lived several hundred miles away from home, in boarding school and in college. Not having resided with his father or mother since he was sixteen, he received minimal firsthand guidance from two parents who should have been helpful role models.

Without such guidance, Roscoe often relied on artifice. His obsession with appearances and his tendency to make superficial judgments about others and their choices was an indication of his own insecurities. From the letters that he wrote to his parents, and later to Clara, it is evident that he yearned for "greatness" in his career and life—the kind of greatness that he thought his parents had enjoyed. Unfortunately, as a young man, he had little sense of how to get there or what he would do with it once he achieved it.

It had become evident while Roscoe was at Exeter that he enjoyed seeking intellectual challenges and those who he thought were his intellectual equals. Shunning the sports activities that were popular at the prep school, he focused his attention on the *Exonian* newspaper and the *Literary Monthly*, where he worked his way up to editorial management positions.[6] He did the same at Harvard, where he avoided athletics and instead advanced to president of the Varsity Debating Club and vice president of the Republican Club.[7]

But what started to become obvious once he had left the Northeast and arrived in Tuskegee, Alabama, was that not only did he prefer the company of intellectually gifted people, but that he was simply incapable of enjoying himself around those who lacked sophistication and those who failed to recognize his classical background. He was simply bored by ordinary people and their ordinary problems, and he was unwilling even to address or discuss their concerns. In fact, as much as he loved her, he was unwilling to address even the problems that were facing his own, now middle-aged, mother.

For example, in the fall of 1902, just months after his college graduation, he was settled into his new job at Tuskegee Institute, a position that he presumed would allow him to leapfrog over entry-level administrators and instantly take on the weightier cerebral issues that would face a full college professor. His mother, widowed now for four years, was writing to him often, to report on her business problems at home. It was hard for her to manage the staff on the Mississippi plantation, as well as to run Kelso Farm in Maryland and maintain her own Washington town house and lifestyle.[8] But while she never asked for constructive assistance from Roscoe, none of her overtures to him seemed to move him toward even providing her advice or empathy. In fact, despite her having paid for his education, gotten him the position at Tuskegee, and continuing to support him financially, he seemed unwilling to engage physically or emotionally with her plight.

This lack of concern for his mother's situation was evident in a November 25, 1902, letter that he wrote to his girlfriend, Clara, while she was a student at Radcliffe.

My dearest,

A letter from Mother alarms me about the condition of the plantation. She seems to be thoroughly dissatisfied with Woodford and his management of the business. Just what will be the outcome I'm sure I don't know. I hope that Mother will summon to her aid the utmost patience and tact. I have just bought Reed's Modern Eloquence, *and find the book well worth reading. Some of the speeches are quite commonplace, but many exhibit that rare quality we call eloquence.*[9]

Roscoe was so unwilling to deal with his mother's problem, he was barely able to discuss it, treating it as a minor distraction or nuisance. He was able to say only that he hopes she uses "patience and tact," a response that sounded both condescending and remote. Since many of his letters refer to his mother's problems with the same dismissive tone, he appears to be too self-absorbed to care, or simply too immature to know how to advise her during this difficult time. Since he was, by then, a very bright twenty-three-year-old with some insights worth offering his mother, one is left to conclude that youth was no longer an excuse for his lack of empathy.

What became apparent is that Roscoe often ignored everyday practical problems and, instead, quickly retreated to the security of topics that he preferred: esoteric or intellectual subjects that had no relation to the issue at hand.

Unlike his father—the ultimate pragmatist—who made a career of finding practical solutions to impossible barriers, Roscoe was more the nineteenth-century intellectual dandy who dismissed those laboring over the practical. His father had been raised a slave, performing manual work for himself and others who owned him or hired him. Roscoe, on the other hand, never even had a part-time job or household chores until he was an Exeter student.[10] His father had to drop out of Oberlin College in order to work full-time, because he couldn't pay the tuition.[11] Roscoe, on the other hand, spent four uninterrupted years at college, where his mother paid all his expenses. Blanche had bought his own home and over a thousand acres of investment property long before he was married, whereas Roscoe's official residence would remain his mother's Washington town house until the day of his wedding. He would eventually move back into her home when he and his wife lacked the finances to maintain a home for their own children.

Everything about Roscoe, by this age, seemed to resist practicality and normal convention. Just as he liked to lace his letters home from boarding school in the 1890s with French phrases, he later filled his epistles to Clara with references to books or essays written by European intellectuals or American professors.[12] More than half of the letters that he wrote to Clara during his time at Exeter and Harvard contain references to scholarly books that he was reading, or that he insisted *she* should be reading.

Evidently fancying himself a black Anglophile who would be carrying intellect into the wilds of Alabama, Roscoe apparently had almost given up on Booker T. Washington's students, faculty, and school before he had even begun his full-time position as head of the institute's Academic Department. In January 1902, he was visiting Tuskegee before he was to take up residence there. He wrote to Clara, warning her, in a letter replete with dramatic declarations, that there was no way he could work in an environment that fell so far short of his intellectual and cultural standards:

> *My darling, I expect to leave Tuskegee this next Saturday morning at 6 o'clock and to arrive in Boston Sunday night at 11 pm . . . the fact is that I have learned at least something of all the essential things in this miserably organized institution and there's absolutely no use in my staying here after this week . . . Tonight at Chapel there was held a kind of revival—that is to say a reversion into barbarism! The antics of the preacher and the students were disgusting. Such nonsense ought to be stopped at once . . . Such a proceeding is an insult to a man of culture . . . The miserable preacher declared as loudly as he could "The worst Christian is better than the best sinner." I hope most fervently never to descend to such a depth of ignorant tolerance. . . . Don't write to me dearie, after you receive this letter, as I shall in all probability leave here before your letter would arrive . . . Devotedly, Ros*[13]

After the last six years of his life had been steeped in the New England formal traditions of Exeter and Cambridge, it was no doubt a major culture shock for Roscoe to find himself in the grips of an all-black, heavily Baptist, rural Southern college campus like Tuskegee, but his response to the challenge seemed to be riddled with bigotry and condescension. His visceral response upon his arrival on campus was that the school was intellectually barren and "disorganized." And once he saw the students and faculty during their Baptist church service, he concluded that the people were not only lacking in intellect but were uncouth as well. Despite all this, he did ultimately decide to move to Tuskegee upon graduation—just a few months after the January 1902 letter.

Roscoe's reaction to the lively and animated Southern Baptist church services was probably similar to that of most upper-class blacks at the time. A group that had already begun embracing the Episcopalian and Congregational faiths, the black elite abhorred any church rituals that seemed animated, loud, or spontaneous. It has been argued that this group avoided practices that were, in any way, reminiscent of the religious traditions from slave life (e.g., Negro spirituals, speaking in tongues, or outright displays of emotion). It is also possible that the black upper class simply preferred these particular Christian denominations because they required more complex educational requirements for their certified clergymen.

At the time, the Episcopalian and Congregational Churches did demand more rigorous training and formal education than did the Baptist and AME denominations. The Baptist and AME groups, however, performed far greater outreach on behalf of blacks. Roscoe himself had been raised primarily in Josephine's Episcopalian faith. But it became obvious that Roscoe not only seemed to be contemptuous of the black Baptist church service, he also seemed to deride any person who demonstrated a true devotion to religion. In fact, he was unashamed to admit that he was quite pragmatic about religion—one of the rare subjects to which he applied pragmatism. In a letter to Clara, he said, "As for my religion, I have little. I believe in God, Freedom and Immortality, though should be loath to defend logically my beliefs. I seize upon them because in my judgement they are metaphysically valid . . . You understand my religious status and you love me—what more?"[14]

Roscoe was unapologetic about his lack of interest in the church and God. When taken together with his contemptuous reaction to the black Baptists at Tuskegee, his own approach to religion made him appear arrogant and patronizing.

Even though Roscoe complained about many elements of his life at Tuskegee, his arrival on campus in the fall of 1902 began an important chapter of his career. As the new head of the college's Academic Department, he was finally the teacher and no longer the student. For the first time, he was earning an income, and he was no longer under the strict supervision of parental figures.

In 1902, Tuskegee Institute was gaining national recognition as a leading black institution for postsecondary education. Much of this recognition was derived from its founder's controversial autobiography that had been published a year earlier. When Booker T. Washington wrote about, and continued to lecture on, his life story, *Up from Slavery*,[15] he advanced the name and reputation of his school. And more important, he continued to popularize the concept of the black industrial training institute.

Unlike the more prestigious black liberal arts colleges, such as Howard, Fisk, Spelman and Morehouse, which focused on providing blacks with the same academic education that students received at white universities, Tuskegee focused on teaching its black students about the trades: farming, building, plumbing, cooking, and so forth. In other words, the school embraced Booker T. Washington's appeasement theory, popularized in his 1895 Atlanta Compromise speech, that blacks should not seek the same academic education or opportunities that whites—and some well-to-do blacks—were privy to.

While many liberal whites and educated blacks in the middle and upper classes were offended by the condescending notion that it was a waste of time for blacks to take academic courses in history, biology, or literature in a good college, there were many more whites who agreed that black students would make better use of their time at an industrial trade school like Tuskegee Institute.

The pragmatism embraced by Washington and his school was at times attacked by black scholars as being both anti-intellectual and cynical. At worst, he was called an "Uncle Tom." What made Washington and his school even more controversial among black thinkers and the black elite was that it attracted the support of wealthy whites throughout the nation.

W. E. B. DuBois, the black intellectual who had earned his PhD from Harvard, argued that white industrialists and segregationists liked Booker T. Washington's views because he "practically accepts the alleged inferiority of the Negro race."[16] DuBois, as well as others, like Atlanta University president John Hope, believed that blacks deserved the same higher education and the same employment opportunities as whites, and that Washington's approach simply gave whites permission to continue their discrimination. In February 1896, Hope had said, "I regard it as cowardly and dishonest for any of our colored men to tell white people and colored people that we are not struggling for equality."

So, as the 22-year-old Tuskegee Institute raised thousands of dollars through Washington's speeches and appeals to important whites like Andrew Carnegie, J. G. Phelps Stokes, and George Foster Peabody, its detractors became more outspoken about the way in which Washington and his institution undermined racial advancement in the nation.[17] In fact, many of them noted that because Washington now had the ear of white philanthropists, he was telling them to stop contributing to black colleges that taught the sciences and liberal arts and instead to contribute only to black schools that taught the industrial trades.

But, to Booker T. Washington, his approach made complete sense in a 1902 United States, which he believed offered few alternatives for black people. The nation was becoming even more segregated following the 1896 Supreme Court case *Plessy v. Ferguson* that advanced the "separate but equal" treatment of blacks.[18] Although 90 percent of the nation's 8.8 million blacks lived in the South, the few blacks who had begun migrating North for employment were faced with racial violence and threats.[19] There was not yet a National Urban League to focus on black economic needs. The NAACP would not be founded for another seven years. There were only a few high-profile black individuals arguing for the equal civil rights of blacks. And the nation that Dr. Washington and Roscoe Bruce were living in was still not ready to offer equality. And Booker T. Washington was not going to demand it. His Tuskegee Institute approach was an implicit acknowledgment of that.

What does remain ironic, however, is that while Washington and Tuskegee clearly embraced and advanced the industrial-training school approach for blacks who wanted a postsecondary education, Roscoe Bruce's life focus had always been on the intellectual. His postadolescent experience had been committed to a life of academic rigor. Exeter and Harvard were the premier academic institutions in the nation in 1902, and yet he was now suddenly working at a black institution that argued against that form of training for blacks. It would have been more logical for him to have joined Howard or Fisk or Atlanta University—all superior black schools that embraced the notion that blacks should receive the same rigorous academic postsecondary education that whites received. But for him to have joined Tuskegee shows dramatic contradictions to what he claimed to believe up to that time.

There was no question that Roscoe, a magna cum laude Ivy League college graduate, had been able, and would continue, to demonstrate great intellect in the classroom. And he had an insatiable desire to read and surround himself with the literature that popular intellectuals of the day were discussing. Even his choice of Clara Burrill as a girlfriend and future wife, a woman who was possibly even more gifted, in both an intellectual sense and a practical-life sense, surely demonstrated his desire to be challenged. Despite the fact that he had begun working for Booker T. Washington—mostly as an informant on Washington's Northern detractors—while still in his senior year, it nevertheless seems that Roscoe should have found his intellectual interests to be too at odds with his joining the Tuskegee faculty.

There were possibly three factors that affected Roscoe's decision: first, Washington's charge to Roscoe that he should both launch and lead the school's first Academic Department;[20] second, Roscoe's desire to be close to a man who was now the most powerful and influential black American since his father; and third, Roscoe's realization that he had no other employment offers, since discrimination had prevented him from obtaining the jobs that his white classmates at Harvard were getting.

When Booker T. Washington first gave him the chance to perform part-time work for Tuskegee while Roscoe was still in college, the offer was probably made because Josephine had recommended it to him and because he needed a trusted ally in Boston, to observe and report back about those black Bostonians who were speaking out against Washington's accommodationist theories. What had not been expected was for Washington to be so impressed with Roscoe's work that he would immediately name him head of the institute's Academic Department upon his graduation from college. It is true that Roscoe followed Washington's advice during his junior year to supplement his political science major with additional courses in education, but neither Josephine nor Roscoe knew that these early conversations and correspondence would lead to such an important position. If Roscoe had to work at an industrial-training school, he must have been grateful that his position was to lead whatever academic curriculum the institute was willing to offer its students.

The second important factor influencing Roscoe's decision to accept the position in Tuskegee was his desire to enhance his relationship with the man who had become the most popular and most powerful black man in America. Roscoe had grown up in a household that understood the value of power, wealth, and fame. It had given him, his father, and his mother access to important blacks as well as powerful whites. Now that his father was no longer alive, he sought new opportunities to capitalize on the connections that his father had established. To the extent that his mother could provide these connections, she did, but Roscoe probably recognized that he needed to develop a mentor-protégé relationship with someone who was vibrant and who could provide guidance and fresh ties to new power brokers. Booker T. Washington was the person who could do that. Roscoe was eager to get to Tuskegee and engage with his mentor.

The first chore that Roscoe tackled was recruiting instructors who could teach those few academic courses that he would be introducing through his Academic Department. He reviewed his own contacts, which included bright young Negro graduates of good schools, and he corresponded with others who might identify other graduates that he didn't know. In February 1902, he wrote to Booker T. Washington to describe some people whom he thought would be good additions to the Tuskegee faculty. Among them were some former classmates from M Street High, Exeter, and Harvard. He wrote:

> I had a long talk with [Leslie Pinckney] Hill. He is unmistakably a man of force. He has determined . . . to remain at Harvard one more year, then, he would like very much to come to Tuskegee—even at a smaller salary than he could get at Lynchburg. I shall keep him in view.
>
> [Paul Calvin] Pinn is really eager to come to Tuskegee and will be at our service after the present year. He is competent to give a course in the history of education with special reference to Negro education, a course in morals, and work in English composition

and literature. I feel that the work in the history of education
would be a valuable contribution to the Normal department . . .
Pinn is just the man to give a good rousing course in morals.
    I shall write to Doctor Rankin of Howard in reference to
Mr. Baugh. I understand that Mr. J. A. Bluford, a post-graduate
in Science of Cornell . . . is a good man. I'll look him up.[21]

Of the people that Roscoe recommended for recruitment that
month, several were old friends. Paul Calvin Pinn had been a year
behind Roscoe at Exeter and Harvard College.[22] Leslie Pinckney Hill
was another one of Roscoe's Harvard friends.[23] Dr. Jeremiah Rankin,
who would end up recommending potential teachers to Roscoe, was
the white president of Howard University and had been a close friend
of Roscoe's father when the senator had sat on the university's board of
trustees in the 1880s and 1890s. Though Roscoe was only a college
senior at the time that he wrote this letter to Washington, it reveals his
confidence and enthusiasm about the job that he would begin six
months later at Tuskegee Institute.

Throughout this time, Roscoe consulted Clara on his strategy for
bringing academic-minded teachers to Tuskegee. As an economics
major with a strong interest in the law, Clara was not very enthusiastic
about industrial education, but she encouraged Roscoe with his plans.
Because of her own pragmatism, she recognized that while she and her
future husband had always pursued the intellectual challenges that
their schools had put before them, their academic experiences would
not translate into the kind of employment opportunities that would be
available to their white classmates. She knew that the teaching profession and the trade professions were going to provide the majority of the
jobs to the black population. It was not a pleasant realization for an
aspiring lawyer, but it was a fact nonetheless.

As Roscoe began to establish himself in his very first job, it must
have occurred to him that, at some point, others would ask him how he
planned to follow in his father's footsteps. They were questions that he
often addressed in letters to Clara and Josephine: Did he want to return
to Washington? Did he plan a political future? If so, did his ambitions
include elective office? Did he need to begin building a network of
black advisers? Whatever his thoughts were regarding a political
future, it was clear that the political landscape for blacks had changed

more in the five years since his father's death than it had in the prior twenty-five years.

When Blanche Bruce had been nominated for the Senate in 1874, there had already been four blacks elected to the posts of lieutenant governors and seven other blacks elected to Congress. These numbers would grow substantially over the next several years. But by January of 1903, the black political movement had been stopped in its tracks by the Ku Klux Klan, the Southern Democrats, and strong white resistance in virtually every state. In fact, the white backlash against Reconstruction's advances for blacks was so severe that by 1903, there was not a single black in Congress or in a lieutenant governor position. President Theodore Roosevelt's support of the notion that black people were the white man's "burden" and his open belief that blacks were inferior all served to further undermine black achievement in the political arena.

It must have been obvious to Roscoe that even if he had held ambitions to follow his father's career path, reality was stacked against him. A career in academia, an area well suited for a bright young man who enjoyed only the company of bright people, was preferable to seeking support from a black and white public that was becoming increasingly segregated.

CHAPTER FIFTEEN

❧◐◑◐❧

1903

A Marriage of the Second Generation
and Life in Tuskegee

ROSCOE HAD AN IDEA THAT HIS MOTHER, JOSEPHINE, WORRIED ABOUT
his marrying Clara or any other woman who did not come from an
equally wealthy family. After all, Josephine had seen her own brother's
wife abandon him a few years earlier, with all of his possessions in tow.

For Josephine, this was a tragic example of how mismatched mates
could end up, and it is likely that she feared that her much wealthier
son could be the victim of a young woman eager to capitalize on his
family background and money. Although Clara's family enjoyed a
middle-class background and demonstrated no interest in Roscoe's
apparent wealth, Josephine had quietly hoped that he would choose a
young woman from a richer family.

As Roscoe arrived at the Tuskegee campus, he saw his mother's
reluctance to embrace Clara Burrill in the way she had embraced some
of the daughters of their wealthier friends. But Roscoe was unwilling to
change his plans. At a corner of the campus, where three elm trees
stood shading a small lot, was half of a brick foundation for a house
that was to be his and Clara's once they were married. At this moment,
lumber was stacked at the front along the sidewalk, and bricks were
lined neatly under the trees. The three-bedroom house looked to be six
months from completion, but the school said it would be ready in just

over thirty days. It would be built completely by Tuskegee students and their class instructor.

Roscoe discounted his mother's concerns about Clara. He himself had no doubts. What Roscoe was having second thoughts about was the way in which his colleagues, and Booker T. Washington failed to respond to Roscoe's questions and concerns. Dr. Washington had made many promises about his salary, his benefits, and his professional opportunities, but things were moving much too slowly, and at a standard that failed to impress Roscoe. Earlier that morning, he had written a letter to Clara at Radcliffe, voicing some of his concerns: "The school owes me a good deal of money but they haven't yet paid me one cent. Our house won't be completed for a month. The builder tells me that now, but I don't know . . . I shall continue to board at the horrible school dining room."[1]

Roscoe quickly learned that keeping the school's faculty and administration happy was a low priority for Washington. The greater goal for the "Wizard of Tuskegee" was building his own power and influence. And he got that through creating what came to be known as the "Tuskegee Machine," a political organization that he built in order to gain influence with elected officials, the most important one being the president of the United States. Already, Washington was able to wield enough influence to make himself the first black man ever to be invited to dine at the White House.[2]

When Theodore Roosevelt became president in 1901, Washington's autobiography, *Up from Slavery*, was simultaneously capturing the attention of the white public. With his historic 1895 Atlanta Compromise speech behind him and this new book offering whites an opportunity to see how their "Negro problem" could be solved, Washington had managed to offer himself to white leaders as the conciliator who could get black people to do what white people wanted them to do.

He already had the ear and trust of wealthy whites. Now, Washington wanted the ear of powerful elected officials, like the president. He had succeeded to some extent with President McKinley, but he wanted to take it even further with Theodore Roosevelt, so he set out to do this by making himself useful to Roosevelt, a Republican who was determined to beat back any Democratic opposition that might threaten his power or the power of his party. Recognizing this, Washington pointed out how important black support would be to the Republicans. He promised to use his influence with blacks in various cities and establish black Republican clubs throughout the nation. This necessarily meant that less time and focus was given to local matters on campus. The Tuskegee Machine set about identifying black lieutenants who could help their cause in cities throughout the South and wherever else there were large black populations. As Washington increased the number of these black Republican organizations, Roosevelt became more grateful and more interested in hearing Washington's opinions.

Although Roosevelt believed that black people were inherently inferior, and he had previously offended many black Americans when he refused to acknowledge their contributions in the Spanish-American War and the Battle of San Juan Hill, he knew that it was politically expedient to reward a few blacks with patronage jobs in the nation's capital. He relied on Booker T. Washington to tell him which blacks to reward.

Just as Washington had earlier advised President McKinley (and later, President Taft) on several of his black appointments, he was now offering Roosevelt lists of names that should or should not be considered. This access gave the Tuskegee Machine unprecedented power in the black community, and it accounted for the appointment of many of Roscoe Bruce's acquaintances and contemporaries, including Robert Terrell, who was named Washington, DC's, first black city judge, and John Dancy, who was named recorder of deeds in the nation's capital.

And it was probably because of Booker T. Washington's influence and the power of his Tuskegee Machine that so many black intellectuals and black civil rights leaders resented him. Although he was helping to get a few blacks into government jobs, he was doing it at a stiff price to his faculty back home who were operating in his absence, and to the larger black community in the nation. This was probably one of the reasons why the 1903 publication of W. E. B. DuBois's book *The Souls of Black Folk* was so controversial, and so eagerly anticipated by Washington's detractors. Not only did it outline where blacks needed to turn in order to improve their condition, it clearly criticized Booker T. Washington's "national" policy of white appeasement.

A graduate of Fisk University, Harvard College, and Harvard's graduate school, where he earned his PhD in history in 1895, DuBois was a well-respected scholar who strongly opposed Washington's arguments that blacks should limit their education to industrial schools. He also disliked the way in which Washington encouraged blacks to surrender their fight for equal rights and for an end to discrimination. He said,

> Mr. Washington represents in Negro thought the old attitude of adjustment and submission; but adjustment at such a peculiar time as to make his programme unique . . . and Mr. Washington's programme practically accepts the alleged inferiority of the Negro race . . . Mr. Washington distinctly asks that people give up three things—First, political power, Second, insistence on civil rights, Third, higher education of Negro youth—and concentrate their energies on industrial education, the accumulation of wealth and the conciliation of the South.[3]

By the middle of 1903, it was plain to everyone, including Roscoe, that Booker T. Washington and DuBois despised each other. Not only had the DuBois book become immensely popular, but it turned DuBois into a literary star. The more attention DuBois received for his critique of Washington, the more aggressive the Tuskegee boss got. He was determined to make sure that DuBois and other detractors did not embarrass him to the point that his wealthy white supporters lost interest in his school and programs. To a great extent, he did not care that the black elite was shunning him. After all, they didn't bankroll his activities, and they refused to send their children to his industrial school. The people who mattered principally to Washington were his white benefactors, many of whom attended his famous 1903 fundraiser for Tuskegee Institute in New York City's Madison Square Garden. The crowning event for Washington took place on April 24, when Carnegie gave $150,000 (worth almost $2.5 million in today's dollars) to Washington and his family for their personal use, and then another $450,000 in U.S. Steel bonds to Tuskegee Institute.

Although the fund-raising activities for 1903 were already a financial triumph for Washington, it angered his detractors even more when they saw how many whites were willing to invest in a man who was undermining the rights and future of the Negro race. It also upset the Tuskegee teachers who felt that although the funds were being used to build their school, their leader was rarely on campus. This internal and external resentment led to increased popularity and sales for DuBois's book. But despite attacks on his programs, Washington pretended to be unconcerned by DuBois and his writings. In fact, Washington harbored great resentment toward DuBois. It was during the planning for an upcoming series of lectures by DuBois at Tuskegee Institute's summer school session that Washington expressed his dislike of the man and his new book. In a note to Roscoe, Washington wrote:

> *Dear Mr. Bruce: Under all the circumstances I think it will be well to pay Dr. DuBois' traveling expenses to Tuskegee and return for the sake of his lectures. If he chooses to be little we must teach him a lesson my bearing greater and broader than he is.*[4]

When Roscoe was not trying to gain the attention of his boss, his mind was focused on his beloved Clara in Cambridge. Having gotten engaged on December 27, 1902, Roscoe had been laying out plans for their future together for several months. They corresponded with each other almost weekly. She had written to him in January that she was looking forward to their marriage:

> *My darling,*
> *The sweet letter that I received this morning from you I have read and reread many times. It is perfectly true dearie, that if I were not so deeply in love with my sweet [future] husband, I could do ever so much better work at Radcliffe. Often when I should be studying, I am writing a letter to you ... What can one expect of a girl whose soul is at Tuskegee and whose body alone is in Cambridge?*[5]

By the beginning of 1903, Clara Burrill had been teasingly referring to Roscoe as her "dear husband" or "sweet husband" in her almost weekly correspondence with him in Alabama. Although they were not to marry until the end of the year, their frequent love letters revealed a strong emotional attachment that was mutual and seemed not to be hindered by the thousand miles that lay between them. What was also obvious about them was that they appreciated each other's intellect, as they debated over current events and intellectual theories.

Two years Roscoe's junior and a native of Washington, DC, Clara

Burrill was, in many ways, very similar to her fiancé. The daughter of educated black middle-class parents, John Henry Burrill and Clara Eliza Washington, Clara grew up in a conservative household that embraced education and self-discipline. Although her family was neither powerful nor wealthy like the Bruces, they did make sacrifices so that Clara, her sister, Mary, and her older brother, Edmond, would have the best education available to blacks at that time. Like Roscoe, she attended M Street High School, where children of Washington's black elite had attended for many years.[6] Although they had met when she was ten years old, they did not become close friends until they had been in high school together in 1895 and 1896.[7]

Whether he realized it or not at the time, Clara was the ideal mate for Roscoe and, in many ways, was as valuable to his career as his mother, Josephine, had been to his father's public life. From the time she graduated M Street High School in June 1897, Clara continued to improve herself intellectually. Just as Josephine Willson had sought early training as a teacher, so did Clara. Like many black high school graduates who planned a teaching career, she attended West Chester Normal School in Pennsylvania for a two-year teaching degree. There, she took courses in, among other things, Latin, English, German, geometry, and physics.[8] In September 1899, at the same time that Roscoe began Harvard and Josephine began her position as lady principal at Tuskegee Institute, Clara entered Howard University with the plan of taking enough courses to transfer into Radcliffe as a sophomore. Around this time Clara had another experience that would draw her closer to Roscoe: her father died, leaving Clara, her sister, her brother, and their mother alone in Washington.

It must have been comforting for Roscoe to know that he and Clara had so much in common. They shared their families' emphasis on education, their Washington childhood friends,[9] and their understanding of the black upper classes. By early 1903, Roscoe was certain that she was the right woman for him. The only serious dispute the two had experienced was a short 1900 bout with Roscoe's jealousy over Clara's male friends and suitors who lived in Cambridge near Radcliffe.[10] He was ready to propose, marry, and plan a life together.

Others were not so supportive of the match. Despite Roscoe's reputation as an intellectually gifted student, there were some who felt that Clara Burrill was significantly smarter and might not be satisfied with taking on the role of a passive, adoring wife. There were even those who found Clara to be too cerebral and, hence, intellectually threatening. In fact, in 1902 Clara wrote a letter to Roscoe, telling him that people in Washington and Boston were trying to stop their marriage. "I despise Archibald Grimke . . . He is saying to Anita [Hemmings] that your mother is against my marriage to you. Grimke also told Anita that we shouldn't marry because I am too intellectual to make a good wife."[11]

While there is no proof that Josephine made openly aggressive moves to prevent Roscoe's marriage to Clara, it is conceivable that the senator's widow would have found Clara a little too liberated and more cerebral than the typical mate for a traditional man at that time. Clara was certainly unlike Josephine when the latter became engaged to the senator in 1877. Like other upper-class women, Josephine had been noted for her wealth, beauty, charm, and potential as a Washington hostess for her husband and his political friends. Clara was not likely to shine in any of these areas in the way that Josephine had done so many years before.

While she was attractive and poised, no one would have called Clara a great beauty, as they had labeled Josephine. In fact, in a society that valued slender women with small waists, Clara did not fit the ideal. At twenty years old, she weighed 157 pounds and stood at five feet five inches. Certainly, it was a normal weight, but not one that fit the conventionally sexist view of "slender beauty." While they were dating, and even after they became engaged, Roscoe would write to her about the "beautiful and fair" Anita Hemmings, the daughter of a well-to-do Cambridge family that often entertained black Harvard and Radcliffe students at their home. He even took it upon himself in one letter to explain Anita's beauty to Clara.[12] In what must have been both insulting and humiliating to Clara, Roscoe detailed the Cambridge girl's good background, long hair, slender body, olive complexion, and talent at singing and playing the piano. The only flaw that Roscoe could find in Anita was the fact that she was not as bright and interesting as Clara. The fact that Josephine liked Anita and Anita's mother was another factor that weighed against Clara Burrill. And although Clara could converse with anyone, her tendency to challenge and demand intellectual rigor from others would not be appealing to those who expected an obsequious or deferential hostess.

If Josephine had, indeed, told the famous Harvard Law School–

educated Archibald Grimké, who later helped found the NAACP, that she did not find Clara to be a suitable wife—and it is likely that she did tell him so—it was a somewhat ironic statement. After all, Clara may not have resembled the twenty-five-year-old woman who married Senator Bruce in 1878, but she definitely resembled the more mature Josephine Bruce who had stepped out from behind her husband's shadow in 1898. It is possible that Roscoe's mother found Clara's intellect and confidence both disconcerting and threatening. It is also possible Josephine sensed that Clara was independent enough to insist that her future mother-in-law stay in the background and allow her to conduct her own household as she pleased. Only months later, Clara wrote to Roscoe, "When your mother comes in the fall, I shall realize what it means to be sole mistress of my household. Mothers-in-law may be well-intentioned—but they are still mothers-in-law."[13]

Notwithstanding Josephine's alleged worries, Clara would ultimately prove to serve her husband in ways that only a bright woman could. She would eventually edit his writings while he was teaching at Tuskegee, redraft his speeches while he was school superintendent in Washington, and even serve as his adviser and assistant after he was hired by John Rockefeller to manage the Dunbar apartment complex in New York during the 1930s. There was no question that she would eventually add value to his career. In a fall 1902 letter, Roscoe revealed that his mother had evidently capitulated, and he used this opportunity to state that his mother did not see Clara's great intellect as a problem. He wrote to Clara, "Our unspoken prayer is answered: Mother loves you, she has said so in so many words again and again. She is rejoiced in your scholarly ambitions . . ."[14]

Only weeks after Josephine's alleged complaint about Clara's suitability as a spouse, it was clear that Clara was aiding Roscoe's work. She wrote from Radcliffe about the most recent editing assignment she had performed on his behalf: "I went to the printer this morning and asked him to change 'mountain whites' to 'poorer whites' . . . Tomorrow morning he promised to have the speech in final form for me. I selected a very pretty gray cover and the paper is good . . . Instead of having *The Work of Tuskegee* separated and two words put on left page and two on right, your [future] Wife decided that it would look better to have *The Work of Tuskegee* written across the left and right pages. That isn't very clearly expressed, but you know what I mean."[15]

There was a confident air of no-nonsense efficiency that permeated Clara's letters to Roscoe. Even though she was still in school, and he was now employed by Tuskegee Institute, she did not hesitate to make decisions that she felt would enhance his professional assignments. She eloquently challenged the books that he sent to her, and she demanded greater honesty and intellect in the papers he was writing at Tuskegee. Demonstrating once again that she was more than his intellectual equal, Clara wrote in one letter the following:

> *I have been reading your Ward's Sociology. I haven't read enough of it to be able to intelligently criticize it. As yet I haven't come across anything startlingly new. In fact I have been impressed lately that very few of the great books are made up of other than commonplace things . . . I read the article in the Congregational Work. It was supposed to have been written by Professor J. P. Bond. But he [obviously] didn't write it. You wrote it. There are certain phrases that you use constantly—they always appear in whatever you write. It may be effective, dearie, and yet it gives a little too much sameness to your writing. Don't you think so? Is not Matthew Arnold criticized for the constant repetition of certain phrases.*[16]

Clara's eloquence and insight were intellectually dead-on, and she was unafraid to question what Roscoe and others put in front of her. Whether in person or through her letters, she was frank and clear about what she believed.

It is also clear that Roscoe relied heavily on Clara's guidance. Several days after she made changes in one of his speeches, he wrote back and paid her high compliments:

> *My dearest,*
> *President Eliot*[17] *said the other day that Alice Freeman Palmer*[18] *was the bravest woman he ever knew; my wife is brave— brave in thought and deed. We shall both strive with all the strength that is in us to be brave and good and sensible.*
> *I am highly pleased with the form in which the Boston speech appears. You are right in saying that "citizen" should be*

"citizens" . . . The gray cover is just the thing. I hope you'll give
Sie [Syphax] three or four copies.[19]

Comparing Clara with the admired Alice Freeman Palmer, president of Wellesley College, was possibly the highest compliment that Roscoe could offer to Clara, who was demonstrating her devotion to him. What is also evident in their correspondence of this period is their sense of greatness—of trying to be great by striving to do good and be courageous. He says that the two of them should try to be "brave and good" as if they were about to enter battle. Similarly, in a late January letter written by Clara to Roscoe, she ends the letter saying, "I hope we may be of great service."

Although neither one had spoken of repeating the senator's life in public service, it is clear Clara and Roscoe recognized that such a possibility existed for them even if not through elective office. They expressed admiration for individuals who presided over colleges and who advanced intellectual discourse, so it is reasonable to believe that these two young adults saw their own futures as including great deeds. Their ambitions, while lofty, were not haughty or unreasonable. They both sounded thoughtful and sincere in their hope to do great things in the world together.

Despite his declarations to be "good and sensible," and despite his articulated devotion to Clara, Roscoe seemed to change dramatically as the wedding plans began to unfold in the winter and spring of 1903. He started to reveal a petty, selfish, and unforgiving side. It all seemed to relate to the wedding expenses and his unwillingness to assist with them despite knowing that Clara's father was deceased and her mother, Mrs. Burrill, was unable to afford the extravagant wedding he and Clara had discussed.

Although he spoke of greatness and being "good and sensible," he fell short of being a generous suitor. In fact, not only was he not generous in addressing the cost of marrying Clara, he evidently was also not generous in welcoming her mother and brother into his family. Clara implored him to be nicer to her mother and less harsh on her brother in Roscoe's demands that Edmond bear all the expenses for his sister's wedding. She wrote, "Ed is very good to offer to help in our wedding expenses . . . one mustn't expect too much of Ed."[20]

She already felt that her brother had held his tongue about their decision to marry so soon. In order to spare Roscoe's feelings, Clara did not tell him how devastated she, her mother, and her brother were about Roscoe's insistence that she leave Radcliffe before graduating. Her brother had written to her several months earlier, expressing his disappointment. He wrote, "Dear Carrie, How is Edith Smith and all the Radcliffe girls with the funny and catchy names? Mama tells me that you are going to give up college to get married. I have refrained from mentioning it until I felt able to make some comments."[21]

Clara hid her own and her family's disappointment regarding Roscoe's request that they marry before she graduated. She hid it because she felt that Roscoe had already waited a year for her. She was afraid to ask him to wait an additional year. But because of this compromise, both Clara and Ed felt that Roscoe owed them some generosity and a display of agreeable behavior.

This was the beginning of Roscoe's three-month-long bout of selfishness. For the next several weeks, he sent Clara letters replete with complaints about her mother and brother.

It would have been inconceivable for Roscoe's father to level such treatment upon the Willson family when he courted Josephine and presented himself to them. Even though Josephine's father was well able to afford an elegant wedding, Blanche spent a great deal of money to ease the burden on her and her parents. As an employed young man with few expenses and a wealthy mother, Roscoe could have afforded to show greater generosity. Instead, he leaned on tradition, pleading and even demanding that Clara's family bear the expenses of the wedding. Following the best role model for "greatness" that existed for him, Roscoe should have known that his father would never have conducted himself in such a manner.

Early on, Clara asked Roscoe to be nicer to her widowed mother. She put some of the onus on herself, but her point was clear: Roscoe had made Mrs. Burrill feel like an outsider. She wrote, "neither you nor I have been as patient with them as we should have been . . . I want mama to feel that as long as we have a home, she has one too. I hope you'll let her know dearie, that she will always find a welcome in our home."[22] By this point, Clara's brother already had offered to assist in the wedding expenses, but it appeared that Roscoe was not satisfied.

Recognizing her family's financial situation, in late January, Clara suggested that they postpone their marriage until she had completed Radcliffe and they had more money for the wedding. Clara's pragmatic response to the situation—her brother's limited funds and her own desire to finish school—demonstrated her maturity and composure, but Roscoe was not interested in hearing about Edmond's lack of funds and even less in her plea for patience. He instead sent a strongly worded letter to her, stating that Edmond should not be permitted to travel, move out of town, or incur any expenses until they had established a wedding date and Edmond had paid all the expenses.

The letter was written on official Tuskegee Institute stationery that featured the names and titles of the top administrators and board members. It read:

> *I wrote to you in some detail with perfect candor . . . I hope your reply will be equally detailed . . . As a plain matter of fact Edmond is every whit as responsible for the well being of the family as is your mother . . . until his duties to his family are discharged . . . An essential part of those duties is a reasonable provision for your marriage. No decision of yours can truly release him from these duties.*

The letter, fierce and almost threatening, goes on to say that Clara should not excuse Edmond from this financial responsibility even if it is true that he has been supporting the family as well as loaning Clara's mother money since before Clara entered college. Roscoe wrote, "If it be said that he has already 'loaned' your mother certain hundreds of dollars, I reply that a son cannot *lend* his mother a cent. He and all he has are (in the absence of his marriage) thrice mortgaged to the woman who gave him birth and nourished him."[23]

How ironic this letter would have sounded to Josephine if she had ever gotten to read it. Although Roscoe argued persuasively about a son's responsibility to a mother and family in the absence of a father, he himself had always avoided his responsibilities as they related to his mother and her ongoing challenges with the plantation and their other properties. On many occasions and in many letters, he complained to Clara that his mother was asking too much of him with her queries for advice and counsel. It was both hypocritical and disingenuous for Roscoe to say that Edmond was being selfish for not placing his sister's wedding plans and expenses ahead of his own career plans to work and study in Europe. At no point had Roscoe put his family's needs ahead of his own. And what made Edmond's actions even more sympathetic—and Roscoe's less so— was the fact that Clara had said several times that she was willing to postpone the wedding planning and marriage date until after she completed Radcliffe and there was less of a financial burden on her family.[24]

And still trying to offer solutions in the face of her family's financial burden, Clara continued to pare back her dreams in response to Roscoe's demands that the wedding take place despite her brother's meager finances. Clara made compromises that she couldn't possibly have enjoyed: she said that it would be all right if they didn't go on the honeymoon they had planned; she reduced the guest list from three hundred to forty people; she also told Roscoe that he need not buy her a bracelet. And, finally, she asked if he really had to buy her a wedding ring.[25]

In the short term, Roscoe's selfishness would prove to serve his goals and usurp Clara's. Despite the fact that many considered Clara to be the smarter half of this couple, she would not succeed in graduating from Radcliffe College. Because of his demands that they marry immediately and his insistence that she leave Radcliffe at that time and follow him to Tuskegee, she gave up an important goal that she and her family had set.

Despite his own wealth and the apparent financial strain on Clara's family as they attempted to allocate money for a wedding while also paying her college tuition, Roscoe never offered to assist in the expense. In fact, he cunningly avoided the possibility by telling her that such an act on his part would be unacceptable. He wrote, "Edmond would be the last person in the world, let me once more say, to permit me to pay all the bills for our wedding."[26]

So overbearing was he in his correspondence to Clara that he attacked her and her family in every way, even questioning her moral character for offering to postpone the wedding. He wrote, "In the name of our love, I solemnly insist that come what may, you become formally my wife in June 1903. We have come to a point now, dear, when shuffling hesitation is actually immoral. If you love me (and I know you do), you will not hesitate . . . I beg you once more never again to intimate in a letter that you could conceivably agree to the postponement of our marriage."[27]

Still, a month later, in February, when Roscoe learned that Clara's brother was being considered for a Foreign Service position in Switzerland, he complained and asked, "Who will pay for the wedding if he's gone and who will take care of your mother?"[28]

All of this was made worse when Roscoe told Clara that since he himself was short of money, she should ask the treasurer of Radcliffe College to give her a rebate for the month of June, since she would be leaving the school one month before completing the year.[29] Possibly recognizing that this was an audacious request, and possibly worried that this letter would also be a permanent record of his alleged meager finances, he wrote in the postscript at the bottom of the page a large note, "Tear up this letter." In this letter, he also spoke to Clara about the new house they would live in on the Tuskegee campus, and informed her that he would like to host a friend's wedding there the week after they arrived from their own wedding.

Several weeks later, the dispute ended because the Syphax family offered to host the wedding at their Washington home. This lessened the financial burden on Clara's brother, ended Roscoe's complaints, and allowed Clara to invite her original list of three hundred guests.[30]

Also a major issue of discussion was their anticipated sexual intimacy, an uncomfortable subject for Roscoe. In early May, he wrote to Clara, asking her to seek guidance regarding their first night together. He wrote, "At this time, it is important for you to speak to someone about the personal aspect of marriage. . . . Perhaps you should talk to a doctor at Radcliffe who can advise you. I will speak to Dr. Francis who shall advise me on this uncomfortable subject."[31]

In her characteristically direct manner, she answered him, "Our college has no regular physician. Dr. Bond who lectures there occasionally is out of town at present. I am not a prude, dearie. I do not object to you writing to me about those matters . . . Let me know what Dr. Francis tells you."[32]

A more pressing issue for Clara during the spring of 1903 was the wedding and reception. Because of their families' ties to the black community in Washington, most of the guests would be people that they had known as children. But they also invited classmates and black neighbors from Cambridge, as well as several of Roscoe's Tuskegee colleagues. Understandably, Roscoe would use this occasion to reconnect with many of his parents' affluent and well-connected black society people, like Louisiana Lieutenant Governor P. B. S. Pinchback, who had moved to Washington; Harvard's first black graduate, Richard T. Greener; members of the Memphis Church family who were the wealthiest blacks in the country; and, of course, Booker T. Washington, his new boss.

From the tone of Roscoe's letters regarding the guest list, it was obvious that he enjoyed remarking on the value of certain guests. He wrote,

> *Yes, let's invite Mr. and Mr. T. H. Carver, Mr. & Mrs. A. Hart, Mr. & Mrs. Pinchback; Mr. & Mrs. Theodore Green of Washington; Mr. Richard Greener, U.S. Consul at Vladivostoc, Russia; the Bentleys—they are the Chicago Bentleys. Don't you think we ought to invite your former beau—that Philadelphia doctor. . . . I'll try to get Mr. and Mrs. Booker T. Washington to attend the ceremony; they'll appreciate the invitation. I don't think it will matter if I distribute the Tuskegee invitations from here; these folks aren't up to snuff.*[33]

In this letter, it was first suggested that Roscoe's former Exeter schoolmate, T. John Syphax, might be removed from the list of ushers for the wedding. Although it is not clear if Syphax remained an usher—because he was still a close friend to both Clara and Roscoe— Roscoe wrote to Clara, "Yes, let's omit Sie from the list of ushers; he *would* be embarrassed."[34] It is possible that this referred to the fact that, around this time, the light-complexioned T. John Syphax began to pass as white.

Around the time that he left Trinity College in 1903, Syphax had begun to deny his racial identity to the extent that when he entered Columbia Law School in New York, he identified himself as racially white. Upon marrying a white woman, he misrepresented his true racial background. Syphax also altered his name to T. John McKee, assuming his grandfather's last name. It is quite possible that Syphax had recognized that he could not participate in such a high-profile black wedding—one that was to be chronicled in the black and white press—if he was about to begin living as a white person. As many upper-class black families and friends did during this period, Clara and Roscoe evidently made a "gentleman's agreement" with Syphax to assist him in executing his plan to disguise his racial identity. It was a disguise that Syphax/McKee would maintain for 45 years.

When the wedding finally took place at 7:30 p.m. in Washington, it was officiated by Rev. Archibald Grimké of Boston, and the 8:30 p.m. reception was attended by more than two hundred members of Washington's black elite. Immediately following the reception, the couple were taken by horse-drawn carriage to their hotel, and the next day they boarded a train bound for Atlanta, and then for Tuskegee, Alabama. In the end, proving that Roscoe's and Josephine's worries about the Burrill family finances were groundless, Clara's brother and mother paid all the wedding expenses.

CHAPTER SIXTEEN

಄ඖ

December 1903–1906
Roscoe and Clara Build the Next Generation

"MY DARLING MOTHER . . . I SOMETIMES THINK THAT PAPA IS FAR away in some higher and better world, looking down upon me with a certain disappointment."[1] This was how Roscoe thought about himself and his constant reliance on his family as he wrote to Josephine from Tuskegee Institute in 1903.

The Tuskegee Machine continued to grind on in 1903, attracting supporters, crushing detractors, and collecting money from white Northerners who liked to hear the words of the great accommodationist from Tuskegee. With a team of bright, ambitious lieutenants to assist him, Booker T. Washington was unstoppable. His assistant, Emmett Jay Scott; his friend, the New York publisher T. Thomas Fortune; his treasurer, Warren Logan; and he himself all used various kinds of subterfuge, media manipulation, bribes, espionage, and a variety of underhanded techniques to maintain their control as the country's black power brokers. They did whatever they had to do in order to silence their black critics, because their greatest fear was that white benefactors would cease supplying them with money and white political leaders would stop seeking their advice.

Since the most vocal critics of Washington were still the coeditors of the black Boston newspaper *Guardian*, W. Monroe Trotter and George Forbes, Washington and his lieutenants funded the creation of at least two other black Boston papers that would publish frequent pro-

Tuskegee articles. Since many of his benefactors lived in the Boston area, it was important for Booker to demonstrate that many of the blacks in Boston did, in fact, like him and subscribe to his beliefs. It was irrelevant that most black Bostonians actually disagreed with him; what mattered was merely that local whites had the general impression that he was the preeminent spokesperson for the black community.

In order to silence Trotter and Forbes, Washington encouraged all types of activities to undermine their paper.[2] He encouraged a black Yale student, William Pickens (class of 1904), to sue the paper after the *Guardian* criticized a speech in which Pickens had said that Haitians were not ready for independence.[3] Washington had his own attorney work on Pickens's behalf. Furthermore, after Trotter caused a near-riot at one of Washington's Boston speeches, the pro-Washington lieutenants put pressure on the local authorities in Boston to have Trotter arrested and put in jail for several days. One of the outspoken critics of Trotter at that time was Washington's young friend William H. Lewis, who had graduated from Dartmouth and Harvard Law School. Washington would later reward Lewis for his loyalty by convincing President Taft, in 1911, to name Lewis the first black assistant attorney general of the United States.[4]

It is likely that since Roscoe had aided Washington while he was still in college, he knew of the powerful Tuskegee Machine before he arrived in Alabama. But what probably wasn't so obvious was how broad-reaching Washington's power was, and how aggressively he would work not only to silence detractors but also to spread propaganda about himself and his school.

Once they were settled in their modest three-bedroom wood-frame house on the Tuskegee campus, Roscoe and Clara were able to dig into their work and responsibilities as the bright new Northern couple on campus. Early on, just before their marriage, Roscoe had warned Clara of his responsibility as a new young faculty member and role model for the students. He had said, "Our home would soon constitute itself as the social center for the teachers and for a carefully selected group of students. I do not mean that we are to be overrun by visitors. I mean simply that semi-occasionally our house will be thronged."[5]

But Clara did not know what to expect at Tuskegee. First, there was the mythical reputation that the campus held in the general population because of all the things she had read in articles that either quoted Booker T. Washington or profiled his rise as the chief "spokesman for colored America." He and Tuskegee's prominent benefactors had spoken of the school as though it was a black version of Harvard and Radcliffe.

And then, there was the Tuskegee that Roscoe had described as narrow, backward, and uncouth—a place where it was hard to find even a decent fountain pen for writing. Only months before, he had written, "My difficulty here is to get hold of a pen that is respectable; I've tried a good deal but as yet haven't succeeded."[6] Clara had received letters from Roscoe that derided the institution and its people:

"Radcliffe offers you information and discipline that married life in this narrow place, Tuskegee, could not offer you."[7]

"The antics of the preacher and the students were disgusting."[8]

"I have just found it necessary to administer to [George] Jenifer and Miss [Hermione] Garvin [two junior Tuskegee faculty members] a severe rebuke for their having become so conspicuously interested in each other . . . Miss Garvin is permitting her reputation to suffer . . . Like most 'educated' Negroes, Jenifer has no common sense."[9]

"The fact is that I have learned at least something in this miserably organized institution."[10]

"My hesitation is that in taking you away from Radcliffe . . . I should be doing violence to your own best interests, seeing that Tuskegee isn't Cambridge."[11]

What had she gotten herself into? Clara had just given up the opportunity to complete the last few months of a bachelor's degree at the nation's most prestigious college for women and had abandoned an environment rich in intellectual rigor and urban sophistication for a rural trade-school campus in the Deep South. She'd left her family and friends in Washington and her accomplished classmates in Boston. Having grown up in DC, and spent the rest of her years on the campuses of Howard and Radcliffe, Clara was, indeed, not ready for what she found on the rustic Tuskegee campus.

Within days of her arrival, Roscoe requested that she open their small home for the wedding of two junior faculty members. Clara must have been surprised at the time, since this was the very couple that only months earlier, in a November 25, 1902, letter, Roscoe had derided as "Negroes with no common sense."

Clara was, nevertheless, happy to be settled. The two-story house looked small from the outside, but the interior was sufficiently spacious, and because it was new, it was fitted with an up-to-date kitchen and bathroom on the first floor. Also on that floor were a parlor, a dining room, and a library "running the whole length of the house with very high ceilings. The side windows open upon a fine porch."[12] The second floor had three small bedrooms, a sitting room, and a bathroom.

When Clara arrived, she discovered that Roscoe's housekeeper, a Mrs. Kelly, had decorated and arranged the rooms in a way that did not appeal to Clara. It was also clear to her that Roscoe had begun to rely heavily on Mrs. Kelly. Only a month earlier, Clara had said that she did not want a housekeeper, because the woman would inevitably disagree and start to challenge Clara's authority as the new lady of the house. She had said, "We shall of course have a maid, but no housekeeper. I will make the decisions on housekeeping."[13] For the next several weeks, Clara concentrated on making the home their own. She decided to save her foray into the town and the rest of the campus for the fall months.

The town had been settled in 1830, and like many of the small towns of Macon County, it consisted mostly of farms and plantations that grew peas, corn, cotton, and potatoes. There was a small center of town, which was populated mostly by middle-class white store owners and workers tied to the local agricultural economy.

The school, however, was distinctly rural. Located close to the eastern border of Alabama, only a few hundred miles from the Georgia state line, the rustic campus was quite large—roughly 1,400 acres. There were approximately thirty-five buildings of varying sizes; the oldest ones were wood frame, but the newest ones were substantial red-brick buildings about four stories tall. There were eight hundred students coming from twenty states. Because the school billed itself as an industrial trade institute that taught carpentry, plumbing, masonry, painting, and farming, a great deal of the students' training was in the practical application of these skilled trades. Therefore, students had the responsibility of helping to build the dormitories and classroom buildings, as well as erect walls and fences. They even made their own bricks at the campus brickyard and kiln.

The school's students farmed more than six hundred acres of the institute's property. Rather than study in libraries and learn primarily in the classroom with books and professors, the students at Tuskegee were sewing on sewing machines, sawing lumber at the school's saw-mill, and learning how to care for livestock that were raised right on the grounds. In fact, by 1902, the school owned two hundred horses, mules, and cows, and was breeding more than seven hundred hogs and pigs.[14]

Of course, there was classroom teaching for some of the curriculum, but it was to instruct on the practical skills of a particular trade. For example, students interested in building were required to take courses that taught architectural drawing, plastering, and house painting. Women who hoped to work in dress shops were given courses in clothing design, sewing, and simple bookkeeping.

Clara must have found the style of teaching as far from the intellectual rigor of Radcliffe as possible. A few years earlier, Booker T. Washington had described the school in an article he wrote for the _Atlantic Monthly_. In it, he said that Tuskegee Institute "has emphasized industrial or hand training as a means of finding the way out of present conditions . . . the school furnishes labor that has an economic value, and at the same time gives the student a chance to acquire knowledge and a skill while performing the labor. Most of all, we find the industrial system valuable in teaching economy, thrift, and the dignity of labor, and in giving moral backbone to students. The fact that a student goes out into the world conscious of his power to build a house or a wagon, or to make a harness, gives him a certain confidence."[15]

In essence, this was a form of education that was well outside the culture of the black middle class and black upper class that the Burrill and Bruce families had come from.

As Clara and Roscoe adjusted themselves to Southern living at Tuskegee, there was a lot to observe. The school was going through an important growth period. Faculty and staff numbered roughly ninety people. By that point, the campus property was valued at $700,000, and the endowment was $1 million—a truly astronomical number for a black college in the early 1900s. With white philanthropists and industrialists still responding positively to Washington's lectures on how the black race should cease asking for equality or an end to segregation and discrimination, and instead focus on self-reliance, Tuskegee was blessed with thousands of dollars from Northern donors. In fact, Clara and Roscoe arrived just in time to see the spanking-new crown-jewel campus building open its doors: the Andrew Carnegie Library, a building that the industrialist had paid for with a $20,000 check two years earlier. The striking red-brick Georgian colonial with large white columns was reminiscent of a Southern plantation mansion, and it reinforced the perception that the school was becoming the most important black institution in America. It stood across the road from Washington's private residence, an imposing Victorian mansion named The Oaks.

In one sense, Roscoe could not have asked for a better role model in his first boss. Currently at the pinnacle of his power and influence among wealthy whites and the educated black population, Washington was a diplomatic leader who outlined a policy for his followers and persuaded them to follow it. He understood that whites wanted the black community to embrace self-reliance and second-class citizenship. And he developed speeches, letter-writing campaigns, a national network of well-scripted supporters, and a school curriculum that would advance his goals.

While he never attacked white racism in the way that Roscoe's father was occasionally willing to do in the Senate and thereafter, Washington was able to portray himself, to black people and others, as the leading spokesman for blacks. While he was conservative and accommodationist, his methods for persuading whites and most blacks that he could solve the "Negro problem" were relentless and extremely effective.

Booker T. Washington always stopped short of asking whites to make up for the disadvantages that two hundred years of slavery and discrimination had created for the black race. In fact, at times he suggested that white Southerners could not be blamed, because they were also victims of the institution of slavery. His argument focused primarily on what blacks should do to help themselves. He put the onus on them. Long ago, Blanche Bruce had been at odds with this aspect of Washington's message. Instead, Bruce had stated that both whites and the national government needed to make amends with blacks by improving black schools and investing in the black community.

In 1887, Blanche had told the *Philadelphia Times*,

To tell you just how the Negro is doing ... I shall have to ... point out the fact that during their 200 years of servitude, the individuals of the race acquired some knowledge ... but it was acquired at second hand, was at best crude and inadequate

for him as a freeman and citizen. The period has been reached
when the national authority should intervene in the interest of
this [Negro] people . . .

The power that gave them freedom should afford them
such educational facilities as will render that gift invaluable.
Good government, good order and the preservation of free
institutions alike demand immediate action . . .[16]

While Senator Bruce was never considered radical or militant, he
was at least willing to tell white people that their past wrongs necessi-
tated their assistance in making things right: changing laws so that
blacks were given equality, protecting blacks in the South, investing in
black communities, improving black institutions, et cetera.

Booker T. Washington, on the other hand, argued for self-
improvement and patience in the black community. Never insisting on
equal rights or respect, he told whites that blacks would be satisfied
with second-class citizenship and never demand equality. Unlike
Blanche, who argued that two hundred years of slavery had put blacks
at a severe disadvantage compared to whites, Washington insisted that
whites and blacks were both victimized by slavery. In his book, *Up from
Slavery*, he went so far as to excuse the white plantation worker who
had raped his mother and never acknowledged Booker, the child that
was born to her. He wrote, "I did not even know his name . . . Whoever
he was, I never heard of his taking the least interest in me . . . He was
simply another unfortunate victim of the institution which the Nation
had engrafted upon it at that time."[17]

The willingness to turn the other cheek for white racism and those
who practiced it stood in stark contrast to the manner in which he dealt
with blacks. Whether they were family members, colleagues, employees, or strangers, Washington was dictatorial, controlling, and vengeful.
The idea that white Southerners should not be taken to task for their
past and current racism and their ongoing efforts to segregate blacks
was not only preposterous in itself but inconsistent when taken
together with the way in which the vindictive and harsh Washington
dealt with even his most beloved family members.

For example, his relentless attempts to completely control the
movements of his two oldest children would eventually cause them to
rebel by leaving Alabama and picking spouses who would help them

break free of his hold on them. And when Washington couldn't punish his children for their actions, he struck out at others. When his oldest son, Booker T. Jr., eloped without his father's knowledge, an angry and humiliated Washington issued a memo two days later to the entire school staff stating that any faculty member who married without his knowledge would be dismissed from the school immediately.[18] Since he couldn't reverse his son's action, he would make others pay for the transgression. As time went on, he became less tolerant of people who challenged his authority or acted without his blessing.

There was much about Booker T. Washington that also made him a difficult person to embrace as a mentor. In many ways, Roscoe found him to be as distant as his own parents had been while he was an adolescent. Just as Blanche had always been on the road, giving speeches around the nation while Roscoe was a child and then in prep school, Washington was also constantly away from home and family. And although controlling and unrelenting with his demands on the family and associates around him, Washington was strangely disengaged from any aspect of their lives that lay outside of the school or his work.

Within a ten-year period, Washington was married to three different women. The first two had died from natural causes at relatively early ages, yet he never seemed to lose his focus on expanding the school.

One reason why his personal life never got in the way of his work was, perhaps, because he made sure that they were one and the same. A year after founding Tuskegee, in 1882, he married his first wife, Fannie Smith, and she began working at his school just before giving birth to their daughter, Portia. After Fannie died in 1884, he married his school's chief fund-raiser, Olivia Davidson, in 1885. After giving birth to their sons Booker T. Jr. in 1887 and Ernest in 1888, she continued raising money for the school. After Olivia died in 1889, Washington began dating, and then married, his head female teacher, Margaret James Murray, in 1893. Margaret would be elevated to the role of lady principal of the school and remained in that job until Josephine replaced her in 1899. So, Washington really made the school his life, and vice versa.

What Washington failed to do with his family—a fact that did not go unnoticed by Clara—was apply the practices that he claimed to embrace. Despite his alleged belief that blacks should accept segregated schooling and embrace industrial education, none of his three children were raised in those traditions. Furthermore, none of them demonstrated the drive that he said was important if the race was to advance through self-reliance. His youngest child, Ernest, went to the white boarding school Oberlin Academy, in Ohio. His oldest son, Booker Jr., attended two white prep schools in Massachusetts, Rock Ridge Hall and Wellesley School for Boys. After he had been caught smoking in his room, sneaking out at night, lying to the headmaster, and refusing to study, the principal, Edward Benner, asked his father to take him back to Alabama. The following year, he entered the nation's oldest private boarding school, Dummer Academy, in Newbury, Massachusetts, and then later transferred to Phillips Exeter, where he did not even succeed at completing his first semester. Booker Jr. would later attend Fisk University, a distinctly academic college that emphasized a classical and intellectual curriculum, which differed dramatically from Tuskegee. Washington's oldest child, Portia, had attended the all-white Bradford Academy and Wellesley College in Massachusetts, once again highlighting the fact that despite Washington's declarations that all-black industrial-training schools provided the ideal education for blacks, he never applied these beliefs to his own family.

When the *Guardian* learned that Portia Washington was refused housing in a Wellesley dormitory and that she was not allowed to return to the school in 1902 because of her low grades, the Boston newspaper couldn't resist poking fun at the girl and her father. In an October 4, 1902, editorial, the newspaper said Portia left Wellesley because she and the rest of Booker T. Washington's children "are not taking to higher education like a duck to water, and while their defect in this line is doubtless somewhat inherited, they justify to some extent their father's well-known antipathy to anything higher than the three R's for his 'people.' "[19] It wasn't long before others, like the *New York Times*, noticed the irony and began writing stories about Washington's failure to follow his own advice about industrial education.

Although Clara was still not sold on the school's curriculum, she and Roscoe were mesmerized by the unrelenting schedule that was in place for the students on campus. Unlike the relatively unstructured days at Harvard and Radcliffe, where students took classes, activities, and study time at periods that differed from student to student, the daily routine at Tuskegee Institute was lockstep. From the rising bell at

5 a.m. until the bedtime bell at 9:30 p.m., it had the air of a military school. The scheduled periods highlighted the nonintellectual aspects of Tuskegee life, because a great portion of the "class" work was simply practical physical labor interspersed with "study time." The day went as follows, with each period announced by a ringing bell:

5:00 a.m.	Wake Up
6:00 a.m.	Breakfast Begins
6:20 a.m.	Breakfast Ends
6:20–6:50 a.m.	Cleaning of Rooms
6:50 a.m.	Work Begins
7:30 a.m.	Morning Study Hour
8:20 a.m.	Study Hour Ends
8:25 a.m.	Inspection of Male Student Toilets
8:40 a.m.	Chapel Prayer
8:55 a.m.	Daily News Reports
9:00 a.m.	Class Work Begins
12 noon	Class Work Ends
12:15 p.m.	Dinner
1:00 p.m.	Work Begins
1:30 p.m.	Class Work Begins
3:30 p.m.	Class Work Ends
6:00 p.m.	Supper
7:10 p.m.	Evening Prayers
7:30 p.m.	Evening Study Hour
8:45 p.m.	Evening Study Hour Ends
9:30 p.m.	Retire

A day that began at 5 a.m. and ended with a total of sixteen and a half fully scheduled hours was more physically demanding than any schedule Roscoe had ever encountered. Since the classes focused on skills like carpentry, sewing, brick making, cooking, and house painting, the students were physically exhausted by their classroom assignments. So, even though they found it intellectually lacking, he and Clara were impressed by the sheer industry demonstrated by the school, staff, and students.

As his first order of business, Roscoe set about reviewing each department of the school and each of the courses offered to the students. He evaluated the instructors teaching the courses as well as the content of their presentations. A strict adherent to proper grammar and diction, he insisted that the instructors place greater emphasis on their students' writing and public speaking, even though the courses focused on trade skills. Since he was new to the school, it took a great deal of time to observe the classwork and be present for the hands-on aspect of each class—many of which were conducted outdoors or in buildings that were not conducive to study. Whether it was for a class on brick-making, tailoring, horticulture, or Bible study, which was taught in the school's Phelps Hall Bible Division, Roscoe offered suggestions on introducing additional reading, writing, and intellectual rigor to the course work.

Simultaneously, Roscoe was charged with identifying and recruiting additional teachers who would enhance the Tuskegee faculty rolls and bring greater prestige to the school.

As eager as Roscoe was to launch into his new position and strengthen his relationship with his boss, it quickly became evident that it would be difficult to move into the tight circle that was drawn around Washington by Emmett Jay Scott and Warren Logan, respectively Washington's private secretary and school treasurer. While Roscoe held the lofty title of head of the Academic Department, he was both young and new to the campus. Furthermore, he had arrived in town with academic and social credentials drastically superior to those of the deeply entrenched faculty, who had already proved their loyalty to Tuskegee. This certainly did not endear him to Scott or Logan.

Scott, a twenty-nine-year-old native of Houston, Texas, who had graduated from Wiley College, had worked as the private secretary for Washington for six years. And Logan, a former instructor of book-keeping, had been at Tuskegee since 1884 and had been serving as the school's treasurer for several years. Along with people like T. Thomas Fortune and Charles Anderson in New York, Scott and Logan helped mastermind and execute the public relations program that kept Washington and his school in the black and the white newspapers.

Scott and Logan were no more interested in bringing Roscoe into their inner circle than they had been in bringing in his predecessor, James Dickens McCall. In fact, McCall, who had been a science instructor before Washington elevated him to head the Academic Department, felt the cold shoulders of the top lieutenants and pleaded for them to allow him to return to his prior role of science instructor. Washington discussed his school and outside activities with Scott and Logan, but Roscoe was not a part of these conversations. Roscoe was also not consulted about most of the strategy that was implemented as the school reached out to new white benefactors who enriched its coffers.

Although they probably did not feel that their jobs were threatened by Roscoe's arrival, it is likely that both Scott and Logan were concerned that their backgrounds appeared—and, in fact, were—intellectually inferior to their new colleague's. Having worked two years earlier with his mother when she was lady principal, the staff generally looked at Roscoe as a privileged Northerner who had gotten his job through connections. While most of them were Southerners who had grown up poor and had been educated in Southern black colleges, they noted his Northern childhood, wealthy upbringing, and training in white Northern schools. He could not have been more different from them.

Because Scott was the primary author of much of Washington's correspondence and speeches, he was particularly threatened by Roscoe's eloquence and writing skills. Roscoe's youth also troubled the slight, bespectacled Scott, who had, up to then, been the youngest of Washington's top staff. Scott often kept Roscoe at arm's length, sharing little information and offering little advice. This was the general treatment offered to Roscoe by the Tuskegee staff. Although Roscoe would soon recruit young teachers who promised him greater loyalty, he would never succeed in winning over the school's old guard.

One way that Roscoe dealt with not being accepted by the administrators was by scheduling additional trips to conduct research or to give speeches on behalf of the Institute. In March 1903, he wrote to Clara, "My Darling, I got back from Mobile, Alabama Tuesday, and since my return I have been as busy as a beehive . . . I delivered six speeches. The Negroes of Mobile are, as a whole, in a mighty bad condition with their bad morals . . . I'm [now] busy working on the Summer School prospectus."[20]

It was not long before Roscoe started to see the power that was wielded by Washington and his lieutenants. Along with this power came a certain amount of vindictiveness toward anyone who crossed Washington, Scott, or Logan. Roscoe saw what happened to Margaret Murrell, a teacher who had worked in the Academic Department and who had come to Tuskegee at the same time he did. When she received an offer to teach in the Washington, DC, public schools, and quit her job at Tuskegee, Booker T. Washington began a campaign to discredit her and have her new employer rescind its job offer.

First, he wrote to Bettie Cox Francis, a black member of the DC Board of Education, and asked Mrs. Francis to immediately dismiss Miss Murrell because she had not gotten Washington's permission to accept the new job. Ironically, Francis was a close friend of the Bruce family, as her husband, Dr. John Francis, had been Senator Bruce's personal physician for many years. In his letter to Mrs. Francis, Washington attacked his former employee's moral standards, manners, and lack of gratitude. He said of Miss Murrell, "To me it is inconceivable how an educated person can act in such a manner . . . I do not believe that a person with such loose ideas of moral obligation can be teacher in the broadest and strongest sense . . . Further, I believe that by making an example of such persons that the lesson would be impressed upon them . . ."[21]

When Washington failed to get the response he wanted—an immediate firing of his former teacher—he wrote to Mrs. Francis's husband four days later, insisting that he do something, because Washington was insulted that Miss Murrell had not been dismissed. Shortly thereafter, the Board of Education rescinded its offer and made her rehiring contingent upon her satisfying Booker T. Washington's concerns. On May 3, he wrote Miss Murrell that he had written her employer in order "to teach [you] a lesson for the future . . . to yourself and to others."[22]

When Roscoe and other young teachers, like Paul Calvin Pinn, would later attempt to leave before their boss was ready to let them go, they would also face the jealousy or resentment of Tuskegee's old guard.

But Roscoe had to concern himself with his own family's affairs, too. Clara had given birth to their first child, a baby girl named Clara Josephine, on March 21, 1904. Clara Sr. kept herself busy by taking care of her daughter and entertaining the young faculty members that Roscoe had recruited to the school.

And Roscoe heard almost weekly from his mother about the financial problems being caused by their Mississippi plantation. She had moved to Mississippi more than a year earlier, in order to bring some organization to the business that had been left in the hands of neglectful managers and workers. Although the plantation, which grew cotton and several types of produce, also provided income through the operation of several cabins rented out to black farmers, the maintenance of the property required great expense. As an absentee owner with no background in farming, home repair, or dealing with the culture of the Deep South, Josephine was completely unfit for the job of managing the land and the workers. As an upper-class woman who was attempting to stay more involved in her women's club affairs, she was reluctant and unprepared to deal with the various banks, cotton factors, and other middlemen that most plantation owners usually had to negotiate with.

Since Roscoe demonstrated little interest in the plantation except for the income it generated, Josephine turned to her sister Emily, who was married to A. L. Harang, for guidance. Harang and his business partner, A. W. Hebert, were hired to assist Josephine in maintaining the plantation buildings and the cabins, as well as to help with the workers, farm equipment, and cotton that was being produced and later sold in Memphis.

Even with the help she was getting, Josephine's time and money were quickly consumed by tenants who defaulted on their rent, a string of crops that failed, as well as equipment that was destroyed during a fire in her cotton gin building. Having to pay the bills—particularly a $7,500 bill her plantation owed to Godfrey Frank & Company, a cotton factor who had advanced her money earlier—she found herself strapped for ready cash, and in early 1905 contacted one of her banks about taking out a mortgage on her home in Washington. This was the town house at 2010 R Street NW, the four-story Dupont Circle home where she and Blanche had lived until he died in 1898.

James Hood, an officer of American Security and Trust Company, wrote to her at the Bruce plantation in Josephine, Mississippi, on February 10, 1905:

> *Dear Madam:*
> *I have this morning received your favor of the 4th instant. We would lend you upon your R Street house $4500 for a term of three or five years, at your option, at 4½ %, or should you desire a loan of $5000 we would lend you that amount for three or five years at*

5% interest; in either event charging you a commission of 1% and all expenses of title papers to be borne by yourself.[23]

Two months later, Josephine secured the $4,500 loan on the property and had the money forwarded to Godfrey Frank. Still anxious to maintain the Bruce plantation as his customer, Frank extended an offer for services the following year in an April 5, 1905, letter. He wrote, "We do not know whether you yourself will operate your lands this year in Bolivar County, but if you do we will be pleased to negotiate with you . . . for the necessary advances."[24]

By the beginning of January 1906, Josephine was thoroughly exasperated by the problems on her plantation. Even with the assistance from her brother-in-law, she was barely earning a profit from the land and the rented buildings. Harang wrote to her, expressing his frustration with the black tenants as well as with the black plantation workers:

> *Dear Sister, We have just returned from Memphis and found the worst condition of affairs for planters known in many years. The merchants . . . are out of vast sums of money.*
>
> *We have exhausted our credit, have no money and don't know what to do about getting something to eat for the darkies. Of course they don't know the condition of things, but if something is not done soon it is bound to come out. I am doing all I know to keep things going and not give in to suspicion, but things can not be worse with us. We will owe about two thousand dollars outside of what we owe you. If we could have collected one half of what is owed u, we would not be in this fix. I think of one tenant like Mr. Oden who owes us over $800 and we received only half . . . about the same with other plantations.*
>
> *Now, in regard to these darkies and the church,* don't you do one thing—they are not entitled to my consideration and not worthy of notice. *They have no regard for moral obligations, and let no advantage go by . . . Made you and I lose thousands of dollars here, because they could take advantage of some infernal law . . . I say, let them go to H . . .*[25]

It was obvious that, like Roscoe, both Josephine and her brother-in-law felt as disconnected from the black plantation workers as did white plantation owners. The racial identity of their workers made them no more sympathetic to their plight. Whether it was because of their own frustrations over finances or because the class differences between themselves and poor blacks were too great, Josephine's family demonstrated a contempt for their black workers that nearly matched that of white employers. Referring to them as "darkies" and "immoral," and dismissing their plight by saying "let them go to H," Harang ultimately advised his sister-in-law to hold back on paying the black plantation workers, despite the fact the workers had no recent wages and little to eat. Hoping not to lose her workers and, hence, devalue her plantation—one section of which, Harang told her, would bring at least $45,000—Josephine responded by paying the black workers. In this instance, she raised money by selling three other parcels of land in Bolivar County.[26] At the time, she was eager to return to her club work with the National Association of Colored Women, an organization founded by educated black women who wanted to aid less privileged black children and families.

One of Josephine's last pleas to Roscoe regarding the plantation came in a letter where she sought his advice on breaking a contract with one of her poorly performing plantation managers. She wrote:

> *I should have been obliged to tell him that there were*
> *two parties to a contract and it was possible that either could*
> *break the contract. In his case, he had broken it by his inability*
> *to carry out his part of it and that he could hardly expect to be*
> *retained in a business, not that he was ruining, but that he had*
> *already ruined.*
>
> *In his innate brutality and disregard of truth he put the*
> *result of his own worthlessness on me, which in itself proved his*
> *unworthiness.*
>
> *I feel like begging pardon every time I speak of the man.*
> *Mother*[27]

Although Josephine kept Roscoe apprised of the physical and financial burdens that were placed on her, he was unable to offer her money—or time. In fact, by late 1905, his job barely left him enough free time to focus on the needs of his wife or child. Not only was he working the sixteen-hour days that students followed on each of their

Monday-to-Friday school schedules, but also he had night work, an extra burden that many teachers complained about to Washington. And the school provided no summer break or significant school-year vacations to Roscoe. Not only was such a schedule grueling for this new father, it did not allow for his own scholarly pursuits of reading literature and writing articles—an exercise he had hoped to partake of while in this position.

By the fall of 1905, Clara and Roscoe knew that it was time for him to leave Tuskegee. It was clear to him that he was not going to move beyond head of the Academic Department, the job he had started in 1902, and he knew that Washington's advisers, Scott and Logan, as well as his outside lieutenants T. Timothy Fortune and Charles Anderson, were not going to grant him any additional authority. Most disappointing to the young administrator was the realization that Washington had intentionally misled him regarding the degree to which he would introduce an academic component into the school's industrial curriculum. Roscoe had arrived with dozens of suggestions, but they were met with resistance.[28] He was not even certain that Washington would fully support the plans Roscoe had outlined in late 1904 for a book that Washington had edited. Roscoe's boss was completing a book that laid out the theoretical underpinnings, and successes, of Tuskegee Institute. Titled *Tuskegee and Its People: Their Ideals and Achievements*, it included a chapter "Academic Aims," wherein Roscoe wrote about the purpose and the mechanics of the academic curriculum he was developing for the school.[29]

What also should have been an impetus for leaving—although it is not clear that he realized this then—was that it was becoming increasingly obvious to others that Washington had merely hired Roscoe for a specific goal: to attract prestige to the school. Just as Washington had hired Josephine in 1899, he hired Roscoe three years later so that he could enhance the school's reputation of attracting blacks who were held in high esteem in the white community. Washington was always concerned about addressing two image problems for his school: first, that it lacked the prestige of the elite black academic universities like Fisk, Atlanta, and Howard; and second, that its anti-intellectual industrial trade approach would make it hard to attract intelligent instructors from top white universities. But by hiring the Bruces—famous black people whose names were respected in both black and white circles, and who also had credentials from top white institutions—Washington addressed his concerns directly. If a school could attract the interest of a U.S. senator's socialite widow and of a Phi Beta Kappa graduate of Phillips Exeter and Harvard, then it must be on equal footing with Fisk and Howard, if not better.

Roscoe consulted his mother about leaving Tuskegee, and she was in complete agreement. Having worked there as lady principal, Josephine was well aware of the school's limitations. She believed that it was an intellectually inferior school, and she also knew firsthand that Booker T. Washington was a difficult and duplicitous boss. When Roscoe had first accepted the position, Josephine had written to him and warned him that her colleagues had not been happy at the school, and that the faculty was much happier at Hampton Institute. While she was still serving as lady principal at Tuskegee, she wrote him after he visited Hampton to see for himself. She said, "My Darling, Just received your letter from Hampton. Hampton is beautiful because the civilization of several thousand years finds expression there. Dr. Frissel [the dean] is a rare man much beloved . . . I want you to take him for your model. What makes life so barren down here [in Tuskegee] is the lack of love and a lack of sympathy and consideration."[30]

The following week, Josephine reemphasized her point that people were not as happy at Tuskegee as they were at schools like Hampton. She said,

> I am glad you have had this visit at Hampton. The teachers there are indeed magnificent. It is an inspiration to know such people. Many of these teachers here [at Tuskegee] are taking comfort in your coming. They are simply enduring the present. Really it is terrible. We have a little Miss Smith who cries herself sick . . . Miss S says that at Hampton everybody is so considerate and they love Miss Hyde [lady dean]. Her way is to say "now we will do so and so."[31]

Josephine was emphatic in pointing out that Booker T. Washington ran his school without much consideration or compassion for his faculty or students. She knew that the experience of working at Tuskegee would be valuable to herself and her son, but she knew that it was not going to be a place where he would want to stay for long.

Clara was eager to leave Tuskegee for other reasons. She still had not bought into Washington's philosophy, and could not see raising her children and continuing to live in the anti-intellectual vacuum of a campus that put economics and industry above everything else. She had already moved away from her family and sacrificed her Radcliffe degree because Roscoe would not allow her to stay a few extra months at the school. And despite Roscoe's original promises, Clara's ambition of pursuing advanced studies in economics and law was not realizable on the Tuskegee campus.[32]

She also must have questioned the contradictions of her husband's boss. It must have struck her as odd that Washington criticized blacks who attended either black or white liberal arts schools in lieu of black trade schools, yet he sent his own daughter, Portia, to the all-white Wellesley College in 1901, and then an all-white junior college in New England right after. Although he scoffed at blacks who excelled in the arts, he helped launch his daughter's career as a pianist. And while he said that blacks should focus on being tradesmen rather than seek white professional jobs, he expressed great pride in the fact that his son-in-law was an architect, and that his younger son, Ernest, had said, while still an adolescent, that he hoped to be a physician.[33]

Despite Booker T. Washington's popularity, Clara was not alone in questioning the quality of Tuskegee and the logical inconsistencies that she saw at the school. Despite his support of Washington, Harvard President Charles W. Eliot gave the Tuskegee leader some stinging criticisms about the school's academics and accelerated growth. He questioned the quality of teachers and curriculum for four of the departments, and he pointed out the dangers of the school's antipathy toward intellectual rigor. In a September 7, 1906, letter, Eliot said,

> *Dear Mr. Washington, I find that there have remained in my mind . . . a few ideas about the Institution: 1) It seemed to me doubtful whether Tuskegee offered any adequate training for the profession of the ministry. Is it best to spend money in providing an inadequate training for that profession?*
>
> *2) I felt much doubt about the training Tuskegee is able to offer for nurses . . . Ought Tuskegee to offer any training for nurses when it is visibly incapable of providing the best training? . . .*

1. Elected to the U.S. Senate in 1874, **Blanche Bruce** had been a slave for twenty-three years. By purchasing an 800-acre plantation and many rental properties, he became a very wealthy man. He later gained appointments under four presidents, and was the first black man to have his name printed on U.S. currency.

2. **Josephine Willson** was born to well-to-do black parents in Philadelphia and married the senator in 1878. Her light complexion won her acceptance among white Republicans and socialites, but worked against her when she ran for the presidency of the National Council of Colored Women.

3. **Roscoe Conkling Bruce** was the only son of Blanche and Josephine. He entered Phillips Exeter in 1896 and graduated Harvard Phi Beta Kappa in 1902. While still in college, he would become both a spy and a protégé for the powerful Booker T. Washington.

4. Although he was not invited to his brother's wedding, **Henry C. Bruce** (left) remained close to Blanche for most of his life. He ran for Kansas State Legislature in 1880 and later wrote a popular book detailing his life as a slave and an active member of the Republican Party.

5. Blanche already owned an 800-acre Mississippi plantation and other properties by the time he and Josephine moved into 909 M Street NW (right) in 1878. The red-brick Washington town house is now a landmark.

6. In 1888, Josephine asked Blanche to buy her a second Washington town house at 2010 R Street NW (left). Here she held teas for her women's groups and entertained her husband's political friends.

7. **Frederick Douglass** was already a celebrated figure through his abolitionist work by the time he befriended Blanche in the 1870s. He became president of the Freedman's Bank the same year Blanche was elected to the Senate.

8. **Adelbert Ames** was one of Blanche's first mentors when he entered Mississippi politics. A liberal Republican, Ames served as governor and U.S. senator.

9. Although **Sen. James Alcorn** had originally aided Blanche's rise in the Republican Party, he refused to walk Blanche down the aisle in the Senate chamber on the day that Blanche was sworn in.

10. **President Ulysses S. Grant** gave Bruce and other black officials the support they needed to advance Reconstruction policies, but the tide turned against them in 1877. Grant later hosted the Bruces in Europe during their 1878 honeymoon.

11. Unlike Bruce, **Hiram Revels** was born a free black man. He would serve a short, twelve-month term in the Senate, in order to complete the term first held by Jefferson Davis. Revels would leave politics altogether in order to become a college president.

12. The powerful **Senator Roscoe Conkling** from New York was Blanche's longtime adviser and mentor in the Senate. Blanche would name his only son after the white senator.

13. **U.S. Rep. John R. Lynch** was born a slave and served three terms in Congress. Bruce's closest Mississippi adviser and the owner of more than 1,700 acres of Mississippi property, Lynch later used his wealth to lecture and write about the contributions made by blacks during Reconstruction.

14. & 15. After his Senate term, Bruce became register of the Treasury. Never before had a black man's name appeared on American money. B.K.'s signature is shown above on a five-dollar bill (and enlarged, at right).

16. **Senator George Hoar** of Massachusetts was a liberal Republican who fought for black equality. He helped Bruce oppose an 1879 bill that limited the immigration of Chinese people. Hoar also used his family's connections to get Roscoe into prep school and college.

17. & 18. After his term in the Senate, Bruce convinced **Presidents James Garfield** and **Chester Arthur** (top, left and right) that he should serve as register of the U.S. Treasury. He held the position from 1881 to 1885. Bruce's new position gave him an office in the Treasury building and a staff of nearly two-hundred people. The job also put his name on U.S. currency.

19. & 20. Head of his own black dynasty, **James Wormley** (left) was a friend to Blanche. He was a wealthy man and owned the famous Wormley Hotel (below) at 1500 H Street NW in Washington, DC. Opened in 1871, the hotel was the site where politicians agreed to end Reconstruction with the Compromise of 1877.

21. & 22. Howard University was the gold standard in education for the black elite since its founding in 1867. Each generation of the Bruce family kept a tie to the school. Blanche sat on its board, Clara Sr. and Clara Jr. attended it before entering Radcliffe, and Roscoe Sr. lectured there often while he headed DC's colored schools.

23. A longtime friend to Senator Bruce, **Pinckney B. S. Pinchback** was a black New Orleans newspaper publisher. Born in Georgia to a black slave woman and a white man, he served as Louisiana's lieutenant-governor and then as governor in 1872 and 1873. He later moved to Washington and built a mansion that dwarfed Bruce's home.

24. **President William McKinley** (right) agreed to appoint Bruce as register of the Treasury in 1897 after pleas from Booker T. Washington. With the Supreme Court upholding segregation in the Plessy case, Democrats strongly opposed black appointments in the capital.

25. **Dr. John Francis** (left) was one of DC's best-known black physicians. A graduate of the University of Michigan Medical School, he was Senator Bruce's doctor, and was later a friend to Roscoe when they both joined the Sigma Pi Phi Boulé fraternity in 1911.

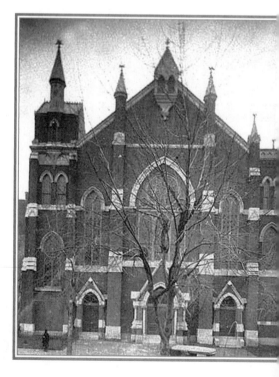

26. Metropolitan AME Church at 1518 M Street NW was the site of Senator Bruce's funeral in 1898. Two decades later, it was where Washington's black middle-class families gathered to ask for Roscoe Bruce's resignation as superintendent of the city's colored schools.

27. Roscoe Bruce entered Harvard six months after his father died in 1898. Six blacks were in his class.

28. **T. John Syphax** (left) was Roscoe's closest black friend at Exeter. He refused to come to Roscoe's wedding after deciding to change his name and pass for white. Forty years later, he admitted he was black in order to claim an $800,000 inheritance that had been left by his black grandfather.

29. & 30. Roscoe's black pals in prep school and college included **George Shaw** (right) from South Carolina and **Bruce Green** (far right) from Virginia.

31. From 1899 to 1902, Roscoe lived in Holyoke House, a five-story Harvard dormitory. When his son, Roscoe Jr., applied twenty years later, black and white freshmen were no longer allowed to live together.

32. & 33. Wealthy, handsome, and smart, Roscoe broke Harvard's racial barriers as president of *Harvard Magazine* (top: seated in front row, center) and as a Phi Beta Kappa member (bottom: seated in front row, second from left). He and Clara were dating at the time.

34. **Booker T. Washington** was the powerful founder of Tuskegee Institute, where he advised presidents and philanthropists. He hired Josephine in order to bring prestige to his school and he later picked Roscoe to head his academic department.

35. **Margaret Washington** was Booker's third wife. She was Lady Principal before Josephine Bruce took the job. Rich and accustomed to getting her way, Margaret was upset when Josephine ran against her for the presidency of the National Council of Colored Women.

Epsilon Boulé of the Sigma Pi Phi Fraternity. 1912.

36. As superintendent of DC's colored schools, **Roscoe Sr.** (above: back row, far right) had one of the best jobs available to a black in Washington. One of the advantages of his new status was that it got him invited in 1911 to join the premier black men's fraternity, Sigma Pi Phi Boulé.

37. Dunbar High School (right) was the crown jewel of Washington's colored school district. Formerly known as M Street High, it sent many of its graduates to ivy league colleges. Roscoe used its reputation as evidence that he was a skilled superintendent. His daughter and oldest son attended the school.

38. **W. Calvin Chase** (left) ran the capital's black newspa *The Washington Bee*, without fearing the power elite. Distrustful of most whites, he supported Senator Bruce, led the movement to fire Roscoe when it appeared that I was nothing more than a puppet of the elite whites who on the city's school board. A graduate of Howard Law School, he ran the newspaper for forty years.

ead, Mrs. Johnson said, and the death of Dr. Minton last McKee became the last living randson of Col. McKee. Kee, whose offices are at 84 am St., lives with his wife, ormer Aimee Bennett, who tedly knew nothing of his y history, in a four-room ment at 230 E. 48th St. occupant of the building the McKees lived quietly with rently few social activities with few visitors. McKee, said tenant, always appeared abid in business and is coned a genial, but quiet man. sidents of the building were le to confirm the report that McKees have two sons, and remembered the sons visit them. Mrs. McKee, who is e, was not at home yester.

Continued on Page 10

"At that time," Mrs. Johnson, a cultured Philadelphia Negro, declared, "he was preparing to attend Trinity College."

McKee was admitted to the New York bar following his graduation from Yale Law School in 1904 after attending exclusive Trinity College in Hartford.

McKee, Mrs. Johnson declared had four brothers — three of

Did You Happen to See...
BARRINGTON SHARMA

39. & 40. The Bruces had ties to many prominent blacks who passed for white. Roscoe's black friend, T. John Syphax (above left) is shown here after changing his identity to "T. John McKee, a white Wall Street lawyer." McKee later admitted to being black in a high-profile 1948 court case. Roscoe's daughter eloped with black classmate, Barrington Guy (above right), who appeared in many black plays and movies in the 1920s and 30s. He changed his identity to "Barrington Sharma, a half-white, half-Indian actor" in order to appear in white theaters after 1941.

41. & 42. Clara Burrill (right) married Roscoe Bruce (left) after leaving Radcliffe College in 1901. Wanting her own career, she later entered Boston University Law School and became the first black editor-in-chief of the *Law Review*. She worried that their three children lacked her ambition.

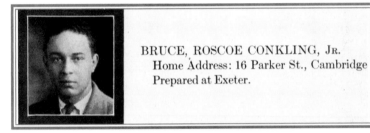

BRUCE, ROSCOE CONKLING, Jr.
Home Address: 16 Parker St., Cambridge
Prepared at Exeter.

43., 44. & 45. Roscoe Bruce Jr., (above) as he appeared in Harvard's 1926 freshman book. Despite top credentials and contacts, he went to prison after a sensational 1937 embezzlement trial. His sister, Clara Jr. (below left, from her Radcliffe yearbook) opposed her father by marrying a black movie actor who passed as white. Youngest brother, Burrill (below right), became a lawyer, but had to beg the Rockefellers to help pay for his last year at Harvard Law School.

46. When Harvard President **A. Lawrence Lowell** (left), told Roscoe Sr. that his son would not be allowed to live in the freshman dorms because he was black, a national debate was launched. After Franklin Roosevelt, W. E. B. Du Bois, and others sided with Roscoe, the school integrated its dormitories.

47., 48. & 49. Radcliffe's **LeBaron Briggs** (above) told Roscoe Sr. that they ran out of dormitory room and could not house his daughter, but the Bruce family remained devoted to the Harvard (left) and Radcliffe (bottom) campuses.

50. **John D. Rockefeller Jr.** (left) built the Dunbar Apartments in Harlem in 1925 and then hired Roscoe and Clara to manage the complex because they would bring class to the all-black, upscale development.

51. Russell Sage Foundation executive **Mary Van Kleeck** (left) introduced Roscoe to Rockefeller in 1926 and served as a reference for Clara Jr. at Radcliffe. Van Kleeck's black protégé, Harriet Butcher, would have an affair with Roscoe that nearly cost him his job and his marriage.

52. & 53. **Clara Bruce Sr.** (left) in her Harlem office shortly after she published her first piece in the *Saturday Evening Post*. She continued to write while helping Roscoe manage the five-hundred-unit Dunbar Apartments (below) at 150th Street in Manhattan.

54., 55. & 56. The Dunbar Apartments were a sought-after New York residence for black professionals from the 1920s to the 1950s The Bruces took interior photos of their own well-decorated seven-room apartment to promote the Dunbar lifestyle to potentia purchasers. Roscoe had the power to handpick the tenants who first populated the six-building development.

57. When Rockefeller founded Dunbar Savings Bank (right) for the black middle class, he put Roscoe Sr. on its board. Soon the Bruces left the bank because of a suit that forced them to sell their shares. That and Roscoe Jr.'s 1937 trial for embezzlement would nearly bankrupt the family.

58. **Roscoe Sr.** attached this postage stamp–sized photo of himself to a letter that he sent to John D. Rockefeller just before Roscoe and Clara applied for public assistance with New York City's Department of Welfare. The family had lived lavishly for seventy years and depleted their fortune on homes, cars, legal suits, and expensive schools.

*4) I felt some concern lest at Tuskegee the manual labor side had
an excessive development as compared with the mental labor
side . . . lest industrial training should unduly impair academic
training. Is it not important that the graduates . . . [acquire] not
only a trade, but the power to read and cipher intelligently, and a
taste for reading?*[34]

So, even though Washington was able to persuade the general public that his school was a panacea for black America and its children,
there were many intellectuals who recognized the flaws at Tuskegee.

After learning about the availability of a position as principal of a
school in Washington, DC, Roscoe recognized that he finally had an
opportunity to escape the Alabama campus and return North. Still
quite intimidated by his boss, he wrote to Booker T. Washington on
August 26, 1905, asking Washington if he would support his leaving
Tuskegee for the new job. He wrote:

*My dear Mr. Washington, I write to ask if you would
countenance my accepting the principalship of the Armstrong
Manual Training School, in case it were proffered me. For three
years I have sought to serve you and Tuskegee to the very best of my
ability, and I realize clearly and willingly the profound obligations
your courtesy and generosity have placed upon my shoulders.*

*I place the situation frankly and freely before you, requesting
your consent and approval . . . You have always treated me with a
consideration that is almost fatherly.*
Sincerely yours, Roscoe C. Bruce[35]

In a letter Washington wrote less than a week later, he offered a
response to Roscoe's request. Although worded in a respectful tone,
Washington offered not a single compliment to Roscoe for his three
years of faithful service. And not only was Washington unwilling to
thank Roscoe for his contributions or congratulate him on the job offer,
he said that "it is a compliment to our work at Tuskegee" that Roscoe
was being given this new job in the nation's capital. In other words,
it was Booker T. Washington's accomplishments—not Roscoe's—
that accounted for the job offer. And in a request of great audacity, he

told Roscoe that if he should accept this new position, he should not start it for another twelve months, when the next school year was to begin.

> *Dear Mr. Bruce: I have your letter of August 26, regarding the possibility of you being appointed as Principal of the Armstrong Manual and Training school . . . I take into consideration that it is natural for you to look upon this in the light of a promotion, and a promotion is something every man should crave or value. Again I always consider that when a teacher of ours receives an offer in the direction of a promotion, it is a compliment to our work at Tuskegee.*
>
> *What I am trying to say is this . . . if the offer comes to you in a definite way that you will see your way clear to remain with us this year, or until after the time of the Twenty-fifth Anniversary.*[36]

Although Washington made the incredible request that Roscoe stay for another twelve months before departing, it was clear that this "request" was, in fact, a demand. Since the Armstrong school was coincidentally named for Booker T. Washington's most important white mentor and benefactor, General Samuel Chapman Armstrong, who founded and presided over Washington's alma mater, Hampton Institute, Roscoe probably knew that his boss had the power to squelch the new job offer if he was so inclined. To the consternation of Clara and his mother, Roscoe agreed to remain at Tuskegee for another year.

In fact, so reluctant was Washington to assist Roscoe in gaining the new position that he waited a full year to write a letter of recommendation on Roscoe's behalf to the Washington, DC, Board of Education.[37] And it appears that Booker T. Washington wrote that September 4, 1906, letter only because he learned from a September 3, 1906, letter that W. E. B. DuBois was also being considered for the appointment. That letter was sent by James Cobb to Booker's assistant Emmett Jay Scott, and said, "DuBois is turning heaven and earth to be appointed assistant superintendent. . . . the friends of DuBois are trying to oust [W. S. Montgomery] and place DuBois in his place. Mrs. Terrell hasn't slept any since . . ."[38]

Motivated more by his dislike of DuBois than by his affection for Roscoe, only a few days before Roscoe was to settle in his new job,

Washington acquiesced and sent a letter on his behalf, saying, "I shall be very glad indeed if you decide to appoint Mr. Bruce to a Supervisorship. I feel quite sure that he will perform the service well and satisfactorily." Always stingy with compliments for anyone who left his employ before he was ready to dismiss them, Washington offered only lukewarm remarks for a bright young man who had devoted the last three years of his life to Washington's school and his cause. Though disappointing to Roscoe, it accurately captured his complicated relationship with a powerful man whom he had wanted to respect and admire.

CHAPTER SEVENTEEN

❧⟨ტ⟩ოუ

1906–1914

A Triumphant Return to Washington Life:
The Bruce Family's Second Generation Emerges

WHEN ROSCOE ARRIVED IN WASHINGTON, THERE WERE VERY FEW
black institutions that rivaled the prestige of the city's Colored Schools.
The black public schools in the city were started soon after the end
of the Civil War and were run by a succession of illustrious black
and white educators who had graduated from the best schools in the
North.

The city's school district was completely segregated when Roscoe
and Clara returned in 1906, just as it had been in 1867, when Vermont-
born John Kimball, a white Congregational minister, was originally
appointed superintendent of the Colored Schools. Working for the
same Washington, DC, school board that the superintendent of the
white schools worked for, Kimball had been selected because of his credentials from Dartmouth College and Union Theological Seminary
and his work as a Congregational minister in ethnically diverse New
York City.

For several generations, Washington, DC, had been home to many
well-educated free black families, and they ultimately provided some of
the first black teachers in the city's segregated schools. This group,
which made up the city's black elite, included several wealthy families
who ran businesses or worked as lawyers, doctors, dentists, caterers,
and educators. Black families like the Wormleys, the Francises, the

Langstons, the Syphaxes, and the Cooks—the richest black family in the city—all valued and took seriously the quality of the education available to black children. Many of these families in the 1870s, 1880s, and 1890s were friends with Roscoe's parents. In fact, Senator Bruce was among the handful of blacks that had been chosen to sit on the city's board of education in its early years.

By the late 1860s, this small black aristocracy—many of them free-born blacks—had clamored loudly enough to actually get the board to give them a black person to head the Colored Schools. Although black citizens believed that Superintendent Kimball did his best in advocating for, and soliciting equal funds for, the black elementary schools and high school, they knew that the board would always reserve greater resources and facilities for the whites. They therefore decided that they might as well insist that a black person be given the opportunity to represent their schools.

In 1870, the all-white board of education picked a member of one of the city's wealthiest and most respected black families to serve as superintendent of the Colored Schools: George F. T. Cook. Cook was a graduate of Oberlin College and a son of a free black man, John Francis Cook, who had founded the city's Fifteenth Street Presbyterian Church. George's brother, Samuel, was a Washington physician who had graduated from University of Michigan's Medical School. His older brother, John, was an entrepreneur who later became the wealthiest black man in Washington—holding real estate and assets worth even more than those held by Blanche Bruce. George Cook, who had socialized with Roscoe's parents until his father's death, eventually held the superintendent position for three decades.

The board of education also put in place a special board of trustees that was charged with assisting the Colored Schools. The first chairman of that board was yet another friend of the Bruce family: William Syphax. The father of Roscoe's best friend and classmate at Exeter, Theophilus John Minton Syphax, William worked as a clerk in the U.S. Department of the Interior and came from another black family with an important history. A pillar of the DC black community for many years, Syphax had known Roscoe's father when Blanche first came to the city in 1874. He was the son of Charles Syphax and Maria Carter Custis, who had both been left land by Maria's father, the wealthy grandson of Martha Washington, and owned several acres of land that later contributed to the expansion of Arlington National Cemetery.

Also working with Cook and Syphax in the new Colored Schools was William H. A. Wormley. Wormley's father, James, was the owner of Wormley House, one of Washington's best hotels during the late 1800s.

These three black men—George Cook, William Syphax, and William Wormley—devoted themselves to launching a superior black school system in the city. What they became best known for was the Colored School's crown jewel: the Preparatory High School for Colored Youth, which they opened in 1870. During its history, the Preparatory High School operated under several names, including the Charles Sumner School, M Street High School (beginning in 1891 and located at 128 M Street NW), and Dunbar High School (beginning in 1916 and located at First and N Streets NW).

Soon after Cook took his position as superintendent of the Colored Schools, he oversaw the building of the city's first structure for black children, the 1872 brick building known as the Charles Sumner School Building. Created in order to house grammar school classrooms and the office for the superintendent of the Colored Schools, it was named for the liberal U.S. senator Charles Sumner of Massachusetts, who was an advocate for equal education for blacks.

During Cook's tenure, a significant number of black teachers were hired into the district. Even more important, a superior school curriculum was developed and was used to establish the best-known black academic high school in the country. Although its longest-held name was Dunbar High School (the same school attended by Roscoe and Clara's two oldest children), by 1906, M Street High School, was already *the* school for children of the black intelligentsia on the East Coast. With a rigorous curriculum and demanding teachers, the all-black high school ultimately became a feeder school for the Ivy League universities and Seven Sisters colleges, as well as Oberlin, Williams, and top black colleges, including Howard, Fisk, Morehouse, and Spelman. Not only did the high school send many graduates in the late 1800s to schools like Harvard, Amherst, Wellesley, Radcliffe, and Dartmouth, it also attracted these same Ivy League graduates to return as the school's teaching faculty.

Just six years before Roscoe was appointed superintendent of Colored Schools, the city's board of education began reacting to the anti-black backlash that was sweeping throughout the country in the wake of the *Plessy v. Ferguson* "separate but equal" Supreme Court decision. As the ruling in the 1896 case encouraged even greater segregation and discriminatory policies against blacks, both Washington, DC, and its school district began penalizing black residents; one response was to remove blacks from nearly every important administrative position in the schools.

Mary Church Terrell, one of Josephine Bruce's closest friends, had served on the school board at the time when the virtually all-white board outvoted her and decided to take power away from DC blacks in the same way other cities were doing at the turn of the century. Terrell, who was a black graduate of Oberlin and the daughter of Memphis's Robert Church, the nation's first black millionaire, was infuriated but powerless as the board humiliated her by stripping blacks of their jobs in the schools. Several years later, in 1906, during a speech to the United Women's Club in Washington, she spoke out about the incident:

> From 1870 to 1900, there was a colored superintendent at the head of the colored schools... The directors of the cooking, sewing, physical culture, manual training, music and arts department were colored people. Six years ago, a change was inaugurated. The colored superintendent was legislated out of office, and the director-ships, without a single exception, were taken from colored teachers and given to whites... Now, no matter how competent or superior the colored teachers may be... they can never rise... can never hope to be more than an assistant.[1]

During the period that Terrell described, the board had installed undistinguished white administrators who had little concern for the academic welfare of the black students. But the year that Terrell gave her speech was the same year that the district hired Roscoe as principal of the Colored Schools' Armstrong Manual Training High School. It would be another year before he was actually named the head of all the Colored Schools in the city. Terrell was no doubt happy that Bruce was brought to town, since she had been friends with both Josephine and

Blanche. It is quite possible that her well-publicized and controversial speech forced the white board to ultimately consider Bruce for the assistant superintendent position.

But as enthusiastic as the black community was when Roscoe arrived in Washington, it was obvious that the duties he would soon inherit as superintendent had changed dramatically since his father and Mary Church Terrell had served on the board years before. Not only was there greater contempt for blacks from the white board and leadership, but also there had been a school reorganization that served to ensure that the Colored Schools and the related black faculty and administrators never gained too much power or control.

Just as Roscoe arrived, they fired the bright and talented M Street High School principal Anna J. Cooper, who had headed the school for several years. One of the few black women in the nation with a master's degree in classics at the time, Cooper had received her bachelor's degree from Oberlin in 1884 and was hired by Superintendent George Cook in 1887 to run the prestigious high school.[2]

Cook knew that Cooper would bring the same standards to the school that were brought to it by one of its past principals, Richard T. Greener, who had become principal soon after becoming the first black graduate from Harvard College in 1870. But like Greener, Anna Cooper had great ambitions for her students at the black high school. She wanted her students to be trained by the same challenging curriculum that was available to students in the city's white high schools. When she opposed the white board's attempts to weaken the high school's academic curriculum and introduce anti-intellectual, Booker T. Washington–type industrial trade-school courses, Cooper stood up to the white board members and the white politicians of the city. They responded by firing her and humiliating her in the press. Although Cooper would later receive her PhD and return to the school in a less prominent teaching role, the white board made it clear to her and other blacks in the city that they placed a very low priority on maintaining high academic standards in the Colored Schools.

Even with all of his family's connections to the Washington hierarchy, getting the job of principal at Armstrong High School had been difficult for Roscoe, because of Booker T. Washington's reluctance to let him leave Tuskegee Institute. Despite Roscoe's pleas for Washington's support in light of his need to earn more money for Clara and their growing family, it was only Washington's dislike of another person that caused him to finally support Roscoe's departure. Once it became known that Washington's archenemy, W. E. B. DuBois, was being considered either for the Armstrong principal position or for the assistant superintendent job in charge of the Colored Schools, Washington was willing to support Roscoe for the post of principal—with the hope that Roscoe would eventually win the assistant superintendent position as well.

When Roscoe and Clara finally arrived in Washington during the fall of 1906, they both were ecstatic to be out of Alabama. They were a young couple who had desperately missed the energy, culture, and sophistication that existed in a city like Washington. Roscoe was confident that the city's black residents would be excited about his return, and he was also certain he would be able to manage them as skillfully as his father had. The young couple prepared to move into his mother's four-story town house with their two-year-old daughter, Clara Jr., their four-month-old son, Roscoe Jr., and their nurse.

Roscoe felt triumphant after his three years in Tuskegee. In Washington, he had good memories of growing up in a family that was respected and feared. No longer under the thumb of Booker T. Washington's lieutenants, he felt confident and important now that he was in his new position as principal of the Armstrong Manual and Training School. Although the school was not within walking distance from his mother's home, it was a well-built, four-year-old building with all the modern conveniences. He was also grateful to be back in a large community of educated middle-class and upper-class blacks that shared his tastes and intellectual curiosity.

But the city that Roscoe and Clara returned to did not resemble the Washington that he had left ten years earlier in 1896. The city and the nation had become much more racially segregated. There had not been a black serving in Congress in more than five years. White resentment was growing as more Southern blacks moved north looking for jobs. Many poor blacks had left farms and sharecropping in Georgia, Alabama, and Mississippi, and were now populating Washington in huge numbers. These were people with rural skills who were yet hoping for higher-paying industrial and government jobs. Their hopes were quickly dashed as they realized that the city's employment opportunities were few. To make matters worse, these new residents were forced to live in the alleys behind and between unkempt urban dwellings. These newly segregated neighborhoods were neglected by the white-controlled city and were left crowded and unsanitary.

Josephine Bruce was well aware of what had happened to the city during her son's absence. She had seen the neighborhood around their former home on M Street NW deteriorate as poorer people had crowded into the small living areas along Blagden Alley nearby. Except for her short tenure working at Tuskegee and her visits to the planta- tion and to her family, who now lived in Indianapolis, she had remained a resident of the capital. She had also remained active in the Washington-based National Association of Colored Women, and had even published speeches and scholarly essays on race and education in Washington and other urban centers.[3] Josephine was astute enough to understand that blacks in the city had little to celebrate at the time, and she knew that although the tight circle of black elite families in Wash- ington were grateful that the board had brought a talented and enthu- siastic black educator to their schools, they believed Roscoe to be somewhat young and a bit too arrogant to recognize and manage the political nuances that lay before him.

At the time of his arrival, Josephine was living in both her Wash- ington town house and at Kelso Farm, which was located near Hyattsville, Maryland. She had recently returned from the Mississippi plantation, where she had to pay for the repair of the cotton gin and for the replacement of roofs on several of the workers' cabins on the prop- erty. Josephine told her son and daughter-in-law that having spent a great deal of her time performing work for the National Association of Colored Women, she was contemplating running for the national pres- idency of the organization. Since Booker T. Washington's wife, Mar- garet, had been active with the association during Roscoe's time in Tuskegee, he and Clara already knew a great deal about the organiza- tion's activities.[4]

By the beginning of 1907, after only a few months in the principal's position, Roscoe had sufficiently impressed the white school board members with his hard work and discipline; they finally decided to name him superintendent of Colored Schools, with the job to take effect for the September 1907 school year. But in recent years the white board had sufficiently changed the superintendent of Colored Schools position that it was no longer on equal footing with that of the white superintendent who managed the white schools. There was now a superintendent for the entire school district who was in charge of both the colored and the white schools. Under him was an "assistant superintendent" who ran the day-to-day operations of the Colored Schools. Roscoe had to answer to both the superintendent and the powerful school board.

Even with those limitations, it was still an important job, with the power to hire and promote. And Roscoe was happy to accept the position. It was among the most prestigious jobs available to a black man in Washington at the time, and it suddenly put Roscoe on a footing that approached that of his parents' within the black community of the 1880s and 1890s. His office was located at 1201 17th Street NW, at the corner of M Street, in the handsome red-brick Charles Sumner School building, a structure built in 1872 for the city's black children.

Still in his midtwenties, as superintendent of the Colored Schools, Roscoe was suddenly earning an impressive salary and was a sought-after guest in important black circles, as well as among liberal white educators and political leaders. With their own Washington family ties, their East Coast school credentials, and the imprimatur that came with having worked with Booker T. Washington, Roscoe and Clara were a popular new couple in their old hometown. They were living in Josephine's spacious recently puchased house at 1327 Columbia Road NW and spending occasional weekends at Kelso Farm in nearby Hyattsville, Maryland, while Josephine continued to manage the paperwork and finances of the Mississippi plantation. Since Roscoe's new position was too demanding to allow any free time, Josephine was alone in making decisions about the property, and she was making them from hundreds of miles away, relying on written reports and queries from managers that she had hired.

Finally earning a comfortable income, Roscoe soon purchased an expensive new 1906 four-seater Cadillac touring car. At that time, only about four thousand models were being manufactured each year; mainly purchased only by the well-to-do, each car cost $2,500. With his new job and new standing in the community, Roscoe and Clara began to entertain and socialize with the friends that they had known several years earlier.

As he moved around the city, Roscoe finally saw that the city of

Washington had changed for the worse since he had left for boarding school in 1896. With increased segregation, the mobility of blacks in 1907 Washington was even more limited than before. For example, although his office was located in the all-black Charles Sumner School at 17th and M Streets NW, the actual board of education and the superintendent of all the city's schools held their board meetings a few blocks away at the all-white Franklin School at 13th and K Streets. Although Roscoe was allowed to attend meetings at both schools, the black board of trustees that governed the black schools was not permitted to meet at the white school.

As educator Mary Church Terrell had pointed out the past autumn during her speech to the United Women's Club, even the wealthiest blacks living in the capital were forced to face daily indignities. Hotels and inns did not rent rooms to black Americans of any socioeconomic background, though Chinese, Indian, Japanese, and Filipino people—regardless of their citizenship status—could all get hotel accommodations. Even though she was the daughter of a millionaire, the wife of an attorney, and a well-known member of the school board and other groups, Terrell and other blacks were allowed to stay only in the few black-owned boardinghouses.

Similarly, many of the white churches, movie theaters, trade unions, and restaurants barred blacks, who by then made up nearly 25 percent of the city's population. And as Terrell further noted at the time, "With the exception of Catholic University, there is not a single white college in the national capital to which colored people are admitted."

The situation in 1907 Washington was equally bad for blacks in the field of employment, since the department stores, banks, insurance firms, restaurants, and most government offices were unwilling to hire blacks in any capacity where they would have contact with, or be seen by, white patrons. The rare exception was when blacks were employed to clean floors or empty trash, because restaurants did not allow them to wash or touch dishes, and stores did not want them to touch merchandise that was to be sold. Even the jobs of nurse and maid were suddenly being denied to black women, because segregated facilities like theaters, parks, pools, and concert halls no longer wanted to permit black nannies caring for white children, or black maids assisting white adults, to sit with their charges in the "white sections" of their properties or buildings. The result was that white families began to replace their black caregivers with white nurses and maids. The Jim Crow laws also continued to push black people into the back seats of the city's streetcars, the side entrances to movie theaters, and the back rows or balcony seats of most churches.

Though Josephine's real estate holdings provided a decent income and an enormous amount of prestige for the family, the Bruce plantation in Bolivar County, Mississippi, was an ongoing drain on her energy and resources. Her mother's recent death and the strain that came with it only made her realize that the properties were more than she could handle by herself. Every six months, there seemed to be a new problem that plagued the plantation, which had been enlarged by the purchase of additional acreage, and was now a parcel of several thousand acres located in the northwest quadrant of Mississippi. In the summer of 1908, a fire ravaged two of the buildings on the property and resulted in several thousand dollars' worth of damage.

Even though she had a bright, capable son living with her, Josephine had to solve these problems with the help of lawyers and managers she employed in Washington and Mississippi.

On October 8, 1908, she received a letter from one of her Mississippi attorneys, Roy Church, who wrote to her regarding the insurance that covered part of the loss from the plantation fire. From her lawyer's comments, one gets a sense of how deeply Josephine had to involve herself in the financial affairs of the plantation and its operation. He says to her:

> Dear Madam . . . I went to the plantation yesterday with the insurance adjuster and . . . money will be paid at the end of 60 days . . . and will be turned over to Mr. Goldfarb only on a showing that he has applied the $2700 to rebuilding. He has most of the lumber on the ground to rebuild . . . In regard to what you ask about discounting rent notes, I think most of the banks here will discount any rent notes which are good or are endorsed by responsible parties . . . If you will be more specific as to the notes you wish to discount, I will take up the matter with some bankers . . .
>
> Mr. Goldfarb has the plantation in fairly good shape, certainly much better than it was last year . . . he has plenty of feed,

*including 100 tons of pea hay, and seems to have plenty of labor
in sight as there were two new families applying yesterday. I
arranged with him to insure the gin in the name of yourself and
your son, for $3000, so you will have that much more security . . .
I will sign the application for the gin insurance as your
agent . . . Yours very truly, Roy Church.*[5]

So complicated was the plantation and Josephine's land holdings
outside Washington that not only did she have to employ people like
plantation manager L. T. Goldfarb to hire the families who would live
and work on the plantation, but she had to hire attorneys and rent collectors to oversee the plantation manager to ensure that he was keeping
the property maintained, insured, and productive. As a woman who
had spent the last thirty years as the nonworking wife of a senator and
Washington dignitary, she was not well suited for such a job.

In the meantime, Roscoe was spending a great deal of his time corresponding with, and reporting back to, the district's mostly white
board. He also seemed to work hard to remain close to his string of
white bosses: William Estabrook Chancellor, William Davidson, and
Ernest Thurston. Always charming and obsequious in the company of
powerful whites, Roscoe was adept at winning over the white board
members as well as the numerous white superintendents who held the
job during Roscoe's early years as assistant superintendent. With his
"white" academic credentials and his own ability to espouse conservative, almost anti-black attitudes, Roscoe was able to engender enthusiasm and support from the white board members, who felt that he
spoke their language and represented their kind of black.

Roscoe failed to offer such attentions to the important black educators or black board members in the city. Never a favorite with the
larger black community, he further antagonized them by making little
or no effort to seek their input on the Colored Schools and their curriculum. After he had been in the job less than five years, black newspapers around the country were beginning to report regularly on his
controversial position in the black community. In September 1911, the
New York Age offered a front-page story that began with the sentence
"The annual fight to oust Professor Roscoe C. Bruce as Assistant
Superintendent of Colored Schools is on, led by the three colored members of the Board of Education . . ."[6]

By being dismissive of the black board members, teachers, and parents, Roscoe tended to undermine his own contributions. Following his own sense of what was needed, he brought improvements to many of the schools and raised the hiring standards for teachers and administrators. Given his work in Tuskegee's Academic Department, his greatest interest lay in enhancing the programs in the upper grades, and was thus focused on the Armstrong Manual and Training School, as well as M Street/Dunbar High School and the Miner Normal School, which prepared many of the students for future teaching careers.

While M Street High School was still considered the favored institution among the Colored Schools, there was now a growing prestige associated with the Miner Normal School as well. Many members of the black elite were sending their daughters to the school. One such family was the Loftons, whose daughter, Euphemia Lofton, entered during those early years when Roscoe's school contributions were still being praised by segments of the black community.

Euphemia, who would one day be the first woman to chair the DC school board, became one of the most famous graduates of the Miner Normal School when she finished in 1909. She went on to Smith College, where she received a bachelor's degree in mathematics in 1914, and then received a master's and a PhD from the University of Chicago and Catholic University, respectively. Although Roscoe did not know it at the time when he was heralding Euphemia's accomplishments as a Miner School graduate, she would later chair the math department at Dunbar High School and marry Harold Appo Haynes, the man who would be named to Roscoe's job after years of dissension between Roscoe and the black school parents.

Although he enjoyed the early support of Calvin Chase, the powerful publisher of the black weekly *Washington Bee*, it was not long before Chase began to feel that Roscoe conducted himself like Booker T. Washington in that he seemed only to court white people for their support. Chase and others had early on discouraged Roscoe from attempting to weaken the Colored Schools' academic curriculum and replace it with industrial education. They feared that blacks would be left with nothing but a curriculum full of trade-school classes.

As a means of managing some of the criticism that came from the black community about his ongoing interest in the Booker T. Washington–inspired industrial curriculum, Roscoe reached out and brought the beloved Anna J. Cooper back to the Colored Schools in 1911. Although she never regained her position as high school principal, she did teach for two more decades at the school. But even these gestures were not grand enough as the larger black population accused him of favoring light-complexioned blacks from old Washington families over other blacks, and favoring whites over everyone. It was an accusation that his own parents had heard thirty years earlier. And it wouldn't be long before Calvin Chase and others started launching an even broader campaign against Roscoe, taking him to task for the way in which the young black superintendent dealt with the black community as a whole.

Early in 1911, Roscoe was asked if he would join seventeen other prominent black men in the city and form the Washington chapter of a national organization that had been founded seven years earlier. Roscoe was asked not to discuss the group with anyone other than his wife, and even she was not to be given details of the group's mission or activities. He could, though, tell her who else had been asked to participate. The organization was a men's fraternity called Sigma Pi Phi Boulé.

Clara recognized the names her husband mentioned. They were all black Washingtonians who had attended top universities, but they all worked in different professions. Dr. French Tyson was a successful physician. Judge Robert Terrell was a prominent attorney who was married to the wealthy Mary Church Terrell. And the best-known name, Dr. Carter Woodson, was a history scholar who had worked as a school principal before becoming publisher of the *Journal of Negro History*.

Founded in Philadelphia in 1904 by a group of physicians and attorneys, Sigma Pi Phi Boulé was considered the most prestigious, by-invitation-only social organization for upper-class black men. When Roscoe was asked to join the group in 1911, there were only four other chapters—in Philadelphia, Chicago, Memphis, and Baltimore.

"For years, colored men of training, of culture, of ideals and ambitions, in various sections of this country have felt the need of some organization that would bind them close together," began Professor Carrington Davis of Baltimore, as he welcomed Roscoe and the sixteen other Washingtonians who had assembled that evening to be installed as new members—known as "archons"—in Sigma Pi Phi.[7]

Davis, who had graduated from Harvard before becoming a Greek professor and the president of the Maryland Educational Association, was anxious to inspire Roscoe and his fellow black colleagues with a sense of the black fraternity's purpose and stature in colored society.

The first black Greek-letter fraternity, Sigma Pi Phi differed from the school fraternities that would be started a few years later for black men in that it was not aimed at college students. It was, instead, created for men who had graduated and already established themselves as leaders in their fields. Their purpose was to discuss scholarly topics, current affairs, and issues that related to the improvement of the larger black community. While not intentional, the fraternity had the added benefit of serving as a social and professional network of prominent black men. Three generations later, with chapters in virtually every major American city, Sigma Pi Phi would include the nation's black millionaires, the first black corporate CEOs, as well as the most respected black mayors, congressmen, and college presidents in the country. Black scholar W. E. B. DuBois would be invited to join the fraternity the year after Roscoe Bruce.

Roscoe was intrigued as he noted the credentials not just of the members but also of their parents, spouses, and siblings. He was most fascinated by the name of the man who was the founder of the fraternity: Dr. Henry McKee Minton. When Roscoe learned that Minton was from Philadelphia, that Minton's father's name was Theophilus, and that this prominent black doctor was an 1891 graduate of Phillips Exeter, he immediately realized that Minton was the first cousin of his old Exeter buddy, Theophilus John Minton Syphax. Roscoe would also learn that Dr. Minton's wife was none other than Edith Wormley of the Washington Wormley family. Her own brother, Sumner, was being inducted with Roscoe.

"The joining of men in such a union as this, however," Professor Davis continued, "brings solemn obligation to each one of us. Fidelity, honor, discretion, fortitude and faith must be the golden apples of our quest . . ." Although he had traditionally turned to a small cadre of white people for advice and direction when he was in school and once he had arrived in Washington, here finally was a group of blacks whom Roscoe could consider representative of his own background and ambitions. Perhaps he was hoping that these men, many of them older than him, would be a sympathetic group; a fraternity of like-minded men who would be there for him as he and Clara advanced through the Washington social network.

Among the group of new members were men who would bring great pride to black America. Along with Roscoe, the other seventeen new archons included such men as James Cobb, assistant U.S. district attorney; Dr. Ernest Just, a Dartmouth graduate who was professor of biology at Howard; Dr. Austin Curtis, a Northwestern Medical School graduate who was on staff at Freedman's Hospital; Dr. John Francis, the graduate of the University of Michigan Medical School who had been Blanche's physician; Dr. Kelly Miller, a professor of sociology and dean of the college at Howard University; as well as Dr. G. Sumner Wormley, a graduate of Howard.

Barely six months after Roscoe was welcomed into the fraternity, he was making front-page headlines that underscored the black community's dissatisfaction with his work as assistant superintendent in charge of the Colored Schools. His white boss, Dr. William M. Davidson, became concerned when he saw Roscoe on the front page two days in the same week. Davidson was upset that blacks in the city were critical of Roscoe, and that the articles were running not just in the *Washington Bee* but also in the *New York Age*, as well as in papers published in Baltimore and Pittsburgh.[8]

Davidson didn't want to hear excuses. He had known that the Colored Schools had been a source of controversy even before he had joined the district himself, and Roscoe Bruce never seemed to have the black parents on his side.

For the next several weeks, as the black board members worked together to publicly humiliate Bruce, various high-ranking blacks in the community weighed in with their opinions. Fellow Sigma Pi Phi Boulé member Kelley Miller, the dean of Howard University, appeared on the front page of several papers, saying that he was an admirer of Bruce's but that he respected the right of his colleague, black board member Dr. William Tunnell, to attempt to oust Bruce if he felt it was to the benefit of the Colored Schools and their students.

With such tepid support coming from the black community, Roscoe was able to keep his position only because of the solid backing he received from white board members and white administrators who felt that he always followed their instructions and sought their advice before acting. In essence, he was just the type of black that they wanted to run the Colored Schools. They weren't certain that they could find another black who would be so agreeable to their demands. Conservative in demeanor and obedient and deferential in the presence of his white bosses, Roscoe rarely disagreed with the whites who put him in power, and who demanded that he carry out their dictates.

Since virtually the first day Bruce started in his position as superintendent, blacks identified him as someone who wouldn't play ball with them. They perceived that he felt no more kinship with them than a white administrator would have felt. In fact, the current problems with one of the black board members—Mr. R. R. Horner—could be traced back three years, to when Horner had asked Roscoe to see if Booker T. Washington would endorse Horner's candidacy for the city's recorder of deeds position. Horner was incensed that while Roscoe was quick to call on connections for his own purposes, he would not do so for any other blacks—not for those within the schools and not for those outside. The other blacks on the board and in the district felt similarly about Roscoe.

Clara knew that Roscoe's tenuous standing in the black community made it essential that the white board members remain unified behind him. But even she knew it would be difficult for them to stand by him if they continued to see so many important members of the black community to criticizing him.

Roscoe knew this was a legitimate point, but he was fairly confident that the board wouldn't want to replace him, because that would only be surrendering to the vocal colored community, and the board didn't want to give the impression that they could be bullied by blacks.

What seemed to anger the black residents even more about Roscoe was his determination to embrace Booker T. Washington's philosophy that the majority of Negro students were better off being educated in trade schools rather than in academic schools that emphasized English, history, science, and math. This was antithetical to the black families who had found pride in their renowned school system. Since many black professionals in Washington were graduates of academic high schools and top colleges, they were insulted by the idea of transforming academic high schools into trade schools that taught cooking, carpentry, and plumbing. They saw Roscoe and the white administrators as being in a hurry to relegate black students to this second-class status.

Interestingly, Roscoe probably reached this conclusion for much different reasons than his white colleagues or his mentor, Booker T. Washington.

While Washington seemed to sincerely believe that all blacks should manage their ambitions and aim their careers toward the trades, Roscoe's philosophy appeared to offer a dichotomy of ideas. Unlike Washington, Roscoe did not seem completely able—or willing—to argue that all blacks should accept a subservient role. Perhaps because his background was so wildly different, he truly believed that blacks deserved to compete with whites in every arena. While Roscoe was, indeed, living the life of a wealthy senator's son, he was also surrounded by a cadre of blacks in prep school and college who had similarly lofty ambitions. It was a black world completely foreign to Booker T. Washington.

So, as Roscoe advanced the idea of turning more of the colored high schools in Washington into training institutes, it was not with the wholeheartedness that his mentor would have argued. Roscoe had developed a hybrid version of the black accommodationist's theory. He believed that *many* blacks—but not *all*—were better suited to the trades and, therefore, should attend high schools that prepared them for such careers. But he also believed that there was *another* type of black individual—black children who came out of privilege, like himself and his circle of elite blacks—who should do all that they could to compete in white or mostly white academic and professional settings.

In 1909, Roscoe gave a controversial speech to the Howard University alumni in which he called for the university to close its preparatory department—a division that offered a precollege curriculum. He felt that Howard was compromising its status as a premier college by offering courses aimed at high school students—thereby making it too easy for less-prepared black students to associate themselves with a prestigious university. "Is it desirable to continue the policy of offering high school opportunities here at Howard?" Roscoe asked in his May 26, 1909, speech to the alumni. "A Howard man should invariably be something more and better than a high school graduate. My impression is that the reputation of a university is not enhanced by graduates of its high school department, however worthy that department may be. The Howard man is the ambassador of the University to the Nation. I do now with due humility venture the prediction that the progressive well-being of this great university of ours demands the devotion of all its resources to the enrichment and elevation of the colleges and the professional schools. The vital service of the preparatory department in making the college possible none may question. Twenty-five years hence, however, all will realize that this was the scaffolding of the structure of the university. And who shall then think of marring the beauty of the noble structure by retention of the scaffolding."[9]

Even though his comments were probably intended to buttress his theory that a select segment of black America should compete with whites while the rest of the black community should accept its second-class status, the audience at Howard perceived his remarks to be nothing more than a critique of this superior black institution. Both the Howard alumni and local black Washingtonians were insulted by his questioning of a division of Howard that had educated so many of them. Even his wife had attended that particular program at Howard.

Remarks like these only exacerbated the negative feelings that the black school board members in Washington already held for him. For them, and for many black school parents, this was further evidence that he looked down on the black citizens of Washington.

Five years later, he was still defending himself from these accusations when, in 1914, he was criticized for raising the necessary qualifications for black teachers to a level that exceeded the level required for white teachers who were teaching in the same grade. Although most teachers in the nation at that time were not required to have a college degree in order to teach black or white children at the elementary level, Roscoe decided to implement a new rule that required college degrees for teachers who were instructing high school students, as well as for teachers who were instructing grammar school children.

Given that the impact of this new rule would apply only to the teachers in his Colored Schools, it infuriated the black teachers, who were already angry that they were being paid far less than their white counterparts in the same city. The black teachers further argued that this new rule was really meant to give Roscoe the power to reward his few black elite teacher friends who had degrees from white Northern colleges. The response was swift, direct, and overwhelming.

"Roscoe C. Bruce is facing the most serious opposition of his career—opposition from fully three hundred colored teachers," declared a front-page article in the *New York Age*.[10] "The colored teachers have organized . . . and let it be known that Mr. Bruce's alleged unfair treatment of them can only be penalized by his removal." All three hundred teachers signed the petition that listed their demands to the board. The article further stated that Roscoe was accused of managing his own publicity by writing favorable articles and letters about himself and his work, and then anonymously submitting them to various newspapers.

It was not long before some of the white board members began to wonder if Roscoe should be removed from his position. They saw that he invited so much black criticism that, they reasoned, blacks wouldn't be much angrier if it was a white person, in fact, who ran the Colored Schools. After the white board experienced some disagreements with the principal of the Miner Normal School, the district's well-regarded school that prepared black students for the teaching professions, they were disturbed by the fact that Roscoe did not step in and immediately dismiss her. Soon after, the press started to accuse him of straddling the fence between the black teachers and his white bosses—and failing to please either group. Newspapers reported, "In [Bruce's] endeavor to satisfy everybody, he develops weakness and unreliability . . . A committee of citizens headed by Daniel Murray of the Library of Congress is looking about for a man to succeed Mr. Bruce as superintendent . . . Unless differences are settled within the Negro schools, the result will be an elimination of the Negro as a school official and that a white will be put in charge of the Negro schools."[11]

With the constant public attacks on her son's work as head of the Colored Schools and the continuous drain on her energy in managing the Mississippi plantation, sixty-year-old Josephine began to look for ways to simplify her life in Washington. Once Roscoe and Clara began to need even greater financial assistance with the arrival of their youngest child, Burrill, Josephine realized that the best solution would be to sell the plantation. In early 1913, Josephine received a letter from Clyde Denton, her rent collector who worked at the Sunflower County Title Company in Indianola, Mississippi. Despite all that she was paying him, he was coming back with problems, new expenses, and complaints about plantation tenants who were defaulting on their rents.

> *Dear Madam, I am enclosing a statement showing the amounts I have collected during the year 1912 on your house and the amounts I have paid out. You will note that I have not charged my*

*regular commission because the negro who was renting the cabin
was unable to pay me . . . I carried him along in hope that I could
get him to pay out but it was hopeless and I finally put him out . . .
I am also enclosing you a receipt . . . for repairs on the fence. I
am also enclosing a receipt for $4.25 that I had to spend for repairs
on the cabin . . . I am enclosing you the tax receipts for the County
and Town taxes on this place . . . I have talked with Mr. Pitts about
his buying the place and he has promised to let me know soon . . .
    Yours truly, Clyde T. Denton*[12]

It was not a surprise that Josephine, as an absentee owner with no
experience in real estate management, was less successful than her husband at profiting from their vast land holdings. As a widowed black
woman living several hundred miles away, she was easy prey for the white
Southern businessmen who were hired to "manage" her property while
she resided in Washington. Given her Northern rearing in large cities, she
did not understand Southern plantation life, and she did not have friends
or family in Mississippi who could advise her on how to protect her investment. In each piece of correspondence sent to her by these various rent collectors and money managers, there were multiple references to "surprise"
unanticipated expenses for which they needed reimbursement—sometimes reducing the plantation's income to suspiciously low figures.

But there was nothing Josephine could do so long as she relied on
these men. She was not willing to move to Mississippi, nor was Roscoe
prepared to help her, so she had no choice but to acquiesce to their
demands for additional moneys for improvements that she never really
saw and expenses that she could never verify. Roscoe, rather than someone for her to lean on, had become an added burden. Not only was he
asking her for more money to supplement his income now that he had
three children, ages ten, eight, and five, but he was also facing rising
opposition from parents, teachers, and the black publisher of the *Washington Bee*, Calvin Chase, who had launched a campaign to begin black
neighborhood Parents Leagues. Their sole purpose was to force Roscoe
to resign as assistant superintendent of the Colored Schools.

Josephine must have known that, in many ways, she was all alone
in solving the family's problems. Her son's triumphant return to Washington was doing very little to bring back the magic of her prior life in
the capital city.

cᴐＯＧＤＪ

1915–1922
Roscoe's Downfall in Washington

The Negro peasant is wholly unprepared for the complications,
the competitions, the moral stress of city life, and little or no
provision is made to train him in theatres and industries
by which he might sustain himself.

—*The Washington Bee*, June 7, 1919
Letter to the editor from Roscoe C. Bruce,
Superintendent of the Colored Schools[1]

ALTHOUGH ROSCOE HAD ALREADY INVITED DERISION AND ANIMOSITY
from black school parents, the black newspaper publishers, and black
board members who felt that he looked down on them and dismissed
their concerns in favor of the concerns of white board members, Roscoe's
most severe problems began in 1915, when his mentor Booker T.
Washington died shortly after returning from a speaking tour in New
York City.

Ever since he had arrived from Tuskegee in 1906, black and white
Washingtonians had been led to believe that Roscoe enjoyed the ongoing support of the powerful Booker T. Washington. His mother had
been lady principal of Tuskegee Institute from 1899 until 1902; Roscoe
had headed the school's Academic Department from 1903 until 1906;
and Booker T. Washington had several times communicated his sup-

port of Roscoe to the white DC superintendent William Chancellor and others, during Roscoe's early tenure. Even though Washington continued to travel around the country, raising enormous amounts of money from white benefactors and still advocating that blacks embrace self-reliance, few people, including Calvin Chase, publisher of the *Washington Bee*, would dare criticize him or the man they thought was his protégé. Through interviews, speeches, and writings, Roscoe had invoked Washington's name with sufficient frequency to suggest that he had the Tuskegee Wizard's full support over the years.

But the black professional class in Washington had grown weary of the disdain Roscoe had shown for them and for the less-affluent Washingtonians, and of his constant pandering to the white citizens of the city. Once the *Washington Bee* labeled Roscoe "the most despised man in Washington" in 1915, it was clear that people now had permission to openly attack Roscoe and the policies he was implementing as head of the Colored Schools.

Only days after Booker T. Washington died in November 1915, Roscoe was left without the cloak of protection that had previously been provided by the country's most famous black educator and adviser to presidents.

Now that the Tuskegee founder was gone, the people of Washington could openly criticize and chastise Roscoe without fear of retribution. Black parents accused him of ignoring them, of favoring a certain class of people in his selection, promotion, and retention of teachers, and of populating the schools only with teachers who were light-complexioned, who were from the city's older, wealthy families, and who had been educated at schools that he favored.

Most of the white school board officials were nevertheless still smitten by the charming Roscoe who spoke with eloquence and exuded a university professor's intellectual demeanor. Here, they thought, was a colored man who didn't "act colored," "sound colored," or even "think colored." Here was someone they could completely understand and utterly control. For now, Roscoe's problems lay with the black teachers and parents. In between the twice-a-month board meetings, Roscoe worked long hours putting together detailed memos and reports in his office at the Franklin School at 13th and K Streets NW.

Earlier in the year, Roscoe had faced a major setback when he was injured in a near-fatal car crash while driving through Maryland. On

April 21, 1915, he was traveling from Washington to Baltimore for a school-related conference in his late-model Cadillac sedan. On a winding road in Relay, Maryland, he made a sharp turn, lost control of the car, and was thrown thirty feet from the vehicle. He landed on the ground, fracturing his skull. The accident required a long recuperation, but there was a great deal of gossip that followed among black parents and other teachers when it was revealed that also in the car were some of the very teachers that Roscoe had been accused of favoring in the schools. He had earlier denied having any special ties or friendships with the teachers in the district.

Traveling with him and his secretary were three female teachers, who were injured in the accident: Miss Jessie Wormley, Mrs. Miriam Wormley Lewis, and Mrs. Wormley Anderson. Because these women teachers were all members of the wealthy, light-complexioned Wormley family—the very sort of people that other teachers said Roscoe was favoring with special attention, promotions, and perks—much of black Washington used the succeeding weeks to argue this entourage was further evidence that the assistant superintendent did, in fact, have special friendships with certain members of the teaching staff. The public argued that but for personal connections there was no justifiable reason for Roscoe to have selected these teachers over other teachers to have traveled with him in his car.

By the time Roscoe had recovered from the accident, he had yet another controversy to address within the black community. It related to Roscoe's November 7, 1914, dismissal of Dr. W. Bruce Evans from the position of principal of the Armstrong Manual Training School.[2]

Even though Roscoe and Evans had some legitimate differences, many believed that Roscoe had gone too far with his public criticism of the popular black educator when he said that Evans had "a meager education," was disobedient to his superiors, and "was not the master of any subject taught in a high school."[3] It was not uncommon for Roscoe to unleash such venomous insults on those he disliked, but he greatly miscalculated the backlash that would follow his attack on Evans. Furthermore, Roscoe made two grave errors. First, he had not anticipated that Evans would respond by suing both Roscoe and the school board. Second, he hadn't realized the power of Evans's family members and friends.

In addition to being a popular fixture among the city's black professional class for many years, Evans was brother-in-law to Daniel Murray, an influential Baltimore native who was now among the ten richest blacks in Washington. An independently wealthy man, Murray was assistant librarian at the Library of Congress and a well-regarded historian. Murray's closest friend was black Ohio state senator John P. Green, a DC socialite as well as a friend and adviser to John D. Rockefeller. The three men—Evans, Murray, and Green—had, in 1901, displayed their influence in Washington when they hosted an all-black inaugural ball that honored incoming president Theodore Roosevelt.

With Evans's cronies working against Roscoe, his reputation in the black community suffered greatly. They set up a committee of people who would help fan the anti-Roscoe flames. They wrote dozens of critical letters to the press, and spoke negatively about Roscoe at numerous gatherings that were host to both prominent blacks and whites in the city.

It was during this period that Clara began to limit the time she spent advising Roscoe on his professional affairs. Instead, she, began to pursue interests that advanced her own ambitions. She had invested a great deal of her time into Roscoe's career, but correspondence with her husband later revealed that she was anxious to pursue her own professional goals. By this time, her children were thirteen, eleven, and eight and were a bit more independent, allowing her to explore issues like the law and international affairs. She'd been reading a great deal about the ongoing war in Europe.

In 1917, as the United States was entering the war, black men who had volunteered to serve were met with hostility from army officers and other whites who wanted to maintain the rules of segregation both here and abroad in their facilities. Since white officers wanted to limit black recruits to performing menial labor, and didn't want them to mingle with white recruits, they first assigned them to join French divisions. The Americans decided that they would rather lose the additional manpower than change their policies of segregation.

Once the U.S. Army acknowledged that it needed all the manpower it could get, including from their black recruits, it established two segregated black divisions, the Ninety-second and the Ninety-third. During 1917 and 1918, approximately 2.3 million black men registered with the U.S. Army, and nearly 400,000 of them actually served. Unfortunately, their presence was resented by white officers and by the white citizens living wherever the black units or regiments happened to be stationed in

the United States. Although the French treated the black American servicemen equally and without regard to race, when they returned home
to the United States, they were once again subjected to Jim Crow laws
and discriminatory treatment. With Klan activity still continuing, and
with Southern whites angered that black servicemen were coming back
to their Southern towns and seeking jobs formerly held by whites, some
returning black military men were lynched in their uniforms as a message to let blacks know that their service in the army was not going to
afford them any new benefits or prestige at home.

Back home during the war, when the United States finally joined
the Allied troops, most black civilians were still more focused on
domestic issues in the American South, where lynching, race riots, and
discrimination in housing and work were the more immediate problems for them. Few of them engaged in the debate over the American
government's role outside the United States; so much bigotry and
unequal treatment was being aimed at blacks here on American soil,
there was little reason for black Americans to turn their concern or
sympathy toward abuse that was being directed at people in foreign
lands. This changed slightly as more blacks were permitted to register
in the armed forces.

Another issue that held different weight in the American black
and white communities was the women's suffrage movement.
Although it first gained great attention in 1848, with the Seneca Falls
Convention in upstate New York, it was not until the end of World
War I that women's demands for the right to vote were taken seriously.
Black Americans had long been disenfranchised because of ongoing Ku
Klux Klan activity, bogus poll taxes, or other schemes to discourage
black voters, so very few blacks were joining in the debate on giving
women the right to vote. Since blacks had been denied the vote even
after allegedly being given the right with the Fifteenth Amendment in
1870, it was difficult for them to muster outrage over the lack of successes in the women's suffrage movement.

But, interestingly, all of these topics captured the interest of Clara
Bruce. As a feminist with a strong interest in world affairs and economics, she sought out literature, organizations, and speakers who
would educate her on these issues. It was at this time that she became
involved with the League of Women Voters, and she began following
the writings of Louis F. Post, a known American anti-imperialist who

would later serve as the assistant secretary of labor under President Woodrow Wilson.

Post, one of a handful of liberal whites who helped found the NAACP in 1909, became a controversial figure in the Wilson administration when he challenged J. Edgar Hoover's and Attorney General A. Mitchell Palmer's arguments and demands that deportation be used as a simple and logical solution for dealing with people living in the United States who had possible ties to the Communist Party. Arguing for due process, Post would eventually force the federal government to respect citizens' rights to privacy and freedom of association. Before Post had joined the administration, he had been best known for publishing a magazine that Clara read with regularity. Written for the liberal intelligentsia, Post's magazine was called *The Public: A National Journal of Fundamental Democracy*. Published between 1898 and 1919, *The Public* was a popular journal for socialists, union supporters, and people who opposed American imperialism.

By 1917, Clara had become so significantly enamored with *The Public* that she tried to submit several creative pieces for publication. By 1918, she was able to get the magazine to accept her work. The first to be published was a rather lengthy poem that offered a strong statement on the issues of race and war. Titled "We Who Are Dark," the poem attempted to lay out the abuses perpetrated against black people, and the effects of these abuses. She suggests that "we" dark-skinned people empathize with the downtrodden—in this case, the Europeans being abused by the Germans—because we have also been abused. But the most poignant part of the poem is near the end, when she points out that blacks receive only a qualified acceptance from white people when the blacks march off with them to fight in a war that their white brethren have asked them to support. The ironic twist comes in the last lines, which point out that while the black and white soldiers march together to victory, they will be bringing a freedom and an equality to foreigners that the black soldiers don't even get to enjoy in their own homeland of the United States.

WE WHO ARE DARK

We who are dark and know the lash
On bodies worn, insensate made

Through years of wrong; That feel no more
The scourge, the whip—
  We who are dark and know the hurt
Of pitiless scorn on souls that live
And feel the dart and thrust of wrong . . .
  We who are dark and know the urge
Of blinding rage and fury red,
That eats and burns the ache of hands
Pressed on by hearts on vengeance bent—
  We've won your praise that side by side
With those who taught us all our woes
We bravely march . . . Brothers-in-arms
  As we march forth to Victory,
Bearing aloft to foreign lands
A freedom sweet that's not our own.[4]

Having written a large collection of short stories, essays, and poetry since her years at Radcliffe, Clara had come to express most of her views about race and politics through her creative writing. Already a great fan of socialist and progressive thinkers who demanded equality between the genders, races, and across all economic backgrounds, Clara continued to both read and write essays that addressed these issues. Given Roscoe's sensitive position vis à vis the white board members, and his own cautious stand on racial and political issues, this was the extent to which she was able to express her liberal views. Years later, she turned to writing less politically charged pieces and began submitting them for publication in the popular mainstream magazine *Saturday Evening Post*.

By 1918, it was becoming evident that Roscoe and Clara were both falling out of step with Washington's black elite community, Josephine Bruce's well-regarded position there notwithstanding. Unlike his mother, Roscoe did not embrace the institutions that the old black families held dear. Although he remained a charter member, Roscoe became less involved with Sigma Pi Phi Boulé. The prestigious secret organization included some of the most powerful black men in the city but Roscoe stopped reaching out to this circle of strong black men. He withdrew from the black community in still other ways. For example, rather than vacation with the many upper-class black families in Highland Beach, a black resort community on the Chesapeake Bay that had been popular since the 1880s, the Bruces chose to vacation quietly, by themselves, on their Maryland farm.

Roscoe was not a member of any of the black college fraternities, nor was Clara a member of any black sororities, since they had not graduated from black colleges and had not availed themselves of the events sponsored by the groups after their pre–World War I development. In fact, neither Roscoe nor Clara had strong affiliations with any black organizations. They did not even maintain ties to a church. Along with their three children and Roscoe's mother, Josephine, the Bruces were still a very important family among the black elite, but this was more because of the strong black affiliations that Blanche and Josephine had established in prior years, when Blanche served on the board of Howard and when Josephine was an officer with the National Association of Colored Women. Left on their own, Roscoe and Clara did little to make their way into the powerful black networks of the city. Their indifference would eventually work against them.

"We want him out of here." This was the rallying cry from black residents in Washington when nearly fifteen thousand of them crowded into the city's Metropolitan AME Church on the evening of June 10, 1919, in order to demand the firing of Roscoe Bruce from his position as assistant superintendent of Colored Schools.

People in the church's pews distributed copies of the June 7 issue of the *Washington Bee*. Many of them turned to the editorial page and signed their names and addresses on the dotted line of a mail-in form that was printed at the bottom of the page. It was a form that specifically called for the ouster of Bruce. There was a rumor many of them believed, that he had allowed a strange perverted white man to visit their schools and take nude photographs of young black schoolgirls, and among the girls were Bertha Young, Helen Saunders, and Ruth Barnaby, known by many of the adults in the church.

In fact, Bruce and several other prominent black educators had permitted a white man, known as Professor H. M. D. Moens, to take photographs of black teenage female students as a part of his study to show the physical similarities between Negroes and whites. To the surprise of the black community, it was revealed that the photographs showed the young girls at various stages of undress—many of them with no clothing at all. It had been argued during a criminal trial in March and April that not only had Moens been taking the photographs, but also he was having illicit relations with the older girls—dancing nude with them and writing sexually provocative letters to them.[5]

It was further revealed that Moens kept no data or statistical records of his alleged research, and during cross-examination, it was shown that he had no background in medical or scientific research. The trial uncovered that for some unknown reason, he had deposited several thousand dollars in bank accounts in such countries as Germany, Belgium, and Russia. He had invited one of the young girls to go to Europe with him, alone. In essence, the trial had determined, the defendant was nothing more than a sexual deviant who had duped Bruce and other black school officials that felt flattered to be assisting a white man who feigned an interest in their colored schools. It was this event that the *Washington Bee* used in order to call for his resignation. They had been running an advertisement for several weeks that read:

To the Board of Education and Superintendent
of Public Schools of the District of Columbia:

 We, the undersigned, members of the Parents' League of the District of Columbia, most respectfully represent as follows:
 That Roscoe C. Bruce, Assistant Superintendent of Colored Schools of The District of Columbia, during his administration of said schools, has, by his many acts of omission and commission, forfeited the confidence and lost the respect of the parents of the children in the Public Colored Schools in the District of Columbia.
 That the said Roscoe C. Bruce has lost his usefulness in the schools, and we therefore ask his immediate removal for the good of the service.
  Name: . . . .
  Address: . . . .

[cut out and send to 1518 M Street N.W.]

Not only was the black press advancing the campaign to humiliate and remove Roscoe, but the black public was also asking Congress to take a position and force an overhaul of the city's schools. Many blacks were even asking that a white person replace Roscoe because, as some said, a white man would not have any less regard for Negroes than he did.

As Roscoe showed his lack of remorse and refused to resign his seat, editor Calvin Chase widened his attacks and directed the public's animosity toward the black professional families who were governing the schools. His articles and editorials were written to demonstrate that the larger black community could not trust the black intelligentsia to protect their children's interests, because these "elitist" leaders would never give poor black children the same respect and treatment that they gave their own offspring. He also pointed out that the black elite would always use the working-class blacks as their "scapegoats." He used the Moens scandal as an example, because, while it was true that the fake researcher had clearly duped many people before he took the nude photos, it was a fact that many of the girls and women who allowed themselves to be photographed were members of the black elite. His point was that the educated black families were all too eager to participate in this white man's "research" without first asking about his credentials, and that they were also quick to keep the press from publishing their own names and willingly permitted the board to release the names of poor black girls and women who had been photographed.

Chase wrote the following in an April 26, 1919, editorial in the *Washington Bee*:

> There are individuals going around the city declaring that this one or that one was not mixed up in this Moens case . . . The *Bee* takes this opportunity of saying that the servant classes had no connection with the Moens case. The actors and actresses were the wives and daughters of doctors, lawyers, preachers, educators who constitute the so-called leading colored people in society.
>
> It is said that only the lower class posed for Moens. It was the so-called intellectual social classes that exposed themselves and now they realize they have committed a notorious blunder. They were told they had white blood in their veins and their symmetrical form would make a great picture. This intelligent class fell to this propaganda . . . which a monkey would have repudiated.

The black press went on to argue that not only was the black professional class a corrupt and selfish group, but that Roscoe Bruce was their leader. Months later, the *Bee* began reprinting excerpts from various old letters and speeches that served as evidence that Roscoe was contemptuous of black working people. It reprinted a July 22, 1909, letter that he had written after poor blacks in Washington accused him of removing too much of the academic curriculum from their schools. Brimming with condescension, Roscoe's letter began, "The Negro peasant is wholly unprepared for the complications, the competitions, the moral stress of city life, and little or no provision is made to train him in theatres and industries by which he might sustain himself." He went on to explain that it was in their best interest to focus their studies on basic industrial skills rather than the study of history, science, and literature, which should be reserved for whites and more affluent blacks.

For many months leading up to the beginning of 1921, the *Washington Bee* continued its weekly attacks on Roscoe through its editorials and articles, until it convinced the larger black community and the white board that Roscoe was representative of a small black elite that looked out only for itself. With pressure from black board members, the black press, the powerful Parents League group, and certain influential blacks, like former principal W. Bruce Evans, the white board and its superintendent Ernest Thurston finally capitulated and demanded Roscoe's resignation in the spring of 1921, within days of his daughter Clara's graduation from Dunbar High School, the school district's premier school for black students.

Completely humiliated by his forced resignation, Roscoe blamed his predicament on the Parents League and a group of black elite figures that remained well connected in the Colored Schools, Howard University, and the important social groups of old black Washington. Oddly enough, Roscoe had every opportunity to solicit support from Howard University and its power brokers, but he was too proud to do so. Although his own father had once sat on the board of trustees of the school, Roscoe was too contemptuous of the school's leaders to compromise or work with them.

During the next several months, Roscoe and Josephine launched an aggressive campaign to find a new job for him, but it quickly became clear to both of them that Roscoe was being "blackballed" by the city's black elite. Few people were willing to meet with him, and those who did offered only vague promises to recommend him for jobs. In a lengthy letter to his mother, he complained that neither her friends nor his were helpful in his search:

> You know, Mama, these folks of mine lack—what shall I say? Imagination. They are so niggardly in speaking in your behalf. To do the magnificent thing—they cannot. They know me thoroughly; they know my work; they know how outrageous the persecution and the punishment have been . . . We don't need their old help anyhow. Yet, these Negroes who know all the facts, begin to hem and haw!!![6]

By the fall of 1921, with Roscoe out of his job, the Bruce family began to experience their first real financial problems. Although Josephine still owned multiple properties and maintained comfortable savings, her income was barely sufficient to pay her own bills, much less those of her son's high-living five-member family. Roscoe was unwilling to relinquish his plans to purchase another Cadillac, or to consider a college other than Radcliffe or Wellesley for his daughter, or a high school other than Phillips Exeter Academy for his older son. He simply refused to economize.

Realizing that there was nothing available for him in Washington, Roscoe applied for a principal's position in a black school district in West Virginia. Despite his controversial past in the nation's capital, the poor rural community of Kendall, West Virginia, was grateful to attract a person with Roscoe's experience to their Browns Creek District High School. Their gratitude was met with his characteristic condescension. In fact, as soon as Roscoe arrived in West Virginia, he immediately began searching for better opportunities, first at black schools in the Southeast, then in the Midwest. His greatest efforts were made in applying for a job at Lincoln University in Jefferson City, Missouri. Although the school had less than five hundred students, it was a far better choice than his position in West Virginia, where Roscoe found the people and environment intolerable. He complained in a letter to his mother about the situation in early 1922:

My darling Mother. . . . So, I am praying with desperation for the success of the Lincoln University project. Jefferson City cannot conceivably be as sooty as this veritable coal mine. Here the soot is external, internal and eternal . . . Mama dear, I do not want you and Caree [Clara Sr.] and dear little baby Woogs [Burrill] to be mixed up in this Negro society of the coal mine. It would be exceedingly humiliating to me. The only way you could get a friend [here] to talk with who'd understand your language, would be to take the train and go a thousand miles from here. That's a fact.

Roscoe's resentment and bitterness over his banishment from Washington was palpable in his description of his new job. As was customary in his letters, his use of the word "Negro" continued to be his disparaging way of referring to the types of black people that he believed were not worthy of his respect.

Roscoe was earning a meager salary in his new position in West Virginia, but in addition to paying for his housing there, the family had to maintain Kelso Farm in Maryland, properties in Mississippi, and a town house in Washington. Added to that, there were the anticipated expenses for educating his children, since Clara Jr. had begun her freshman year at Howard University in September of 1921 with plans for transferring to Radcliffe College in September 1922, and Roscoe Jr. was about to leave Washington's Dunbar High School in order to begin his first year at Phillips Exeter Academy. The responsibility for all of these expenses fell to Josephine, who, unbelievably, was still buying clothes for her forty-two-year-old son.

In a 1922 letter, Roscoe thanked his mother for clothes that she purchased and sent to him in West Virginia. He wrote, "How can I thank you enough for that elegant overcoat? And it certainly imparts to my modest figure the grand air!" In that same letter, he thanked her for having bought a new car for his wife and children in Washington, but even in showing his appreciation, it was obvious that his main concern was maintaining appearances for the black Washingtonians who had chased him out of his job. He wrote, "as for the purchase of the Ford, I think that your action was simply heroic. What would the children have done in getting to and from school without it? It has distressed me a very great deal to think that you and Clara had only the old truck in which to ride when going to town. I have always feared that some of the Parent Leaguers might see you only to exalt over the discomfiture, etc."[7]

So evident were the family's financial problems that sixteen-year-old Roscoe Jr. wrote to his grandmother when he realized there might not be enough money to send him and his sister away to school at the same time. By this time, sixty-seven-year-old Josephine had grown exasperated by the amount of money she had given to her son and daughter-in-law. Although she had allowed them to move onto Kelso Farm with her in suburban Maryland, the closer they got to her, the more of her money they spent. After paying their expenses, buying them clothes, and giving them a new car, she had evidently considered leaving Washington and moving elsewhere by herself—or perhaps to West Virginia with her son—and had indicated this when writing to her grandson in a prior letter. He wrote back to her from Exeter in the fall of 1922:

Dearest Grandma, I just got your letter. Please tell me why you are leaving. I won't tell anyone. Isn't Clara going to school any more? If we haven't money enough to send us both, send Clara and I'll stay home until she finishes because Clara won't want to go to school when she is 20 or 21 and I won't mind it . . . I really cried when I read your letter . . . Your grandson, Roscoe[8]

Although the family had not fully informed Roscoe Jr., they had decided that Clara would have to take a year off from school between her one year at Howard and her first year at Radcliffe.

These were the financial problems that, no doubt, precipitated one of the worst betrayals that Roscoe and Clara were likely to face with regard to their daughter. Born at a time when little was demanded of young girls except to be attractive, poised, and obedient, Clara Jr. was raised by parents and a grandmother who doted on her during her childhood years in Washington. She took piano lessons and ballet lessons alongside girls from the other black professional families. She was dressed in beautiful clothes and driven around the city in her parents' Cadillac. As the granddaughter of a senator and the child of the Colored Schools' superintendent, she was invited to participate in cotillions that were sponsored by society groups in both Washington and Baltimore. And, naturally, she attended the respected Dunbar High School, her parents' alma mater.

Her father had been superintendent of Washington's Colored Schools for the entire thirteen years that Clara attended the public schools. Her father's position, added to the fact that her grandmother Josephine maintained an active social life among the city's black elite, brought special favors and attention for Clara as a child. But this unwanted attention also revealed her shy demeanor, as her father's reputation in the schools and among the city's black families became more controversial. She was barely seven years old when the black press first demanded that her father resign. She was only fifteen when her father was implicated in the 1919 Moens trial. By the time Clara entered her senior year at Dunbar High School in September 1920, she was a somewhat withdrawn girl who was eager to escape the scrutiny imposed by Washington's small black upper-class community.

In her high school class, there were many other children from prominent black families with ties to Howard, Sigma Pi Phi Boulé, the MuSoLit Club, and other important black institutions. Among them were Montague Cobb, who went on to become chairman of Howard Medical School's Anatomy Department. He had graduated from Amherst College in 1925 and earned his MD at Howard and PhD at Case Western. Another one of Clara's Dunbar classmates was William Henry Hastie, who went on to become the nation's first black federal judge after graduating from Amherst and Harvard Law School.

With few choices offered to young women at the time, Clara was expected to repeat the same life decisions that her mother had made for herself. Like her mother, she was expected to graduate from Dunbar, attend Howard University for a year of college preparatory studies, and then apply to Radcliffe. And while at Radcliffe, she was expected to become engaged to some eligible black Harvard student from Washington or Atlanta, and then get married. Her brother Roscoe was expected to do exactly as his father had done: attend Dunbar for two years, then enter Exeter, and upon graduating, enter Harvard University. Despite the fact that they lacked their parents' ambition and superior intellect, both Clara Jr. and Roscoe Jr. followed the exact same paths as their parents had done a generation earlier.

Although Clara's parents wanted her to find a suitable Washington beau whom she could maintain contact with while away at college, in the same way that her mother had done upon graduating from M Street High School, Clara Jr. was in no position to choose among the best black families when she graduated in 1921 or while she was enrolled for the one year at Howard University. Following those years of scathing criticism from the *Washington Bee*, as well as from Washington's more prominent black families, Roscoe had lost his esteemed place in black Washington. Being named "the most despised" colored man in the nation's capital by the black press and then finally being forced out of his job in early 1921 in a publicly humiliating manner, Roscoe brought embarrassment and shame to his daughter within her social circles. There was no way that she could now attract the interest of a boy from a respected family.

Recognizing that her father's humiliation and loss of his job was putting her own future marital choices in jeopardy, Clara was no doubt terrified, and became even more withdrawn from her Dunbar High and Howard social circle. On February 23, 1922, Clara applied to Radcliffe College, telling the admissions office that she had three reasons for wanting to attend the school:

> Because my mother was a student at Radcliffe and my father is a graduate of Harvard class of 1902. Because of the high rank of the college. Because of the opportunity of coming in contact with the able educators who form its faculty.[9]

Lacking her own parents' drive and intellect, Clara had no real sense of who she was or why she wanted to attend Radcliffe—or any college, for that matter. In all fairness to her, very few girls—black or white—in the 1920s were being encouraged to attend four-year colleges.

By the time Clara was admitted to Radcliffe in June 1922, her father had been driven out of Washington and was trapped in a community that offered few social possibilities for Clara and her siblings. Roscoe's position as principal of the poor black high school in Kendall, West Virginia, was humiliating for all of them. Since he was earning a very meager salary, the lifestyle that he, Clara Sr., and the children had grown accustomed to in Washington was clearly coming to an end. Although she had completed her year at Howard and was admitted by Radcliffe and expected to begin in September, her parents made it clear to her that she might have to wait another year before entering, because their finances were so short.

Once it was suggested that the children and Clara Sr. would have to relocate to West Virginia with Roscoe, Clara Jr. made a desperate decision that ended up altering her life, betraying her parents, and further humiliating her father. News of this decision came in the form of a letter to her father, dated October 24, 1922, from Nathaniel Guy, the father of Barrington Guy, one of Clara's black schoolmates from Dunbar High School:

> *Dear Sir,*
>
> *There are persistent rumors afloat that Clara and Barrington are married. I have questioned Barrington and he just as persistently denies it . . . I will be more than glad to join you in a concerted effort to bring about an annulment, for I am very sure you had other plans for Clara . . . We could not have wished for him a more charming girl, nor we a daughter whom we could possibly love more, but we feel that Barrington, at least, is too young to assume marital responsibilities.*[10]

For a man who embraced tradition and respectability above most everything else, it must have been devastating to learn that his daughter had married in secrecy and without a proper wedding. Knowing that this was the second humiliation that he had to endure in front of the tightly knit Washington community, Roscoe was certain that tongues would be wagging as soon as the word got out about Clara's elopement. Although the Bruces knew that Clara was dating Barrington, a man almost three years her senior, he was not someone they would have selected for her. Planning for a career on the stage, Barrington was hoping to be an operatic singer and theater performer. His parents, Nathaniel and Louise, were very much outside the black elite circles of the Boulé crowd and of the privileged black alumni who had been educated at private white colleges in the Northeast. His father was a drama teacher who had performed in local Shakespeare productions produced in the Washington area.

But it wasn't just that Clara had failed to marry into a prominent family; it was that she was jeopardizing her future at Radcliffe. Like most of the top colleges for women at the time, Radcliffe did not welcome married students. Fearing that marriage would distract students from the rigorous course work as well as introduce a social and sexual sophistication that was unwelcome on these conservative campuses, schools like Radcliffe were very clear about their policies. And Roscoe knew that if the school was ever to learn of her marriage, they would rescind her offer to attend.

Immediately after learning of the union, Roscoe hired a lawyer with the intent of having the marriage annulled. Knowing that he had the stated support of Barrington Guy's father in bringing about an annulment, Roscoe immediately sought advice from Frank Stephen, a Washington attorney who also happened to live in Prince George's County, near the Bruces' family farm in Maryland. When talking to Stephen, he tried to find out the various ways to annul a marriage, and wanted to know if a justice of the peace could legitimately marry two people without a clergyman present. In his correspondence, he used no names and was careful not to reveal that his daughter was the woman who had just eloped. In Stephen's October 25, 1922, letter, he told Bruce that "to make a marriage valid in Maryland there must be some sort of a religious ceremony performed and I take it that a marriage by a Justice of the Peace, would not be held to be a religious ceremony."[11]

This was surely encouraging news for Roscoe, who was willing to do what was necessary to end the marriage even though he felt rather powerless so many miles away, in rural West Virginia. Two days later, he wrote to Barrington's father, Nathaniel, and outlined what the attorney was planning. Clearly concerned that his daughter's name and reputation would be tarnished, he was careful not to mention Clara's name or his relationship to the young couple being discussed. Roscoe wrote,

> My understanding is that these young people went out to Rockville sometime during the latter part of August and went before a Justice of the Peace. In each instance, the surname was correctly given; but the given name, the residence, the place of birth and the age were incorrectly stated.
>
> I agree with you in the judgement that, to protect the parties at interest now and in the future, it is desirable that the whole proceeding be annulled by decree of Court. My Maryland attorney is Frank M. Stephen, Esq. and I suggest that you and I jointly employ him for the purpose of effecting this annulment.[12]

At the end of the letter, Roscoe added a postscript pointing out that Clara, his wife, and his mother were all in West Virginia at the time, but rather than write their names or suggest that his family was involved in this, he cryptically stated, "Under the circumstances, the ladies of my family have decided to spend the vacation periods here in West Virginia."

Only a day after Roscoe sent the letter to Barrington's father, Barrington surprised them all and showed up in West Virginia. Although anxious to annul the marriage, Roscoe was evidently not hostile toward his daughter's handsome new husband. Barrington's father, Nathaniel, though, was furious that Barrington had defied him, and he was also disturbed that Roscoe was pleasant to his son, given the elopement and the trip to see Clara. What Roscoe had not expected, however, was that Nathaniel was so angry with all of them that he had now decided not to contest the marriage. He evidently was annoyed that Roscoe had decided to assume the position of the "kind in-law," thus leaving Nathaniel Guy to look like the only in-law who was pushing for the annulment. It was likely that Roscoe had taken this position because he knew that his daughter was already sufficiently upset with him over the many months of humiliation she had to suffer in front of her Dunbar and Howard friends as her father was forced to resign from his job, and then the additional embarrassment of her having to stay out of school another year because he lacked the money to send her to Radcliffe after she had been admitted.

Nevertheless, Nathaniel Guy made it clear that he was no longer going to assist Roscoe with the plans for an annulment. He wrote back on November 6,

> *My dear Mr. Bruce:*
>
> *I was surprised to learn that Barrington was in your town, but extremely glad to know that he was safe. The trip was taken without my knowledge and not only without my consent but in positive defiance of my will. That he took the trip knowing how opposed I was to such a step convinces me that the attachment was far deeper than I thought. For this reason I wash my hands of the whole affair . . . [Yet] I fail to appreciate your idea of disgrace.*
>
> *From what I have said you can readily understand that I will take no step now toward annulment. You will . . . do whatever you will without help and without hindrance from me.*[13]

When Roscoe now realized that he would not be receiving any help in getting the marriage annulled, he sent a scathing letter to Nathaniel

Guy, accusing him of backing out of an agreement to hire an attorney. He wrote on November 9, "My dear Mr. Guy . . . Let me remind you, however, that you made a definite proposition to me upon your own motion. That proposition I immediately accepted without condition. If that doesn't make a binding agreement, I don't know what does."[14]

Even though Roscoe kept his daughter from living with Barrington during her four years at Radcliffe, the young married couple would later move to New York and live openly as husband and wife. Barrington would continue his stage acting, eventually appearing in several New York– and Hollywood-produced films, as well as a 1932 Hollywood movie that featured an all-black cast. The movie, directed by well-known black director Oscar Micheaux, was ironically titled *Veiled Aristocrats* and told the story of a light-complexioned woman who brings shame and embarrassment to her prominent black family when she falls in love with a dark-complexioned black man from modest beginnings.

Although the film was an adaptation of a popular novel by Charles W. Chestnutt, the story's elements of race, class, respectability, and tradition were similar to the same issues that Roscoe was addressing as he saw the final humiliating chapter of his Washington life come to a close.

CHAPTER NINETEEN

⟳⟲

1923–1924
Roscoe Struggles with Harvard's President,
His Family Finances, and His Children's Success

Dear Mr. Bruce:
Your letter to the Registrar about your son has been given to
me. I am sorry to have to tell you that in the Freshman Halls,
where residence is compulsory, we have felt from the beginning the
necessity of not including colored men. To the other dormitories,
and dining rooms they are admitted freely, but in the Freshman
Halls I am sure you will understand why, from the beginning, we
have not thought it possible to compel men of different races to
reside together.[1]

ROSCOE WAS DEVASTATED WHEN HE RECEIVED THE LETTER FROM
Harvard University's president A. Lawrence Lowell. After being
chased out of Washington by the Parents League and the black establishment that despised what he had done to compromise the academic
curriculum and reputation of their schools, Roscoe never imagined that
his children would also be subjected to an ostracism that approached
his own. Harvard's new policy on the treatment of black freshman students would prove otherwise.

It was December of 1922, and Roscoe was contemplating how he
would address the situation that was just put before him by the presi-

dent of his alma mater. Had this been two years earlier, when Roscoe was flush with cash and still had his own political power and prestige, he would have pressed forward and boldly demanded that the school change its policy and allow his son to live in the freshman dormitories alongside white students as they had done when he was a freshman in 1898.

Roscoe was clearly stunned as he read the letter that had been written to him by Lowell, Harvard's twenty-second president. As a class of 1902 Harvard alumnus who had graduated with a stellar Phi Beta Kappa record, Roscoe had been looking forward to seeing his son follow in his footsteps at the Ivy League school. Roscoe had proudly proclaimed this to Clara several months earlier, after their son had announced that he wanted to attend both Exeter and his parents' alma mater, rather than go to Yale with several of his friends.

Roscoe Jr. had entered Phillips Exeter Academy in September of 1922 and had just finished his first semester. Although there were fewer than five black boys among the six hundred forty students at the prep school, Roscoe Jr. was enjoying an experience that was slightly less parochial and segregated than the semesters endured by his father twenty-five years earlier. For one, black students were no longer required to live off campus, as they had been previously. Unlike his father, Roscoe Jr. was able to live in Hoyt Hall, a handsome four-story red-brick dormitory just steps away from the main Academy Building, where classes were given.

Not only was Roscoe Jr. permitted to live alongside his white Exeter classmates, he also found himself in a school that was considerably more sophisticated and worldly. The student population had grown by 150 percent since his father's day, and now included students from countries like Mexico, China, and Japan. Previously, more than one-third of the student body had come from New Hampshire and Massachusetts. By 1922, when Roscoe Jr. entered, New York had come to supply nearly 20 percent of the students, with Midwestern and West Coast cities also serving as feeder communities for the prestigious school.

Now Roscoe Jr. was planning a future at Harvard, where black students were forbidden from living in the freshman dormitories. Although the school had been admitting black students since 1865, and had long embraced a liberal outlook on racial integration for its students, President Lowell was altering Harvard tradition by establishing his own Jim Crow policy on campus, with the intent of appeasing a segment of white Southern students.[2]

Roscoe Sr. had lived in the Harvard campus dormitories for his sophomore, junior, and senior years, and it was in Holyoke House, a handsome building in the southern end of the Yard, along Massachusetts Avenue, where he felt he had gotten to bond with the larger Harvard community.

The Harvard values that President Lowell was now ushering in were a giant leap backward for the campus and its students. For a forty-year period, from 1869 to 1909, the school had been governed by its twenty-first president, Charles Eliot, who had encouraged greater numbers of public school graduates and young men who came from families outside the elite, old-money WASP set.

President Lowell, who had taken office in 1909, had something else in mind. He chose this year, 1922, to implement policies that would affect two groups of Harvard applicants: Jews and blacks. The policy for Jews was straightforward. There would be a quota that would limit the number of Jewish students admitted. For blacks, the policy would be more convoluted. There would be no spoken quota or limit on the number admitted, but the rule for all black freshmen would be that they would not be allowed to live in the freshman dormitories in the Yard, even though all other freshmen would be required to live in those dormitories. Black sophomores, juniors, and seniors, on the other hand, would be allowed to live in dormitories where white students lived.

When Roscoe Sr. had attended the college, some students (approximately 10 percent) lived in campus dormitories, but no one was required to live there. Toward the end of Charles Eliot's presidency, though, a segment of the administration and faculty, including Lowell—who was then teaching in the Government Department—suggested that there would be greater cohesiveness to the school if they could house more of the students on campus rather than having so many of them cast off to neighboring boardinghouses and residence halls that offered no feeling of a Harvard community. In fact, Lowell had said several years earlier, "the tendency of the wealthy students to live in private dormitories outside the Yard, involves great danger of a snobbish separation of students . . . bringing about a condition of things that would destroy the chief value of the College. I fear . . . the loss of that democratic feeling which ought to lie at the basis of university life."[3] Given the bigoted policies that Lowell would soon establish for the student dormitories, this would prove to be an ironic statement.

During a major period of physical expansion in the early 1900s, more than a dozen dormitory buildings were built on the campus. Freshman dorms, like the massive Wigglesworth Building, were built in the Yard. And through the generosity of Edward Harkness, a Standard Oil millionaire, many of the upperclassmen's dormitories were erected in order to implement Lowell's "house system." But what was also changing on the campus and in the nation was an increasing desire to segregate the races—and, to some extent, non-Christians.

In 1898, when Roscoe Sr. was a freshman, there were less than a dozen Jewish students in the incoming class. By 1920, that number had more than tripled. Enough of a Jewish presence was established that it was duly noted in 1902, when New York businessman Jacob Schiff provided the money to build the school's Semitic Museum. Some of the more conservative alumni were not happy with the growing Jewish population, so Lowell's response was to introduce a quota to keep the Jewish contingent at the college to a minimum.

The number of black students was so small that the only attention it drew was from the growing Southern white population at the school. When Roscoe Sr. was at the college, there were typically only three or four black students in each class of four hundred fifty men. That number had grown only to about ten or eleven students per class of five hundred men in the early 1920s. But there was an increasing Southern presence at the school, now that Harvard's admissions process attempted to attract beyond the New England and mid-Atlantic states. Lowell had issued a new rule that freshmen would have to live on campus, but he worried that the white Southern boys would object to living in the same dormitory with black students, hence his new policy.

By the time Roscoe Jr. was accepted at Harvard, the nation had become more segregated than ever before, and racial discrimination at Harvard was now worse than it had been when his father went there.

In 1896, just two years before Roscoe Sr. began his freshman year, Harvard awarded its first honorary degree, to Booker T. Washington, and several prominent blacks of his own generation had graduated from the school around that same period: Washington judge Robert Terrell, who was a friend of Roscoe's parents, had graduated in 1884. New York intellectual W. E. B. DuBois received bachelor's and master's degrees in 1890 and 1891, respectively. Boston lawyer Clement Morgan received bachelor's and law degrees from Harvard in 1890 and 1893, respectively. Boston publisher W. Monroe Trotter, an outspoken critic of Booker T. Washington, graduated in 1895. And graduating its first black student, Alberta Scott, in 1898, Radcliffe was also making a positive impression on the black community during the turn of the century.

During the late 1800s, blacks at Harvard lived a life that was racially separate from the students who came from the WASP and Boston Brahmin families, but because Irish, Jewish, and Italian students were also excluded, it was not so painfully obvious that blacks were not accepted into the mainstream student population. As W. E. B. DuBois explained, "I was happy at Harvard, but for unusual reasons. One of these was my acceptance of racial segregation . . . In general, I was encased in a completely colored world, self-sufficient and provincial, and ignoring just as far as possible the white world which conditioned it."[4]

As the twentieth century arrived at the Harvard campus, so had the expectation of black students that they would be accepted more into the mainstream. In fact, there were at least a few blacks in every entering freshman class from 1890 to 1930. Even though Roscoe Sr. was holding a relatively unimportant job in West Virginia, when he got the letter from Lowell, he was not about to take this racial slight lightly. He wrote back a lengthy letter that included an articulate argument against the policy. He said,

> *My delay in responding to your letter is occasioned by my endeavor to recover from the shock of your decision to refuse my son placement in the Freshman Halls specifically because he is an American of African descent . . . I have lived and labored in the South so long since my graduation from Harvard College over twenty years ago that . . . I had cherished the illusion that New England was enriching rather than impoverishing her heritage.*
>
> *The policy of compulsory residence in the Freshman Halls is costly indeed if it is the thing that constrains Harvard to enter open-eyed and brusque upon a policy of racial discrimination . . . To proscribe a youth because of his race is a procedure as novel at Harvard until your administration as it is unscientific . . .*[5]

In this letter, Roscoe wrote flatteringly of Harvard's past and of the education and experience that he had enjoyed during his four years, but he was unrelenting in his criticism of the policy and the mentality that it sought to encourage. He had never argued against the white establishment before, and perhaps it was his paternal instinct to protect his son that caused him to sidestep his normally cautious approach when challenging white people's racism. Clearly angered by the potential effect such a policy would have on the psyche of his child and other young blacks who entered the school, Roscoe argued that the policy would cause some light-complexioned blacks to attempt to pass for white, deny their race, and thereby nullify the policy of exclusion with deception. He added forcefully, "be assured, no son of mine will ever deny his name or his blood or his tradition."

Still, the president was unmoved. A few days later, Lowell sent a condescending letter to Roscoe that made it clear that the discriminatory rule would remain in place. In it, he said, "I am sorry you do not feel the reasonableness of our position . . . We give [the colored man] opportunities for room and board wherever it is voluntary. To maintain that compulsory residence in the Freshman dormitories should not be established for 99½ percent of the students just because the remaining one-half of one percent could not properly be included, seems to me an untenable position . . ."

Roscoe then immediately shared President Lowell's letter with the NAACP, as well as with white Harvard alumni who appeared to have liberal leanings. He also forwarded it to national newspaper columnists, for them to comment on in their pages. Roscoe Sr. was particularly incensed because he had been an active alumnus who regularly contributed to the Harvard Endowment Fund.[6]

By the beginning of 1923, the issue surrounding the segregation of Roscoe Jr. and other incoming black freshmen had become a national one. Some of the most prominent Harvard alumni, and several members on its board, spoke out against this new, discriminatory policy. Future president Franklin D. Roosevelt, then a member of the university's board of overseers, was annoyed that President Lowell had not told him or other board members that such a racist policy was being implemented. Recalling that black students were not segregated when he had been at Harvard, Roosevelt wrote, "There were certainly many colored students in Cambridge when we were there and no question ever arose." And Roosevelt was not alone in being surprised by this policy because, after all, black students in the past had lived in the freshman dormitories as well as the upper-classmen's dormitories.

As Roscoe's campaign against Lowell continued, details began to emerge regarding the genesis of the policy. It seemed that the policy was actually formulated by Lowell in the fall of 1921, when five black freshmen were entering the school. One of the students, William Knox Jr. of New Bedford, Massachusetts, was assigned to a room in Standish Hall, one of the freshman dormitories. When the school realized that Knox was black, they sent him a telegram telling him that the room was assigned to him mistakenly.[7]

Finally, Harvard's dean Philip Chase told Knox that although black students had lived there in the past, they would no longer be permitted to live in the freshman dormitories. Knox asked a black friend, Edwin Jourdain, who graduated in 1921 and who had lived in the freshman dormitories in 1917, if Jourdain would help him argue his case with President Lowell. Lowell explained to Jourdain and others that a growing number of Southern students were attending the school and that they opposed social equality with blacks, and would therefore not live in the same building as black students.

It is likely that Roscoe Sr. got wind of this policy through friends, or, more likely, that Roscoe Jr. heard rumors about it from his many Exeter classmates who had plans of attending Harvard the following year. It is unknown if Roscoe Sr. was writing to check the rumor's validity or to learn if an exception would be made for his son. What is known is that his letter was the impetus for dozens of newspapers and high-profile individuals to weigh in on the controversial issue.

What also made President Lowell's position so unpopular with white Harvard alumni was that it was aimed at the class of black people that these liberal alumni were actually proud to welcome to their alma mater. The original six black freshman students who were being excluded from the dormitories were not the children of poor, illiterate families from the Deep South. They were six young men from educated families and middle-class backgrounds. Roscoe Jr.'s parents had gone to Harvard and Radcliffe, and his grandfather was a senator. Edward Wilson was the son of an attorney who had also attended Harvard. Cecil Blue was the son of a Washington physician. Pritchett Klugh was the son of a Boston clergyman who had graduated from Yale. And the other three were children of professional families from New England communities.

Articles published in the *New York Times*, *New York Post*, the *Nation*, and the *New Republic* all criticized Lowell and his policy. Roscoe's press campaign against the school was gaining traction. The *Nation* said that both Lowell and the university were "accepting and preaching the Southern doctrine that every man with Negro blood in his veins is inferior to every all-white man."[8] That same month, the board met and soon ruled that "equal opportunity for all" was Harvard's goal, and that such a dormitory policy undermined it completely. Finally, under pressure from the alumni, the board of overseers, and the public, President Lowell rescinded the policy of keeping black freshmen out of the dormitories. It was a humiliating loss for the university president, but he remained in his position for another dozen years after the incident.

Even before the dust had settled on Roscoe's fight with President Lowell, Roscoe Sr. and Clara Sr. began to see that dormitory life was not going to be any easier for their daughter at Radcliffe. In fact, the women's college seemed to be even less informed than Harvard, regarding segregation. While Harvard's policy was to keep black freshmen out of the dorms yet permit black sophomores, juniors, and seniors in the dorms, Radcliffe did not permit black women of any class year in their campus housing. This was the general practice at most of the Seven Sisters colleges,[9] but the equally prestigious Wellesley College allowed black women to live on their campus. And although Radcliffe would later distinguish itself—in the 1940s and after—as the more progressive and welcoming of these seven elite women's colleges, its treatment of black women through the early 1900s lagged considerably behind both Wellesley and Smith. In fact, not only had Roscoe written to Clara Sr., when they were students, urging her to go to Wellesley instead of Radcliffe, Roscoe also knew that Booker T. Washington's daughter, Portia, had attended Wellesley.

Considering how offended Roscoe was by Harvard's housing policy for black freshman boys, it seems odd that he did not outright reject Radcliffe as a choice for his daughter, since their policy was even more egregious and would discriminate against his daughter for the entire four years of her schooling there. The only other difference between the policies was that Harvard's was stated and Radcliffe's was not. To verify the policy, Roscoe went so far as to write to Radcliffe's president, LeBaron Russell Briggs, in May of 1922 and ask if Clara could live in the dormitories when she began.

Rather than respond directly, President Briggs waited several days and then sent Roscoe a three-sentence letter that sounded suspiciously vague, as if he was looking for a way to pass the problem to someone else. He said, "I have delayed answering your letter because I am not quite sure how to answer it. Meantime I send this bare acknowledgment with a view to writing a little later when I know more . . . The subject is one with which I have little or nothing to do."[10]

It is obvious from his letter that President Briggs had never before been compelled to answer the question regarding their housing policy, so it appears that he clumsily stalled for additional time to develop an acceptable answer. What is also obvious from the letter is that President Briggs was desperate to avoid creating a "paper trail" record that even mentioned the subject matter of the correspondence, or Clara's name. Briggs, who had been on the faculty since the 1890s, was skilled at university politics. In addition to his role as president of Radcliffe, he had served as English professor, dean of Harvard College, as well as dean of the Harvard Faculty of Arts and Sciences. He knew that he had to be very cautious about acknowledging that the school embraced discriminatory housing policies. Finally, after passing several pieces of correspondence back and forth from one office to another during the subsequent days, President Briggs responded with a "nonresponse" that never answered Roscoe's important question. He avoided admitting that their policy was to keep black girls out of their dormitories, and instead wrote the following to Clara's father:

> *Dear Mr. Bruce:*
>
> *With oral explanation to the Dean, I sent your letter to the Committee on Dormitories, of which Committee she is chairman. I learned in the first place that when your application came there were already forty applications ahead of it, and there is no chance for any applicant this year who did not apply earlier.*

The question this year, therefore, settles itself. The underlying question which I know to be in your mind I want some time to talk out with you if you come to this part of the country as I hope you will . . . Sincerely yours,
       LeBaron Russell Briggs[11]

It also must have been clear to Roscoe that Radcliffe's recently retired dean, Bertha Boody, had been somewhat bigoted and unwelcoming to black students. In fact, a current Dunbar High School teacher and friend of his, Mary Gibson, had endured offensive treatment from Dean Boody when she entered Radcliffe in 1913, and during her time there. A native of Washington, as well as a graduate of Dunbar High School, Gibson was the daughter of a lawyer and a former Tuskegee Institute professor. While she was in high school, Gibson's father died, leaving her mother, a retired professor, with too little money to afford the Radcliffe tuition. Despite the fact that she was a top student at Dunbar—and also at Radcliffe—and although many white students were given need-based scholarships, Dean Bertha Boody refused to offer Gibson a scholarship. The dean told the teenage Mary Gibson that the only way the school could assist her was to help her find a job as a maid working for a local family. As a child of professionals, who knew that many white girls were offered scholarship assistance or campus jobs in the library, Mary was insulted by the dean's insistence that the only suitable job for her was to work as a maid. Mary and her mother were also disturbed to learn that Dean Boody, a Southerner with little affinity for blacks, was able to discourage President Briggs from helping her, by suggesting that Mary and her mother were acting "uppity."[12] Ironically, Roscoe Bruce had written Gibson's letter of recommendation, so he surely knew the details of the school's recent treatment of black girls who attempted to live on campus.

Outsiders might have wondered why Roscoe would send his daughter to a school where the segregationist policies were so firm, but those who knew him understood that he believed in following family traditions even under the most difficult circumstances. As a man who yearned for greatness, he felt that a true dynasty needed to have traditions that were repeated from one generation to the next, regardless of what was best for the individual.

Since her mother had gone there and her father had gone to Harvard, it made sense to Roscoe that Clara attend the school as well, despite the discriminatory treatment.

One thing had become clear to Roscoe even before he took up the dormitory fight with Harvard: so long as he was working in West Virginia, a place that he detested, the family would have to continue relying on his mother for financial assistance. When he wasn't asking her for money, he was busy overdrawing his various bank accounts in Washington. This pattern had begun at the conclusion of his tenure with the Washington schools. And despite the strong warning he received at the time from Washington's Second National Bank on April 16, 1921, it continued there and at other banks. At the time, bank president Cuno Rudolph had written to him, "It is with a great deal of regret that I observe constantly that you draw checks against us for which you have not provided sufficient funds . . . I must ask that you desist from this practice [or] it will be necessary for us to ask that you close your account with us."[13]

Roscoe continued to ask his mother for help—both professionally and financially. Even though she was nearing seventy years of age herself, Josephine remained the steady support system for Roscoe's constant needs. As he continued his pursuit of a job at Lincoln University, hoping that she would use whatever contacts she still had, he wrote to her frequently with requests. In an early 1922 letter, he asked her to help him with his job search, as well as with Howard University, because he was trying to get the school to award him a master's degree based on school credits he had earned while at Harvard and through lectures and work he had performed in Washington. He wrote, "My Darling Mother: Yes, I do wish you would talk confidentially with Cox about the Lincoln University situation and the A.M. The committee of the Howard University Board of Trustees having charge of degrees consists of Grimke, Moorland (who is no friend of mine!), Atkinson, Purvis (always a problematical person), Durkee . . ."[14] In addition to noting the antipathy held for him by powerful board members Jesse Moorland and Dr. Charles Purvis, Roscoe's letter later also stated that others, like former superintendent Davidson, wouldn't respond to his correspondence.

As was typical of his letters to his mother, this one raised the issue of money. In the postscript, he wrote: "P.S. 1327 is worth at least $15,000 today." This number was evidently a reference to her home at 1327 Columbia Road NW. It is likely that he was encouraging her to sell it, since she was getting older and he was in need of additional cash. By this point, it appeared that the family no longer had the R Street town house but was using Columbia Road as Josephine's residence and Kelso Farm in Hyattsville, Maryland, for Clara and the children while Roscoe lived in West Virginia. Josephine would eventually sell her Columbia Road home and move permanently to West Virginia with Roscoe in 1923, but Clara and the children would move there for only a short time as they shuttled back and forth to Kelso Farm and then, eventually, to Cambridge, Massachusetts.

At around this time, Roscoe relied heavily on his mother to manage the activities and finances of the farm where his wife and children lived. He asked her to deal with his creditors, perform errands around the city, and to mail packages as if she were still young. One of his letters to her said, "Would it be possible for you to drive by the Southern Building Supply in order to find out what credit they would give me— I mean *cash!*—for half a car or more of bituminous coal. Please inquire and let me know . . ." In the same letter, he noted that his wife had told him that Sears Roebuck was demanding payment for an overdue bill, but that they didn't have enough money to pay it, "so, please do *not* forward draft for $100 to Sears Roebuck as suggested in my note today."[15]

As Roscoe was encouraging his mother to sell her own property in order to raise money for his family's expenses, he was also attempting to either sell Kelso Farm or find a real estate mortgage company that would exchange it for a town house or apartment house in the city of Washington. Such a move would put his family closer to school and businesses. In his letter to the Stone and Fairfax real estate management company, he laid out his rather novel idea and described Kelso Farm's value, "As a residence for cultured people, it is ideal . . . the estate of an English peer, adjoins me on the West . . . In a word, if you can see your way clear to offer in exchange for the farm an apartment house conservatively appraised at, say, fifty or sixty thousand dollars, I should be interested."[16]

By the end of 1922, it became obvious that Josephine was too old to manage her various properties any longer, and she sold her Washington home and then moved to West Virginia to join Roscoe. Her move had been preceded by Clara's, who brought the children to Kendall, temporarily, with the plan to move to Massachusetts in the fall when they all would return to school. By this point, Roscoe Jr. had already been enrolled for a semester at Phillips Exeter Academy. Clara Jr. would be entering Radcliffe in the fall, and Burrill would be entering public school in Cambridge. But the plans being made by Clara Sr. came as a shock and something of a disappointment to Josephine. After years of putting her ambitions behind those of Roscoe, Clara had decided to pursue a legal career. When she joined the children in Cambridge that coming fall, she would be enrolling at Boston University Law School. As the only black woman in her class, she would eventually become the second black woman in the state of Massachusetts to join the state bar.

None of this sat well with the ailing Josephine, who imagined her son being abandoned by both his children and his wife when he was at his neediest. But before the family had been settled long in West Virginia, Josephine suddenly became ill. Already overwhelmed by bills and the anxiety of knowing that his wife and children would be leaving for Boston within the next few months, Roscoe began to panic. Working in a job that paid little money, and living in a community that lacked culture and sophistication, Roscoe was unable to create a comfortable home for his aging mother, and he knew it. As they lived together in a mountainous neighborhood, just minutes from Roscoe's school, they endured the cold winter months uneasily. Finally, on February 15, 1923, Josephine suffered a heart attack and died in her sleep.

Josephine's death was a devastating blow to Roscoe, who had grown accustomed to her professional guidance, emotional support, and financial assistance. At the time of her death, he had been seeking her advice on his plans to enter the legal profession and attend the law school at the University of Chicago. Only a few months prior, he had proudly told her of his legal career plans. He wrote, "Today I had a long talk with the Judge of the Circuit Court about conditions governing admission to the Bar in this State. He was just as nice as he could be, seeming anxious that I should enter upon practice here . . . I got the new book which you forwarded. It is *Warren: Cases on Property*. So, now I have all my Law books. Modifying a suggestion from Charlie Houston, I am attempting to complete one subject at a time."[17]

With the burden of paying for the rather costly education of his wife and children, Roscoe was never able to pursue his own legal career. Although he had been admitted to the University of Chicago's law school, his focus after his mother's death was to find a job that would allow him to return to life in an East Coast city. In the absence of that, he decided in May 1923 to resign his principal's position in West Virginia and relocate to Kelso Farm alone, since his wife and children were all moving to Cambridge, Massachusetts.[18]

By the fall of 1923, Roscoe Sr. was beginning to fall into a serious emotional depression. Not only was his beloved mother gone, but he felt he was doing a poor job as the new head of the Bruce dynasty. Certain outside appearances suggested that things were just fine. His daughter was at Radcliffe. His elder son was at Exeter. His wife was getting top grades as a first-year student at Boston University Law School—the only black woman in her class. And he himself had emerged victorious in the public fight with Harvard's president. The university had been forced to capitulate to Bruce's demands that his son be permitted to live in a freshman dormitory when it was time for him to matriculate at the school. It finally made Roscoe look like a man who not only stood up to white people but also would speak on behalf of the black people's cause.

And further, Roscoe Sr. still had an open invitation to attend the University of Chicago Law School, after being admitted to the school's class of 1926.

To the outside world, the prestige of the Bruce family and its association with some of the most elite institutions of the nation seemed to be as intact for the second and third generations of the black dynasty as it had been when the senator and his wife were the toast of Washington in the late 1870s. The family's ongoing tradition of living outside the typical black experience also appeared to be consistent. In both Tuskegee and Washington, while leading a privileged lifestyle, the Bruces still lived amid black people, socialized with them, and sent their children to the black segregated schools. On the Tuskegee campus, they mingled and worked only with the blacks who were affiliated with the school. In Washington, the segregated school system was where they educated their children. Just as they had both been raised amid the capital's black elite families and sent to the top high school in the city's segregated school district before going away to prep school and college, their children had been raised in a mostly black setting: both Clara Jr. and Roscoe Jr. attended Dunbar High School, the elite black school in the city's still-segregated school district. Even when they had prior ties to some white institutions, they still were anchored at home amid the black elite community. But things were different now.

Having been chased out of Washington, Roscoe's wife and children no longer had a foothold in the black community. By late 1923, their world had become almost uniformly white. Clara Jr. was in a white college; their youngest son, Burrill, was in a mostly white public school in Cambridge; Roscoe Jr. was in a white boarding school; and Clara Sr. was in a white law school. Mother and children resided in a mostly white Cambridge neighborhood, at 16 Parker Street. Similarly, in an attempt to maintain a low profile in a Washington that had only two years earlier given him the boot, Roscoe remained on the Maryland farm, where few blacks resided.

Although she had the primary responsibility of caring for her children—with Clara Jr. and Burrill living with her and Roscoe Jr. an hour away at Exeter—Clara's independence and confidence soared as she finally accomplished her goal of furthering her education beyond her years at Radcliffe. Still, she had to rely on the weekly allowance that her husband sent her; Clara was responsible for paying the rent, purchasing coal for the heat, buying the children's clothing, preparing their meals, and helping with schoolwork.

Hundreds of miles away in Maryland, Roscoe Sr.'s primary family responsibility was to send money to his wife and children. Still not earning an income that could pay all of their expenses, he relied on the assets left him by his mother's estate. If Roscoe had not already felt exhausted by the loss of his job in Washington, the death of his mother, and the fight with Harvard's president, his role in his family left him feeling quietly emasculated. He was six states away from them, unable to pay all their bills, and mostly unaware of their daily activities.

In one sense, Roscoe Sr. had become the absentee father that his own father had been for so many years. While the senator had spent most of Roscoe's childhood in the Senate or in Washington-based presidential-appointed positions, his government meetings and political speeches had kept him either out of the house or on the road for long periods. It was Josephine who had to pick up the slack left by the senator's absence. In the case of Roscoe's children, it was Clara who had to step in during Roscoe's absence.

Josephine was originally a mother who clearly exhibited greater skill and interest in being a hostess and socialite than the typical mother of her period. Clara was originally a mother who clearly exhibited greater skill and interest in pursuing intellectual challenges and a legal or writing career than the typical mother of her period. Both of them—during their midforties—were put in the position of managing their finances and their children: Josephine because of her husband's death, and Clara because of her husband's job losses.

But both of these black women seemed to mature and rise professionally at the time of their husbands' departure. Josephine immediately took charge of her husband's properties while resuming her teaching career by becoming lady principal at Tuskegee Institute. Clara took sole charge of her children's lives and began her legal career by enrolling at Boston University Law School, where she eventually became the editor of the law review. Both of these professional routes were rare possibilities for black women of the period; in fact, they would have been equally unusual for white women of that time.

The balance of power between Clara and Roscoe shifted with the changed responsibilities. No longer focused on advising him on his career or entertaining his colleagues, Clara turned to Roscoe mostly to ask for money or to keep him informed of the family's financial condition. It no doubt left him feeling emotionally detached and unloved, since his older son, Roscoe Jr., communicated with him for the very same reasons.

In the spring of 1924, while Roscoe Jr. was on break from Exeter, he wrote to his father in Maryland, asking him to buy him a motorcycle for $285, a substantial amount of money for a teenager to be requesting at that time. During that period, his father was trying, unsuccessfully, to raise chickens on Kelso Farm, and Roscoe Jr. offered a dubious explanation for why he could use a motorcycle: in order to get a part-time job delivering mail for the local post office.

> *Dear Pop,*
>   *Say, why don't you write to me? I'm not going to write you a letter after this one until you have written at least two letters to*

begin paying me back for all of my letters. Say, I'm writing to you about a business proposition. I'll tell you the situation . . .[19]

Not only was $285 an extraordinary amount of money for an eighteen-year-old, but given the financial hardships that the family was already enduring, it seemed particularly galling when Roscoe was paying three private-school tuitions.

It was probably true that Roscoe Jr.—a spoiled teenager who got mediocre grades and never distinguished himself at Dunbar High School, Exeter, or Harvard—was playing fast and loose with his father, trying to extract whatever money or expensive toys he could during his absence. Never before had he held so much as a part-time job. And there was no reason to believe he would seriously seek one while he was in the midst of his college studies. Along with his requests for money, the boy attempted to layer in remarks about his serious nature and earnest desire to help the family. He said,

The reason I am so anxious is because I will be able to buy my own clothes, and I need some. Don't think I'm complaining at all, for I'm not, but I'm thinking of what I could do to help out. I was thinking, if it was impossible now, about the money you would get from the F.L.B. . . . . if you can spare any of it. Don't forget this is strictly business.   —Roscoe[20]

It is clear that Roscoe Sr. had little day-to-day involvement with Roscoe Jr's rearing at this point. In fact, not only did the father fail to write regularly during this period, he did not even attend his son's school graduation ceremony. His wife wrote to him on June 13, 1924, to tell him about the event. In the same letter, it became obvious that Clara was on such a tight budget that she had to apologize for her itemized expenses and plead for more money so she could pay the rent. She itemized everything she had bought over the past month, including the graduation suit she had purchased for Roscoe (whom the family often called "Woogs").

Dear Roscoe,
I am running short of money. Although I'm sick, I am also trying to hold off paying the rent since I will be short $13.10. I am sorry for

*not having enough money, but I had to buy Woogs' new graduation
suit. Went last night to see Woogs graduate. He looked as sweet in
his little suit all pressed and with new shoes and stockings. Will tell
you more about it tomorrow.*

*Here are my expenses: $70.60 for train tickets, $3 for the trunks
to be transferred, $9.35 for gas since the coal gave out, $10 for milk,
$4.85 for laundry, $38 for rent and $6.50 for cleaning Burrill's suit
and Clara's dresses. I have tried to be responsible with the money
you gave me, but I simply need more.*

*I thought I might ask Mr. Forsythe to wait for his rent. In that
way, I could manage to pay all these other bills, and then have
something to keep us going until Wednesday . . . With lots of Love,
Carrie*[21]

Clara's next letter to Roscoe—only two days later—again revealed
how tight money was and how out of touch Roscoe was with his children. In the letter, Clara tells him what she gave to their son for his
graduation present, and she also tells Roscoe the name of his son's best
friend, a white classmate, whom Roscoe Sr. was hearing about for the
first time—even though the school year had just ended.

*Dear Roscoe, Woogs has gone to the theatre. I gave him $1.25 for his
graduation present. He used $1.00 to pay off a trip to Wollaston,
Massachusetts with one of his schoolmates, "Fordy" John Ford Jr.
whose father is the Vice President of a publishing corporation. Fordy
is Woogs' best friend—in fact his shadow. The other 25 cents Woogs
saved in order to go to the theatre today—Charlie Chaplin I think.
Burrill is out playing baseball and KahKitten [Clara Jr.] is here with
me reading the* Saturday Evening Post . . .   *With love, Carrie*[22]

This letter, which was sent only three months after Roscoe Jr. asked
his father for a $285 motorcycle, revealed that the family was in no posi-
tion to spoil their eighteen-year-old son with extravagant presents. His
mother's graduation gift to him amounted to only $1.25, since she was
struggling to pay the rent, so it was clear that the family was failing to
give its children a realistic sense of their financial situation. Like Roscoe
Sr., Clara Sr. also derived a great deal of pride from her son's being able
to socialize with wealthy white children. Unfortunately, neither one of

them considered the ultimate effect of his trying to live up to the economic lifestyles enjoyed by wealthy young boys like John Ford Jr.

Something that neither Clara nor her husband wanted to acknowledge was that their children were at a much greater disadvantage than Roscoe Sr. had been when he was attending prep school and college. While it was true that during the late 1800s and early 1900s blacks had never been fully embraced by the student bodies at these institutions, Roscoe Sr. had at least arrived on campus with the secure financial backing and mainstream social status of a national political leader's child. He was the son of a senator and of a mother and father whose businesses and properties were enhancing their wealth. Roscoe Jr. and Clara Jr., however, did not arrive on their campuses with the same status or financial clout, and these factors were extremely relevant in such institutions. Rather than being known as the grandchildren of a former senator—a fact that few whites in the North recalled or cared about since his death twenty-five years earlier—they were more likely thought of as the son and daughter of the black alumnus who fought with President Lowell over the segregated housing. Even though their parents had impeccable credentials, they were the credentials of educators and intellectuals. Being the child of a West Virginia school principal and a Boston University law student did not rival the status derived from being the child of a Washington socialite and a well-known senator who had worked for several presidents.

In addition, when Roscoe Jr. and Clara Jr. got to college, although their family property included a Mississippi plantation, a Maryland farm, and a Washington home, they had very little cash and lived modestly from month to month on their father's small salary and their grandmother's savings. In later years, when prep schools and Ivy League colleges intentionally reached into the middle and working classes for their student population, children with a weak financial status like the Bruce children might have been commonplace. But in the 1920s, these elite Northeastern schools were primarily populated by wealthy families who had top credentials, as well as substantial wealth. Yes, there were a few children of intellectuals, but the student bodies were mostly the children of rich industrialists. Their fathers were bankers, department store owners, manufacturers, and vast landowners. Those who were senators and governors also happened to be members of families who had businesses that could finance their low-paying political careers. By the third generation of the Bruce family, such money-producing businesses had disappeared. Roscoe Sr. had already spent much of his mother's money, and he lacked the talent to run the plantation and farm at a profit.

While much more resourceful than her husband, Clara was not interested in the family businesses. For the many years that the three children were in prep school, college, and graduate school, the family was cash-poor. This would change in the early 1930s, when they relocated to New York City, but from 1923 until 1929, school tuitions, multiple homes, and mismanaged businesses would soak up the family savings and Roscoe's income.[23]

At the same time that Clara, who herself was in graduate school, was writing about her need for additional money, her husband was receiving hostile letters from lawyers and bill collectors representing vendors that had not been paid by the plantation or the Maryland farm.

Smith & Kline Incorporated, a Washington, DC, building-supplies company, had sent Roscoe multiple letters, attempting to collect on a $352.50 bill that he had owed since the prior year. By June 14, the company president became exasperated, writing, "Unless we have something definite from you within the next few days, we will be forced to . . . resort to legal methods to obtain what is justly due us."[24]

Five days later, Roscoe received a letter from the Washington, DC, law firm of Leckie, Cox and Sherier, which represented yet another company that he owed money to. Acting as counsel to the Asher Fireproofing Company, the lawyers had sent multiple letters regarding a $170 bill that was several months overdue. As Roscoe had explained to all his creditors, including the lawyers, he would be able to pay his debts once he had found a buyer for his deceased mother's Washington home, a property she had already partially mortgaged while helping to finance Roscoe's lifestyle years earlier. When Roscoe finally sent a partial payment of $100 after months of stalling, the Leckie attorney was unmoved by Roscoe's claim to be waiting for a house sale. He wrote for the final amount:

> *My Dear Mr. Bruce:*
> *I am in receipt of your communication of June 17th, with regard to your indebtedness to the Asher people . . . and when we may definitely expect payment.*

*You must bear in mind that the unpaid balance is only $70,
and surely so small an item as that should not enter into the selling
of a $15,000 house. As I told you, we have no desire to impose any
hardship on anyone who plays fair with us, but I feel there has
been a great deal of unnecessary correspondence in this particular
matter—the unpaid balance really is not very much, has been
running a long time.*[25]

Realizing that unpaid bills, as well as the upcoming tuitions for
Clara Sr., Clara Jr., and Roscoe Jr. were facing them, Roscoe finally
capitulated and applied for a substantial loan—$7,000—in the summer
of 1924. Even the lending company, Stone & Fairfax Real Estate, found
the amount to be rather high, given Roscoe's meager principal's salary.
The company treasurer wrote back to Roscoe, "We are obliged by your
letter of July 8, and enclose herewith an application for loan of $7,000.
We think the loan is rather more than might be readily made,
but . . . we will endeavor to obtain it."[26]

What was also becoming obvious about the third generation of the
Bruce family was that they didn't have the drive and the intellect that
their predecessors had exhibited. While it is unclear how the youngest
son, Burrill, fared in his early schooling—he did later attend New York
University and Harvard Law School—it was obvious that Roscoe Jr.
and Clara Jr. were lacking either in motivation or academic talent by
the time he reached prep school and she reached Radcliffe.

CHAPTER TWENTY

⌈☙◉ᑤᐣ

1925–1929

The Family Moves to Cambridge and New York,
and Roscoe Builds an Alliance
with John D. Rockefeller Jr.

LIVING ALONE AND HAVING NO JOB, ROSCOE SR. WITHDREW TO KELSO
Farm in relatively remote and rural Prince George's County. Not only
did he feel disconnected from his wife and children, who had been living the past eighteen months apart from him, in New England, but for
the first time he also felt removed from those people and places that his
mother had previously integrated into his existence almost daily during
the last forty-four years. When Josephine was alive, she anxiously
served as his link to her own immediate family of parents and siblings.
She had acted similarly to keep him associated with, and informed on,
the old black Washington families that had known and respected his
father. Once Roscoe had been chased out of Washington in 1921, her
deep ties to the city's old families had still kept him in touch with
names and stories from their past. Now he had no "comrade" to meet
with and keep him informed on the "locals." Because of his own past
failure to build or maintain relations with his father's relatives in Missouri and Kansas, he also had no contacts that kept him informed of his
family members.

His lack of family relationships beyond his mother, wife, and children had never been so apparent until 1925, when his nuclear family
was living apart from him in Cambridge. In fact, since Blanche had

never insisted that his son or his wife establish relations with Blanche's mostly working-class family, Roscoe had only a few childhood memories of two or three visits to relatives in Brunswick, Missouri, where his paternal relatives—all of them former slaves and many of them sharecroppers—still lived. Josephine, however, made sure that her son developed relationships with her parents and sisters. Because they were all educated and lived a middle-class or upper-class lifestyle, she and Blanche had even encouraged Roscoe to spend summers with her family members.

Once Josephine's parents relocated to Indianapolis, where their daughters Mary and Victoria resided, Josephine made frequent trips with her son to that city. Their other daughter, Emily, remained in the Deep South where her husband, A. L. Harang, ran the business affairs of the Bruce Plantation and other properties. Although Roscoe had attended grammar school in Indianapolis for one year and spent multiple summers there during college, he never seemed to develop a tie to the community independently of his mother.

As Roscoe began rearing his own family and relying more heavily on his mother for advice and money, she reduced her trips to Indianapolis. In fact, as her husband had when he was still alive, Josephine began receiving numerous letters from siblings that complained of her failure to remain in touch with them. Her sister Mary sent such a letter on January 1, 1923, just six weeks before Josephine died. She wrote, "Dear Josephine, Here it is the beginning of another year and I have not heard from you for four months. I hope you like your new quarters. I fear things seem quite primitive, but you must set that thought aside if you find simplicity and kindness, hospitality and genuineness in the people. Such people are superior to the pompous, false hearted, sneaking people of the great cities who . . . are ignorant, jealous and narrow."[1]

During Josephine's life, Roscoe would be kept apprised of his relatives' activities, but he expressed little interest in her family after her death. He thought this was his mother's province, just as he came to believe that it was Clara's job to be responsible for the activities of their children. He had basically relinquished all his day-to-day parental duties when it became necessary for him to live apart from the family, but he and the children would eventually pay the price. By June 1925, it became clear to Roscoe and Clara that they had made a serious mistake in having their daughter transfer from Howard University to Radcliffe College. Not only was Harvard's sister school infinitely more expensive than the black college, it was also significantly more rigorous in its academic demands.

The financial and emotional toll that the experience had on the family was palpable. And it disturbed Roscoe that his wife had not been able to get Clara Jr. to focus more on her studies. In his letters to her, he accepted no blame for the situation, because he was not living with them in Cambridge, even though it was his idea that she attend the rigorous school rather than stay at Howard or attend a less challenging white university.

Like her husband, Clara Sr. was stunned by the grades that their daughter, Clara Josephine Bruce, had just received for the 1924–25 academic year. The grade report that listed Clara's courses for the year— English 41, German 1a, Greek, Philosophy A, Philosophy B, and English 73—revealed a discouraging record.[2] There was not a single grade over C. Clara was disappointed, but not as much as her husband was, because Clara knew that a lot had been working against her daughter during those last two years.

For one, she knew how intimidated Clara Jr. had been when she first arrived at the college, in a class where she was one of only three black girls. Never before had the young girl attended a school with white students. She had never been taught by white teachers. From the all-black Dunbar High School she went to the all-black Howard University, and now was in a college where the students, faculty, and administrators were all white. Even though her father claimed to have endured the same circumstances, he actually had not. By the time he entered college, he had already attended a boarding school that featured a white student and faculty population, and he knew what it was to live and study among whites. He had two years to prepare himself for the experience of being a rather lonely, alienated black college student.

Furthermore, Clara's college experience differed from her father's in that Harvard allowed black men to participate in most aspects of campus life, while Radcliffe allowed almost no involvement of black women. Under much greater scrutiny and with students who were far more outspoken on race issues, Harvard seemed to welcome black men into its social fabric slightly more than its sister school, such that even in the late 1800s, there were high-profile and popular black male students being selected as class orator, class marshal, and captain of the football team. At Radcliffe, even well into the 1930s, there were still white female students who complained about allowing the one or two black female classmates to eat their meals in the dining halls, a policy that had been race-neutral for the men since the 1890s.

Black Radcliffe graduate Muriel Snowden (class of 1938) would later recall her devastation when the school refused to let her live in a dormitory. Even though her family was paying for her tuition and housing without any scholarship assistance, the school did not allow Snowden to live in the dorms until her sophomore year, whereby she reportedly became, in 1935, only the second black to be given permission to live in a Radcliffe dormitory.[3] Twelve years later, in 1947, Radcliffe would see its first black class president when Elizabeth Fitzgerald (class of 1948) was elected by her classmates. So, while the school was more progressive than many other white women's colleges of the time, it was well behind its brother school four blocks away.

Another problem that complicated Clara's first years even further was the fact that she was secretly married yet not permitted to live with her husband, or to even acknowledge his existence out of fear that the school would expel her. The pressure that came from having to leave Barrington in Washington while she spent the next four years away in college was immense.

Roscoe, on the other hand, had expected his daughter to have done better since she had entered the school in 1923 with college credits in history, English, and French from Howard University. But for two years, Clara's grades were just barely passing. Roscoe was particularly embarrassed by her performance in light of the fact that just two years earlier, he had staged a very public battle with Harvard's president over the equal treatment of blacks in the dormitories. He feared that her intellectual failings would only serve to undermine his arguments for equal racial treatment.

At the end of that school year, Roscoe took a train to Boston to visit Clara Sr. and the children for several days as he prepared to relocate from Kelso Farm to New York City. He had just received a job offer that required him to move to New York before the summer. He had been hired to edit a new volume called *Who's Who in Colored America*.[4] To be published by the Phyllis Wheatley Publishing Company in New York, the volume would include profiles of hundreds of accomplished black Americans. This new directory was conceived as a black version of the respected reference volume *Who's Who in America*, and it would offer short biographical profiles of black people from the worlds of science, politics, education, journalism, business, law, medicine, the arts, religion, civic affairs, and foreign diplomacy. His job was to select the individuals who would be profiled.

It is likely that Roscoe was chosen as editor because he had become known as an excellent researcher and as a person who would be well suited for discerning which black Americans ought to be included in a volume focusing on the black elite. He was proud to be the gatekeeper of what was clearly going to become the list where prominent blacks would want to be mentioned. He told the *New York Times* in May 1926 that the only people he would include would be truly accomplished individuals for whom the facts of their "Negro descent is clearly demonstrated."[5]

While Clara Sr. and the children remained in Boston, Roscoe transported some of his possessions from Maryland to an uptown apartment in New York City and immediately started his new position with the company that was set up to publish *Who's Who in Colored America*. The only other executive publicly attached to the business was the well-connected black New York political boss Ferdinand Q. Morton, who had been the highest-ranked black ever to work for the city's district attorney. Morton had not only been named an assistant district attorney in 1916, but by 1922, he had become chief of the Indictment Bureau in the DA's office. More important, he was an old acquaintance of Roscoe's.

Two years Roscoe's senior, Morton had also grown up in Washington and attended Phillips Exeter as well as Harvard. Like Clara, he had attended Boston University Law School. Following his schooling, he came to New York to practice law and moved up the ranks in the New York Democratic Party. With the support of the black paper, *The New York Age*, Morton became an important power broker who advanced the causes of blacks in Manhattan.

Once Roscoe landed in New York to start his new job, he began compiling lists of prominent black Americans who had excelled in various professions. With letters and phone calls, he began to solicit submissions from these individuals. And before long, many prominent blacks from around the nation began to hear of the project and started submitting their profiles or nominating others who they thought would deserve inclusion in the prestigious volume. This new role immediately brought him prestige in black New York circles. And it was not that his income allowed him to socialize with the wealthier black doctors, lawyers, or businessmen that he was profiling; it was simply that many of these individuals reached out to him as a means to ensure that their profiles appeared in the book.

Because of financial problems at the publishing company, Roscoe had to make frequent requests to be paid his salary. Eventually he threatened to quit because of the company's inability to pay him. It is not entirely clear at what point he actually ceased editing the volume, but by the time of the release of the first edition of *Who's Who in Colored America* in 1928, Roscoe was no longer with the company. Although a biographical description of his wife, Clara, appears in the volume, he was not profiled in it and he was not named as editor. It is not clear how much of that edition had been edited by Roscoe before he left the company.

Given Roscoe's unrelenting focus on how the outside world perceived him and his family, he was probably upset at his daughter and his wife. Since he had to forgo his own plans for law school, he was no doubt both envious of his wife's law school success and resentful of her inability to keep their daughter's grades at a respectable level. He was probably upset that his savings—and his mother's money—were being depleted, without an idea of how they would be replenished.

The conventional 1920s American father would not have supported the role that Clara was playing. Most would have argued that she should be raising her children and living with her husband. But, in reality, it was she who had the greater challenge and was making the greater sacrifice. Not only was she raising the three children on her own, she was also in law school at Boston University, where she was serving as an editor for the school's law review. She was the one who worked out weekly budgets and paid the monthly bills. At this time, Roscoe wrote to her on more than one occasion to express his own interest in becoming an attorney, and he went so far as seriously considering an enrollment after being accepted by the law school at the University of Chicago.

Roscoe must have been frustrated that he was not finding career success, not living with his family, and not blessed with children who were academically gifted. All his life he had taken his family legacy more seriously than anything else. While growing up in Washington, while away at school, he was always conscious that whatever he did, his acts would reflect on his father and their family. When his father was being considered for presidential appointments, he was cautious about what he said or did, because he believed that his own actions—the actions of a child—might have some bearing on his father's future success. Why didn't his children understand that?

Clara felt sorry for her husband. She knew that many Washingtonians thought he had an exaggerated sense of his own importance. But what they didn't know was that Roscoe was never focused on elevating himself for his own sake. His focus, in fact, was on preserving and enhancing the family's legacy of excellence. Even while he was the superintendent of Colored Schools in Washington, DC, what he cared about most as he considered his legacy was that he did not let down his mother or the memory of his father. He was, first, the son of the Senator and Mrs. Bruce. Everything else—his professional position, his credentials, his accomplishments—came second. So, when he said that his daughter was making them look bad by her poor performance at Radcliffe, he meant that she was not living up to the standards that Senator and Mrs. Bruce had set fifty years earlier, as they presented Washington, the national press, and the bigoted Southern whites with a gold standard that no black family ever presented for the world before or since.

To Roscoe, it was quite simple. What he expected of her was to have added greater prestige to the family name. He had expected her to attend college, develop a love for the classics and history, earn good grades, and meet nice girls from accomplished white and colored families; and at the end of junior year, he expected her to be introduced to black society in Washington or New York at a debutante ball, or, like the Wormley daughters, at a formal tea. And by the end of senior year, he expected that she would be engaged to a nice Harvard senior or recent Harvard graduate who came from a good Negro family—a good Negro family with class and background that would further enhance her own bloodline. Instead, she was a poorly performing student, already stuck in a marriage to an actor, which she could not acknowledge publicly.

During the fall of 1925, while Roscoe was fully moved into Harlem and learning about New York, Clara Sr. was spending most of her time in the law library at Boston University. Between her course work and caring for her children, she was researching a law review article that she was preparing on current employment issues.[6] Her article on workmen's compensation would be her third published law review piece and would give her the respect of her professors and classmates. The next semester, Clara Sr. made history at both Boston University and in the law review world when she became the first woman to edit Boston University's law review and the first black person to serve as editor in chief of any law review in the nation.[7] Working alongside her were a group of white male students that included Paul A. Dever, a future governor of Massachusetts. In the meantime, her daughter was barely keeping afloat at Radcliffe, Roscoe Jr. was doing poorly at Exeter, and only her youngest son, Burrill, was maintaining a good average in the Cambridge public schools.

In May 1926, Clara Sr. had realized her dream of graduating from law school. Not only was she selected the class day orator, as her husband had been two decades earlier at Harvard, she was also praised in the pages of her 1926 school yearbook, which said the following about her: " 'All, Hail to the Conqueror!' That is the way this lady should be addressed. Not only is she an honor student of the first rank, but she has achieved a distinction never conferred on a woman before—she is Editor-in-Chief of the Law Review."[8]

For so many years, Clara had expressed her disappointment at having left Radcliffe just months before she earned her degree. She had gotten over her resentment that Roscoe had convinced her to leave the school and join him in Tuskegee, but she continued to regret that she had not completed her bachelor's degree with the rest of her class. Now she could hold her head up and proudly announce that she had an even greater honor. Several months later, she passed the Massachusetts Bar and became the second black woman in the state ever to have accomplished that feat.[9]

Although Roscoe Sr. was still in New York City, all of his immediate family members were living five hundred miles away in Boston. In fact, shortly after Clara Sr. graduated and was admitted to the bar in Massachusetts, her son Roscoe Jr. was preparing to enter his freshman year at Harvard. It had been three years since the school's president A. Lawrence Lowell had launched a public dispute with Roscoe Sr.

over the school's policy of preventing blacks from living in the freshman dormitories. But even though Lowell had been overruled by both alumni and the school's board of overseers, who decided black students must be allowed to reside in the dormitories, the issue was on everyone's mind as they saw this long-awaited black legacy student—Roscoe Bruce Jr.—enter with his fellow freshman classmates from the class of 1930.

Though twenty-eight years had passed since his father had started his freshman year at Harvard, it was immediately obvious that the racial makeup of the campus had not changed very much. When Roscoe Sr. had entered in 1898, there were 3 other blacks in his class of 471 students. In 1926, Roscoe Jr. also had 3 black classmates—but the class size had nearly doubled, with a freshman class size of 929 students. Though he was the only black student to enter the college that year from Phillips Exeter, the other black freshmen had gone to well-respected high schools. Howard Naylor Fitzhugh had graduated from the prestigious Dunbar High School in Washington, the same school which had once been called M Street High School, and which had been both Roscoe Sr.'s and Clara Sr.'s high school.[10] The other two black students, Edward Fiske Hutchins and Thomas William Patrick, had graduated from the well-known Boston Latin School.

Still drawing its members from old powerful WASP families, the class of 1930 included a heavy percentage of young graduates of Andover, Exeter, Groton, and Saint Paul—many of them still coming from New England and New York. Another famous offspring was James Roosevelt, who had grown up in Hyde Park, New York, and graduated from Groton School. His father, the future president Franklin D. Roosevelt, had been at Harvard with Roscoe Sr. twenty-five years earlier.

Although the family had just celebrated Clara Sr.'s graduation from law school and her preparation for the bar exam, their happiness was to be short-lived. On the afternoon of December 8, 1926, Clara was shopping in Shepard's, a downtown Boston department store, when she entered the store elevator and it plummeted five flights, injuring her and several other shoppers. Shattering the bones in her legs and hip, the injury left her hospitalized for fourteen weeks and gave her a lifetime disability that required her to use a cane when walking.

Despite Clara Sr.'s serious injury, Roscoe did not visit her or the children in Cambridge with great frequency. He was enamored with New York and his life there. And, in 1927, it finally became evident to Roscoe Sr. that he would be staying in New York when he learned of a possible job opportunity in Harlem. John D. Rockefeller Jr., the wealthy philanthropist, was building a five-hundred-family apartment complex in Harlem that was aimed at middle-income blacks who wanted to own, rather than rent, their homes. Considered a type of urban race experiment, the Paul Lawrence Dunbar Apartments were named after the famous black Harlem Renaissance poet and were built on a square block running between Seventh and Eighth Avenues along West 149th and 150th Streets. Roscoe hoped that the new development might bring employment opportunities that he could consider.

While Clara remained in Cambridge with their three children, Roscoe moved again, this time to a modest downtown Manhattan apartment at 18 East 10th Street, just off Fifth Avenue. It was early 1927, just after Clara had gotten out of the hospital and he had ceased working for *Who's Who in Colored America*.

Though Roscoe had little money, he entertained himself by dining out and attending art galleries, movies, and cultural events. New York offered the urban sophistication that he had not seen in Tuskegee, Washington, or West Virginia, and he made the most of it. In Clara's absence, he began to socialize and developed a close relationship with a woman he had known from Washington who now lived in New York and worked as the building superintendent of the Russell Sage Foundation on East 22nd Street. Harriet Shadd Butcher was a very light-complexioned black woman who had grown up in Washington with both Roscoe and Clara, and later was employed as a teacher while Roscoe was superintendent of the Colored Schools. Harriet's parents, both well-connected black professionals, had been close friends with Clara's parents for many years. One of her relatives, Mary Ann Shadd, had become the nation's first black woman lawyer in 1870 after graduating from Howard University Law School.[11] Another relative, Marion P. Shadd, had been teaching in the Washington, DC, Colored Schools since 1877, and eventually retired in 1926, after advancing to the level of assistant superintendent of elementary schools.

Although Roscoe escorted Harriet to many black social gatherings during the months they spent together in New York, he suspected that the light-complexioned woman was probably passing as white in some of her activities in the city. In her job at the prestigious Russell Sage Foundation, a philanthropic organization founded in 1907, which used its initial $10 million endowment to advance urban planning issues and improve poor people's social and living conditions, Harriet was responsible for the operation of the foundation's ornate nine-story red-sandstone building on the corner of Lexington Avenue and East 22nd Street. Although it would have been unusual at that time to find a white-run organization in midtown Manhattan that hired a black woman to serve as its building superintendent, it is likely that the liberal foundation made such an exception because of Butcher's family connections and the fact that she could pass as white when confronted by many of the building's neighbors. Because of her steady salary and her own personal family wealth, she was the ideal female companion for Roscoe, who was now very short on cash. The two of them spent evenings and weekends together in black uptown clubs, theaters, and restaurants in Harlem. It was a relationship that would later take a toll on Roscoe's finances, marriage, and public image.

During one of these visits to Harlem, Roscoe learned more about the new housing complex that John D. Rockefeller Jr. was building in Harlem for the black middle class. Roscoe and Harriet watched as the $3.5 million development rose from the ground, knowing that Rockefeller had recently announced that he was searching for a manager who could take on the job of hand-selecting the development's first black residents. Having received a medal from the American Institute of Architects for building the apartments and dedicating them as a place for blacks who wanted quality homes in Harlem, Rockefeller knew that he needed a black manager who would be discerning in his selection of upstanding applicants and who himself would bring prestige to the reputation of the complex. It was an important venture for the Rockefeller family, who were interested in improving certain impoverished areas.

Although Standard Oil founder John D. Rockefeller Sr. had provided financial support to a black Baptist church in New York in the late 1800s, it was not until his son, John Jr., contributed $12,000 in 1920 to a Harlem shelter for black unwed mothers that the family had targeted Harlem as a community they wanted to assist.

As the black migration brought more black Southerners to Northern cities, urban areas like Harlem became congested with job

seekers who had little money. As white Harlem residents moved out of
their elegant stone town houses and apartment buildings, the white
building owners subdivided the previously spacious apartments and
turned them into cramped rooming houses. They charged their new
black residents high rental fees to live in basements, attic rooms, and illegal single-room apartments. Charitable and civil rights organizations,
like the NAACP and the Urban League, along with black newspaper
editors, complained often of the poor housing choices available for black
New Yorkers. Because of the city's policies on racial segregation, even
middle-class and somewhat affluent blacks, who could afford to pay for
better housing, were forced to live in substandard Harlem housing.

The Rockefeller family, originally from Ohio, now settled in New
York City, was one of the supporters that black groups and influential
Harlem citizens reached out to as they searched for solutions in their
crowded community. Since John D. Rockefeller Jr. had already invested in
and built, other housing developments in New York, it was not a surprise
that he chose Harlem as a site for one of his complexes. Conducting his
businesses and philanthropic activities with the help of a well-educated
army of white businessmen, Rockefeller assigned Charles O. Heydt, one
of his real estate advisers, to lead the effort to develop additional housing
for blacks in Harlem. He and Heydt launched their plans back in the
spring of 1926, when they quietly bought the large parcel in Harlem along
busy Seventh Avenue.

Even before it was completed, Harriet Shadd Butcher encouraged
Roscoe to apply for the position as manager of Rockefeller's development in the spring of 1927. Without fully explaining the extent of her
friendship with Roscoe, Harriet even got her white boss, Mary Van
Kleeck, who was a director at the foundation, to write a letter of recommendation on Roscoe's behalf. This was fortunate, since the foundation itself had helped finance a housing development just two decades
earlier, and understood what Rockefeller was trying to accomplish. Van
Kleeck was a well-respected name in New York's liberal white society.
Only four years younger than Roscoe, she was a 1904 graduate of Smith
College and a leading expert at the foundation on labor issues and
work conditions for women, children, and the poor. Van Kleeck's
May 18, 1927, reference letter for Roscoe was sent to Rockefeller's chief
lieutenant on the Harlem project, Charles O. Heydt. In her letter of

reference, she quickly stated the unique credentials of this colored job applicant: "He is a son of former Senator Bruce of the United States Senate."[12] Not knowing many people in New York, Roscoe relied heavily on Harriet and Van Kleeck to advise him on how to pursue the manager position at the Rockefeller development.

Heydt, who was based at Rockefeller's headquarters at 26 Broadway, had the title of vice president at Rockefeller's Empire Mortgage and Trust Company. He and Rockefeller were immediately intrigued by Bruce's impressive background, and they began serious correspondence with Bruce even before they made the decision to hire him. It is likely that they hoped to first gain ideas on how to run and manage such a development, since he was clearly a representative of the type of upscale black that they hoped would reside in their buildings. Eager to impress Heydt, Roscoe sent correspondence every few days. The letters served to outline Roscoe's qualifications, as well as to advise Rockefeller on how the development should be managed, decorated, and named.

In a June 2, 1927, letter to Heydt, Roscoe provided Rockefeller's people with details on the salaries that various New York City–employed blacks earned.[13] His intent was to give Rockefeller a sense of how much money potential residents would be able to pay for the apartments. Roscoe also attached his Harvard transcript, a letter of recommendation from the vice principal of Tuskegee Institute, details from his job as Washington, DC, superintendent of Colored Schools, and letters from two other Washington, DC, educators.

Only four days later, on June 6, 1927, Roscoe wrote to Heydt again. This two-page, single-spaced memorandum outlined his specific advice for the launch and management of the "Housing Project for Negro Harlem," as he described it.

Although the apartments were expected to open in October 1927, the development still did not have a name. Throughout the summer, the Rockefeller executives had tried to decide between various important black figures to honor when naming the project. Although Rockefeller had made it clear that the Harlem-based development needed to pay tribute to an important black person, Roscoe responded on July 25 with a bizarre suggestion. His eleven-page letter to the Rockefeller executives advised, "The entire Rockefeller housing project for Negro Harlem may fitly be called 'The Abraham Lincoln Garden Apartments.' "[14] In his typical assimilationist style, Roscoe suggested naming this all-black housing development in the midst of black Harlem after a white man. Frustrating the Rockefeller office even further, Roscoe came up with additional names for each of the five buildings that the apartment complex comprised. Although he did concede that it would be good to name one of them the Frederick Douglass and another the Booker T. Washington, he also recommended naming the remaining buildings after international luminaries: Aleksandr Pushkin of Russia, Samuel Coleridge-Taylor of England, and Alexandre Dumas of France. While these respected individuals were of black ancestry, Rockefeller's people were exasperated by Bruce's elitism and inability to grasp that the black Harlem community and average Harlem resident would have a greater appreciation for modern-day black heroes from their own country than they would for nineteenth-century composers and writers from Europe.

In the same July 1927 proposal, Roscoe outlined his reasons why his discriminating eyes would make him the ideal manager. He would know how to pick the best tenants. He wrote, "Fill the Harlem apartments with unselected Negro tenants, and the beautiful structures would soon become filthy, disorderly, a bad example to the new Harlem, a disgrace to the city of New York."

And, most important, in his letter Roscoe stipulated that as the resident manager of the new complex, he would have to be provided an apartment suite of no less than seven rooms. He explained his need for such a large space by stating that it was "not only for the accommodation of my own family but also in order that Mrs. Bruce and I may entertain from two to four of the tenants at a time . . . The educational value of such systematic hospitality not only to the tenants but also to the management cannot be overestimated."[15]

With Clara's college and law school credentials, and Roscoe's experience of selecting and profiling famous blacks for *Who's Who in Colored America* and his own elite background, the Bruces symbolized the ideal Negro family for Rockefeller, who was probably doubly intrigued by the fact that they currently had two children at Harvard, a school he had given $5 million to in the prior year.[16]

Finally, on August 16, 1927, with less than two months before its opening, the Rockefeller apartment complex offered Roscoe the job as resident manager. Taking Roscoe's prior requests seriously, Charles Heydt also agreed to hire Roscoe's wife, Clara, as the development's assistant manager. He wrote,

> Dear Mr. Bruce,
> We are ready now to engage you and Mrs. Bruce as Resident Manager and Assistant, respectively, of the new colored community development on the block between Seventh and Eighth Avenues, 149th and 150th Streets at the rate of $6000 per annum for your own salary, and at the rate of $3600 for Mrs. Bruce's salary. We are to provide an office for you and Mrs. Bruce, together with equipment, also a Clerk . . . You are also to have charge of the selection of tenants, whether on a cooperative or on a straight rental basis.
> As you already realize, this work is of vital importance to the Colored race . . . You can proceed to investigate all the applicants and weed out those whom you think will not be desirable tenants.
> Very truly,
> Charles O. Heydt[17]

Although Roscoe and Clara were happy to finally receive a steady income for the family (worth approximately $100,000 in today's dollars), they had considerable debts and expenses from their children's tuition, and the many bills from their Cambridge home.

Within a week of their appointment to their jobs at the development, the Rockefeller executives accepted one of Roscoe's suggestions and finally settled on an official name for the apartments. Named for the famed black poet who had been born in Washington, DC, the Paul Lawrence Dunbar Apartments of New York opened officially in the fall of 1927. Roscoe quickly produced a beautifully detailed brochure that discussed the standards for daily living at the Dunbar. It was illustrated with photographs of handsomely outfitted doormen, well-dressed children playing in the Dunbar playground, manicured flower beds in the courtyard, well-appointed bedrooms and dining rooms, and storytelling time in the building's basement nursery, as well as special rooms for Girl Scout meetings, a women's club room, and a room for boys to use for sports and exercise. Roscoe issued memos to the Rockefeller executives, apprising them of the specific number of professionals and blue-collar tenants who lived in the buildings, dividing them into specific jobs: attorneys, dentists, schoolteachers, post office clerks, pharmacists, chauffeurs, nurses, et cetera. He also began publishing an elaborately typeset newspaper, the *Dunbar News*, which featured photographs, advertisements, and well-written news stories about issues of interest to black New Yorkers. The newspaper even carried social announcements—many of them regarding the more important Dunbar residents. Roscoe felt he had hit his stride with this new position.

Clara Jr. remained at Radcliffe for the 1926–27 school year, living at 16 Parker Street in Cambridge with both of her brothers, while her parents lived in New York. With Roscoe Jr. enrolled a few blocks away at Harvard College, they were a unique pair in that they were the first black brother-and-sister Harvard-Radcliffe "team" who were also the children of black Harvard-Radcliffe alumni. From the outside, they looked like the perfect representation of the Bruce family's successful third generation. Building on their grandfather's record of being the first of their kind to break down racial barriers, they maintained a foothold in both the black world and the white. Unfortunately, Clara was not doing well during her fourth year, either. Having already declared English as her concentration, she took six English courses as well as math, Slavic, and Greek that year. The rigorous course load was overwhelming for her. Unlike her father, who had maintained an A average, or her mother, who had maintained a B average at the school, Clara Jr. during four years had been stuck mostly in the C+ range of grades, with a few Bs in courses like education and botany.

At the end of her fourth year, in June 1927, the dean of Radcliffe informed Clara that because she had already been at the school for four years—but had earned only enough credits to count as having gotten through her junior year—she would have only until February 1, 1928, to complete her final course credits for her bachelor's degree. Since she had fallen short of credits after the 1923–24 school year, she had not been given sophomore status when she returned in the 1924–25 year, but then caught up with her class by increasing her workload. In a curiously unforgiving move, Dean Bernice Brown made it evident in her letter of July 5, 1927, that Clara's Radcliffe degree would be awarded only if she earned her credits in a four-and-a-half-year period. The fact that her family was willing to send her to the school for an additional year, so that she would have gained all her credits, fell on deaf ears. Dean Brown wrote to Clara that July, saying,

> *My dear Miss Bruce: I understand that you have not yet met the algebra requirement, the French elementary language requirement, or the requirement in physical education. You also need two courses, one of them completed with a grade of C . . . I hope this summer that you will be near the ocean or a swimming pool, in order that you can pass the swimming test as soon as college opens in the fall.*[18]

It is hard to know if this treatment would have been dealt on white students as well, because it seems unlikely that the college would have been so dismissive of a family that had already sent several of its members to the university. But the facade was quickly fading for both brother and sister. With their parents living in New York neither Clara Jr. nor Roscoe Jr. had the support or pressure to succeed. Lacking the ambition of their grandparents Josephine and Blanche, and the intellectual gifts that both of their parents had enjoyed, the brother and sister began to neglect their studies and fall behind in their work. By the end of the school year, it was clear that Roscoe Jr. was not performing well, either. In September 1927, Clara's poor study habits became so evident to her father that he wrote to the Radcliffe dean asking if Clara could take her general examinations in May 1928 instead of February 1928, when they were originally scheduled.

Given the fact that Clara had completed her junior year and was the daughter of Harvard alumni, and that there were virtually no blacks at Radcliffe at the time, it seems surprising that the administrators would have been so unforgiving—particularly when it was not entirely clear whether the college required all its students to complete the credits within a specific four-year period or forgo receiving the degree altogether.

It is extremely likely that the family's race entered into Radcliffe's decision. After all, Radcliffe's treatment of blacks thus far had been dismal: when Clara arrived on the campus, black women were still not allowed to live in the school's dormitories. On her own mother's transcripts at the top of the page above her name, the registrar had written the word COLORED—and underlined it for emphasis. Just two years before Clara Jr. was admitted, Dean Bertha Boody made it very clear to the family of black Radcliffe student Mary Gibson that she was unwelcome there, and that, despite her good record, she would never be considered for a scholarship. Meanwhile, scholarships were awarded to white girls whose records were weaker and whose need was less.

And it was likely that Radcliffe was even less inclined to accommodate Clara since her family had already taken Harvard to task over its racially discriminatory housing policy for young men. The racial prejudice existing at the school during that time was reason enough for the administrators to be thinking of ways to ease her out of the school.

Black high schools were never equipped with swimming pools, and segregation made it virtually impossible for black children to use public swimming facilities or many beaches, so the college swimming test was sometimes used as an additional ruse or roadblock for white schools to keep blacks from entering or graduating certain colleges on time.

Clara Jr. was prepared to return in the fall and complete her senior year, and since her parents were once again earning a substantial income as the managers of the Dunbar Apartments, her father wrote to Dean Brown and asked if she could attend the school in the fall and stay until June 1928, rather than try to finish all her credits by February 1928. In asking for this simple four-month extension, Roscoe Sr. offered an understandable explanation for this request in a September 18, 1927, letter:

> *My dear Dean Brown: My daughter, Clara Josephine Bruce, was unable to prepare herself for her General Examinations at Radcliffe this June because of her duties in connection with the grave illness of her Mother, resulting from the dropping of a Boston department store elevator December 8, 1926 . . . Under all the circumstances, I am very earnestly hoping that it may be possible for her to take the Generals at the end of the scholastic year 1927–28.*[19]

Evidently, the dean was unwilling to grant this request. Hence, Clara did not return for her senior year and did not receive her Radcliffe diploma, even though she had entered the school with college credits from Howard and had spent four full years at Radcliffe.

It appears that Roscoe Jr. and Clara Jr. both moved to New York

City, where they joined their parents and Clara's husband, Barrington, who was by then performing in New York nightclubs. Now finally able to live openly with Barrington as her husband, Clara Jr. became pregnant with their first child in early 1928. The child, a boy named Barrington Jr., was born later that year, the same year as Clara's youngest brother, Burrill, graduated from public school.

Although the family was new to New York City, and had grown accustomed to living in a city where everyone knew them, and where they pretty much knew the more prominent citizens, the Bruces had surprising success at meeting the more prominent Harlemites. Because of their neighbors' desire to get apartments in the Dunbar, and Roscoe's past position as editor of the *Who's Who* book, Roscoe and Clara were welcomed and immediately embraced by black New Yorkers. What is apparent, however, is that beyond the NAACP, neither of the parents appeared to make an effort to join the black social clubs that were active during this important Harlem Renaissance period. Although there was an active chapter of Sigma Pi Phi Boulé, which he had joined in Washington, Roscoe never transferred to the New York chapter. Similarly, neither his wife nor any of his children joined black sororities or fraternities.

John D. Rockefeller Jr. was so pleased with Roscoe's and Clara's management of the development that he invited them to dine on March 26, 1928, at his private Manhattan mansion, a nine-story town house at 10 West 54th Street.[20] Joining them that evening was Roscoe's Exeter friend Leslie Pinckney Hill, who was now on the faculty at a Pennsylvania teacher's college.

It was less than two years before New York's Wall Street would reach its economic downfall, but right then, Roscoe's wife and children were living well, and finally living together—in Harlem. Roscoe had, by now, seen two successful years as manager of Dunbar Apartments, where he was now making $6,000 per year, a substantial salary for that time. Clara Sr. was paid $3,600 to work as his assistant, and she also edited a newspaper for the apartment complex residents. She also volunteered her time working with the New York League of Women Voters.

The Bruces' stars were surely rising. By running the Dunbar with a focus on services for the upwardly mobile Harlem resident, they had brought elegance and sophistication to the Harlem community. Their weekly newsletter and their monthly teas, classes on parenting, home decorating, and proper etiquette all served to enhance the Dunbar's reputation. Roscoe would regularly draft detailed memos to the Rockefeller executives, updating them on his new projects and ideas. One of his suggestions was for the building owner to consider expanding his empire in Harlem. Roscoe suggested that Rockefeller might open a bank or insurance firm that could serve the upwardly mobile residents.

Shortly thereafter, Rockefeller announced that he would, in fact, be launching a new project in the Dunbar community, the Dunbar Savings Bank, which was intended to serve as another pillar in this fast-growing black enclave. While black-owned banks had been established in many cities, including New York, long before the 1920s, Dunbar would be a hybrid. It would be founded by whites with the clout of John D. Rockefeller's money and name, but it would be managed by blacks. Or, at least, that was the plan initially publicized in the black community. In actuality, Rockefeller's advisers were planning for the bank to be run by whites, with a few blacks working in the office or serving on the board. A letter sent by Charles Heydt to the chief national bank examiner at the Federal Reserve Bank in New York explained the concept:

> *My Dear Mr. Reeves,*
>
> *I am wondering if I may call upon you some time in the near future about a project which Mr. John D. Rockefeller, Jr. has in mind for establishing a bank in Harlem for the benefit of negroes. It is not our thought to make this a large institution. We hope, however, to secure the cooperation of the better negroes in Harlem and also possibly to have a few of them on the Board of Directors. It is our thought generally to have capable white men as the responsible officers of the bank, with a number of negroes as clerks.*
>
> *Mr. Rockefeller is willing to undertake the financing of such a bank, having been requested by a number of prominent negroes . . .*[21]

Roscoe was not sure if he would be permitted to play a role at the bank, but he was pleased to see how quickly Rockefeller's attorneys and advisers were working to bring the project together. In late May, Rockefeller's lawyer, William Conklin of Van Doren, Conklin & McNevin, provided an update to Charles Heydt on the establishment of the bank. He wrote,

> *Dear Mr. Heydt,*
>
> *I had luncheon today with Mr. [Charles C.] Huitt, Mr. Finley J. Shepard's Secretary, and in the course of conversation he told me he was very much interested in the plan for the negro bank . . .*
>
> *Mr. Huitt has had experience with negroes as he comes from the South. He says that we should certainly have a white President and he believes all the other officers should be negroes; that if we had a negro President, he and all the other officers would become so haughty and autocratic that it would be difficult for negroes to get along with them; that if there is a white man at the head they hesitate to take on this autocratic attitude.*
>
> *Further than that the negroes themselves prefer to deal with an institution which has a white man at the head of it. He seems to have some very good ideas as to the method of handling these people.*[22]

During the next few months, Rockefeller would, indeed, open the Dunbar National Bank of New York, with its first office located next to the Dunbar Apartments on 150th Street at Eighth Avenue. With its first-floor windows framed by ornate brass bars and finials and its interior walls lined with handsome marble and polished mahogany, the Dunbar Bank's public areas looked like a Wall Street office. Uniformed black doormen and security guards welcomed patrons as they sought to conduct business at the windows or with the bank executives in the front or rear offices. Black Harlem residents were excited about having the new bank in their neighborhood.

Happy with the job that Bruce was doing, Rockefeller named him to the board of directors of the Dunbar National Bank. It was a clear sign to Roscoe and his family that although they did not fully engage in the culturally black organizations and movements of Harlem, they were certainly having their own type of renaissance, which they had never thought was possible after their humiliating departure from Washington seven years ago.

When Roscoe joined the bank's board, he was asked to purchase forty shares of stock in the bank. Recognizing that he lacked the necessary cash—money that the white board members already had from their own hefty incomes—the Rockefeller organization lent him a sufficient sum to purchase the minimum amount of stock to be held by a bank director.

In the spring of 1929, the Bruce family was hit with an accusation that threatened to bankrupt the family and break up Roscoe and Clara's marriage. Although the Bruce family had become even more respected and welcomed in New York's black community once Clara had fully established herself as Roscoe's assistant manager and "lady" of the Dunbar Apartments, there was one woman who became infuriated by Mrs. Bruce's presence: Roscoe's friend Harriet Shadd Butcher.

It is not clear how far Harriet and Roscoe had carried their romantic affair during the months that Clara and her children were living in Cambridge, but there is strong evidence that Harriet was enamored of Roscoe and had done certain favors for him with the expectation that he would show a romantic interest in her. Not only had Harriet arranged to have her boss at the Russell Sage Foundation write a strong letter of recommendation for Roscoe when he applied for the Dunbar job, she had also written a letter of reference to Radcliffe, when Clara Jr. applied for admission. In addition to getting him invited into the homes of the city's black society families, she had introduced him to New York's nightspots and used her own steady salary to pay for many of their "dates."

All of this came to a head when, according to Roscoe, Harriet asked him to leave his wife, and he refused. In an April 29, 1929, letter to John D. Rockefeller Jr.'s assistant, Charles Heydt, Roscoe explained that a vengeful Harriet was infuriated by her inability to get Roscoe to leave his wife for her, and demanded a payment of $3,000 to keep her from exposing their affair to the newspapers. He explained,

> *All went well until Mrs. Butcher definitely found that Mrs. Bruce was to join me . . . After Mrs. Bruce came, Mrs. Butcher went out of her way to treat my wife with the utmost insolence, attempting to discredit Mrs. Bruce in Harlem "society." . . . she continued to gossip about us scandalously, not omitting one of our three children . . .*[23]

Roscoe further explained that Harriet made a false claim that she had loaned him $3,000, and that in order to press her false claim, she

had cleverly hired J. Douglass Wetmore, the black attorney who represented the New York *Amsterdam News*. A beloved newspaper in
Harlem, the *Amsterdam News* had recently published articles critical of
the Dunbar Apartments and Roscoe's management of the complex. In
his letter to the Rockefeller office, Roscoe argued that although Harriet's initial intent was to get Roscoe to leave his wife, her plan soon
turned into one of extortion. Roscoe said that she told him that if he
didn't give her $3,000, she would encourage the *Amsterdam News*,
through her attorney, Mr. Wetmore, to continue publishing negative
articles about the Dunbar. Roscoe said that she claimed to have given
$3,000 to him in a series of loans, but Roscoe argued that he had never
borrowed money from her, and that she was demanding $3,000 because
she had recently learned that Roscoe had been awarded that exact
amount in a personal injury suit that Clara Bruce had filed when she
was injured in an elevator accident at a Boston department store two
years earlier. He continued,

> *After the Negro newspapers reported the winning of Mrs.*
> *Bruce's suit against Shepard's Stores in Boston and the award to me*
> *of exactly $3000 to cover the expenses [of the suit], Mrs. Butcher*
> *began telephoning me in imperative tones to come and see her at*
> *once . . . she made demand upon me to sign a Note in her favor for*
> *$3000 . . . Mrs. Butcher telephoned me to say that Wetmore was*
> *rendering wonderful assistance by holding the newspaper in check.*[24]

Roscoe insisted to his wife and all others that he had never borrowed
money from Harriet. He did, however, admit to the Rockefeller executive
that he had spent time with Harriet on numerous social occasions the year
before. Worried that his frequent "dates" with Harriet might compromise
his relations with the Rockefeller people, Roscoe characterized his time
with Harriet as merely a few innocent get-togethers when he escorted her
to short public events or advised her in her office duties. He wrote, "She
was lonely here in the big city and wanted some dependable escort when
she went, as she did constantly to the theater, to entertainments both
downtown and in Harlem. So, I acted for her in that capacity. At the same
time, I formulated practically all of Mrs. Butcher's official reports, tabu-
lated and interpreted her statistical data, drafted much of her official correspondence, and rendered various other services."[25]

Roscoe's defense of his actions further enraged Harriet, and she aggressively argued that she had proof of her loans to him. Although her "proof" did not include any receipts, canceled checks, or signed notes, her insistence was loud enough to gain the ear of her Russell Sage bosses and her friends in the Harlem community. Harriet had, indeed, employed a well-connected lawyer, but there is no evidence proving that either she or her lawyer was able to influence the *Amsterdam News* to write negative stories about Roscoe and the Dunbar.

Even though Harriet's only evidence of financial loans to Roscoe were some hand-scribbled notes in her bank-account book about cash amounts that she had given to Roscoe between May 1925 and September 1927, Roscoe was afraid that the story might jeopardize his job. To settle the matter, he asked Harriet to agree to an arbitration proceeding, to be conducted by her boss at Russell Sage. When she refused that, he asked if she would allow her aunt, a respected Washington educator, to serve as arbitrator over the dispute. Harriet and her lawyer again objected. Finally, the two parties decided on a hearing in front of the American Arbitration Association.

At the November 1929 hearing, Harriet was represented by four attorneys, including Douglass Wetmore and Francis T. Christy, who belonged to the Wall Street firm of Murray, Aldrich & Webb. Roscoe was represented by one lawyer, James W. Johnson, who practiced in a small office at 200 West 135th Street. Johnson did not mount an aggressive challenge regarding Harriet's lack of written receipts. He acted as though her lack of canceled checks or written proof would serve as sufficient evidence for Roscoe. He was wrong. Whether by design or coincidence, one of Harriet's attorneys, Francis T. Christy, was a well-connected Manhattan lawyer who worked closely with the Rockefeller organization in developing the sprawling Rockefeller Center office building complex in midtown Manhattan. It is not clear how she was able to gain the support of such an influential attorney.

Because of Roscoe's inferior legal representation, Harriet easily persuaded the arbitrators in her favor and won a judgment of $3,026.55 against Roscoe. It was a humiliating defeat for the Bruce family, because not only did it launch gossip throughout Harlem about a possible affair between Harriet and Roscoe, it also meant that this once well-to-do family would again fall into debt. Harriet demanded a court order that would garnishee Roscoe's salary at the Dunbar Apartments so that he would lose $11.54 each week from his salary. Roscoe was required to send these payments regularly to the New York County sheriff.

But Harriet still wasn't done with Roscoe and his family. She further humiliated him by spreading a well-substantiated rumor that Clara was filing for divorce from him. The story was advanced so aggressively that on November 30, 1929, the *New York News*, a black weekly, published a front-page article with a headline reading "Divorce for Mrs. Bruce?" Other headlines attached to the story also read "Bruce-Butcher Scandal Is Exposed," and "Dunbar Apartment Head Is Threatened with Wife's Divorce Suit Based on Shadd Exposé."

Although it is quite possible that Clara was angry when she discovered the depth of Roscoe's friendship with Harriet during her own three years with the children in Boston, it is not likely that she would have seriously considered divorcing him, since her own income and livelihood were tied to Roscoe's ability to keep his Dunbar job. In an effort to secure both of their positions, Clara wrote to Rockefeller executive Charles Heydt to say that she was demanding a retraction from the newspaper, because she was not seeking a divorce from Roscoe. On December 14, the paper ran a front-page headline that said "Mrs. Bruce Denies Divorce," and it printed Clara's letter stating, "I protest as emphatically as words permit against the publication of this altogether misleading, false, scandalous, malicious, and libelous article . . ."[26] According to the paper, she denied "the existence of any facts justifying in any way an alleged rumor that she has ever contemplated or had the slightest reason to contemplate suit for a divorce."

CHAPTER TWENTY-ONE

1930–1939
The Third Generation Makes News,
and the Senator's Grandson Goes to Prison

WHAT WOULD I BE?

I'd be the music of your lyre,
Silvery sweet;
The upward darting of your fire,
The chanson for your feet.

I'd be the silence of the grief
Enfolding you;
I'd be the faith of the belief
Upholding you.
I'd be the guerdon of your joy,
A laughing sprite;
The flaming gold of your alloy;
The day for every night.
I'd be the victory awaiting you,
When the battle's done;
I'd be the crown of laurel, too,
When the race is won.

—CLARA BURRILL BRUCE,
Saturday Evening Post
April 22, 1933

CLARA HAD BEEN A TALENTED WRITER HER ENTIRE LIFE, AND SHE saw no reason to hide her expression simply because no law firm or business could make use of the skills she had honed a few years earlier as a star law student and editor of her school's law review. Being black and female might have weighed against her in the business world, but she was unwilling to surrender her creativity and eloquence. Since her teens, she had been writing poetry, and was able to publish some of it commercially during World War I. And now, she was being recognized by a famous publication: the *Saturday Evening Post*.

The April 22, 1933, issue of the handsome magazine featured a cover illustration of a rosy-cheeked white woman looking demure and sophisticated. In this issue was also a story by Pearl S. Buck, the famous novelist and essayist who covered Chinese culture and other international topics, as well as the poem by Clara Bruce, her first published piece in several years. "What Would I Be?" was just one of many poems that Clara would send to the Curtis Publishing Company in Philadelphia, but this one was especially romantic, a great deviation from her normally cerebral written expression. This particular poem is also rather ironic, since it speaks of the devotion she has for the love of her life—certainly an interesting piece for her to write after a long and publicly humiliating suit strongly suggested that Roscoe had carried on an affair with another woman while she and their three children were living in Cambridge.

By the beginning of 1930, the Depression was being deeply felt in most corners of the United States. The Bruce family had, by now, fully relocated to New York, and they, too, were feeling the economic pinch. Although Roscoe and Clara were earning respectable salaries for managing the Dunbar Apartments, they were still suffering from the financial losses that Harriet Shadd Butcher had brought to them. In March 1930, it was revealed in the *New York Amsterdam News* that Roscoe had been so short on cash when he had been forced to satisfy the judgment against him that prior November, he had to sell his forty shares of Dunbar Bank stock. Without the bank stock, he was required to step down from the bank's board of directors.[1] Since he had been the bank's first black director, the loss of the stock was an emotional as well as an economic disappointment.

But even with the setback regarding the Harriet Shadd Butcher suit, Roscoe and Clara were well regarded, both at the Dunbar and among their bosses at the Rockefeller offices.

Burrill was preparing to enroll as a freshman at New York University. Roscoe Jr., having left Harvard College after less than two years, was a sophomore at City College of New York, which was minutes away from the family's West 150th Street home. And Clara Jr., while still helping her parents perform their job at the Dunbar, was living with her husband, Barrington, and their two-year-old son, Barrington Guy Jr. It must have been both obvious and disappointing to Roscoe Sr. and Clara Sr., by now, that their two oldest children had not become the hardworking, gifted adults they had hoped for. Both of them had been given every financial, social, and academic advantage.

The only child who seemed to escape the heavy scrutiny and pressure of Roscoe Sr. and his wife was their youngest son, Burrill, who always seemed to be a little out of step with the family's historical settings and institutions. And although he was later to become the most successful of the three children, he was, ironically, the one who gained the least from the family's past wealth.

For example, while virtually every member of the three generations had ties to important black Washington institutions, like Dunbar High School and Howard—Blanche was on Howard's board; Roscoe Sr., Clara Sr., Roscoe Jr., and Clara Jr. all went to Dunbar High School; Clara Sr. and Clara Jr. both attended Howard University; and all of them, including Josephine, spent an important part of their adult (or young adult) lives in Washington—Burrill's life was spent mostly in Boston and New York City. While two generations of men had attended prep school at Phillips Exeter, Burrill attended public schools in Cambridge. While Roscoe Sr., Roscoe Jr., Clara Sr., and Clara Jr. all went away to college at Harvard, Burrill lived at home and attended the plebeian New York University. In fact, so parochial was his experience that rather than attend the university's main campus at Washington Square in lower Manhattan, he took his classes at the school's Bronx campus, which was just a few minutes north of his parents' Seventh Avenue Harlem apartment.

For the most part, unlike his parents and his siblings, Burrill was raised neither with the black elite nor with the white elite. With resources being stretched to pay for the family's two oldest children, there seemed to be nothing left for the youngest child. Burrill's first taste of the privilege that the Bruce family had come to embrace as their own occurred when he was twenty-five years old and entered Harvard Law School in September 1934. Unfortunately, the family could not afford to pay for the entire three-year term, and he left the law school in June 1936, at the end of his second year.[2] This was unfortunate, because, of all the third-generation siblings, he seemed to be the most ambitious and gifted. During his first year at law school, a notoriously rigorous two semesters of civil procedure, contracts, torts, and property, he maintained a solid B average.[3]

Since the family had no ties with, or contacts at, New York University, it is likely that Burrill made his own case for being accepted by the school. And it was, indeed, an odd choice for a black child of his family's background. At a time when most well-educated black parents were sending their children to black colleges in the South or elite white schools in New England, such as Harvard, Yale, and Amherst, it was an unusual decision for the Bruces to send their child to New York University. While it went on to greatly distinguish itself in later years, in the early 1930s, when Burrill attended it, New York University was a mediocre school for whites and an extremely unlikely choice for blacks with means. It lacked the prestige of other New York institutions, such as Columbia, Cornell, or Colgate. At that time, it was simply not a school that black professionals would normally have selected for their son.

Nevertheless, Burrill distinguished himself at NYU's College of Arts and Pure Science by writing for the university's *Daily News* newspaper for two years, and serving on the YMCA council beginning as a freshman. The YMCA council ran a freshman summer camp and hosted lectures, recreational gatherings, and student-faculty teas. Burrill continued in those organizations and eventually joined the Adam Smith Society, an organization for students majoring and interested in the field of economics. By his senior year, Burrill was treasurer of the school's YMCA council. Like his brother and sister, Burrill was being educated in a mostly white school setting, but unlike at Radcliffe and Harvard, the NYU student body consisted mostly of New Yorkers and, with regard to Burrill's organizations, of Jewish students—the YMCA included.

Roscoe Jr. would work with his father at the Dunbar for two years, learning how to interview applicants, collect rents, hire staff, and take care of tenants' needs. In September 1930, at the same time as Burrill was entering his freshman year at New York University, Roscoe had entered City College of New York. Because of his low grades at Harvard, Roscoe was unable to transfer many of the credits to his new school. During the next three and a half years, he would concentrate in the Romance languages, taking many advanced courses at City College in French and Spanish. In the midst of the Depression, Roscoe Jr. spent the money he made at the Dunbar quite freely, and was known as a ladies' man among his school friends. Riding his motorcycle between home and campus, he cut a dashing figure, as he was a few years older, a bit wealthier, and considerably more sophisticated than many of his classmates, who had generally been graduates of New York public high schools and who had spent their entire lives in Brooklyn, the Bronx, Queens, or Manhattan.

At the time, Roscoe Sr. and Clara Sr. were short on cash and beginning to fall behind in their rental payments for their apartment. Clara's brother had recently died, and because he had little insurance, it was her responsibility to pay for funeral expenses.[4] The fact that their son spent money so recklessly was particularly troubling to them.

Soon after graduating from City College in February of 1933, Roscoe Jr. met an attractive young woman from Lynchburg, Virginia, named Bessie Humbles. At the time, Bessie herself was new to New York. Although such things didn't matter to Roscoe Jr. as much as they did to his father, Bessie came from a well-known black elite family in Virginia that was responsible for funding the creation of the Virginia Seminary and Theological College. Bessie's relative Adolphus Humbles Sr. of Lynchburg was a vast landowner, as well as the owner-operator of a wood-and-coal business in central Virginia. The Humbles family had lived in Appomattox County since before 1860, and they settled an area very close to the courthouse where the Confederate Army had surrendered at the end of the Civil War.[5]

Soon after the Humbles family purchased a large plot of land in Lynchburg, they gave it to the college, which was founded in 1886. One of the school's major buildings, Humbles Hall, was named in honor of the family's contributions to the school. Like many other Washingtonians, Roscoe's father first became aware of Bessie's family when Adolphus Humbles underwrote the bond to build the True Reformer Building in Washington, DC. The thirty-thousand-square-foot office building became famous when it opened in 1902, because it was the first American office building to be fully developed by blacks. The architects, the developers, the contractors, and the Humbles family—as the financiers—were all black. It would gain additional attention in 1905, when Booker T. Washington's National Negro Business League chapter met there, and later, in the 1930s, when First Lady Eleanor Roosevelt rededicated it to be used by Washington's Metropolitan Police Department and its Boys' Club.

Although the girl was not the intellectual equal of his own wife, Roscoe Sr. seemed to be pleased with the prestige that Bessie's family name could add to the Bruce family history. Unfortunately, this prestige did not come without a price. For the first two years of their relationship, from February 1933 until April 1935, Roscoe Jr. did not hold any full-time or part-time job to help support himself or even to pay for dates out with Bessie. That expense fell to his father, Roscoe Sr., who seemed to be enamored of the Humbles family.

But just as intriguing—although for vastly different reasons—was Clara's mate, Barrington Guy, who by now was performing in local clubs and theaters as a singer and dancer, and as a handsome leading man in small plays and nightclub acts. Although Roscoe had originally opposed their elopement several years earlier, he was pleased that Barrington was finally making a name for himself as a performer. In 1931, the actor was contacted by black movie producer Oscar Micheaux, who had purchased the rights to Charles W. Chestnutt's book *The House Behind the Cedars*. And because he liked a particular title of another book, Micheaux had recently purchased the film rights to Gertrude Sanborn's 1923 novel *Veiled Aristocrats*. Using Sanborn's title but Chestnutt's story, the final film told the tragic story of Rena Walden, a light-complexioned black woman from a respectable black elite family in North Carolina, who surprises her mother and brother by announcing that she is in love with a dark-skinned black man named Frank Fowler. Their planned engagement invites laughter and derision from the town's light-skinned black elite families and brings shame and humiliation to the older brother, John, who is a respected attorney in South Carolina, where he lives and passes for white. The brother takes Rena to his home in South Carolina, presents her as his white sister, and tries to marry her off to a wealthy white man named George Tryon.

By this time, Micheaux had made several full-length black feature films, including *Body and Soul*, which launched Paul Robeson's career, and *The Millionaire*. He was a filmmaker, writer, and editor, and his first film, adapted from the Pulitzer Prize–winning novel *Birthright*, told the story of a Harvard graduate's experience with racism.

Micheaux asked Clara's husband, Barrington, to perform the role of George Tryon, the only white character in the film, which also starred popular 1930s black actors Lorenzo Tucker and Laura Bowman. The screenplay was ultimately adapted by both Micheaux and Charles W. Chestnutt, the novelist and short-story writer who had authored *The Conjure Woman* and who had won the NAACP's well-regarded Spingarn Medal.

Now the mother of four-year-old Barrington Jr., Clara was certain that this would be her husband's big break—after several years of working in local clubs that brought little money and no prestige to their Harlem household. The film was released in 1932 and made little commercial impact, except within the black moviegoing audiences.

Despite his melodic baritone singing voice, his good looks, and the Shakespearean training he had received from his father and other acting teachers, there were simply no decent parts available for a black of Barrington's complexion. In fact, although this movie features only black actors, Barrington actually plays a character who is supposed to be a white man with Scottish background. So, even when he had the chance finally to appear in a feature film, he was too light-complexioned even to be believable as a light-skinned black man. They could only cast him as a white character. As Barrington later admitted, his early career had brought him success on the stage in front of white audiences because he was light-complexioned enough that customers and the owners of the Keith theaters had assumed he was white, and gave him decent roles. When it was discovered that he was actually a Negro, he was no longer allowed to perform in their theaters. And even though there were occasional roles for blacks to play servants, slaves, or buffoons, directors would not hire him, because his skin was too light and his hair too straight for him to be perceived as an authentic-looking black person. Disappointed and disillusioned, Barrington returned to performing in black Harlem nightclubs, like the Plantation, and other local spots where audiences would accept a talented black singer who did not epitomize the shuffling, wide-grinning stereotype that was in demand on stage and in films.

Among the many New York stage productions that he appeared in during the 1930s were an operetta called *Africana*, a comic play named *Brain Sweat*, and a musical titled *Black Rhythm*.

When Roscoe Sr. finally saw *Veiled Aristocrats*, the film that featured his son-in-law, he no doubt saw the ironies of the story and how it appeared to mirror his own daughter's life. What he couldn't have known at the time, though, was that his own daughter, like Rena in the film, would have to choose between passing as white in order to live with her man, and living as a black woman to remain true to her family. In the end, Clara Jr. would decide to deny her racial identity and pass for white as a way of helping her light-complexioned husband.

At the end of 1936, the Rockefeller executives informed Roscoe Sr. and Clara Sr. that they were selling the Dunbar Apartments, and the Bruces' services would no longer be needed. It is not clear why Rockefeller wanted to let go of the complex, but it is likely that the Harlem race riot of 1935 played an important role. In March of 1935, rioting began along 125th Street after it was reported that a black boy had stolen a knife from a store and that white police officers had beaten him badly as punishment. By the time it was learned that the story was mostly rumor, black residents had already started to express their rage over the long-standing bad treatment they had accepted from the all-white police force that patrolled their community. During the unrest, many stores and homes were damaged, and dozens of people—mostly black—had been arrested by the white police officers. This incident, along with the fact that black unemployment was growing, surely must have been discouraging news to the Rockefeller real estate team. They recognized that the black middle class in Harlem was quickly shrinking and might not be able to afford the rents at the Dunbar as the economy worsened.

Roscoe sent numerous obsequious letters to Rockefeller's famed "Room 5600," the family office that sat atop the 30 Rockefeller Plaza office tower, with the hope of getting the executives to hold on to the Dunbar or, at least, to somehow hold on to the Bruce family. One such letter was sent to Rockefeller executive Frank Staley on November 25, 1936.

> *My dear Mr. Staley:*
>   *At this, the zero hour in the history of the Dunbar when it looks as if our relations with Mr. Rockefeller and his business associates are on the verge of terminating because of the foreclosure sale, Mrs. Bruce and I wish to assure you one and all of our heartfelt appreciation of the opportunity you have given us here and of the veritable education we have received at your hands . . .*
>   *To the end of our lives we shall take great pride in having served Mr. Rockefeller and his associates, however humbly. . . . Nobody who is at all familiar with the history of housing in America up to now, can honestly deny that the provision Mr. Rockefeller was so good as to make for the most disadvantaged element in our nation's life, in founding the Dunbar Apartments, has proved a powerful influence for good . . .*[6]

Although it was surely not his intent, such fawning letters only made Roscoe appear phony and pretentious, and they further proved that he really was not suited for any position that required him to make ordinary people feel at ease.

Despite nearly ten years of service to them, Roscoe was not liked by the Rockefeller advisers, and was therefore given a paltry parting gift—three months' salary, ending in January 1937. Roscoe would later say that he had *voluntarily* stepped down from his position as manager at the Dunbar Houses—a fiction that few should have believed, since his finances were in such bad shape. Given that it was widely reported that Roscoe had placed his wife, daughter, and younger son on the Dunbar payroll, earning the family in excess of $20,000 a year in addition to receiving free housing for the first few years in the cooperative buildings, it is certain that Bruce would have stayed in the job if he had been able to convince the Rockefeller advisers. In fact, Roscoe pleaded with Heydt and others to at least recommend him and Clara to the new owners—but the pleas failed to gain them even an interview.

Although Rockefeller's sale of the Dunbar certainly was the primary reason for the Bruces' departure from the building, there was also the fact that most of the apartment dwellers simply did not like Roscoe. Snobbish and elitist in almost every sense, he looked down on the black residents who lived in the development and elsewhere in Harlem. This reputation put him out of favor with local ministers, editors at the black-owned *Amsterdam News*, and other prominent blacks who might have come to his aid. He was also high-handed and duplicitous when dealing with his bosses at the Rockefeller organization. After a year working in his position, he was required to pay rent for his own space, and he was perpetually late with his rent payments. He wrote bombastic letters with outrageous explanations for his tardiness. The fact that he often laced his letters with references to his children's tuition expenses at Radcliffe, Exeter, and Harvard did not sit well with conservative white bosses who clearly must have envied the fact that this black man had such "white-shoe credentials."

Complaints about the "autocratic" manner in which he selected tenants and governed them once they had moved into the exclusive apartment complex also probably precipitated Roscoe's departure. From the very beginning, it had been Roscoe's intent to admit only black elite families with good credentials into the buildings. While Roscoe's elitist airs and stringent requirements for getting in and staying in made the building even more desirable to families, it had the simultaneous effect of making him extremely unpopular among certain residents and other Harlemites who resented his snobbery. A November 6, 1937, article from the *New York Amsterdam News* reported: "Dissatisfaction with the management was also made public . . . with assertions that it was too autocratic." As the paper pointed out, "Almost from the beginning there were rumblings of discontent in the community concerning the apartments. Despite the fact that they were originally reported to have been built as a pioneer low cost housing experiment, they were filled by high salaried persons."

Just as Roscoe had zealously guarded entry into the *Who's Who in Colored America* directory when he was editor of the historical volume, he had similarly culled the personal and professional biographies of families as he had determined who could live in the Rockefeller-financed development. Such a role made him both a social arbiter and a resented troublemaker for those kept on the outside.

When Roscoe and his wife were replaced as the Dunbar managers by two men, Roger Flood and Wilbur Coleman, owner-developer John D. Rockefeller Jr. changed the buildings from cooperative ownership to rental units.

Although Roscoe tried desperately to publicly explain his departure from the Dunbar in favorable terms, soon after Rockefeller sold the development in early 1937, a Bruce family scandal led to the eventual and complete humiliation of Roscoe Sr. and Clara Sr. It had all begun in April 1935, when Roscoe Sr. got Roscoe Jr. a job working as the manager of a black housing development in Newark, New Jersey. Named in honor of the black actor and 1930 NAACP Spingarn Medal winner, the Richard B. Harrison apartments were rental units built and owned by the Prudential Insurance Company. Having trained under his father at the Dunbar, Roscoe Jr. was given the manager's job of the New Jersey development just one year after graduating from college.

Such a position was clearly too complex and demanding for the young man. To begin with, he had never been responsible with money. And it was well-known to his father and mother that he was unable or unwilling to pay his own bills. In June 1933, Roscoe had moved into his own first-floor apartment at the Dunbar and began renting it for $40 per month.[7] Only a year later, his account was $65 in arrears, and his father had to send him a letter stating, "my instructions from the auditor are to dispossess you by summary action unless you pay $50 upon account before the end of this month."[8] Although his parents came up with money to pay the debt, only a year later, the young man was again displaying a blatant disregard for his debts. Haughty and sarcastic, Roscoe Jr. was often disrespectful of his own hardworking parents. And the fact that his parents continually bailed him out of his problems may have made him even more inconsiderate.

When he finally obtained the job as manager of the Harrison Apartments at 59 Somerset Street in Newark, New Jersey, in April 1935, he was already once again well behind in his rental payments at the Dunbar. Despite the fact that his father, Roscoe Sr., had warned him that Rockefeller's people were filing a suit against him for back rent, Roscoe Jr. decided to spend money to furnish a second apartment for himself and his young wife at the Newark apartment development. In a June 28, 1935, letter to Roscoe Sr. on the son's fancy new letterhead that included the engraved words "Roscoe C. Bruce, Jr., Manager" and "Edward D. Duffield, President—The Prudential Insurance Co.,"

Roscoe Jr. wrote unapologetically about his inability to pay the past due rent. In fact, his tone was almost belligerent toward his father:

Dear Mr. Bruce:
    I wish to acknowledge your letter of this morning . . . As I stated in my recent letter to you I am unable to make any payment on account now. From my pay check of this month I have left exactly ten dollars. I cannot give you that.
    . . . While it is true that my father-in-law died last year and left my wife and me quite a large sum of money, we are not permitted to touch any of this money . . . As I explained, I have had to spend a large amount of money in furnishing up an apartment . . .
    Very truly yours,
    Roscoe C. Bruce, Jr.[9]

How ridiculous and insulting this letter must have appeared to Roscoe Sr. when he received it from his son. It must have been particularly humiliating to the father to be forced to turn it over to the Rockefeller office as evidence that his son's rent was still unpaid. Not only did it elicit letters from Rockefeller to the son, but Roscoe Sr. was also taken to task by Charles Heydt. In Heydt's letter, Roscoe Sr. was told that his own job at the Dunbar might be in jeopardy if the family did not start paying their rent on schedule.

Dear Mr. Bruce:
    Your son's letter of June 28th addressed to yourself, is received. It seems to me if I were in your position, I would not countenance such an attitude as that letter reveals. Your son evidently had sufficient funds . . .
    You and your family have been chronically in arrears for many months. We have had to check up each one of you on numerous occasions. None of you has lived up to the spirit of the agreements which you signed. . . . Unless you and your family find means of meeting your obligations, you will endanger the continuance of your relationship with the Apartments as Resident Manager . . .[10]

Two days later, Heydt sent a similarly worded letter directly to Roscoe Jr. in Newark. In that letter, he noted that members of the Dunbar board of advisers were equally disturbed by Roscoe Jr.'s treatment of fellow tenants and "have justly made criticisms of your attitude as well as that of your sister."[11]

A review of Roscoe Jr.'s rent records from the Dunbar office reveals that throughout the entire time that he resided in the apartments, he was at least one to three months behind in his rental payments. He maintained a practice of sending his father partial payments in the form of checks that were postdated by a month or more—and even those checks would be refused by the bank because of insufficient funds. At some point after Roscoe Jr. vacated the apartment and moved to Newark yet still owed considerable back rent, his father refused to supplement the payments and simply forwarded the postdated checks to the Rockefeller office.

Finally fed up with Roscoe Jr., one of the auditors working for Rockefeller, R. H. Wilkens, ordered Roscoe Sr. to begin legal proceedings against his son. On June 5, 1936, he wrote to Roscoe Sr.: "At the request of the Directors of our corporation, you are asked to institute garnishee proceedings against Mr. Roscoe C. Bruce, Jr. . . . As you are aware, there has been considerable passing back and forth of checks issued us by this former tenant."[12]

Evidently, the threat was enough to get Roscoe Jr. to pay his final debts to the Dunbar. Of course, he had already caused additional damage to his parents' credibility as managers at the Dunbar—damage that was soon to lead to their dismissal at the end of the year. But by that time, Roscoe Jr. was already deeply entrenched—and overwhelmed—at his job as manager of the Harrison Apartments in Newark.

Clearly a position that was far too demanding for an inattentive and coddled young man, Roscoe Jr.'s job required that he maintain an office staff as well as manage workers who performed numerous jobs around what was then described as a "swank" rental development. He was paid in excess of $3,000 a year, a sum that was considered quite substantial for a recent college graduate with no previous work experience in the post-Depression years.

Still a socially active young man who remained popular among his Newark neighbors and his college friends from Harvard and City College, Roscoe did not take his job as seriously as his ambitious and fastidious father did. The lack of attention that Roscoe Jr. paid to his office soon took its toll. Even though he had finally paid his debts to the Dunbar, his sloppy record-keeping and inattention to the office workers and financial affairs at the Newark rental office soon led to missing funds. It is not entirely clear if he or his assistant manager, Milton Taylor, actually knew how the shortages developed, but it was eventually apparent that there was a shortage of $1,200 in the rental receipts by March of 1937.

Although Roscoe Jr. was later to tell a different story, it was suggested that he had spent some of the money in order to help tenants he had befriended who were in danger of losing their apartments because they could not pay their rent. However the money was spent, it sent Roscoe Jr. into a panic and caused him to make the matter even worse. Unable to explain the missing funds and his poor record-keeping, which had been out of order since November of the prior year, he came up with a scheme that days later became front-page news.

On the evening of Saturday, April 3, 1937, just past nine o'clock, three masked gunmen broke into the Harrison Apartments' rental office and brandished their guns at Bruce, his night clerk, and another employee. Disguising their voices and demanding that the employees put their hands up, they ransacked the offices and safe and threatened to kill Bruce and his employees if they failed to remain quiet and turn over all the rental money collected that week. After several terrifying minutes, the armed gunmen locked Bruce and his coworkers in a room and escaped with the money.

For several days, front-page articles in the *New York Amsterdam News*, the *Washington Bee*, and many other newspapers in New Jersey and along the East Coast reported the robbery and repeated Roscoe Jr.'s chilling account of the night's events. With great detail, he gave information on the robbery, telling the police that one of the robbers was around six feet four inches tall, looked to be about thirty years old, and weighed about 200 pounds, and that the other was in his late twenties and seemed to be five feet nine inches and weighing about 175 pounds. Each article referred to Roscoe Jr. in its headlines and quickly identified him as a scion of the Bruce family of Harlem.[13]

Roscoe's wife, Bessie, who lived with him in Newark at 59 Somerset Street, was equally distraught by the robbery and the attention that it brought the family. But eleven days later, on Wednesday, April 14, 1937, the sadness turned to humiliation for his wife and parents when Roscoe Jr. was arrested by Newark police detectives who arrived at his home with a complaint accusing him of hiring a gangster as well as the gunmen who robbed the Harrison Apartment rental office. Also arrested on that evening were two of the gunmen—Willard Gramby and John Hayes of Newark—as well as Milton Taylor and Bernice Baskerville, two of Roscoe's employees who worked in the apartment rental office. When Bruce was arraigned the next day, it was announced that he had also paid Archie Borras, "a master gangster whom Bruce contacted to swing the job."[14]

Police had questioned one of the gunmen, and after a long interrogation, he broke down and admitted that they had been hired by Roscoe to take $600, and that Roscoe had told the police that it had been $2,000, in an effort to hide the fact that he had either embezzled or mismanaged at least $1,200 during the past several months.

"He was too much at ease for a victim who had just been robbed of such an amount of money," said the police as they commented on their interrogation of Roscoe and noted that it was a "smoothly told story, plausible in spots, lacking in truthfulness."[15]

There was an immediate frenzy throughout New York and Washington in the black elite community as news of Bruce's arrest and arraignment became public. His parents, recently retired from managing the Dunbar, saw their names invoked in every article covering the story. After years of building their reputations at Harvard, Radcliffe, Boston University Law School, Exeter, Tuskegee, Washington, DC, and New York, they saw their family become a scandal with front-page headlines like "Young Bruce Out on Bail—in Hiding."[16]

Clara Sr., by this time vastly overweight and in poor health, took to her bed and avoided her friends. Roscoe Sr. reached out desperately to his New York contacts, such as former classmate Ferdinand Q. Morton, and fraternity brothers that he first knew when in Sigma Pi Phi Boulé. Long ago abandoned by Bruce, few of these men were willing or able to help. After years of favoring his few white acquaintances over these accomplished black men, he was finally receiving the sting of their rejection. New York and New Jersey newspaper reporters descended on Roscoe Jr.'s home on Barclay Street in Newark as soon as he was released from jail on a $2,500 bond. When his wife, Bessie, was reached at the front door, papers gleefully reported, "reporters made an effort to interview the youthful Harvard graduate and scion of an illustrious family . . . [and] his wife, the former Bessie Humbles of Lynchburg, Virginia said, 'Mr. Bruce is out of the city. Won't you come back later?' "[17]

After a third gunman, Edward Reddin, was also found by the police, he confessed that he was paid $125 for the robbery. Police revealed that what led them to the various gunmen was a discovery that these men, who were previously rather destitute, had been spending a great deal of money during the past week in various Newark bars and restaurants.

Within days of Bruce's release from jail, he went into hiding. The white executives at the Prudential Insurance Company fired him and merged the management of the Harrison apartments with the management of the Douglas Apartments, another complex that Prudential owned. The executives gave the temporary job to Thomas Puryear, a longtime business rival of Roscoe Jr.

Roscoe Sr. knew that the only way to save his son from jail was to try to hire the best local lawyers, and, being out of a job and low on money, he turned to his childhood best friend from Exeter, Theophilus John Minton Syphax, who had gone to Columbia Law School, and become a successful lawyer in Manhattan.[18] Syphax, who was now passing as a white man after changing his name, was unwilling to meet with Roscoe, but he spoke with him and gave him some suggestions on whom to contact. Syphax, who was then practicing under the name T. John McKee, Esq., in downtown Manhattan, was, like Roscoe, married and living in New York with children and grandchildren. Syphax's first wife, Anna Lois Dixon, was a white woman he had met in 1906 and married in 1908. She divorced him after learning that he was black. Now he was married to a second white woman.

As Theophilus informed Roscoe at the time, his own two sons, Theophilus Jr. and Douglas, were almost the same age as Roscoe Jr. and Burrill. Just as Roscoe Jr. had been sent to his father's alma mater, Harvard, McKee's son had been sent to his alma mater, Trinity College, graduating just one year before Roscoe Jr. From there, the two families' lives diverged dramatically. Roscoe Sr.'s prominence was specifically tied to the black world. Theophilus Sr.'s status was tied to the white world: he was a member of the Bensonhurst Yacht Club, on the board of directors of the Kings County Tennis Club, and had been a member of the St. Mark's Episcopal Church, a white congregation in Brooklyn. McKee's son, Theophilus John McKee Jr., was president of the class during his first year at Trinity, married a white woman weeks after graduating in 1932, and was raising their four children in upstate New York, where he worked as a supervisor in a commercial dairy.

Finally, Roscoe was able to retain Roger M. Yancey, a local criminal defense attorney, to serve as his son's counsel. Throughout the summer and early fall, there were frequent postponements for the trial, and Roscoe and his son used that time to try to gain support from local friends who might wield power in his favor. They considered all kinds of deals—offering to send Roscoe out of the country if the charges were dropped, or to promise that he'd leave New Jersey. The elder Bruce was frustrated by the family's lack of connections in New Jersey, the relevant jurisdiction in this case. Although never affiliated with them in any way, he reached out to the black churches, hoping that those in the Newark or Jersey City communities would lend a hand in asking the Essex County court for leniency. Attorney Yancey also attempted to challenge the validity of Roscoe Jr.'s indictment, but the motion was denied. Both the prosecutor and the owner of the Harrison Apartments—Prudential Insurance—were unmoved and insisted that Roscoe Jr. be prosecuted to the full extent of the law.

By mid-October, it was decided that Roscoe's trial would begin Thursday, October 28, 1937, in the Essex County courthouse, with Judge Daniel Brennan presiding. Scared and somewhat despondent, Roscoe Jr. arrived in the courtroom that Thursday morning and found the seats filled with reporters, photographers, and neighbors from both New Jersey and New York.

He remained seated at the side of his lawyer, Roger Yancey, nervously gripping the side of the defendant's wooden table. His wife, Bessie, was conspicuously absent from the scene, and onlookers speculated that the wife's absence could only mean she no longer supported her husband.

Also seated in the courtroom were the other defendants involved in the April holdup: the middleman Archie Borras; and the three gunmen, Edward Reddin, John Hayes, and Willard Gramby, all street thugs who made Roscoe Sr. seem uneasy as he listened to them enter their pleas of non vult—or nolo contendere—that morning. Roscoe Jr.'s assistant Milton Taylor was also present, but, like Roscoe, insisted he was innocent.

When it was time for Roscoe Jr. to take the stand, he immediately laid the blame for the whole holdup scheme at his assistant's feet. He said Taylor was responsible for "instigating the plan by suggesting that he be allowed to go to Detroit 'to secure a couple of guys who would put the job over properly.' "[19] Roscoe also insisted that, at the time, he had told his secretary, Bernice Baskerville, that Taylor had created the holdup scheme.

Taylor's lawyer cross-examined Roscoe and tried to get him to say that it was he, Roscoe, who had come up with the idea of a fake holdup. But Roscoe stood by his story.

It was the next day, Friday, October 29, that things turned sour for Roscoe. Bernice Baskerville was called as a witness, and she confirmed that it was Roscoe, and not Milton Taylor, who had planned the holdup several months earlier. Policemen who had questioned Baskerville and others at the time of the arrest confirmed that Roscoe was always said to be the strategist for the fake robbery—all to cover up his bad management of rent receipts.

That afternoon, as Roscoe's father and others sat watching, the prosecutor suddenly offered into evidence further incrimination of Roscoe Jr. It was a letter that he had written from jail in late April, following his arrest. The letter was written to his wife, Bessie, and read:

> *Dear Bess,*
> *I did have Borras do the hold-up. Taylor and Baskerville agreed to it as the only way to correct the shortage of over $1000 we could neither account for nor replace. You go on home, dear, and forget me. But please do remember that I have always loved you and always will. Please go home.*
> *Roscoe.*[20]

The courtroom was dead silent as the prosecutor read the letter and then turned to Roscoe Jr. There was nothing more he could say except to change his plea. It was later revealed that the letter had been given confidentially to a representative of the Prudential Insurance Company.

As Roscoe Jr. finally stood with his attorney, Roger Yancey, at his side, the judge asked the slim, pale young man how he was pleading to the charge of conspiracy to defraud his former employer.

"I plead guilty, Your Honor," was Bruce's response.

Yancey repeated it, "My client pleads guilty."

The courtroom buzzed as reporters and onlookers were shocked to learn that Bruce, the college graduate from an esteemed family, didn't have some explanation or argument to justify his innocence. After all, the rumors throughout Harlem society were that someone must have "set up" Bruce as a scapegoat for some other, more complicated scheme. The plea of "guilty" sent shock waves throughout the black communities in New York and New Jersey. And there seemed to be repercussions right at the Bruce family's doorstep in Harlem.

Thoroughly embarrassed by the family that he had handpicked to open and manage the Dunbar, only days after Roscoe Jr. entered his guilty plea for defrauding the Harrison Apartments, John D. Rockefeller abruptly sold the Dunbar apartment development that the Bruce family had managed and been associated with for so many years. Perhaps it was a coincidence, but no one believed that to be the case, because Rockefeller had long refused to sell the complex that had brought him both housing awards and considerable goodwill within the New York black community. Unfortunately, testimony and virtually every news article relating to Roscoe Jr.'s criminal trial made reference to Rockefeller and his hiring of the Bruce family to hand-select residents and manage his elite Dunbar Apartments. Even the letterhead that the Bruce family members used in their jobs as managers of the complex carried Rockefeller's name. The fact that the stories listed Roscoe's prior work experience with Rockefeller's Dunbar Apartments before coming to the Harrison Apartments, probably frustrated Rockefeller even further. After denying that the buildings were for sale, Rockefeller's firm finally sold the famous West 150th Street development to the 320 East Seventy-third Street Corporation for an undisclosed sum.

Rockefeller employees also made sure to minimize the use of the Bruce family name in correspondence related to the Dunbar Bank, which Rockefeller had earlier established and asked Roscoe Sr. to assist in running.

As Roscoe Sr. lost his employment with the Dunbar, he aggressively pursued other jobs while also advising his son's trial lawyers. One job that he applied for was that of manager at the Harlem River Houses, New York City's first federally funded housing development. Aimed at low-income blacks, the new development was just being built on 151st Street at Harlem River Drive. Hoping to land the job at the

574-apartment complex, Roscoe sent an application to the New York Housing Authority. Knowing that federal money were being used to build the development, Roscoe asked John D. Rockefeller Jr. to write a supporting letter to Harold L. Ickes, who headed the Public Works Administration in Washington at the time.[21] Rockefeller sent a strongly written letter in support of both Roscoe and Clara, and he explained that the only reason Roscoe had been released from the Dunbar was because they were undergoing a reorganization in order to "operate more economically." Three weeks later, Ickes wrote back to Rockefeller, stating that he had already selected a manager for the new Harlem project before he received Rockefeller's letter.[22]

It was now clear to Roscoe Sr. and Clara Sr. that all the prestige and success that they had worked for since the day they left Dunbar High School in Washington for bigger and better things was at stake. Their earlier declarations and promises to seek greatness and goodness were being challenged to the very core as their son faced a humiliating criminal trial and a possibility of going to jail. The idea that this family—which had included a United States senator; a bank president; a Washington socialite; a school superintendent; landowners; and graduates of the best prep schools, colleges, and law schools in the country—could be reduced to an *Amsterdam News* headline about a Newark petty criminal was absolutely devastating to them both.

In many ways, Roscoe Sr. was fighting to preserve his father's legacy. He had already sold his father's Mississippi plantation, the Maryland farm, and the multiple residential properties in Washington, Indianapolis, and Mississippi that his mother had left him. He had also already spent his mother's fortune over the years, on high-priced schools for his wife and children, Cadillacs for himself, club and fraternal organization dues for family members, and the generally lavish lifestyle that exceeded his own annual earnings. Two years earlier, Roscoe had asked the Dunbar Bank to give him a $500 loan, and Charles Heydt sent a confidential memo to bank president Charles Huitt recommending that he turn down the loan. He wrote, "I do not think it would be advisable to loan the Bruces any money . . . They are, I believe, very extravagant in their manner of living."[23]

But Roscoe thought he could pull this one off and save his son as well as their family's name. He had beaten the odds before. He had taken his personal battle with Harvard's president A. Lawrence Lowell to the public and beaten the powerful university president's policy on racial discrimination in its dormitories. He had stood up to the Washington papers and the black society families who wanted his resignation from the DC school superintendent job—and while he ultimately lost the war, he won most of the battles during his fifteen-year tenure. Even as a teenager, when his Exeter classmates and others thought he would fall apart after his father's death, he rallied his family contacts with Booker T. Washington and others to ensure that he would get into Harvard. Now, he had to continue to rally and call on his own strength and the strength of others as his son faced the possibility of prison time in New Jersey.

Although Roscoe learned that his son had not even bothered to vote while living in New Jersey, he called on leaders in political circles and in the churches. He managed to get the prominent Rev. William A. Byrd of Jersey City and his First Baptist Church to lead a letter-writing campaign to Judge Brennan.[24] Other prominent New Yorkers who helped Bruce win sympathy were Rev. W. P. Hayes and Urban League executive Dr. Charles Johnson, who worked with the Rosenwald Fund and later became president of Fisk. As the network grew, the Bruce family became hopeful. At that time, it was widely believed that there was enough outside pressure that the judge would not give Roscoe Jr. any punishment greater than five years of probation.

As the family waited for Roscoe Jr.'s sentencing, he remained in a Newark jail, and his father continued to offer comments to the press— hoping that his contrite tone would soften Judge Brennan's resolve to make an example out of his son. At one point, he told reporters that if Roscoe were given a probationary sentence, the family would send him to Paris to study medicine or enter the photography business in another city.[25]

Finally, on November 17, 1937, Roscoe Jr. returned to Judge Brennan's court in order to hear his final sentencing. When Roscoe arrived in court that Wednesday, neither his parents nor his wife were in attendance. His brother, Burrill, was the only family member present among the Newark courtroom's onlookers. Chief among the reporters' conversations was commentary on the fact that the day before, Bruce's assistant, Milton Taylor, had been acquitted of all charges. This did not bode well for Bruce, because he had attempted to convince the court that it was Taylor who had developed the holdup scheme. The fact that they acquitted Taylor meant either that they felt neither man should be held responsible, since it was the gunmen who actually took the money, or that they believed Bruce was lying to hide his own guilt and, hence, was wholly responsible.

And then it happened. After asking Roscoe Jr. to stand and face front, the middle-aged white judge looked down from his desk and scowled at the well-dressed, olive-complexioned thirty-year-old. Looking tired, scared, and gaunt, Roscoe Jr. braced himself against the table and offered a friendly stare. What came next was a shock to him and everyone else in the small courtroom.

In what sounded like a double slap in the face, the judge said to the defendant: "You are suffering from the self-delusion that you are not guilty. Because of your background and training, I am giving you eighteen months in the state penitentiary."[26]

It seemed that what ultimately convicted Roscoe Jr. was the letter he had written to his wife several months earlier. The fact that he wrote the letter of confession, but in the court still denied responsibility for the holdup, evidently incensed Judge Brennan. In the end, not only was Roscoe sentenced to eighteen months in the Essex County Penitentiary in Newark, but his jail time even exceeded that of the middleman and the three gunmen. This was surprising and disappointing to many. Borras and Hayes each received a yearlong sentence because of prior petty convictions on their records, and Reddin was given only a nine-month sentence. Gramby was given five years' probation.

Although they did not have friendly ties to the Bruces, many members of the black professional community took great offense at the judge's action. They understood his statement to suggest that because of Roscoe's education, he should have known better than the other defendants, but they also believed that because this was Roscoe's first offense, and because he had been such a stellar citizen in every other regard, those factors should have weighed in his favor. Why would repeat offenders who actually carried the guns get less of a punishment than a first-time offender? It never seemed to work that way when young, educated white men from good families were first-time offenders. For many members of the black elite in Harlem and elsewhere, even those who disliked the Bruces, there was a feeling that the sentence carried a tinge of racism and envy on the judge's part. In their eyes, it appeared he was trying to penalize this illustrious family and cut them down to size by heightening the humiliation.

Although Roscoe Jr. had originally told friends weeks earlier that he would rather kill himself than serve time in jail, he was far more stoic when the sentence was rendered in court. His father and brother, however, were combative, and they attempted to offer the court, the media, and the public an additional defense that implicated the manager from another Newark housing development. Their arguments were scattered and fruitless, because it became clear that nothing was going to keep Roscoe out of prison.

"Eighteen Months in the Penitentiary for This Harvard Man," screamed the front page of the Washington weekly *Afro-American*.[27]

"Bruce Goes to Jail," declared the front page of the *Amsterdam News*.[28]

"Grandson of Late U.S. Senator Convicted of Fake Holdup!" and "Aristocratic Scion Is Sentenced to Term of 18 Months," were some of the other headlines in Washington.

Interestingly, outside of Washington, virtually no newspaper that ran stories on Roscoe Jr. even made a reference to his grandfather, the late senator and presidential appointee. (It had been only a handful of papers, like the *New York Mirror*, back in the spring, when the crime first occurred, who had made mention of Senator Bruce.) Although it was a pleasing footnote for Roscoe Sr. and Clara Sr., who worked hard to preserve the family's greatest legacy, it was surprising that even the New York newspapers had such a short collective memory of this family's original claim to fame. Mentioning that fact certainly would have created an even more dramatic backdrop to the articles that talked about one generation's fame and privilege and then Roscoe Jr.'s fall from Exeter and Harvard into a New Jersey penitentiary.

During his first few days in jail, Roscoe cried regularly, and was visited by reporters who looked forward to telling the story about his fall from a childhood of privilege. In early December, when his mother was finally able to visit him, he greeted her in khaki prison clothes, in a room where they spoke through a wire screen. It was then that he revealed to Clara that the penitentiary had assigned him to one of the worst jobs at the prison: to break rocks with a sledgehammer on the rock pile. The *New York Amsterdam News* reported, "From other prisoners, it was learned that Bruce cried all day during his first day on the rock pile. And what was three weeks ago a pair of tender hands is now a blistered and callused pair, hardened by the rigor of swinging a pick."[29]

When it looked like matters could not get any worse for the third generation of Bruces, yet another scandal devastated Roscoe Sr. Just as Roscoe Jr. had completed his sentence and set sail for France, Burrill, Roscoe's youngest child, found himself in trouble and on the front page.

An attorney and an officer in his father's one-year-old real estate business, Bruce Realty Company at 209 West 125th Street, Burrill had received a summons and was told to appear in Manhattan's Third District court on Thursday, April 13, 1939, after being charged with bilking a legal client of $500. Harlem resident Mary Robinson had hired Bruce the prior November to represent her in buying a neighborhood building that she was intending to turn into a small rooming house. At the time, she had given him $500 so that he could use it as a deposit on the West 133rd Street building. Burrill had told Robinson that the seller had accepted her offer, but that the sale would take several weeks to go through. After several months had passed and Bruce had not contacted her, Robinson learned that the seller had actually turned the offer down months earlier. Bruce had held on to the money and had continued to claim that the negotiation was ongoing.

On April 13, 1939, the day that Bruce was to appear before Court Magistrate Overton Harris to be charged with unlawfully withholding funds from a client, newspaper photographers were waiting for the dapper attorney. One aggressive photographer from the *New York Amsterdam News* ambushed Burrill in a large, humiliating photo that showed a handsome Burrill with expensive fedora and briefcase, as well as his father, Roscoe, and an unidentified black woman suddenly running from the cameras. The enlarged sidewalk photo scene of the three scurrying subjects carried the embarrassing headline—"B. K. Bruce Accused in Money Deal"—in addition to this mocking caption:

They didn't want to look at the birdie—but definitely. At the sight of the camera, they put on a spreading act but *The Amsterdam News* lensman got'em anyhow. At right is Burrill K. Bruce, accused by a Harlem woman of unlawfully withholding money she turned over to him in a business deal. At left, almost out of the picture, is Bruce's noted father, Roscoe Conkling Bruce. Next to Burrill is a young lady who not only was quick enough to turn her back but also managed to keep her identity secret. The trio was snapped just as they were about to enter the court building.[30]

The schadenfreude that New York's black society was feeling was indeed palpable as yet another member of the Bruces' third generation was brought to his knees. Still, the black media enjoyed stinging the family by reminding them and their readers that the Bruces were not as superior as they thought. Although the newspaper once again neglected to highlight the fact that they were the descendants of United States Senator Blanche Bruce, the editors didn't miss other salacious details when they said, "Court litigation enmeshed the prominent family of Roscoe Conkling Bruce once again this week when the Harvard graduate's son, Burrill K. Bruce, himself a former Harvard student . . ."[31] It was obvious that this family's fall from grace was a story that the New York paper liked to repeat.

It is a mystery why the editors of the *New York Amsterdam News* consistently failed to mention the third generation's ties to Senator Bruce in the 1937 articles about Roscoe Jr.'s trial and incarceration and then again in the 1939 articles about Burrill's litigation. It seems inconceivable that these talented black journalists could report the details of where Roscoe Sr. and his children had gone to school yet not know that their greatest family credential was that they descended from a black U.S. senator.

Because the Bruce family lived much of their lives outside of black circles, it is possible that some of the most obvious and interesting facts about them escaped the notice of the reporters and neighbors who scrutinized them. For example, the fashionably dressed unidentified woman escorting Burrill to court in 1939, the one captured on the photograph as turning away, was almost certainly Burrill's older sister, Clara Jr. Still married and living in Harlem at the time, she had a reason for ducking the media: her husband's fledging career in the New York theater.

Clara's name had appeared in a *New York Amsterdam News* profile of her husband only a month earlier, on March 22, 1939. The last thing she wanted to do was associate her husband's name and struggling acting career with the criminal doings of her younger brother.

In that *Amsterdam News* story, the reporter emphasized how Barrington's light complexion had created a double-edged sword and made it hard for him to succeed in both white and all-black theater productions. The March 1939 story explained that he had earlier success in white stage productions because the white audiences and theater owners had assumed that Barrington was, indeed, as white as the Caucasian characters that he portrayed on the stage.

"I never tried to pass," Guy told the paper. "Folks thought I was white and I didn't enlighten them."[32] As Guy explained, his career had been going well on the vaudeville circuit until people who knew his parents in Washington contacted theater owners, informing them that they had a black man playing onstage opposite white women.

"I had to start all over again," the actor explained to the reporter. He also noted that when a New York theater produced Langston Hughes's story *Mulatto*, the producers turned him down in favor of a full-blooded white actor, because "it would not do for a real Negro to be on stage killing a white man." Guy said that he, therefore, had to satisfy himself with performing in nightclubs. It was not something he liked, yet, as the article pointed out, "Guy detests cabaret work, but he has to eat."

Two generations earlier, the possibilities seemed infinite for the Bruce family. With connections, education, money, and confidence, the senator and Josephine had been able to build a world seventy-five years earlier that seemed stable, even in the face of national prejudice and discrimination. Their son and daughter-in-law had seemed to improve upon it with their own hard work and optimism. But this third generation almost seemed to be crashing down on itself despite the advantages their parents and grandparents had bestowed upon them. Through the fault of ongoing bigotry and their own greed and pride, they seemed to lose track of what the prior generations had done and had intended to do as they built up a proud black legacy of achievement and respectability.

CHAPTER TWENTY-TWO

1940–1967

The Third Bruce Generation
Erases a Proud History

February 8, 1940

My dear Mr. Rockefeller,

I need help desperately and I can't help hoping that in the goodness of your heart you may be willing to come to my aid. I am in the third year at the Harvard Law School but unable to go back because of lack of funds.

My great grandfather, Dr. Joseph Willson, knew your grandfather well in Cleveland many years ago. And my father and mother managed Paul Laurence Dunbar Apartments for your father . . .

My father and I have worked very hard indeed since that time to earn a decent livelihood as real estate brokers in the Harlem Region, but through no fault of our own, without success.

Every member of our family, except the two little boys, is able, willing, eager to work. Thus, my father, a phi beta kappa man from Harvard and past sixty years of age, tried to get a job as a night watchman . . .

Would you be willing to enable us to borrow about as much as my father and mother received each month in salary at the Dunbar apartments?

Most sincerely,
Burrill K. Bruce[1]

By 1940, when thirty-year-old Burrill Bruce wrote a letter to David Rockefeller (who had ironically attended Harvard at the same time as Burrill), asking to borrow money to pay for food and school bills, it had become increasingly obvious to the third generation of the Bruce family that they were no longer held in an exalted place above the rest of their race. Their dwindling finances could no longer exempt them from the experiences of the majority of black America. Not only had elite whites ceased to acknowledge them at public events, but upwardly mobile blacks in New York had also begun to snub them. After living a life of privilege for two generations in Washington and then another dozen years of upper-middle-class comfort in New York, the Bruce family had collapsed financially and was now destitute. In fact, three months earlier, Roscoe and his wife had applied for public assistance with the Welfare Bureau of the City of New York.[2]

The Rockefellers had severed any historic ties that they had once shared with the Bruces when they sold the Dunbar Apartments and closed down the Dunbar Bank. In early 1939, Rockefeller's lawyers laid out a liquidation plan for the bank, which reduced the bank's board to five people and shrank the large staff to four employees.[3] The Bruce family would quickly become a footnote in the Rockefeller files.

Later that year, John D. Rockefeller Jr. received a letter from a New York City welfare case worker, indicating that he was writing in reference to Roscoe and Clara Bruce, who lived with two sons at 32 Morningside Avenue in Manhattan. It read, "Dear Mr. Rockefeller, Mr. and Mrs. Bruce and family are applying to us for assistance at the present time. Mr. Bruce tells us that he, his wife and sons were employed with you . . . from 1927 to 1937 . . . We are writing to ask whether or not you may have some employment to offer any member of the family now."

The Rockefeller executives offered no assistance to the Bruces, and sent a curt note to the city's Department of Welfare, stating, "It is true that they were employed by us . . . However, we paid them high salaries and it is surprising to me to learn that they are trying to go on relief. Our interests in Harlem have been disposed of and we have nothing at the present time for which either of them could be considered."[4]

In Washington, the third generation were thought of as the grandchildren of a senator and the children of the former DC school superintendent. In that city, they were also known to be considerable landowners, as they had owned at least two large city town houses and a substantial farm in suburban Maryland. Their town house at 909 M Street later fell into disrepair, like the once-handsome brick buildings surrounding it. The home, which was later bought and renovated by a white family in the late 1970s, eventually received national landmark status from the U.S. Department of the Interior.[5] Their second town house, on R Street NW, is still today a handsome four-story building in use, just off Washington's bustling Dupont Circle.

In New York, where the valued social currency was more tied to financial wealth and less to family name and background, the only prominence the Bruce family had achieved was the eleven-year position they held as the managers of the Dunbar Apartments from 1927 to 1936. By that time, the local residents of New York had either forgotten that there had been a black U.S. senator sixty years earlier, or they simply didn't care anymore. Outside the South and beyond Washington, DC, a legacy of accomplishment in Reconstruction politics counted for very little.

So, within three generations, a family had risen from slavery and obscurity on Blanche Bruce's side and freeborn upper-middle-class status on Josephine Willson's side to a national stature that brought wealth, power, and prestige to an upper-class black family during the late 1800s, which it enjoyed through the 1920s, all to come tumbling down on the third generation sixty years later.

The 1937 trial and incarceration of Roscoe Jr. had left him divorced and jobless. The cost of his defense lawyers had depleted his parents' savings and aged them significantly. The minor 1939 financial mismanagement suit against Burrill had heaped further humiliation onto the Bruce name and left little luster for the family to enjoy. And the third devastating blow was revealed in the 1939 published acknowledgment by Clara's husband that his acting career was failing because of his racial identity as a black man.

By 1940, the Bruce family's depleted savings and the heightened segregation in the nation made it impossible for the second and third generation to escape the discrimination that other ordinary blacks faced. They no longer enjoyed the association with elite institutions that they had in the late 1800s or as late as the early 1930s. By that time, they no longer belonged to the Boulé, no longer remained affiliated with a church, and had ceased even responding to alumni queries from Exeter, Radcliffe, New York University, and Harvard.

In fact, the only distinction that the Bruces seemed to earn after their departure from the Dunbar was Clara Sr.'s 1938 nomination to the New York State Assembly. Continuing to research and occasionally speak on the same liberal social causes that she had written about, and remaining active in the New York League of Women Voters and Municipal Affairs Commission, Clara impressed many among Manhattan's intellectual and political crowd. Soon, she was approached by members of the small Fusion Party in New York's Nineteenth Assembly District.[6] Despite the party's formal nomination of her in July 1938 and her desire to finally put her law degree to good use, Clara decided not to run for the office of state assemblywoman. With the family's increasing indebtedness, her ill health, and her own fear of a campaign that might attract additional scrutiny for her imprisoned son, Roscoe Jr., the fifty-eight-year-old woman turned down the opportunity and, instead, supported Roscoe Sr. in his failed efforts to launch new entrepreneurial projects.

A telling footnote for the family was Clara Jr.'s eventual decision to fade into the background and join her husband in his plan to completely disassociate himself from the black community and begin passing as half-Italian and half-Indian in 1941—only two years after he was profiled as a light-skinned black in the popular black newspaper *New York Amsterdam News*. Rather than accept a fledging career as a black performer, Barrington—and presumably Clara Jr.—presented himself as a Maryland-born white who had grown up speaking Italian, Hindi, Spanish, English, and German in his multicultural home in Prince George's County.

In a 1941 newspaper gossip column with the headline "Did You Happen to See Barrington Sharma?" Clara's husband gave himself a new background, a revised childhood, a different racial identity, and a fake, foreign-sounding surname. Taking some facts from the Bruce family history, some from his own parents, and inventing others, Barrington Guy now claimed to own a 150-acre farm in Maryland, and recalled growing up performing Shakespearean dramas for his Italian mother while his learned father educated young "Sharma" at home.

"Today," read the article by celebrity columnist Inga Arvad, "he is aspiring to become a second Rudolph Valentino . . . He is tall, handsome in an Oriental way. India is written in the long, dreaming eyes and the shape of his hands."[7] Not surprisingly, Sharma failed to tell the columnist that he had already appeared in the movies, but in "all-colored cast" films under his given name of Barrington Guy.

At this time, Clara and Barrington's children included thirteen-year-old Barrington Jr. and seven-year-old Bruce Guy. By the time this fourth generation came of age, their identification with the black community or their own ties to black history and the black senator were so tenuous as to be nonexistent.

In the same manner that passing blacks were conducting themselves at the time, Barrington and his wife had, by 1940, created a believable ethnic mix to explain their swarthy complexions while rewriting their histories and leaving out associations with actual schools they had attended and communities in which they lived, or family members who might reveal their true racial backgrounds. This probably explains why Clara failed to complete any Radcliffe alumni update or reunion forms beyond her class of 1927 tenth reunion directory in 1937. She and her husband studiously avoided contact with any people or institutions that knew them when they lived as a black couple. Since Barrington was still performing under the made-up Sharma name during the early 1960s, it is possible that she and her children took on the surname of Sharma, which would make it even more difficult to track their identity.

Ironically, it was about this time that Roscoe Sr.'s old friend T. John Syphax, having been passing for years, revealed his true racial background. Roscoe learned about it in the pages of the *New York Daily Mirror*. The story had the peculiar headline, "Family Friend Supports Lawyer as Negro's Kin."[8]

The article revealed that one of New York's most prominent white attorneys on Wall Street was suing to contest a will that was left by a wealthy black man in Philadelphia. As was stated in the article, the white attorney, who was about to undergo surgery at New York's Lenox Hill Hospital, was now claiming to be the black grandchild of the deceased black millionaire, and he wanted to claim the $800,000 that remained from what was originally a $2 million estate.

One of the newspapers said, "Prominent white lawyer T. John McKee was actually born as a black man named T. John Syphax, but changed his name and racial identity after graduating from Trinity College. While a student at Columbia Law School, he became T. John McKee." The articles revealed that McKee was the last surviving child of Douglas Syphax and Abbie McKee Syphax, a prominent black couple. Abbie's wealthy father, Colonel John McKee—a successful caterer and landowner—had died earlier in 1902, leaving an estate worth $2 million, with portions of it intended to go to his daughter, Abbie, and to his seven grandchildren, which included a deceased daughter's son, Henry Minton, and Abbie's children during their lives. Among these grandchildren was, of course, Abbie's son, T. John Syphax. But in 1904, T. John Syphax cut off relations with his family, changed his name, and altered his racial identity to become white, and it was presumed until now that the last surviving grandchild was the prominent black Dr. Henry Minton. After Dr. Minton's death in December 1946, the courts expected to give the rest of the estate (by then, $800,000 remained) to the Catholic Church as stipulated in the will.

This is when white attorney T. John McKee announced that he was actually the "long lost" Negro grandchild who had been passing for the prior forty-four years. He declared that he was the actual Theophilus John Minton Syphax who had "disappeared" years earlier. Syphax/McKee was able to locate a black cousin who had known him as the black Syphax child, thus convincing the Orphan's Court in Philadelphia that he did have the authority to have the will set aside for his benefit.

Over the next several weeks, Roscoe and Clara saw the story of Sie unfold in the New York papers. They must have remembered how close they had all been as teenagers and then how Roscoe relied on him so much at Exeter, and how hurt they were when, at the last minute, he refused to serve as best man at their wedding because he had decided he could no longer socialize with black people or family members.

But during those following weeks in 1948, Roscoe must have considered how his own life had developed in comparison with his friend's. They had lived parallel lives in the same city, yet never came together. They had both come from prominent black families. Their sons were almost the same age—neither one of them able to duplicate the accomplishments of the father—and they had the same number of grandchildren. They were well known in their respective communities: one black and uptown, the other white and downtown. As Roscoe read the stories, he discovered that Sie was divorced from his first wife and married to a second white woman—an Aimee Bennett McKee, who claimed to be surprised by her husband's true identity. Even his white law partner, Irving Berger, and the white residents that lived in Sie's East Side apartment building were surprised to learn he was a black man passing all those years. But in the end, providence would take over when, five months after Syphax/McKee revealed his identity, he died on August 4, 1948, in a Fort Lee, New Jersey nursing home—too soon to claim his inheritance.

With the exception of Clara Sr.'s attempts to write for the NAACP *Crisis Magazine* and her occasional poems or stories related to race, by the 1940s, there was no Bruce family member who was attempting to embrace an important role in the black community—either professionally or socially. Whether it was because they had been so thoroughly humiliated by Roscoe Jr.'s incarceration and ostracized by the black press, or simply because they never developed a meaningful empathy with the black experience that was so alien to their white educational and early social experiences, none of them attempted to consistently live among blacks. They did not establish any presence within the black churches, the NAACP, or the Urban League—all popular institutions for elite blacks living in New York. Roscoe Sr. even ceased any involvement with the prestigious Sigma Pi Phi Boulé, though most of its membership—including the New York chapter—consisted of well-educated and important black men of means.

In fact, Roscoe had descended so far from his past stature that by the mid-1940s, he was working as a presser in a midtown dry-cleaning business. Despite his and Clara's numerous attempts to resurrect a career in education or to find employment as building managers, it became clear that the discriminatory employment practices of New York made it impossible for a black man or woman to hold any such job outside of an all-black Harlem community. Even with his record as a school superintendent, building manager, and Phi Beta Kappa graduate of Harvard, Roscoe was living in a city where black men were hired only as chauffeurs, cooks, elevator operators, custodians, and laborers. The most fortunate of them—particularly those with college degrees—could find work as post-office clerks. Despite Clara's Radcliffe education and law degree, her opportunities were even more limited. For her generation, the only available positions for black women were as maids, housekeepers, seamstresses, or waitresses.

Even Roscoe's attempts to launch a real estate management business in Harlem met with failure, because, though the community was populated almost exclusively by blacks, its buildings and businesses were owned primarily by whites who had no interest in forming business relationships with blacks. In fact, even at this time, there were still Harlem restaurants that served a primarily white clientele—and that refused to seat black patrons, urging them, instead, to buy their meals at the takeout counter.

After two years of working side by side with Clara in the back room of a New York dry cleaner, a frustrated and impoverished Roscoe once again attempted to reach out to the Rockefeller family for assistance. Despite ten years of their service to the Rockefeller-owned Dunbar, the Rockefellers rebuffed every attempt by the Bruces to contact them—often holding them off with cold form letters dispatched by their lieutenants and secretaries.

In the fall of 1946, Roscoe sat in the small backroom of a midtown office that he rented at Madison Avenue and East 43rd Street and drafted a business proposal for opening his own dry-cleaning business that he, Clara, and their sons could operate. He sent the single-spaced typed proposal to John Rockefeller's office, Room 5600 at 30 Rockefeller Plaza, with a cover letter that briefly summarized the attached proposal for the "Incomparable French Dry Cleaning Plant":

> *My dear Mr. Rockefeller:*
>
> *Most sincerely do I hope and trust that you will not deem me importunate in writing to you . . . The members of my family have learned the French Dry Cleaning business the hard way . . . Thus, week after week and month after month I myself have worked as a mere operative twelve and more hours per diem six days a week plus eight hours every Sunday . . .*
>
> *If in the goodness of your heart you should see your way clear to helping me consummate our plans for "INCOMPARABLE", I and all the members of my Clan would never cease to remember you with profound gratitude . . .*[9]

What made the letter and proposal seem even more desperate and pitiful was what the writer had attached to the page: pasted to the bottom of the letter was a small, postage-sized black-and-white photo of an almost unrecognizably aged Roscoe Bruce. The head-shot photograph showed the once-handsome and fit man to now be bald, thin-faced, with wrinkles across his forehead and below his eyes, with creases folding down to his thin, unsmiling mouth. Although he was sixty-seven at the time, he looked at least a dozen years older. Next to the photo was a typed postscript that read, "I have undergone many sorrows through no fault of my own; but, my spirit is unbroken."

In a fashion that had been characteristic for the Rockefeller office in dealing with the Bruce family correspondence, Dana S. Creel of Rockefeller's office responded the very next day, on September 25, 1946:

> *Dear Mr. Bruce:*
>   *I am replying for Mr. Rockefeller . . . As I am sure you realize, Mr. Rockefeller receives a great number of requests from individuals in connection with their business and personal needs. It has necessarily become his rule to decline appeals from individuals, regardless of merit and whether for business or personal assistance . . .*
>   *Sincerely yours,*
>   *Dana S. Creel*[10]

This was to be the last interaction that the Rockefeller office would have with the Bruce family. Whether Roscoe wanted to acknowledge it or not, whatever value he and his wife had added to the Rockefeller properties during their ten-year employment, John Rockefeller and his lieutenants had clearly decided that the relationship was over. It was the end of a chapter for Roscoe Sr. and Clara Sr.

When Roscoe was released from jail in 1939, he had moved to France, studied at the Sorbonne for two years, and then returned to New York, where he moved into an apartment with his parents and brother. His brother, Burrill, also made no special impression on the black community. Although he worked throughout the early 1940s with his father's business, Bruce Realty, which sold and managed a few small black-owned Harlem properties, Burrill's life was mostly outside of Harlem, in downtown Manhattan. He did manage a small legal practice with clients in Harlem, but his social life was far removed from the black community. He lived together with his parents on Grove Street, a downtown area that was populated mostly with whites.

Roscoe Jr., who eventually married a second time, a woman named Jacqueline Moison, had two daughters and lived on Hoe Avenue in a white middle-class section of the Bronx.

And Roscoe Sr., who had treasured the family legacy more than all of them, lived his final years quietly, only occasionally responding to infrequent queries from the black press who wrote about his father, Senator Blanche Bruce.

Clara spent her final years trying once again to regain her own career much the same way she had done when she took the children and moved to Boston to pursue her law career. Unfortunately, despite her historic success at Boston University Law School and her role as head of the law review, Clara was never able to get a job in the legal field. Being both black and female, the only opportunities available to her at the time would have been to teach in a black school or to work at menial jobs in cafeterias and hotels. She spent these years trying to recover from the devastating blow that her son's incarceration had created. Having been overweight for most of her adult life, she had suffered from diabetes during her later years and finally died in 1949. Roscoe Sr. died shortly after, in 1950, of a heart attack.

By the middle 1960s, both Roscoe Jr. and Burrill were working together at their father's former Grove Street address in downtown Manhattan, still keeping a low profile, far away from the black community that they once knew in Harlem. Neither one of them maintained communication with the alumni networks of their former schools, and they did nothing to preserve the records of their father or grandfather, which by then had already been purchased by Howard University from a Bruce family friend.

For almost two generations, there had been virtually no public debate over the history and legacy of Senator Blanche Bruce, despite the notoriety of the two generations of Bruces that followed him. It seemed remarkable that such silence would have enveloped the legacy of Blanche Bruce, given all that he had accomplished and all the barriers he had broken as the first black to serve a full term in the U.S. Senate. In fact, renewed interest in Senator Bruce was not apparent until the election, in 1966, of Republican U.S. senator Edward Brooke from Massachusetts, who became the second black elected to a full term in the Senate.

Despite the legacy that was left by Blanche Bruce and the two generations that followed him, there seem to be very few individuals who continue to claim connections to the senator's family. Given the large number of Bruce siblings who grew up on the Virginia, Mississippi, and Missouri plantations, and the fact that his three grandchildren all married and raised offspring, it is surprising that virtually all of his descendants have disappeared or chosen to obscure their family ties to Bruce for racial or other reasons. In fact, when U.S. Senator Christopher Dodd launched an effort to increase the diversity of portraits in the U.S. Capitol so that more women and people of color were represented in the halls of Congress, he and the U.S. Senate Commission on Art asked renowned black artist Simmie Lee Knox to paint Bruce's portrait, which now hangs at the visitors' entrance to the balcony overlooking the U.S. Senate chamber in the Capitol.[11] In working with the Office of the U.S. Senate Curator, Knox painted the portrait in 2001 by using a nineteenth-century Mathew Brady photograph as a model. When the oil portrait was finally unveiled at a September 17, 2002, Senate ceremony where dignitaries and Bruce descendants were invited to attend, only one relative of the deceased senator responded.

"I was the only descendant of the senator's to come to the unveiling," acknowledged Dr. Norma Rozzelle of Kansas City, Missouri. "It was disappointing, but I have long known that some of his other descendants—my other relatives, that is—live as white people. They simply don't want to acknowledge their relation to the first black man elected to a full Senate term, because that would require that they also announce that they are black."[12] Rozzelle, who is the great-great-granddaughter of the senator's brother James, has met and spoken with some of her light-complexioned relatives who pass as white people. But she also understands that family members who look black, like herself, don't necessarily feel the need to embrace the family history.

"I can see how families lose their collective memory or concern over an ancestor's accomplishments. Even though I took my grandson to the unveiling of Senator Bruce's portrait and showed him a dollar bill with the senator's signature on it," said Rozzelle, "it still did not seem very relevant to him. It is difficult for an adolescent to connect with a world that is one hundred years away. Nevertheless, I continue to collect data on my great-great-grandfather's brother. It is a source of pride for both me and the black community."

So, even as individual attempts have been made to keep the senator's history from slipping away from the nation's collective memory, it is more and more apparent that the black upper-class dynasty he and his wife created more than one hundred years ago was one that broke more social, political, economic, and racial barriers than perhaps any other American family.

Timeline

1841   Blanche Bruce is born a slave on March 1, in Prince Edward County, Virginia.

Joseph Willson (Josephine's father and Blanche's father-in-law) becomes famous after publishing controversial book on black elite, *Sketches of the Higher Classes of Colored Society in Philadelphia*.

1842   Joseph Willson becomes one of the first black dentists in Philadelphia and is aided by his wealthy brother-in-law, Frederick Hinton.

1844   Blanche's slave family are moved to Missouri by slave master Pettis Perkinson.

Joseph Willson marries a free black woman, Elizabeth Harnett, in Philadelphia.

1846   Joseph Willson's son (Josephine's brother) Leonidas is born in Philadelphia.

1847   Blanche; his mother, Polly; his brothers Henry, Calvin, and James; and the rest of his slave family are moved back to Virginia.

Joseph Willson's mother dies, leaving him $23,000 and shares of Bank of Augusta.

1849   Blanche's slave family are moved by their owner to Mississippi.

Joseph's rich mentor and brother-in-law, Fredrick Hinton, dies.

1850   Blanche's slave family are moved back to Missouri and hired out from 1850 to 1854.

1852   Josephine's sister Emily is born.

1853   Josephine Beall Willson is born in Philadelphia to Joseph and Elizabeth Willson.

1854   Josephine's sister Mary is born.

1856   Josephine's sister Victoria is born.

1857   Supreme Court decision in the Dred Scott case.

1863   Blanche Bruce becomes free and moves from Missouri to Kansas.

1864   Blanche opens Missouri's first school for black children.

Blanche's brother Henry escapes from his slave master and marries.

1865   General Robert E. Lee surrenders to General Ulysses S. Grant.

President Lincoln is assassinated. Mississippi creates Black Codes, which penalize newly freed blacks.

Reconstruction begins.

1866   Blanche Bruce enters Oberlin College in Ohio.

1867   Congress passes the first of a series of Reconstruction acts.

1868   Blanche's brother, Henry Bruce, opens a grocery store in Kansas.

Bruce's black friend Pinckney B. S. Pinchback becomes the first black delegate to the Republican National Convention, held in Chicago.

Oscar J. Dunn becomes lieutenant governor of Louisiana, the highest office held by a black thus far. Grant is elected president.

Freed blacks vote in national election for the first time.

1869   Blanche moves to Mississippi on a permanent basis in February.

Blanche is named conductor of elections in Tallahatchie County by Governor Adelbert Ames in the spring.

Blanche's white mentor James Alcorn is elected provisional governor of Mississippi.

1870   Blanche is elected sergeant-at-arms for Mississippi state senate.

Blanche is appointed tax assessor of Bolivar County, Mississippi.

Fifteenth Amendment gives black men the right to vote.

One-fourth of Mississippi legislature is black. Mississippi legislature elects Hiram Revels to fill the U.S. Senate seat formerly held by Jefferson Davis.

Congressman Joseph H. Rainey from South Carolina is seated as the first black congressman.

Harvard College graduates its first black student.

1871   Blanche is elected sheriff of Bolivar County, Mississippi.

Blanche is appointed county superintendent of education.

Josephine Willson graduates from Cleveland's Central High School.

1872   Blanche is elected secretary of the Mississippi State Republican Party.

Blanche is named to the State Board of Levee Commisioners.

Bruce's black friend Pinckney B. S. Pinchback is elevated from lieutenant governor to governor of Louisiana after the impeachment of Governor Henry Warmouth.

President Grant is reelected. Blanche's black friend John Lynch is elected to the U.S. House of Representatives.

Blanche buys nine properties in Mississippi and builds his first home.

Josephine Willson's brother, Leonidas, becomes first black lawyer in Ohio.

1873   Blanche is elected to the Board of Aldermen in Floreyville, Mississippi.

Blanche is asked to run for lieutenant governor with Senator Adelbert Ames, who is the Republican nominee for governor.

Blacks engineer the gubernatorial nomination of Senator Adelbert Ames, along with a ticket that includes three black candidates.

Republicans control governments in Mississippi, Arkansas, Louisiana, South Carolina, Tennessee, Georgia, and Virginia.

Josephine Willson becomes first black to teach in Cleveland's schools.

Josephine's brother, Leonidas, marries a white woman in Cleveland.

1874 Blanche is elected to U.S. Senate (first black elected to a full Senate term).
Blanche takes out a bank loan to buy a 600-acre plantation in Mississippi.
Frederick Douglass is elected president of the already failing Freedman's
Bank.

1875 President Grant sends troops to protect Southern blacks from white residents.
Blanche becomes engaged to a young woman in Cleveland, but she dies
months later.

1876 Blanche is introduced to Josephine Willson in Cleveland.
Blanche's brother Henry, is elected regional treasurer of the Masons in
Missouri, Colorado, Nebraska, Iowa, and Minnesota.

1877 Reconstruction ends when President Hayes gets the support of Southern
Democrats in exchange for his promise to give control of the South back
to the Southern states (the Compromise of 1877). Now, whites reinstate
severe laws penalizing blacks.
Rise in Ku Klux Klan activity against blacks.

1878 Blanche Bruce marries Josephine Willson on June 24, in Cleveland.
Blanche's mother and siblings are not invited to the wedding.
Blanche and Josephine visit former president Grant and other dignitaries
in London, Vienna, and Paris during their honeymoon in Europe.
Blanche and Josephine buy town house at 909 M Street NW in Washington.

1879 Blanche is now the only black in Congress.
So many blacks are being lynched that a number of blacks lead an exodus
to Kansas.
Roscoe Conkling Bruce is born to Blanche and Josephine in Washington.
He is named after Senator Roscoe Conkling of New York, who mentored
Blanche.

1880 Blanche is one of six nominees for vice president at Republican National
Convention, but he withdraws his name. Chester Arthur is selected to run.
James Garfield is elected president.
Blanche chairs Senate subcommittee on the failed Freedman's Bank.
Blanche and Josephine become popular hosts for Washington's black and
white liberal society.
KKK and other whites make it impossible for Blanche to run for Senate
again.
Clara Burrill is born in Washington. She will later marry the senator's
son.
Henry Bruce, Blanche's brother, runs for Kansas state legislature.

1881 President Garfield appoints Blanche as register of the U.S. Treasury.

Blanche becomes the first black to have his name printed on U.S. currency.

Blanche leaves the U.S. Senate.

President Garfield is killed, and Chester A. Arthur becomes president.

Henry Bruce is elected doorkeeper of Kansas state senate.

1882 Henry Bruce moves to Washington for a job in the U.S. Pension Office.

1883 Supreme Court decides that the Civil Rights Act of 1875 is unconstitutional.

Blanche and the black abolitionist Frederick Douglass have public dispute when Douglass accuses Blanche of making disparaging remarks about him.

1884 President Arthur names Blanche as U.S. director of Colored Exhibits for the World's Industrial and Cotton Centennial Exposition.

Grover Cleveland is elected president after promising to embrace segregation.

Blanche and Josephine anger blacks when they serve as witnesses at the wedding of Frederick Douglass to a white woman.

1885 Blanche steps down from Treasury Department post in June.

Blanche travels to New Orleans to manage exhibits at World Exposition.

James Bruce, Blanche's brother, is appointed to represent Missouri at the exposition.

1886 Blanche and Josephine move to Indianapolis with Josephine's parents.

Bruce travels around the United States speaking to Republican groups.

Leonidas Willson's first wife dies, leaving him to raise two daughters.

1887 Blanche, Josephine, and their eight-year-old son, Roscoe, remain in Indiana and join a white Episcopal church.

1888 Blanche and Josephine buy second town house, at 2010 R Street, near Dupont Circle in Washington, for $10,350 and move back to Washington.

Benjamin Harrison is elected president.

Mississippi passes law making blacks and whites use separate public facilities.

Leonidas marries a black schoolteacher from Washington.

Republicans regain control of Senate and House.

1889 Blanche begs President Harrison to give him an important post.

Blanche's mother, Polly, dies in Kansas at age eighty-nine.

Leonidas Willson's second wife leaves him, sneaking away with his money and property when he is at work.

1890 Blanche is named recorder of deeds for Washington, DC, by President Harrison.

Blanche joins the Board of Trustees of the Washington, DC, schools.

Mississippi constitution is changed to keep blacks from voting. This plan is also adopted by other Southern states.

1891   Roscoe meets future wife, Clara Burrill, in grammar school in Washington when she is ten years old.

1892   Grover Cleveland, a Democrat, is elected president.

Elections in Southern states are rigged through ballot stuffing, and by the terrorizing or killing of black voters.

1893   Blanche joins board of Howard University and is given an honorary degree.

Josephine becomes active in the Colored Woman's League, which was founded by Helen Appo Cook, Mary Church Terrell, and Charlotte Grimké.

Blanche visits New York and other eastern cities to address Republican voters.

1894   Blanche opens an investment and insurance business in Washington.

Roscoe Bruce begins attending M Street High School.

1895   Blanche's brother Henry publishes his autobiography, *The New Man*.

Josephine's father, Joseph Willson, dies of diabetes in Indianapolis.

Blanche's colleague Frederick Douglass dies in February, making Blanche the nation's most respected black man.

Booker T. Washington becomes famous and outshines Blanche after giving his "Atlanta Compromise" speech, urging blacks to stop asking for equality.

1896   Blanche's son, Roscoe, enters Phillips Exeter Academy in New Hampshire.

Supreme Court case *Plessy v. Ferguson* establishes "separate but equal" doctrine.

Blanche and Josephine found University Park Congregational Church in DC.

Josephine becomes active in the National Association of Colored Women.

Clara Burrill is a senior at M Street High, and is dating Roscoe.

William McKinley is elected president after Blanche campaigns nationally.

1897   President McKinley reappoints Blanche as register of the U.S. Treasury.

Roscoe becomes editor of *The Exonian* at Phillips Exeter and renews friendship with a black classmate there, T. John Syphax. (Six years later, Syphax will end the relationship and will begin passing as white, after attending Trinity College and Columbia University School of Law.)

1898   Blanche dies on March 17 at age fifty-seven, and is buried in Woodlawn Cemetery in Washington.

Roscoe graduates from Phillips Exeter.

Roscoe begins freshman year at Harvard College.

Josephine temporarily moves to Indianapolis to live with her mother and sisters, Victoria and Mary.

1899   Roscoe is profiled in newspapers in Boston for winning debate team medal at Harvard.

Josephine is appointed lady principal of Tuskegee Institute by Booker T. Washington, and she moves to Alabama.

Josephine takes on management of Bruce plantation and other properties in Mississippi while she is working in Alabama.

Clara Burrill graduates from M Street High School in Washington.

1900   Roscoe becomes president of the debate team at Harvard.

Booker T. Washington gains popularity and financial support from wealthy whites who like his autobiography, *Up from Slavery*, and its themes promoting black inferiority.

Booker T. Washington is criticized by W. E. B. DuBois, Monroe Trotter, and other blacks who say that he has undermined the future of black advancement.

Roscoe is hired, while still a student, by Booker T. Washington to "spy on" Washington's black critics in Boston and Cambridge.

1901   Racial violence breaks out in Northern cities as blacks migrate north for jobs.

Roscoe becomes editor in chief of *Harvard Illustrated Magazine*.

Clara Burrill enters Radcliffe; Roscoe is a junior at Harvard. They continue dating, although he shows interest in girls from richer black families.

Josephine's brother, Leonidas, leaves his law firm and dies in Cleveland.

1902   Roscoe graduates from Harvard Phi Beta Kappa, with a degree in political economy and philosophy. He is chosen as class orator and is still working part time as an informer for Booker T. Washington.

Roscoe is unable to attract employers because of their "whites-only" policies.

Booker T. Washington asks Roscoe to move to Alabama, and hires him as director of the Academic Department at Tuskegee Institute.

Blanche's brother, Henry C. Bruce, dies.

Josephine resigns as lady principal at Tuskegee Institute.

Clara Burrill enters junior year at Radcliffe College and still dates Roscoe.

1903   Josephine moves to Mississippi to manage her plantation and other properties.

Roscoe is working at Tuskegee Institute in Alabama.

Clara Burrill is majoring in economics at Radcliffe; she reluctantly leaves before earning her degree because Roscoe insists that they get married then.

Roscoe and Clara marry in Washington and move into a house at Tuskegee.

1904   Roscoe and Clara's daughter Clara Jr. is born in Tuskegee.

1905   Josephine remains in Mississippi, but plans to buy new house in Washington.

Roscoe upsets Booker T. Washington by asking to leave Tuskegee.

1906 Josephine wants to run for president of National Association of Colored Women but is not supported, because the other women say she looks too white.

Roscoe and Clara's second child, Roscoe Jr., is born on May 16.

Josephine moves to Washington and buys new home at 1327 Columbia Road.

Roscoe Sr. moves his wife and two children to Washington when he is appointed principal of Armstrong Manual Training High School.

1907 Roscoe Sr. is named superintendent of the Colored Schools in Washington. He follows Booker T. Washington's philosophy and emphasizes industrial training rather than academics at some of the schools.

Josephine's mother, Elizabeth Willson, dies in Indianapolis.

Roscoe Sr. and Clara Sr. become an important couple in Washington's black elite community.

1908 A mysterious fire destroys two major buildings at the Bruce plantation.

1909 Roscoe Sr. and Clara Sr.'s third child, Burrill, is born on September 19.

Roscoe Sr. gives a speech at Howard University that insults the faculty and questions their standards.

1911 Roscoe Sr. joins the elite national black men's fraternity Sigma Pi Phi Boulé.

1912 Roscoe Sr. buys new Cadillac and entertains extravagantly with his mother's money and his own salary.

1913 Josephine faces problems from her plantation workers and tenants, who are defaulting on their rents in Mississippi.

1914 Roscoe Sr. dismisses a popular black principal and is accused by black residents and the *Washington Bee* of favoring teachers from certain families. Black parents in Washington organize, and ask school board to fire Roscoe.

1915 Roscoe Sr. named by blacks as "the most despised man in the city."

Roscoe's mentor, Booker T. Washington, dies in November.

Clara Sr. develops an interest in politics and World War I issues.

1916 Although not liked by the black masses in Washington, Roscoe Sr. remains popular among white leaders in education and in Washington political affairs.

Clara Sr. begins to support liberal issues by writing political essays.

1917 The newspaper *Washington Bee* continues to criticize Roscoe Sr. in his role as superintendent of the Colored Schools of Washington.

1918 Clara Sr. publishes a controversial poem about race, "We Who Are Dark," in a liberal political magazine, *The Public*.

Clara Jr. enters Dunbar High School (which was known as M Street High when Roscoe Sr. and Clara Sr. attended it in the 1890s).

1919 Roscoe Sr. is at the center of a court proceeding and sex scandal in the

Colored Schools after it is revealed that he allowed a phony white sociologist to take nude photos of young female students.

1920 White school board members agree with the black community and withdraw their support of Roscoe Sr.

1921 Roscoe Sr. is forced to resign his position as head of the Colored Schools. After being refused jobs elsewhere, he is forced to leave Washington and accepts a job as principal of a black school in Kendall, West Virginia.

Clara Sr. and the three children move into Josephine's summer home, Kelso Farm, in Maryland.

Clara Jr. enters Howard University, but plans to transfer to Radcliffe College.

1922 Roscoe Sr. has serious money problems.

Roscoe Jr. enters Phillips Exeter Academy in New Hampshire.

After Clara Jr. applies to Radcliffe, Roscoe Sr. asks president of Radcliffe if his daughter would be allowed to live in the dormitories, but the request is denied. (Black women will not be permitted to live in Radcliffe dorms until 1926.)

Planning for his son's future at college, Roscoe Sr. asks Harvard's president if black men are allowed to live in the freshmen's dormitories, but is told that Harvard no longer allows blacks to live in Harvard Yard as they did when Roscoe Sr. had attended thirty years earlier.

Josephine, Clara Sr., and Clara and Roscoe Sr.'s son Burrill move to West Virginia to join Roscoe Sr.

Clara Jr. secretly marries Barrington Guy in Maryland. Roscoe tries to get the marriage annulled because Barrington's family is not elite, and because Radcliffe will not accept married students.

Roscoe Sr. is accepted at University of Chicago Law School but doesn't go.

1923 Josephine dies in February while staying with Roscoe in West Virginia.

Clara Sr. takes the children and moves to Cambridge, leaving Roscoe in West Virginia.

Clara Jr. enters Radcliffe and is not permitted to live in dorms with whites.

Clara Sr. enters Boston University Law School.

Burrill enters public grammar school in Cambridge.

Roscoe Sr. has public battle with Harvard's president over the school's new rules for segregating black freshmen. It becomes a national debate in the press and involves Franklin D. Roosevelt and W. E. B. DuBois, who help Roscoe.

Late in the year, Roscoe quits job as principal and moves alone to Kelso Farm.

1924 Roscoe Sr. starts a chicken-and-egg farming business in Maryland at Kelso Farm.

Clara Sr. remains in Boston with her three children and continues at law school.

1925 Roscoe Sr. moves to an apartment on the Upper West Side in New York City, and begins a job as editor of *Who's Who Among Colored Americans*.

Clara Sr. is named editor of the *Law Review* at Boston University Law School; she is the first black in the country to become a law review editor.

Clara Jr. is a sophomore at Radcliffe College.

Roscoe Jr. is at Phillips Exeter. Burrill is at Cambridge Latin School.

Roscoe Sr. begins friendship and love affair in New York with Harriet Shadd Butcher of the Russell Sage Foundation while his wife, Clara Sr., is in Boston.

1926 Clara Sr. graduates from Boston University Law School.

Roscoe Jr. enters Harvard College with five other black students.

Roscoe Sr. asks Harriet Butcher to help his daughter get scholarship money at Radcliffe and to help him get a job working for John D. Rockefeller Jr.

Clara Jr. is told by Radcliffe that her grades must improve.

Clara Sr. is seriously injured in an elevator accident at Shepard's department store in Boston.

1927 Clara Sr. and Burrill move to New York City to live with Roscoe Sr.

Roscoe Sr. and Clara Sr. are hired by John D. Rockefeller Jr. to manage Rockefeller's new Dunbar Apartments in Harlem and select the tenants.

Clara Jr. is a junior at Radcliffe.

Roscoe Jr. is a sophomore at Harvard.

1928 Clara Jr. leaves Radcliffe in February 1928 and joins her husband, Barrington Guy. Until now, she has concealed her marriage from the school.

Clara Jr. and Barrington move to New York.

Roscoe Jr. leaves Harvard and moves to New York City.

Harriet Shadd Butcher asks Roscoe Sr. to divorce Clara Sr.

1929 Clara Sr. volunteers with the New York League of Women Voters.

John Rockefeller puts Roscoe on the board of directors of the Dunbar Bank.

Josephine Bruce's sister (Roscoe's aunt) Mary dies.

Roscoe Sr. is sued by Harriet Butcher and accused of owing her $4,000. He loses the widely publicized case and is forced to pay her $3,000.

New York newspapers report that Clara Sr. has asked for a divorce because of the Harriet Butcher affair. Clara Sr. later denies the news reports.

Clara Jr. and Barrington Guy become parents of a son, Barringotn Guy Jr.

1930 Burrill enters New York University.

Roscoe Jr. enters City College of New York.

Roscoe Sr. steps down from the board of Dunbar Bank because he has to sell his bank stock in order to raise money for Harriet Butcher's suit.

1931 Clara Jr.'s husband, Barrington, has a successful career in New York on the stage and in black nightclubs. He is hired to appear in two feature films.

Clara Sr. edits the monthly *Dunbar News* and continues to write essays and poems on liberal topics.

1932 Clara Jr.'s husband, Barrington, stars in the movie *Veiled Aristocrats*, about a wealthy young black woman who decides to pass for white in order to marry a rich white man.

1933 *The Saturday Evening Post* publishes Clara's poem "What Would I Be?"

Roscoe Jr. graduates from City College of New York.

1934 Clara Jr. works with parents at Dunbar Apartments and has a second son, Bruce.

Burrill graduates from New York University in May.

Burrill enters Harvard Law School in September.

1935 Harlem race riots start in March.

Roscoe Jr. marries Bessie Humbles, whose family funded Virginia Seminary.

Roscoe Jr. is hired by Prudential Insurance Company to manage the Harrison Apartments in Newark, New Jersey.

1936 Rockefeller decides to sell the Dunbar Apartments and fires the Bruces.

Burrill Bruce finishes his second year at Harvard Law School and leaves without graduating because the family cannot afford the tuition.

Josephine's sister Victoria dies in Indianapolis.

1937 Roscoe Jr. mismanages money at Harrison apartments. To hide his losses, he stages a fake holdup. He is found guilty in a widely publicized trial and is sentenced to prison on November 20.

1938 Clara Sr. is nominated for the New York state assembly in the Nineteenth Assembly District.

Roscoe Sr. and Burrill open Bruce Realty in Harlem.

1939 Roscoe Sr. and Clara Sr. apply for public assistance from the New York City Department of Welfare.

Burrill is sued in court and accused of illegally taking a client's money.

Clara Jr.'s husband, Barrington Guy, is struggling as a performer in black theaters and nightclubs.

1940 Roscoe Jr. leaves prison, moves to Paris, and enters the Sorbonne.

1941 Clara Jr.'s husband changes his name to Barrington Sharma and alters his racial identity so that he can gain roles in nonblack theater. The *New York Post* and other newspapers now profile him as being part white and part Indian.

Roscoe Jr. marries Jacqueline Moison.

1942 Roscoe Jr. and Jacqueline become parents of a daughter.

1943 Roscoe Sr. and Clara Sr. get jobs working in New York City at a dry-cleaning business.

1944   Roscoe Jr. and Jacqueline have a second child.

1946   Roscoe Sr. sends a proposal for a dry-cleaning business to Rockefeller.

1948   Roscoe Sr.'s black childhood friend T. John Syphax tries to claim a $4 million family inheritance. To claim it, he must publicly admit that he is actually black but has been passing as white since 1904. He dies before he is able to get the money.

Roscoe Sr. and Clara Sr. are living in Greenwich Village, and Roscoe Jr. is living in the Bronx with his wife and two children.

1949   Clara Bruce Sr. dies of diabetes in New York City.

1950   Roscoe Bruce Sr. dies in New York City on August 16.

1966   Edward Brooke becomes the next black U.S. senator after Blanche Bruce.

2002   U.S. Senate unveils Senator Blanche Bruce's portrait in the Capitol. Bruce family descendants are invited to the ceremony, but only one relative attends.

Notes

CHAPTER ONE

1. John W. Menard of Louisiana was elected to the U.S. House of Representatives but was never permitted to be seated, because although the congressional Committee on Elections agreed that he was fairly elected, they felt it was too soon after the Civil War to allow a black to take a place in the House. The first black man actually permitted to take his seat after being elected to Congress was Joseph H. Rainey of South Carolina, who was seated in 1871.
2. *Jackson Times*, June 8, 1875.
3. *Hinds County Gazette*, March 31, 1875.
4. *Congressional Record*, Forty-fourth Congress, special session (1875), p. 1.
5. *National Republican*, March 6, 1875.
6. June 25, 1878, issues of *New York Times* and *Washington Post*.

CHAPTER TWO

1. Identified on the Certificate of Death for Blanche K. Bruce, March 17, 1898, Health Department of the District of Columbia, Record No. 118058. When Bruce was born in 1841, the State of Virginia did not issue birth certificates for enslaved blacks.
2. After losing that case, Prince Edward County gained national prominence when it closed all of its public schools for four years as a protest against the mandate of allowing blacks into all-white schools.
3. Henry Clay Bruce, *The New Man: Twenty-nine Years a Slave and Twenty-nine Years a Free Man* (York, Pennsylvania: P. Anstadt & Sons, 1895), p. [15].
4. Interview with Dr. Norma Rozzelle, April 11, 2003, Kansas City, Missouri. Dr. Rozelle is the great-great-granddaughter of Polly Bruce's son James, and maintains several records from the Bruce family, including family member information written into the Bruce family Bible dating back to the early 1800s.

5. Interview with Dr. Norma Rozzelle, April 11, 2003, and notes from her conversations with white Bruce relatives residing in Howard County, Missouri.

6. The secretary of the senate George Gorham actually wrote the name "Bruce, Branch K." in the handwritten official U.S. Senate financial ledgers of 1875. It is written again in the Senate ledgers a year later, in 1876, but then corrected in pen. The name was never used in any other public records or documented speeches.

7. Obituary, *Kansas City Star*, unspecified 1889 clipping.

8. Arna Bontemps, *Free at Last: The Life of Frederick Douglass* (New York: Dodd, Mead, 1971), p. 275. Though Douglass's first wife was black, his second wife, Helen Pitts, was white.

9. U.S. Supreme Court majority opinion, *United States v. Cinque*, 1841.

10. Henry Clay Bruce, *The New Man*, p. iv.

11. Ibid., p. 16.

12. Ibid., pp. 20, 21.

13. Ibid., p. 22.

14. Ibid., p. 23.

15. Ibid., p. 25.

16. Ibid., pp. 26–27.

17. As Henry C. Bruce revealed in his 1895 autobiography, *The New Man*, he and Blanche saw their uncle Walt and aunt Martha sold to another owner when their uncle became ill while Pettis Perkinson was bringing his slaves from Virginia to Missouri in 1847.

18. Ibid., p. 61.

19. Ibid., pp. 105–106. In his autobiography, Henry tells of conversations that he and his brother had with Willie Perkinson on the "subject of loyalty" as it pertained to the Union and Confederate armies. After fighting for the Confederacy, Willie was to return to Missouri in 1863 and "find his father dead, his Negroes freed, and stock stolen." Willie would later become a local judge in Brunswick and be known as Judge W. E. Perkinson.

CHAPTER THREE

1. Joseph Willson, *Sketches of the Higher Classes Among the Colored Society in Philadelphia* (Philadelphia: Merrihew and Thompson, 1841).

2. Introduction to 1980 edition of Joseph Willson's *Sketches of the Higher Classes Among the Colored Society in Philadelphia*.

3. James Forten (1766–1842) was among the blacks who founded Saint Thomas Church in Philadelphia in 1794. Forten, who had served in the American Revolution while still a teenager, was also in the real estate spec-

ulation business and was worth more than $100,000 by 1830 (which would be worth in excess of $1.75 million in today's dollars. In addition to being a founder and active leader of the elite Saint Thomas Church, he used a considerable amount of his money to fund efforts to end slavery. He and his wife, Charlotte, sent their children to private schools in Philadelphia. In 1856, their granddaughter, Charlotte Forten Jr., a college graduate, became the first black woman to teach in a white Massachusetts school.

4. Charles M. Christian, *Black Saga* (Washington, DC: Civitas Publishers, 1999), p. 125.
5. *Colored American* September 25, 1841, p. 1.
6. The families of James Prosser and John McKee were early black residents of Philadelphia and were considered leaders of black society while the Willsons lived there. Prosser and McKee owned successful catering businesses, and McKee was worth in excess of $1 million when he died in 1902.

CHAPTER FOUR

1. Blanche K. Bruce, "Washington Letter," *Kansas City Times*, October 17, 1886.
2. Henry Clay Bruce, *The New Man*, p. 31.
3. Ibid., p. 6.
4. Bruce family descendant Dr. Norma Rozzelle believes that Blanche was freed by his white father, Pettis, and never actually had to "escape slavery," while his older brothers, who were, in fact, half-brothers, not fathered by Pettis, were not set free.
5. Blanche K. Bruce, "Washington Letter."
6. Ibid.
7. George Cornelius Smith, "The Man Revealed," *Freeman*, June 27, 1891.
8. Ibid.
9. James Alcorn's inaugural address as governor was given March 10, 1870.
10. *Journal of the Senate of the State of Mississippi*, 1870, p. 24.

CHAPTER FIVE

1. Bureau of the U.S. Census, 1870.
2. *Journal of the Senate of the State of Mississippi*, 1870.
3. *Jackson Weekly Pilot* (Jackson, Mississippi, newspaper), January 22, 1870.
4. This method of electing U.S. senators remained in place until the passage of the Thirteenth Amendment to the Constitution in 1913. After that time, U.S. senators were no longer selected by state legislatures but by the general state population through popular vote.
5. *Natchez Weekly Democrat*, March 10, 1870.

6. Blanche K. Bruce, "Washington Letter."
7. *Annual Report of the Auditor of Public Accounts of Mississippi*, 1872.
8. Wright, who was born in 1840, was elected associate justice in 1870 to a six-year term. Cardozo, who was born in 1837, was elected secretary of state from 1868 to 1872, and later served as treasurer of the state of South Carolina. Ranzier, who was born in Charleston in 1834, was elected lieutenant governor in 1870 and served until 1872. He was then elected to Congress in 1872, for one term.
9. *Jackson Weekly Pilot*, January 29, 1870.
10. Bolivar County Land Records, Bolivar County, Mississippi, county deed books.
11. *Jackson Clarion*, June 19, 1873.
12. The *American Annual Cyclopaedia 1873* reported that the vote was 74,307 for Ames and 52,904 for Alcorn.
13. *Biographical Directory of the U.S. Congress*, 2003.
14. *Mobile Daily Register*, Mobile, Alabama, February 5, 1874.
15. *New York Herald*, March 13, 1876. This newspaper report, which was published more than two years after Bruce's election, suggested that Bruce had purchased state auditor warrants from thirty-three legislators for as much as $170 and for as little as $21, in order to earn their vote for his U.S. Senate candidacy.
16. On December 4, 1874, Mississippi saw one of its largest race riots take place in Vicksburg, when dozens of black residents were killed by the Ku Klux Klan and local white Democrats, who were trying to force the resignation of a black Mississippi sheriff named Peter Crosby. This riot was to shape race relations between blacks and whites in the state for the next several years.

CHAPTER SIX

1. *The Vicksburg Times*, February 15, 1874.
2. *Jackson Weekly Clarion*, February 5, 1874.
3. Most of the prominent black newspapers of the nineteenth and twentieth centuries began after Reconstruction ended, as a result of increased hostility and discrimination against blacks. Among them were the *Washington Bee* (founded in 1882), the *Philadelphia Tribune* (founded in 1885), and *Houston Informer* (founded in 1892).
4. *New York Times Index*, 1874–1875.
5. *New York Times*, June 23, June 25, and December 7, 1878.
6. Born in 1839, Menard was the first black elected to Congress. He later served as inspector of customs for New Orleans. Although he was refused

his congressional seat because of race, he was given his full salary. Walls had won his U.S. House election in November 1872, but the seat was taken away in January 1873. Although Pinchback would eventually serve as both lieutenant governor and governor of Louisiana, he would win both his 1872 U.S. House of Representatives race and his 1873 U.S. Senate race and be refused both seats in Washington.

7. On September 6, 1869, black politician Henry Turner gave a famous speech to the Georgia legislature after that body had refused to seat him and twenty-seven other black legislators who had recently been elected.

8. *Constitution of the United States*, Article I, Section 5.

9. *Constitution of the United States*, Fourteenth Amendment, Section 1.

10. *Congressional Record*, Forty-third Congress, first session (1874).

11. Although Grant sent General Philip Sheridan and the Seventh Cavalry to Louisiana, it was not until January 1875 — months after the ongoing murders by white Democrats of black and Republican officials—that General Sheridan took control of the Louisiana statehouse from the gun-wielding white Democrats.

12. *Congressional Record*, Forty-third Congress, second session (1874), p. 228.

13. *Natchez Democrat*, December 2, 1874.

14. *New York Times*, December 19, 1874.

15. *Natchez Democrat*, November 10, 1874.

16. James S. Pike, *The Prostrate State* (New York, 1874).

17. *Nation*, April 16, 1874.

18. *Congressional Globe*, Forty-first Congress, second session, pp. 1509–10.

19. The special session of the Senate for the Forty-fourth Congress was called by President Grant's executive proclamation. Its term was March 5–24, 1875. The first session of the Forty-fourth Congress was December 6, 1875–August 15, 1876. The second session of the Forty-fourth Congress was December 4, 1876–March 3, 1877. Before 1933, when the Twentieth Amendment to the Constitution was added, Congress was required to begin its regular sessions on the first Monday of each December. This would inevitably lead to a short second session.

20. *Congressional Record*, Forty-fourth Congress, special session (1875), pp. 2–4.

21. *Congressional Record*, Forty-fifth Congress, first session (1877), p. 12. Senate Committee Report excerpts.

22. M. W. Randolph to Blanche K. Bruce, April 10, 1875, Blanche K. Bruce Papers, Moorland-Spingarn Research Center, Howard University, Washington, DC.

23. *Congressional Record*, Forty-fourth Congress, first session (1876), pp. 2100–2101.

24. Ibid., p. 2101.

25. Ibid.

26. Ibid., pp. 2104–2105.

27. *Congressional Record*, Forty-fifth Congress, first session, (1877), p. 12.

28. Ibid., p. 13.

29. Ibid.

30. Ibid., p. 15.

31. Robert Lynch to Blanche K. Bruce, September 21, 1877, Blanche K. Bruce Papers.

CHAPTER SEVEN

1. Multiple newspaper clippings dated June 25, 1898, Sen. Blanche Kelso Bruce Papers, Library of Congress, Washington, DC.

2. Joseph Willson, *Sketches of the Higher Classes of Colored Society in Philadelphia* (Philadelphia: Merrihew and Thompson, 1841).

3. Ibid., chapter 4.

4. Blanche used the term "babies" when referring to Josephine's two younger sisters, Mary and Victoria, who had just begun teaching in a grammar school in Indianapolis, Indiana.

5. Blanche K. Bruce to Josephine B. Willson, December 5, 1877, Blanche K. Bruce Papers, Moorland-Spingarn Research Center, Howard University, Washington, DC.

6. Ibid.

7. John Roy Lynch to Blanche K. Bruce, September 21, 1877, Blanche K. Bruce Papers.

8. "Senators Bruce and Bogy," *Washington Post*, October 24, 1886.

9. John Roy Lynch to Blanche K. Bruce, October 27, 1877, Blanche K. Bruce Papers. Certain passages and remarks here are drawn from this and other letters written between Lynch and Bruce during this time.

10. *Washington Post*, February 27, 1877. Wormley Hotel, a Washington hotel owned by the wealthy black James T. Wormley family.

11. H. C. Bruce to Blanche K. Bruce, November 14, 1876, Blanche K. Bruce Papers.

12. Saks and Company was the original name of the New York–based Saks Fifth Avenue department store. This is one of two canceled checks made payable to Saks during the months prior to Bruce's wedding. The canceled checks are contained in the Blanche K. Bruce Papers.

13. Guest names and their respective wedding gifts are identified in numerous June 1878 newspaper articles published in Washington. Blanche Kelso Bruce Papers, Library of Congress, Washington, DC.

14. "The Wedding," *Cleveland Gazette*, June 26, 1878.

CHAPTER EIGHT

1. "The Capital Social Problem," *Baltimore American*, February 2, 1879.
2. "The Exodus to Europe," *New York Graphic*, June 28, 1878.
3. "Ought We to Visit Her: Society Agitation About the Beautiful Mrs. Bruce," *New York Graphic*, November 20, 1878.
4. "Snobbery," *Central Wisconsin Newspaper*, February 25, 1879.
5. Langston would later be elected to the U.S. House of Representatives from Virginia in 1888.
6. J. J. Bruce to Blanche Kelso Bruce, December 16, 1878, Blanche K. Bruce Papers, Moorland-Spingarn Research Center, Howard University, Washington, DC.
7. Calvin Bruce to Blanche Kelso Bruce, December 18, 1878, Blanche K. Bruce Papers.
8. *Congressional Record*, Forty-fifth Congress, third session (1878), pp. 3–4.
9. *Jackson Weekly Clarion*, January 18, 1878.
10. *Boston Journal*, January 1, 1879. The M Street house was previously owned by former congressman Columbus Delano, who served as U.S. secretary of the interior under President Ulysses S. Grant.
11. *Cincinnati Commercial*, February 19, 1878.

CHAPTER NINE

1. *Congressional Record*, Forty-sixth Congress, first session, Senate seating chart (1879).
2. Ibid., Forty-fifth Congress, second session (1878), p. 1544.
3. Ibid., third session (1879), p. 1314.
4. George F. Hoar, *Autobiography of Seventy Years* (New York: Scribner's Sons, 1903).
5. "Blanche Kelso Bruce: U.S. Senator without a Constituency," *Journal of Mississippi History*, May 1976, p. 183, citation of February 16, 1879, Detroit *Plaindealer*.
6. *Congressional Record*, Forty-sixth Congress, first session (1879), p. 2206.
7. Ibid., second session (1880), pp. 1041–42.
8. Ibid., p. 2248.
9. Ibid, p. 2249.
10. Ibid.
11. "Roscoe Conkling Bruce," *Washington Post*, May 22, 1879.
12. "Naming Senator Bruce's Baby," *Washington Republican*, May 22, 1879.
13. *Boston Advertiser*, society page, May 22, 1879.
14. *U.S. Senate Report*, No. 440, Forty-sixth Congress, second session, April 2, 1880.

CHAPTER TEN

1. George Hoar was on Harvard's board of overseers while he was in the Senate with Blanche Bruce, and was again on the board when Roscoe applied in 1896. Sherman Hoar was a trustee of Phillips Exeter Academy. Senator George Boutwell, another Massachusetts senator who befriended Blanche Bruce, was also on Harvard's board of overseers.

2. Roscoe C. Bruce to Richard Cobb, Esq., April 26, 1898, Harvard College Student File of Roscoe C. Bruce, Harvard University Archives, Harvard University Library. In this letter to Harvard administrator Richard Cobb, Roscoe mentions that Senator Hoar has written to Harvard President Charles Eliot on his behalf.

3. *Congressional Record*, Forty-sixth Congress, third session (1881), p. 1397.

4. Ibid., second session (1880), p. 2195.

5. *Jackson Weekly Clarion*, January 27, 1881.

6. *Proceedings of the 1880 Republican National Convention*, June 2–8, 1880.

7. *Jackson Weekly Clarion*, January 27, 1881.

8. In 1965, Dr. Robert C. Weaver was named secretary of housing and urban development by President Lyndon Johnson.

9. *Congressional Record*, Forty-sixth Congress, third session (1881), p. 1397.

10. Ibid., p. 2375.

11. *People's Advocate*, June 18, 1881.

12. Frederick Douglass to Blanche K. Bruce, August 28, 1883, Frederick Douglass Collection, Schomburg Library, New York Public Library.

13. *Proceedings of Republican National Convention*, Chicago, Illinois, June 3–6, 1884.

14. *New York Times*, November 23, 1884.

15. Personal date book of Blanche Kelso Bruce, 1885, Blanche K. Bruce Papers, Moorland-Spingarn Research Center, Howard University, Washington, DC.

16. "The New Orleans Exposition," *Washington Bee*, February 21, 1885.

17. Ibid., January 31, 1885.

18. P. W. Ray to Blanche K. Bruce, January 9, 1885, Blanche K. Bruce Papers.

19. *Times-Democrat*, December 15, 1884.

20. Blanche K. Bruce to Josephine B. Bruce, September 25, 1885, Blanche K. Bruce Papers.

21. Josephine's third sister, Emily Harang, had evidently moved to New Orleans, and then, for some time, to Mississippi, where her husband managed the workers and business affairs on Josephine and Blanche's plantation.

22. A review of all correspondence written by Josephine Bruce or to Josephine Bruce from the time of her marriage in 1878 until her death in 1923.

23. "Colored Brother: Ex-Senator Bruce Outlines His Present Greatest Need," *Philadelphia Times*, February 29, 1887.

CHAPTER ELEVEN

1. Joseph Willson to Josephine B. Bruce, August 28, 1889, Blanche K. Bruce Papers, Moorland-Spingarn Research Center, Howard University, Washington, DC.
2. Correspondence written by, or to, Josephine B. Willson between 1878 and 1923, Blanche K. Bruce Papers and Roscoe C. Bruce Papers, Moorland-Spingarn Research Center.
3. Henry C. Bruce, *The New Man: Twenty-nine Years a Slave, Twenty-nine Years a Free Man* (York, Pennsylvania: P. Anstadt & Sons, 1895), p. 157.
4. *New York Age*, July 6, 1889.
5. Ibid., October 12, 1889.
6. William Monroe Trotter, along with George Forbes, founded *Boston Guardian* in 1901.
7. *New York Times*, January 30, 1890.
8. *Washington Bee*, February 27, 1892.
9. Ibid., February 1, 1890.
10. "Mississippi Politics," *Washington Bee*, February 27, 1892.
11. *Boston Herald*, January 28, 1893. At Lamar's death, Bruce was interviewed by several newspapers around the nation that asked him to offer his impression of the deceased senator.
12. By the Fifty-third Congress, George W. Murray of South Carolina was the only black man serving in the U.S. House of Representatives.

CHAPTER TWELVE

1. Blanche K. Bruce to Justice John Marshall Harlan, May 1896, Blanche K. Bruce Papers, Moorland-Spingarn Research Center, Howard University, Washington, DC.
2. Y. A. Tufts to Blanche K. Bruce, August 14, 1896, Blanche K. Bruce Papers. Tufts was the secretary of Phillips Exeter Academy.
3. Catalog of the Phillips Exeter Academy, 1897–98, p. 18.
4. Blanche K. Bruce to Roscoe C. Bruce, October 9, 1897, Blanche K. Bruce Papers.
5. Roscoe C. Bruce to Blanche K. Bruce, April 30, 1897, Blanche K. Bruce Papers.
6. Harlen P. Amen was the principal of Exeter, and Dr. James A. Tufts secretary of the board of trustees.
7. Blanche K. Bruce to Josephine Beal Willson Bruce, October 19, 1896, Blanche K. Bruce Papers.
8. Alumni files of Phillips Exeter Academy, academy library.
9. Interview with Eduoard L. Desrochers, archivist of Phillips Exeter Academy, Exeter, New Hampshire, August 9, 2002.
10. Joseph Willson, *Sketches of the Higher Classes of Colored Society in Philadelphia* (Philadelphia: Merrihew and Thompson Publishers, 1841).

11. Multiple newspaper clippings dated June 25, 1878, Sen. Blanche Kelso Bruce Papers, Library of Congress, Washington, DC.

12. Roscoe C. Bruce to Clara Burrill, November 25, 1902, Roscoe C. Bruce Papers, Moorland-Spingarn Research Center, Howard University, Washington, DC.

13. Roscoe C. Bruce to Clara Burrill, January 1902, Roscoe C. Bruce Papers. One of several letters where he makes the statement. (Specific date in January 1902 is not indicated on original letter.)

14. Roscoe C. Bruce to Josephine Bruce, January 1897, Roscoe C. Bruce Papers. (Specific date in January 1897 is not indicated on original letter.)

15. Roscoe C. Bruce to Blanche K. Bruce, January 1897, Roscoe C. Bruce Papers.

16. Acknowledged by a congressional bill in 1866, the Syphax family had inherited land through their family ties to Martha Washington's grandson, George Washington Parke Custis. George's daughter, Maria Custis, married Charles Syphax and was left fifteen acres of land in Arlington, Virginia. The Syphax family members, several of whom later entered the contracting and real estate businesses, eventually gave up the land in the 1940s for the benefit of the Arlington cemetery.

17. *Indianapolis Freeman*, Indianapolis, Indiana, June 15, 1895. In 1895, this black weekly newspaper had ranked Blanche Bruce second to John Cook, a Washington entrepreneur and city tax collector, but over the next two years, through additional acquisitions of land and the success of his claims business, Bruce surpassed Cook as well as the Wormley family, who owned a popular Washington hotel.

18. Trinity College student file of Theophilus John Minton Syphax, class of 1903, Trinity College archives, Hartford, Connecticut.

19. Roscoe C. Bruce to Blanche K. Bruce, several letters from October 1896 to January 1898, Roscoe C. Bruce Papers.

20. Roscoe C. Bruce to Clara W. Burrill, October 20, 1896, Roscoe C. Bruce Papers.

21. Roscoe C. Bruce to Josephine B. Bruce, January 1897, Roscoe C. Bruce Papers.

22. Roscoe C. Bruce to Clara W. Burrill, fall 1896, Roscoe C. Bruce Papers. This letter is undated, but its content suggests its approximate date.

23. Blanche K. Bruce to Josephine B. Bruce, October 21, 1896.

24. The first black sororities, Alpha Kappa Alpha and Delta Sigma Theta, were founded in Washington, but not until 1908 and 1913, respectively.

25. "Tidal Wave Toward Bruce," *Indianapolis Freeman*, July 3, 1897.

26. Blanche K. Bruce to Booker T. Washington, April 15, 1897, Blanche K. Bruce Papers.

27. R. B. Wilcox to Lyman Gage, June 23, 1897. Wilcox was secretary of the McKinley and Hobart Republican Club in Albany, New York.

28. President William McKinley was to appoint Blanche Bruce to the position of register of the U.S. Treasury in November 1897, after being pressured by the liberal wing of the Republican Party.
29. Roscoe C. Bruce to Blanche K. Bruce, January 1897, Blanche K. Bruce Papers.
30. Blanche K. Bruce to Josephine B. Bruce, December 1897, Blanche K. Bruce Papers.
31. Ibid. Letter is undated, but content indicates that it was written on the day Bruce was sworn in as register of the Treasury. It was written on his office's official stationery.
32. Robert H. Terrell, "B. K. Bruce Register: The Great Secret of His Successful Career," *New York Age*, December 9, 1897.
33. According to state and county land records, Blanche Bruce owned more than 1,200 acres of land in Mississippi by 1880. Most of this was plantation acreage, and it was increased during the next ten years. Various nonplantation property deeds relating to land in Floreyville, Mississippi (now known as Rosedale), were also reviewed. While serving as tax assessor of Bolivar County in 1871–74, he was also paid a percentage of any taxes collected.
34. Blanche K. Bruce appointments diary (various years between 1880 and 1890), Blanche K. Bruce Papers.
35. "Blanche K. Bruce Seriously Ill," *New York Times*, March 13, 1898.
36. Josephine B. Bruce to Booker T. Washington, March 15, 1898, Booker T. Washington Papers, Library of Congress, Washington, D.C.

CHAPTER THIRTEEN

1. Rockwood Hoar, an 1876 graduate of Harvard, served as a Republican congressman from Massachusetts. Sherman Hoar, an 1882 graduate of Harvard and an alumnus of Phillips Exeter, served as a Democratic congressman from Massachusetts.
2. Catalog of the Phillips Exeter Academy, 1897–98, page 19, Phillips Exeter Academy library archives.
3. Booker T. Washington to Richard Coff, Esq., April 25, 1898, Roscoe C. Bruce Harvard College student file, Harvard University archives.
4. Harlen P. Amen to Dean Briggs, April 25, 1898, Roscoe C. Bruce Harvard College student file.
5. Roscoe C. Bruce to Blanche K. Bruce, April 30, 1897, Roscoe C. Bruce Papers, Moorland-Spingarn Research Center, Howard University, Washington, DC.
6. Blanche K. Bruce to Josephine Beal Willson Bruce, October 19, 1896, Blanche K. Bruce Papers, Moorland-Spingarn Research Center, Howard University, Washington, DC.

7. Alumni files of Phillips Exeter Academy, academy library.

8. "A Calamity to the Race," *Washington Post*, March 1898. Reprinted in *Indianapolis Freeman*, March 26, 1898.

9. "B. K. Bruce in Indianapolis," *Indianapolis News*, March 1898. Reprinted in *Indianapolis Freeman*, March 26, 1898.

10. Bruce Grit, "The Character of Bruce," *Colored American*, March 26, 1898.

11. John T. Bethell, *Harvard Observed* (Cambridge, Massachusetts: Harvard University Press, 1998), p. 13.

12. Samuel Eliot Morison, *The Development of Harvard University* (Cambridge, Massachusetts: Harvard University Press, 1930).

13. *Annual Report of the President and Treasurer of Harvard College, 1898–1899*, Radcliffe College (Cambridge, Massachusetts: Harvard Board of Overseers), p. 290.

14. Ibid., Harvard College.

15. Ibid., p. 107.

16. After 1899, virtually every freshman class at Harvard had a black student, but in some of these instances, the students were fair-complexioned and chose to pass for white.

17. Alberta Scott was the first black graduate of Radcliffe College. Radcliffe opened in 1879.

18. Samuel Eliot Morison, *The Development of Harvard University*.

19. Charles W. Eliot to Charles Francis Adams [1900]. Adams served on the board of overseers.

20. Student file of Roscoe C. Bruce, class of 1902, Harvard University archives. Terrell was later appointed the first black municipal judge in Washington, DC.

21. Charles A. Wagner, *Harvard: Four Centuries and Freedoms* (New York: E. P. Dutton, 1950), p. 37.

22. Roscoe C. Bruce to Richard Cobb, Esq., April 26, 1898, Roscoe C. Bruce, Harvard College student file.

23. Student file of Roscoe C. Bruce [Sr.], class of 1902, Harvard University archives, Nathan Pusey Library.

24. Ibid.

25. Roscoe C. Bruce to Clara W. Burrill, December 7, 1898, Roscoe C. Bruce Papers. At the time, Clara was a senior at M Street High School in Washington, DC.

26. "Climbing Up the Ladder," *Colored American*, May 6, 1899.

27. DuBois, Trotter, and Hill graduated, respectively, in 1890, 1895, and 1903.

28. W. E. B. DuBois, "A Negro Student at Harvard at the End of the Nineteenth Century," *Massachusetts Review*, 1960. DuBois also taped an oral version of this article for the Harvard University archives.

29. Charles A. Wagner, *Harvard: Four Centuries and Freedoms*, p. 187.
30. Roscoe C. Bruce to Clara W. Burrill, December 28, 1900, Roscoe C. Bruce Papers.
31. Booker T. Washington, "Speech to the Cotton States and International Exposition," September 18, 1895. Booker T. Washington Papers.
32. Josephine B. Bruce to Booker T. Washington, March 12, 1898, Roscoe C. Bruce Papers.
33. Booker T. Washington to Josephine B. Bruce, September 6, 1899, Booker T. Washington Papers, Library of Congress, Washington, DC.
34. Various articles in *New York Times*, *Washington Post*, *Washington Bee*, published during August 1899.
35. Booker T. Washington, *Up From Slavery* (New York: Doubleday & Company, 1901), p. 259.
36. Werner Sollors, *Blacks at Harvard* (New York: New York University Press, 1993), pp. 59, 91.
37. Roscoe C. Bruce to Booker T. Washington, February 8, 1902, Booker T. Washington Papers.
38. Ibid., February 22, 1902.
39. Booker T. Washington to Roscoe C. Bruce, February 1, 1902, Booker T. Washington Papers.
40. Editorial, *Cleveland Gazette*, July 20, 1901, and *Colored American*, July 27, 1901. Also quoted in Booker T. Washington Papers.
41. Booker T. Washington to Hollis Burke Frissell, February 1, 1902, Booker T. Washington Papers.
42. Charles W. Eliot to Booker T. Washington, September 7, 1906, Booker T. Washington Papers. In this letter, Harvard president Eliot spoke of Roscoe's potential and stated that once Roscoe worked in Washington as a teacher, he would be "a more valuable man later for Tuskegee or some other educational institution for negroes."

CHAPTER FOURTEEN

1. Roscoe C. Bruce to Josephine B. Bruce, December 22, 1902, Roscoe C. Bruce Papers, Moorland-Spingarn Research Center, Howard University, Washington, DC.
2. Josephine B. Bruce to Roscoe C. Bruce, 1902–1903. Roscoe C. Bruce Papers. Numerous letters were written during this period by Josephine, as she responded to Roscoe's requests for money. In most of her responses, she lists the amount of cash or size of check she has enclosed.
3. Roscoe C. Bruce to Josephine B. Bruce, December 22, 1903, Roscoe C. Bruce Papers.
4. Blanche K. Bruce to Josephine Bruce, October 19, 1896, Blanche K. Bruce

Papers, Moorland-Spingarn Research Center, Howard University, Washington, DC.

5. Roscoe C. Bruce to Blanche K. Bruce, April 18, 1897, Blanche K. Bruce Papers.

6. The PEAN, Volume XIV, 1898 edition, published by the senior class of Phillips Exeter Academy. (The PEAN is the class yearbook.)

7. Harvard College Class Book of 1902, published by Harvard University, 1902, p. 11.

8. Josephine Bruce to Roscoe C. Bruce, 1902, Roscoe C. Bruce Papers.

9. Roscoe C. Bruce to Clara Burrill, November 25, 1902, Roscoe C. Bruce Papers.

10. Blanche K. Bruce to Roscoe C. Bruce, February 4, 1897, Blanche K. Bruce Papers. In this letter, Senator Bruce expresses surprise that his eighteen-year-old son is serving as a part-time paid tutor. Previously, Roscoe had told his father that he would be willing to work during the summer at a Washington newspaper to earn extra pocket money, but it never happened.

11. George Cornelius Smith, "A Man Revealed," *Freeman*, March 1898.

12. Roscoe C. Bruce to Clara W. Burrill, January 13, 1903, Roscoe C. Bruce Papers. In this particular letter, he asks Clara, "How do you like Harold Rogers' Economic Interpretation of History? Have you read Seligman's book and Carver's criticism of it in the *Journal of Political Economy*?"

13. Roscoe C. Bruce to Clara Burrill, January 1902, Roscoe C. Bruce Papers. The specific day in January 1902 is not visible on the original letter.

14. Roscoe C. Bruce to Clara Burrill, November 26, 1902, Roscoe C. Bruce Papers.

15. Booker T. Washington, *Up from Slavery* (New York: Doubleday Publishers, 1901).

16. W. E. B. DuBois, *The Souls of Black Folk: Essays and Sketches* (Chicago: McClurg, 1903).

17. Stokes and Peabody served on the school's Endowment Committee along with William Baldwin, the president of the Long Island Rail Road.

18. *Plessy v. Ferguson*, U.S. Supreme Court, 1896. It was eventually proven that the "separate but equal" doctrine inevitably discriminated against blacks, because the provisions and facilities that were made for the black race were inevitably inferior in quality and quantity.

19. U.S. Census figures from 1900.

20. Booker T. Washington to Hollis Burke Frissel, February 1, 1902, Booker T. Washington Papers, Library of Congress, Washington, DC.

21. Roscoe C. Bruce to Booker T. Washington, February 22, 1902, Booker T. Washington Papers.

22. Pinn graduated from Harvard in 1903. According to Phillips Exeter Academy's alumni records, he remained a teacher until his death in 1940.

23. Hill graduated from Harvard in 1903. He would teach education at Tuskegee Institute from 1904 until 1907, when he became principal of an industrial trade school in Virginia.

CHAPTER FIFTEEN

1. Roscoe C. Bruce to Clara W. Burrill, April 1903, Roscoe C. Bruce Papers.

2. Although the event elicited a great amount of anger from whites, Washington had been invited on October 16, 1901, to dine with President Theodore Roosevelt at the White House.

3. W. E. B. DuBois, *The Souls of Black Folk: Essays and Sketches* (Chicago: McClurg, 1903).

4. Booker T. Washington to Roscoe C. Bruce, April 21, 1903, Booker T. Washington Papers, Library of Congress, Washington, DC.

5. Clara W. Burrill to Roscoe C. Bruce, January 2, 1903, Roscoe C. Bruce Papers. Clara was a Radcliffe student living at 33 Parker Street, Cambridge.

6. M Street High School was later known as Dunbar High School. Although a public school, it remained the choice of black elite families from the 1880s until the 1950s. Many of its early faculty members were graduates of Howard, Harvard, Brown, and other prestigious Northeastern universities.

7. Student file of Clara Washington Burrill, Radcliffe College, Schlesinger Library, Cambridge, Massachusetts. Clara's student records show that although she was two years younger than Roscoe, she had been advanced at least one year in grammar school and was in his same class at M Street High School.

8. Clara W. Burrill to Roscoe C. Bruce, November 20, 1900, Roscoe C. Bruce Papers.

9. Clara and Roscoe were close childhood friends with children of several black elite families, like the Syphaxes, Terrells, and Wormleys.

10. Clara W. Burrill to Roscoe C. Bruce, January 9, 1900, Roscoe C. Bruce Papers.

11. Clara W. Burrill to Roscoe C. Bruce, fall 1902, Roscoe C. Bruce Papers. The date does not appear on the original letter, but it is clear that Clara is attending school in Cambridge at the time and that they are beginning to make wedding plans.

12. Roscoe C. Bruce to Clara W. Burrill, December 1900, Roscoe C. Bruce Papers.

13. Clara W. Burrill to Roscoe C. Bruce, February 1903, Roscoe C. Bruce Papers.

14. Roscoe C. Bruce to Clara W. Burrill, fall 1902, Roscoe C. Bruce Papers. This ten-page handwritten letter is written to Clara while she is in Cambridge and Roscoe is working in Tuskegee. While it is undated, the contents reveal that it is fall of 1902.

15. Clara W. Burrill to Roscoe C. Bruce, January 2, 1903, Roscoe C. Bruce Papers.

16. Clara W. Burrill to Roscoe C. Bruce, March 1903, Roscoe C. Bruce Papers. In this same letter, Clara reports on a speech that George Washington Carver recently gave for Radcliffe and Harvard students.

17. Charles Eliot was president of Harvard University from 1869 to 1909. He was considered to be friendly to the black Harvard community.

18. Alice Freeman Palmer was president of Wellesley College. The black community knew her name after Charlotte Hawkins Brown, a black educator, named a school—Palmer Memorial Institute in Sedalia, North Carolina—after her. This all-black boarding school catered to children from upper- and middle-class black families in the South, North, and Midwest.

19. Roscoe C. Bruce to Clara W. Burrill, January 10, 1903, Roscoe C. Bruce Papers.

20. Clara W. Burrill to Roscoe C. Bruce, January 1903, Roscoe C. Bruce Papers.

21. Edmond Burrill to Clara W. Burrill, May 20, 1902, Roscoe C. Bruce Papers.

22. Clara W. Burrill to Roscoe C. Bruce, January 1903, Roscoe C. Bruce Papers.

23. Roscoe C. Bruce to Clara W. Burrill, January 29, 1903, Roscoe C. Bruce Papers.

24. Clara W. Burrill to Roscoe C. Bruce, 1902, Roscoe C. Bruce Papers.

25. Clara W. Burrill to Roscoe C. Bruce, February 1903, Roscoe C. Bruce Papers. Clara had originally planned a honeymoon at Arundel by the Bay, a popular black beach resort community also called Highland Beach, situated near the Potomac River in Maryland. Black upper-class families had built and owned cottages there for summer use.

26. Roscoe C. Bruce to Clara W. Burrill, January 29, 1903, Roscoe C. Bruce Papers.

27. Ibid.

28. Roscoe C. Bruce to Clara W. Burrill, February 1903, Roscoe C. Bruce Papers. The content of this letter indicates that it was written in early February.

29. Roscoe C. Bruce to Clara W. Burrill, February 26, 1903, Roscoe C. Bruce Papers.

30. Clara W. Burrill to Roscoe C. Bruce, March 1, 1903, Roscoe C. Bruce Papers.

Although this letter is undated, Clara writes in the text that their wedding date is June 3, then she writes, "our wedding day is only 92 days off."

31. Roscoe C. Bruce to Clara W. Burrill, May 1903, Roscoe C. Bruce Papers.

32. Clara W. Burrill to Roscoe C. Bruce, May 1903, Roscoe C. Bruce Papers. In this letter, she discusses some of the details regarding the wedding day.

33. Roscoe C. Bruce to Clara W. Burrill, March 10, 1903, Roscoe C. Bruce Papers.

34. Ibid.

CHAPTER SIXTEEN

1. Roscoe C. Bruce to Josephine B. Bruce, December 22, 1903, Roscoe C. Bruce Papers, Moorland-Spingarn Research Center, Howard University, Washington, DC.

2. Louis Harlan, *Booker T. Washington: The Wizard of Tuskegee* (New York: Oxford University Press, 1983).

3. David Levering Lewis, *W. E. B. DuBois: Biography of a Race, 1868–1919* (New York: Holt, 1993).

4. When Lewis was appointed in 1911, he became the first black to serve in a subcabinet post for a president.

5. Roscoe C. Bruce to Clara W. Burrill, fall 1902. Roscoe C. Bruce Papers.

6. Roscoe C. Bruce to Clara W. Burrill, 1902, Roscoe C. Bruce Papers.

7. Roscoe C. Bruce to Clara W. Burrill, fall 1902, Roscoe C. Bruce Papers.

8. Roscoe C. Bruce to Clara W. Burrill, January 1902, Roscoe C. Bruce Papers.

9. Roscoe C. Bruce to Clara W. Burrill, November 25, 1902, Roscoe C. Bruce Papers.

10. Roscoe C. Bruce to Clara W. Burrill, January 1902, Roscoe C. Bruce Papers.

11. Roscoe C. Bruce to Clara W. Burrill, January 11, 1902, Roscoe C. Bruce Papers.

12. Roscoe C. Bruce to Clara W. Burrill, March 10, 1903, Roscoe C. Bruce Papers. Prior to their marriage and move to Tuskegee, Roscoe had sent the building's floor plan to Clara with a letter explaining the size and use of each room.

13. Clara W. Burrill to Roscoe C. Bruce, May 1903, Roscoe C. Bruce Papers.

14. Booker T. Washington, *Up From Slavery* (New York: Doubleday & Company, 1901).

15. Booker T. Washington, "The Awakening of the Negro," *Atlantic Monthly*, September 1896.

16. *Philadelphia Times*, 1887.

17. Booker T. Washington, *Up from Slavery*, p. 15.

18. Booker T. Washington to Tuskegee faculty members, January 2, 1914,

Booker T. Washington Papers, Library of Congress, Washington, DC. The letter was written after he learned that his son and a Fisk graduate, Nettie Hancock, had married at a Houston, Texas, courthouse.

19. Editorial, *Guardian*, October 4, 1902.

20. Roscoe C. Bruce to Clara W. Burrill, March 12, 1903, Roscoe C. Bruce Papers.

21. Booker T. Washington to Bettie Cox Francis, April 21, 1904, Booker T. Washington Papers.

22. Booker T. Washington to Margaret P. Murrell, May 3, 1904, Booker T. Washington Papers.

23. James F. Hood of American Security and Trust Company to Josephine B. Bruce, February 10, 1905, Roscoe C. Bruce Papers.

24. Godfrey Frank to Josephine B. Bruce, April 5, 1905, Roscoe C. Bruce Papers.

25. A. L. Harang to Josephine B. Bruce, January 12, 1906, Roscoe C. Bruce Papers.

26. Undated notes and letter written by Josephine B. Bruce; letter from A. L. Harang to Josephine B. Bruce, January 12, 1906, Roscoe C. Bruce Papers.

27. Josephine B. Bruce to Roscoe C. Bruce, January, 1906, Roscoe C. Bruce Papers. Although the letter is undated, its contents reveal that it was written on or about the same date that A. L. Harang sent a January 12, 1906, letter to Josephine B. Bruce.

28. Roscoe C. Bruce to Booker T. Washington, 1902, Roscoe C. Bruce Papers.

29. Booker T. Washington, editor, *Tuskegee and Its People: Their Ideals and Achievements* (New York: D. Appleton and Company, 1905), p. 56.

30. Josephine B. Bruce to Roscoe C. Bruce, April 16, 1902, Roscoe C. Bruce Papers.

31. Josephine B. Bruce to Roscoe C. Bruce, April 21, 1902, Roscoe C. Bruce Papers.

32. Roscoe C. Bruce to Clara W. Burrill, 1902, Roscoe C. Bruce Papers. Roscoe had told Clara that she might be able to pursue advanced studies in Tuskegee if she could obtain the necessary books and study materials from Harvard and Radcliffe.

33. Booker T. Washington, *Up from Slavery*, p. 269.

34. Charles William Eliot to Booker T. Washington, September 7, 1906, Booker T. Washington Papers.

35. Roscoe C. Bruce to Booker T. Washington, August 26, 1905, Booker T. Washington Papers.

36. Booker T. Washington to Roscoe C. Bruce, September 4, 1905, Booker T. Washington Papers.

37. Booker T. Washington to William Estabrook Chancellor, September 4, 1906, Booker T. Washington Papers.

38. James A. Cobb to Emmett Jay Scott, September 3, 1906, Booker T. Washington Papers.

CHAPTER SEVENTEEN

1. Mary Church Terrell, speech to the United Women's Club, Washington, DC, October 10, 1906.
2. Paul Kelsey Williams, "Scenes from the Past," *In Towner*, December 2001, p. 10.
3. Josephine B. Bruce, "What Has Education Done for Colored Women," *Voice of the Negro*, July 1904, pp. 298–300.
4. Josephine Willson Bruce and Booker T. Washington's wife, Margaret, were officers with the National Association of Colored Women, an organization that remains the oldest national black women's group in the United States.
5. Roy Church to Josephine B. Bruce, October 8, 1908, Roscoe C. Bruce Papers, Moorland-Spingarn Research Center, Howard University, Washington, DC.
6. "Making a Fight on Professor Bruce," *New York Age*, September 21, 1911.
7. Charles H. Wesley, *History of Sigma Pi Phi* (Washington, DC: Association for the Study of Negro Life and History, 1954), p. 76.
8. *New York Age*, September 21, 1911.
9. Roscoe Conkling Bruce, speech at the banquet of the alumni of Howard University, Washington, DC, May 26, 1909.
10. "Bruce Charged with Favoritism," *New York Age*, March 12, 1914.
11. "Colored Schools in Bad Condition in DC," *New York Age*, December 24, 1914.
12. Clyde T. Denton to Josephine B. Bruce, January 27, 1913, Roscoe C. Bruce Papers.

CHAPTER EIGHTEEN

1. This was an excerpt from a letter to the editor of the black weekly newspaper *Washington Bee*. Bruce had written the letter in defense against accusations that he was lowering the quality of the black schools. In the letter, he attempts to explain why Washington's poor blacks do not need an academic curriculum and would be better served by courses that taught industrial skills like carpentry, dressmaking, and house painting.
2. "The Evans Mandamus," *Washington Bee*, January 8, 1916.
3. Ibid.
4. Clara Burrill Bruce, "We Who Are Dark," *The Public: A Journal of Fundamental Democracy*, v. 21, December 28, 1918, p. 1552.

5. "Moens Is Found Guilty," *Washington Bee*, April 5, 1919, p. 1.

6. Roscoe C. Bruce to Josephine B. Bruce, April 1922, Roscoe C. Bruce Papers, Moorland-Spingarn Research Center, Howard University, Washington, DC. This two-page single-spaced typed letter is undated but offers specific details that suggest it was written in April 1922. At the time, Roscoe was in West Virginia.

7. Roscoe C. Bruce to Josephine B. Bruce, February 1922, Roscoe C. Bruce Papers. This four-page handwritten letter is undated but offers specific details that suggest when it was written.

8. Roscoe C. Bruce Jr. to Josephine B. Bruce, October 17, 1922, Roscoe C. Bruce Papers.

9. Radcliffe College application of Clara J. Bruce, February 23, 1922, Schlesinger Library, Radcliffe College, Harvard University.

10. Nathaniel Guy to Roscoe C. Bruce, October 24, 1922, Roscoe C. Bruce Papers.

11. Frank M. Stephen, Esq., to Roscoe C. Bruce, October 25, 1922, Roscoe C. Bruce Papers.

12. Roscoe C. Bruce to Nathaniel Guy, October 27, 1922, Roscoe C. Bruce Papers.

13. Nathaniel Guy to Roscoe C. Bruce, November 6, 1922, Roscoe C. Bruce Papers.

14. Roscoe C. Bruce to Nathaniel Guy, November 9, 1922, Roscoe C. Bruce Papers.

CHAPTER NINETEEN

1. Harvard president A. Lawrence Lowell to Roscoe Conkling Bruce, December 14, 1922. Reprinted in the *Harvard Alumni Bulletin, 1923*.

2. In 1865, Richard T. Greener became the first black to attend Harvard College. He graduated in 1870 and later became a philosophy professor at the University of South Carolina and dean of Howard University Law School.

3. John T. Bethell, *Harvard Observed* (Cambridge, Massachusetts: Harvard University Press, 1998), p. 24.

4. W. E. B. DuBois, "A Negro Student at Harvard at the End of the Nineteenth Century," *Massachusetts Review*, 1960.

5. Roscoe C. Bruce to A. Lawrence Lowell, December 1923.

6. David M. Little Jr. to Roscoe C. Bruce, March 9, 1921, Roscoe C. Bruce Papers, Moorland-Spingarn Research Center, Howard University, Washington, DC. Little was executive secretary of the Harvard Endowment Fund.

7. Raymond Pace Alexander, *Opportunity: Journal of Negro Life* (New York: National Urban League, 1923). A prominent black judge in Philadelphia during the 1950s and 1960s, Alexander graduated from Harvard Law School in 1923.

8. *Nation*, v. 116, January 31, 1923, p. 112.

9. The "Seven Sisters" colleges were Radcliffe, Wellesley, Smith, Mount Holyoke, Vassar, Bryn Mawr, and Barnard. The latter three were the last to allow black women to attend their schools, a full thirty or forty years after the other Seven Sisters colleges.

10. LeBaron Russell Briggs to Roscoe C. Bruce, June 1, 1922, Radcliffe College student file of Clara J. Bruce, Schlesinger Library, Radcliffe College archives.

11. LeBaron Russell Briggs to Roscoe C. Bruce, June 7, 1922, Radcliffe College student file of Clara J. Bruce.

12. Mary Gibson Huntley Papers, Schlesinger Library, Radcliffe College.

13. Cuno H. Rudolph to Roscoe C. Bruce, April 16, 1921, Roscoe C. Bruce Papers. Rudolph was president of the Second National Bank in Washington, DC.

14. Roscoe C. Bruce to Josephine B. Bruce [1922], Roscoe C. Bruce Papers.

15. Ibid.

16. Roscoe C. Bruce to John T. Meany, February 22, 1922, Roscoe C. Bruce Papers. Meany was president of Stone & Fairfax in Washington, DC.

17. Roscoe C. Bruce to Josephine B. Bruce [1922], Roscoe C. Bruce Papers. Houston was a well-known black attorney in Washington who taught at Howard.

18. "Roscoe Conkling Bruce and Wife to Study Law," *Cleveland Gazette*, May 26, 1923. This article correctly stated that Roscoe had resigned from his job and that Clara was to study at Boston University Law School, but it incorrectly stated that he was about to enter Harvard Law School.

19. Roscoe C. Bruce Jr. to Roscoe C. Bruce Sr., March 28, 1924, Roscoe C. Bruce Papers.

20. Ibid.

21. Clara B. Bruce to Roscoe C. Bruce Sr., June 13, 1924, Roscoe C. Bruce Papers.

22. Clara B. Bruce to Roscoe C. Bruce Sr., June 15, 1924, Roscoe C. Bruce Papers.

23. Ibid.

24. L. C. Smith to Roscoe C. Bruce Sr., June 14, 1924, Roscoe C. Bruce Papers. Smith was the president of Smith & Kline Incorporated.

25. S. M. Boyd, Esq., to Roscoe C. Bruce, June 19, 1924, Roscoe C. Bruce Papers.

26. Frederic E. Johnson to Roscoe C. Bruce, July 9, 1924, Roscoe C. Bruce Papers.

CHAPTER TWENTY

1. Mary E. Willson to Josephine B. Bruce, January 1, 1923, Roscoe C. Bruce Papers, Moorland-Spingarn Research Center, Howard University, Washington, DC.

2. Grade report from Radcliffe College student file of Clara Josephine Bruce, class of 1927, Radcliffe College archives, Harvard University.

3. "Right to Participate," *Radcliffe Quarterly*, September 1986, pp. 32–33.

4. Roscoe Conkling Bruce Sr. to Ansel Wold, December 11, 1925, Blanche K. Bruce file, U.S. Senate Historical Office, U.S. Senate, Washington, DC. Wold worked for the U.S. Congress Joint Committee on Printing and had corresponded with Roscoe while Wold was updating Blanche Bruce's biographical information for congressional publications.

5. *New York Times*, May 10, 1926.

6. Clara B. Bruce, "Workmen's Compensation," *Boston University Law Review*, November 1925. This would be Clara's third article for the law review, and would be instrumental in getting her named editor in chief of the publication.

7. Boston University School of Law Archives, Boston.

8. Boston University School of Law class of 1926 yearbook, Boston University School of Law Archives, Boston.

9. *Who's Who in Colored America* (New York: Phyllis Wheatley Publishers, 1929), p. 56.

10. After Howard Naylor Fitzhugh graduated from Harvard College, he went on to become the first black graduate of Harvard Business School.

11. Born in 1823, Mary Ann Shadd was the oldest child of Abraham and Harriet Shadd. A lawyer, publisher, and founder of a school for black children, she died in Washington, DC, in 1893.

12. Mary Van Kleeck to Charles O. Heydt, May 18, 1927, Rockefeller Archive Center, Pocantico Hills, NY.

13. Roscoe C. Bruce to Charles Heydt, June 2, 1927, Rockefeller Archive Center.

14. Roscoe C. Bruce to Charles O. Heydt, July 25, 1927, Rockefeller Archive Center.

15. Ibid.

16. Charles A. Wagner, *Harvard: Four Centuries and Freedoms* (New York: E. P. Dutton & Company, 1950), p. 273.

17. Charles O. Heydt to Roscoe C. Bruce, August 16, 1927, Rockfeller Archive Center.

18. Dean Bernice V. Brown to Clara Josephine Bruce, July 5, 1927, Radcliffe student file of Clara J. Bruce, Radcliffe archives, Harvard University. Brown served as dean from 1923 to 1934.

19. Roscoe Conkling Bruce Sr. to Dean Bernice V. Brown, September 18, 1927, Radcliffe student file of Clara J. Bruce.

20. Charles O. Heydt to John D. Rockefeller Jr., March 26, 1928, Rockefeller Archive Center.
21. Charles O. Heydt to O. T. Reeves, February 4, 1928, Rockefeller Archive Center.
22. William R. Conklin to Charles O. Heydt, May 22, 1928, Rockefeller Archive Center. (Charles C. Huitt was president of Ampere Bank in East Orange, New Jersey. Finley J. Shepard was a railroad executive and the son-in-law of Erie Railroad founder Jay Gould.)
23. Roscoe C. Bruce Sr. to Charles O. Heydt, April 29, 1929, Rockefeller Archive Center.
24. Ibid.
25. Ibid.
26. "Mrs. Bruce Denies Divorce," *New York News*, December 14, 1929.

CHAPTER TWENTY-ONE

1. "Heydt Asserts Bruce Gave Up Post as Bank Director to Satisfy Judgment," *New York Amsterdam News*, March 5, 1930.
2. Harvard Law School registrar's records, Office of the Registrar, Harvard Law School.
3. Transcript of Burrill K. Bruce, September 1934 to June 1936, Office of the Registrar, Harvard Law School.
4. Roscoe C. Bruce to Charles O. Heydt, July 6, 1932, Rockefeller Archive Center, Pocantico Hills, NY.
5. Appomattox County History Records, Appomattox County, Virginia.
6. Roscoe C. Bruce to Frank S. Staley, November 25, 1936, Rockefeller Archives.
7. Charles O. Heydt to Roscoe C. Bruce, June 21, 1933, Rockefeller Family Archive Center.
8. Roscoe C. Bruce to Roscoe C. Bruce Jr., June 28, 1934, Rockefeller Family Archive Center.
9. Roscoe C. Bruce Jr. to Roscoe C. Bruce, June 28, 1935, Rockefeller Family Archive Center.
10. Charles O. Heydt to Roscoe C. Bruce, June 29, 1935, Rockefeller Family Archive Center.
11. Charles O. Heydt to Roscoe C. Bruce Jr., July 1, 1935, Rockefeller Family Archive Center.
12. R. H. Wilkens to Roscoe C. Bruce, June 5, 1936, Rockefeller Family Archive Center.
13. "Young Bruce Is Accused in $2000 Steal," *New York Amsterdam News*, April 17, 1937.
14. Ibid.

15. Ibid.
16. "Young Bruce Out on Bail—in Hiding," *New York Amsterdam News*, April 24, 1937.
17. Ibid.
18. Student file of Theophilus John Minton Syphax (later known as Theophilus Vincent McKee), class of 1903, Trinity College Archives, Hartford, Connecticut. Syphax was a member of the Trinity football team, and then was elected by the all-white Trinity senior class to the position of class day orator.
19. "R. C. Bruce Jr. Granted Stay," *New York Amsterdam News*, October 30, 1937.
20. Roscoe C. Bruce Jr. to Bessie Humbles Bruce, April 1937, quoted in "R. C. Bruce Jr. Granted Stay."
21. John D. Rockefeller Jr. to Harold L. Ickes, December 30, 1936, Rockefeller Archives.
22. Harold L. Ickes to John D. Rockefeller, Jr., January 18, 1937, Rockefeller Archives.
23. Charles O. Heydt to Charles C. Huitt, January 4, 1934, Rockefeller Archives.
24. "Hint Probation for R. C. Bruce," *New York Amsterdam News*, November 6, 1937.
25. "Roscoe C. Bruce May Go Abroad," *New York Amsterdam News*, November 13, 1937.
26. "Bruce Goes to Jail," *New York Amsterdam News*, November 20, 1937.
27. *Afro-American*, November 27, 1937.
28. *New York Amsterdam News*, November 20, 1937.
29. "R. C. Bruce's Harvadian Accent Gone!" *New York Amsterdam News*, December 11, 1937.
30. "Burrill Bruce Is Quizzed in Cash Deal," *New York Amsterdam News*, April 15, 1939.
31. Ibid.
32. "High Yaller: Proves as Big a Barrier to Theatre Progress as Ebony Color Skin," *New York Amsterdam News*, April 22, 1939.

CHAPTER TWENTY-TWO

1. Burrill K. Bruce to David Rockefeller, February 8, 1940, Rockefeller Family Archive Center, Pocantico Hills, NY.
2. Julius Levine, case supervisor with the New York City Department of Welfare, to John D. Rockefeller Jr., November 18, 1939, Rockefeller Family Archives. In this letter, Levine writes to Rockefeller to confirm that Roscoe Bruce had been employed by the Dunbar Apartments from

1927 to 1937. He also states that the public assistance application is to benefit Roscoe Sr., Clara Sr., Roscoe Jr., and Burrill Bruce.

3. Barton P. Turnbull to John D. Rockefeller Jr., January 19, 1939, Rockefeller Family Archives.

4. Charles O. Heydt to Julius Levine, November 22, 1939, Rockefeller Archives.

5. "Black Senator's Home Is Dedicated," *Washington Post*, July 19, 1978. Bruce's home at 909 M Street NW was declared a national historic landmark by the National Park Service in 1977.

6. Roscoe C. Bruce to John D. Rockefeller Jr., August 2, 1938, Rockefeller Family Archives.

7. "Did You Happen to See Barrington Sharma?" Associated Press story by Inga Arvad, 1941.

8. "Family Friend Supports Lawyer as Negro's Kin," *New York Daily Mirror*, January 1948.

9. Roscoe C. Bruce to John D. Rockefeller Jr., September 24, 1946, Rockefeller Family Archives.

10. Dana S. Creel to Roscoe C. Bruce, September 25, 1946, Rockefeller Family Archives.

11. "Face Value at the Capitol," *New York Times*, August 13, 2003. Simmie Knox also painted the official White House portraits of President William Jefferson Clinton and First Lady Hillary Rodham Clinton.

12. Interview with Dr. Norma Rozzelle, April 11, 2003.

Bibliography

Ames, Blanche, *Adelbert Ames, 1835–1933: General, Senator, Governor.* New York: Argosy-Antiquarian, 1964.

Aptheker, Herbert, ed., *The Correspondence of W. E. B. DuBois: Selections, 1877–1934.* Amherst, Massachusetts: University of Massachusetts Press, 1973.

Barnard, Harry, *Rutherford B. Hayes: And His America.* Newtown, Connecticut: American Political Biography Press, 1994.

Bennett, Jr., Lerone, *Before the Mayflower: A History of Black America.* New York, Penguin, 1993.

Bethell, John T., *Harvard Observed.* Cambridge, Massachusetts: Harvard University Press, 1998.

Bunting, Bainbridge, *Harvard: An Architectural History.* Cambridge, Massachusetts, Belknap Press of Harvard University Press, 1985.

Bunting, Josiah, *Ulysses S. Grant.* New York: Henry Holt and Company, 2004.

Christopher, Maurine, *Black Americans in Congress.* New York: T. Y. Crowell, 1976.

Cimbala, Paul A. and Randall Miller, editors, *The Freedmen's Bureau and Reconstruction: Reconsiderations.* New York: Fordham University Press, 1999.

Doenecke, Justus D., *The Presidencies of James A. Garfield and Chester A. Arthur.* Lawrence, Kansas: Regents Press of Kansas, 1981.

Douglass, Frederick, *Frederick Douglass: Selected Speeches and Writings.* Chicago: Lawrence Hill Books, 2000.

Douglass, Frederick, *My Bondage and My Freedom.* New York: Penguin, 2003.

Du Bois, W. E. B., *Black Reconstruction in America 1860–1880.* New York: Touchstone Simon & Schuster, 1992.

Du Bois, W. E. B., *The Souls of Black Folk.* New York: Modern Library, 2003.

Du Bois, W. E. B., *The Autobiography of W. E. B. Du Bois.* New York: International Publishers, 1968.

Farrell, Betty, *Elite Families: Class and Power in Nineteenth-Century Boston.* Albany, New York: State University of New York Press, 1993.

Foner, Eric, *A Short History of Reconstruction.* New York: Harper & Row, 1990.

Foner, Eric, *Forever Free: The Story of Emancipation and Reconstruction*. New York: Alfred A. Knopf, 2005.

Foner, Eric, *Freedom's Lawmakers: A Directory of Black Officeholders During Reconstruction*. New York: Oxford University Press, 1993.

Foner, Eric, *Reconstruction: America's Unfinished Revolution, 1863–1877*. New York: Harper & Row, 1988.

Foner, Eric and Olivia Mahoney, *America's Reconstruction: People and Politics after the Civil War*. New York: HarperCollins, 1995.

Fosdick Raymond B., *John D. Rockefeller, Jr.: A Portrait*. New York: Harper & Row, 1956.

Franklin, John Hope, *Reconstruction: After the Civil War*. Chicago: The University of Chicago Press, 1962.

Franklin, John Hope and Alfred A. Moss., Jr., *From Slavery to Freedom: A History of African Americans, Eighth Edition*. New York: McGraw-Hill, 2000.

Gambee, Robert, *Exeter Impressions*. New York: Hastings House, 1980.

Gates, Henry Louis and Anthony Appiah, eds. *Africana: The Encyclopedia of the African and African American Experience*. Philadelphia, Pennsylvania: Running Press, 2003.

Gates, Henry Louis and Evelyn Brooks Higginbotham, *African American Lives*. New York: Oxford University Press, 2004.

Gates, Henry Louis and Cornel West, *The African American Century*. New York: Free Press, 2000.

Gatewood, Willard B., *Aristocrats of Color*. Indianapolis: Indiana University Press, 1990.

Gillette, William, *Retreat from Reconstruction: 1869–1879*. Baton Rouge, Louisiana: Louisiana State University Press, 1979.

Goldfield, David, *Still Fighting the Civil War: The American South and Southern History*. Baton Rouge, Louisiana: Louisiana State University Press, 2002.

Graham, Lawrence Otis. *Our Kind of People: Inside America's Black Upper Class*. New York: HarperCollins Publishers, 1999.

Harlan, Louis R., *Booker T. Washington: The Wizard of Tuskegee, 1901–1915*. New York: Oxford University Press, 1983.

Harlan, Louis R., ed., *The Booker T. Washington Papers Vol. 1–14*. Urbana, Illinois: University of Illinois Press, 1972–1989.

Hoar, George F., *Autobiography of Seventy Years*. New York: Scribner's Sons, 1903.

Isserman, Maurice, *Journey to Freedom: The African American Great Migration*. New York, Facts on File, 1997.

Jordan, David M., *Roscoe Conkling of New York: Voice in the Senate*. Ithaca, New York: Cornell University Press, 1971.

Keller, Morton and Phyllis Keller, *Making Harvard Modern: The Rise of America's University*. New York: Oxford University Press, 2001.

Kelley, Robin D. G. and Earl Lewis, eds., *To Make Our World Anew: A History of African Americans*. New York: Oxford University Press, 2000.

Klinkner, Philip A. and Rogers M. Smith, *The Unsteady March: The Rise and Decline of Racial Equality in America*. Chicago: University of Chicago Press, 1999.

Leech, Margaret and Harry J. Brown, *The Garfield Orbit: The Life of James A. Garfield*. New York: Harper & Row, 1978.

Lester, Julius, ed., *The Seventh Son: The Thought and Writings of W. E. B. Du Bois*. New York: Random House, 1971.

Levine, Michael L., *African Americans and Civil Rights: From 1619 to the Present*. Phoenix, Arizona: Oryx Press, 1996.

Lewis, David Levering, *W. E. B. Du Bois: Biography of a Race, 1868–1919*. New York: Henry Holt, 1993.

Lewis, David Levering, *W. E. B. Du Bois: The Fight for Equality and the American Century 1919–1963*. New York: Henry Holt, 2000.

Logan, Rayford W., *W. E. B. DuBois: A Profile*. New York: Farrar, Straus & Giroux, 1971.

Lynch, John R., *The Facts of Reconstruction*. New York: Arno Press and the *New York Times*, 1968.

Lynch, John R., *Reminiscences of an Active Life*. Chicago: University of Chicago Press, 1970.

McFeely, William S., *Grant: A Biography*. New York: W. W. Norton & Company, 1981.

McPherson, James M., *Ordeal by Fire: The Civil War and Reconstruction*. New York: Alfred A. Knopf, 1982.

Morgan, H. Wayne, *William McKinley and His America*. Kent, Ohio: Kent State University Press, 2004.

Morison, Samuel Eliot, *The Oxford History of the America People, Volume 2: 1789 through Reconstruction*. New York: Penguin, 1994.

Morison, Samuel Eliot, Henry Steele Commager, and William E. Leuchtenburg, *A Concise History of the American Republic, second edition*. New York: Oxford University Press, 1983.

Oakes, James, *The Ruling Race: A History of American Slaveholders*. New York: Alfred A. Knopf, 1982.

Olmsted, Frederick Law, *The Cotton Kingdom: A Traveler's Observations on Cotton and Slavery*. New York: Modern Library, 1984.

Painter, Nell Irvin, *Exodusters: Black Migration to Kansas after Reconstruction*. New York: Alfred A. Knopf, Inc., 1977.

Pereyra, Lillian A., *James Lusk Alcorn: Persistent Whig*. Baton Rouge, Louisiana: Louisiana State University Press, 1966.

Peskin, Allan, *Garfield: A Biography*. Kent, Ohio: Kent State University Press, 1978.

Reeves, Thomas C., *Gentleman Boss: The Life of Chester Alan Arthur*. Newtown, Connecticut: American Political Biography Press, 1991.

Rockefeller, David, *Memoirs*. New York: Random House, 2002.

St. Clair, Sadie Daniel, "The National Career of Blanche Kelso Bruce." Ph.D. dissertation, New York University, 1947.

Salley, Columbus, *The Black 100: A Ranking of the Most Influential African-Americans, Past and Present*. New York: Kensington Publishing Corp., 1999.

Sievers, Harry J., *Benjamin Harrison: Hoosier Statesman*. Newtown, Connecticut: American Political Biography Press, 1997.

Simpson, Brooks D., *Let Us Have Peace: Ulysses S. Grant and the Politics of War and Reconstruction*. Chapel Hill, North Carolina: University of North Carolina Press, 1991.

Smith, Jean Edward, *Grant*. New York: Simon & Schuster, 2001.

Smith, John David, *Black Voices from Reconstruction, 1865–1877*. Brookfield, Connecticut: Millbrook Press, 1996.

Smith, Samuel Denny, *The Negro in Congress, 1870–1901*. Port Washington, New York: Kennikat Press, 1966.

Sollors, Werner, Caldwell Titcomb, and Thomas A. Underwood, eds., *Blacks at Harvard: A Documentary History of African-American Experience at Harvard and Radcliffe*. New York: New York University Press, 1993.

Stewart, Jeffrey C., *1001 Things Everyone Should Know About African American History*. New York: Doubleday, 1996.

Wagner, Charles A., *Harvard: Four Centuries and Freedoms*. New York: E. P. Dutton & Company, 1950.

Washington, Booker T., *Up from Slavery: An Autobiography*. Garden City, New York: Doubleday and Company, 1901.

Welch, Jr., Richard E., *George Frisbie Hoar and the Half-Breed Republicans*. Cambridge, Massachusetts: Harvard University Press, 1971.

Willson, Joseph, *Sketches of the Higher Classes of Colored Society in Philadelphia*. Philadelphia: Merrihew and Thompson, 1841.

Ziff, Marsha, *Reconstruction Following the Civil War: In American History*. Berkley Heights, New Jersey: Enslow Publishers, 1999.

COLLECTIONS AND ARCHIVES

Rockefeller Archive Center, Sleepy Hollow, New York

Archives of Columbia University, New York, New York

Archives of Harvard University, Nathan Pusey Library, Harvard University, Cambridge, Massachusetts

Archives of Phillips Exeter Academy, Exeter, New Hampshire

Archives of Radcliffe College, Harvard University, Cambridge, Massachusetts

Archives of Trinity College, Hartford, Connecticut

Schomburg Center for Research in Black Culture, New York Public Library, New York, New York

Mississippi Department of Archives and History, Jackson, Mississippi

Moorland-Spingarn Research Center, Howard University, Washington, DC

Manuscript Division, Library of Congress, Washington, DC

U.S. Senate Historical Office, United States Senate, The Capitol, Washington, DC

Photography Credits

Photo insert falls between pages 198–199.

Index

About the Author

Lawrence Otis Graham is a nationally known attorney and commentator on race, politics, and class in America. He is the author of thirteen other books, including *Member of the Club* and the national bestseller *Our Kind of People: Inside America's Black Upper Class*. He has written for *U.S. News & World Report*, *The New York Times*, *Essence*, and *Glamour*.

A graduate of Princeton and Harvard Law School, Graham has taught African American studies and American government. He appeared on the cover of *New York Magazine* after leaving his law firm in Manhattan and going under-cover as a busboy at a discriminatory country club in Greenwich, Connecticut.

His wife, Pamela Thomas-Graham, is a novelist and corporate executive in New York City. They have three children and divide their time between Manhattan and Chappaqua, New York. www.lawrenceotisgraham.com